THE SAUDI SOCIAL AWAKENING

THE SAUDI SOCIAL AWAKENING

Explaining Rapid Social Change

Masooda Bano

BLOOMSBURY ACADEMIC
LONDON • NEW YORK • OXFORD • NEW DELHI • SYDNEY

BLOOMSBURY ACADEMIC
Bloomsbury Publishing Plc, 50 Bedford Square, London, WC1B 3DP, UK
Bloomsbury Publishing Inc, 1359 Broadway, New York, NY 10018, USA
Bloomsbury Publishing Ireland, 29 Earlsfort Terrace, Dublin 2, D02 AY28, Ireland

First published in Great Britain 2026

A catalogue record for this book is available from the British Library.

A catalog record for this book is available from the Library of Congress.

ISBN: HB: 978-0-7556-6056-8
PB: 978-0-7556-6057-5
ePDF: 978-0-7556-6059-9
eBook: 978-0-7556-6058-2

Typeset by Newgen KnowledgeWorks Pvt. Ltd., Chennai, India
Printed and bound in Great Britain

For product safety related questions contact productsafety@bloomsbury.com.

CONTENTS

MAP AND FIGURES

PREFACE

Studying institutional change and persistence is central to social science theorizing. Analysing such change, however, presents significant methodological challenges, foremost among them the task of establishing that change has actually occurred. Transformative societal shifts that confront deeply entrenched norms and institutional arrangements, such as the emergence of feminist movements or the consolidation of democratic governance, tend to unfold incrementally over decades, and at times centuries. As a result, they are most commonly examined through longitudinal historical case studies or time-series analyses. On rare occasions, however, scholars gain the opportunity to study institutional change as it unfolds, whether in the context of reform programmes or mass uprisings such as the Arab Spring. This book arises from one such unique moment of real-time transformation.

In 2014, I began researching Saudi Arabia, supported by a €1.5 million European Research Council (ERC) Starting Grant (European Union's Seventh Framework Programme, FP7/2007–2013, grant agreement No. 337108). My focus was on how Islamic scholarly institutions, including Saudi Salafism, were responding to shifting youth sensibilities. During regular visits to Saudi Arabia, I interviewed religious scholars and engaged with university-aged Saudis to understand their views on 'Wahhabi orthodoxy' and state-imposed social norms. I discovered that young Saudis, though firmly grounded in their Muslim identity, displayed remarkably globalized outlooks. Thus, when Crown Prince Muhammad bin Salman introduced Vision 2030 in 2016, followed by major social reforms in 2017, the direction of change was expected; however, the speed and extent of the change were striking.

Since late 2017, long-standing social restrictions, such as those on women's dress, gender segregation and forms of social entertainment that were foundational pillars of the Saudi social milieu, have been systematically dismantled. Even more remarkable has been the enthusiastic embrace of these reforms by a visible segment of a society long regarded as deeply traditional – a process that I continue to observe to date under an ERC Advanced Grant (European Union's Horizon 2020 Research and Innovation Programme, Grant Agreement No. 101019016). While those assessing progress through a Western feminist lens or human rights standards still often highlight the limits of ongoing reforms, the transformation within Saudi society from the pre-2017 social order is dramatic. My engagement with Saudi Arabia since 2014 has enabled me to document this profound 'before and after' transition. This book primarily chronicles the rapid transformation of Saudi social norms between 2017 and 2025. Should the reforms persist, the new social order will consolidate, turning the once-rigid social framework that has defined the kingdom since its 1932 founding into a distant memory. This underscores the importance of documenting the details of this transitional period. Simultaneously, the book explores the state's motivations for implementing these reforms and examines the societal forces that influenced their reception and widespread acceptance.

While the narrative centres on change, it also underscores the importance of what remains unchanged. In line with theories of institutional change, I argue that rapid shifts rarely emerge spontaneously; rather, they are the culmination of gradual, often overlooked developments. Saudi Arabia exemplifies this dynamic: the heavy focus on oil rents and the authoritarian nature of the state has obscured observers' attention to the agency of the Saudi people and to a steady development agenda pursued by the state. I demonstrate that these reforms were not arbitrary top-down edicts but a calculated response to the changing aspirations of Saudi youth, and that they build on a steadily supported development agenda rather than constituting a sudden rupture. Their rapid acceptance stems from the state's strategic responsiveness to local sensibilities and continuous societal feedback, while simultaneously developing an efficient infrastructure to support new choices.

This period of transformation thus calls into question dominant assumptions in Western scholarship on Saudi state–society relations and argues for recognizing the dynamism of Saudi society, as well as of the Saudi state, in order to better understand the country's future trajectory. For scholars who interpret Saudi governance primarily through the rentier state model, such an analysis may be discomforting; yet it is essential to distinguish between benevolence and strategic interest. Reinterpreting state–society relations in Saudi Arabia is not an argument for attributing benevolence to the regime, but for recognizing that the Saudi royal family – like all long-enduring political orders – wants to govern by cultivating consent where possible, because doing so is more sustainable than rule by force.

A Note on Transliteration

The transliteration in this volume has been kept simple in view of the multidisciplinary nature of the expected readership. With the exception of the ‘ to indicate the Arabic letters ‘ayn and ‘hamza, diacritical marks have been avoided. Except for the word ‘ulama’, the plural form of Arabic words is indicated by the addition of an *s* to the singular form. To avoid strain on the eyes and minimize distractions while reading, words that are frequently repeated (such as ‘aqidah) are not italicized except on their first occurrence. Non-English words used only once in the text are defined where they occur, but are not included in the glossary.

Chapter 1

INTRODUCTION

Of the 195 countries in the world, 50 are estimated to have Muslim-majority populations (PRC 2011; Britannica 2023a). Of those, the one most explicitly associated with Islam is Saudi Arabia – home to the two holiest Muslim cities: Mecca and Medina. Carved on the map of the world as recently as 1932, Saudi Arabia has historically gripped the global imagination on account of its religious fervour (al-Rasheed 2002; Champion 2003; Stenslie 2012; al-Shihabi 2016). Until the beginning of the ongoing social reforms, which started in 2017, the ruling monarchy, the Al-Saud family, was seen as legitimizing its rule through skilful manoeuvring of religious authority and the distribution of oil rents (Beblawi 1987; Beblawi and Luciani1987; al-Rasheed 2002; Vitalis 2009; al-Shihabi 2016; Ismail 2021). Its neglect of basic political and social liberties has historically been a serious concern (al-Rasheed 2015, 2021; HRW 2023). Divinely ordained *shari'ah* (the ideal of Islamic law), rather than a modern constitution, defined the law (Brown 2012), and Islamic jurists, rather than judges trained in modern law, ran the courts (Vogel 2000, Mouline 2014). Oil wealth appeared to have insulated the Saudi state from external criticism, whether it was the refusal to allow women to drive or the enforcement of *hudud* (Islamic corporal punishments), including public executions, in a way that other Muslim countries, needing the support of Western development institutions, cannot afford.

Yet in October 2017, this strong defiance of external criticism suddenly gave way without much warning. A young Crown Prince, the first to go beyond the line of succession involving the sons of the founding monarch (Stenslie 2012; al-Rasheed 2015), King Abdulaziz al Saud, set out an ambitious agenda of social and economic reform, referred to as Vision 2030, first announced on 25 April 2016 (GoSA 2016). The first batch of serious social reforms under Vision 2030, announced in September 2017 (Hubbard 2017; Kinninmont 2017; Ottaway 2018), initially perceived by many observers as a way to appease Western critics, have since then developed into an expanded network of social reforms supported by a series of successive royal decrees. Further, as this book will demonstrate, visible segments of the Saudi public have embraced these reforms at an unprecedented pace (The Economist 2023c), which has led to visible shifts in social norms. The Wahhabi religious establishment, historically a partner of the ruling family which enjoyed much control over the social sphere (Commins 2009, 2015; Ménoret

2014; Mouline 2014, 2015), was effectively marginalized within the first year of the announcement of the social reforms (al-Rasheed 2020; Farouk and Brown 2021; Hammond 2021): royal decrees removing social restrictions long defended by Wahhabi scholars are routinely issued without even a pretence of seeking a stamp of approval from the clergy.

Specializing in the study of major Islamic scholarly traditions, including Saudi Salafism (now a more commonly used term than Wahhabism to describe the Saudi religious sphere),[1] I have conducted regular fieldwork in Saudi Arabia since 2014 (Bano 2018e, 2021). Like many other scholars, I was aware that, despite the rigidity traditionally associated with Saudi society, significant changes were underway (Yamani 2000; Haykel et al. 2015b; Bano 2018e). Yet even scholars of this orientation have been surprised by the extent of the reforms in question, which started by giving women the right to drive – a major concession in the Saudi context, announced in September 2017 (al-Jazeera 2017; Hubbard 2017). In another country, the removal of this restriction might appear a minor issue, but for Saudi Arabia, such a reversal, without much warning, was significant for its high symbolic value (al-Saadi 2008; Arab News 2016). The ban on women driving was one of the restrictions most frequently referenced in Western media and also identified by many scholars as a proof of the excessively puritanical zeal of the Wahhabi clergy (Le Renard 2014; Ménoret 2014). The Saudi state had long stood firm on this prohibition, despite the negative publicity that it received on the global stage. On 6 November 1990, the Interior Ministry had formally banned female driving in response to a demonstration by forty-seven women in Riyadh, who demanded more rights for women, including the right to drive (Le Renard 2014; Ménoret 2014). Ménoret (2014) notes how these protests highlighted the politicization of urban spaces and questioned the role of social order maintained through traffic control. It raised the possibility that roads and cars, traditionally tools of policing and enforcing discipline, could also become spaces for gender struggle and alternative public spheres.

Even at the time of the launch of Vision 2030 in April 2016, when quizzed by a reporter about whether the promised social reforms would entail giving women the right to drive, the Crown Prince Muhammad bin Salman al-Saud had argued that the pace of change had to match the realities of each society, and that such changes can only be gradual (Arab News 2016). Yet a year later not only did he announce the abandonment of this restriction (al-Jazeera 2017; Hubbard 2017) but it proved to be just the first step in the promotion of a fast-paced agenda of social liberalization which reversed most of the social restrictions attributed to the Wahhabi way of thinking (Sanchez 2018; The New Arab 2018; Buckley 2019; Graham-Harrison 2019). Neither existing studies on the Saudi religious establishment (Mouline 2015) or religious milieu in general (Ménoret 2020) nor my own fieldwork experience, based on interactions with the wider public, had predicted such a rapid pace of change or such a clear sidelining of the Wahhabi religious elites as we have witnessed since November 2017. In a survey of male Saudi youth responding to ongoing reforms, Thompson (2019) found that 80 per cent of respondents believe that due to Vision 2030-linked reforms, Saudi

Arabia is changing very quickly. Some curbs on the power of the *hay'ah* (religious police) were implemented earlier: in response to public outcry after a video of them went viral in 2016, showing them dragging two girls to a van for not being appropriately covered (Bano 2018e). However, these were primarily viewed as preventive measures to check the abuse of power, rather than as indications of an active move towards promoting social liberalization or consciously rolling back Wahhabi-defined social restrictions. As I show in Chapter 2, the tone for genuine reform was formerly set with the announcements made in September 2017.

More to the point, the scepticism that greeted these policy announcements faded soon. The initial reaction within Western media and policy circles, lasting till early 2021, was that the social reforms were merely aimed at winning good will in the eyes of Western governments by an ambitious young crown prince whose personal image was badly tarnished by his alleged association with the murder of a Saudi journalist, Jamal Khashoggi, in Turkey (Kirchgaessner 2021; BBC 2021). Yet, by 2023, the changes on the ground in terms of how the Saudi social and public sphere is organized, what women can or cannot do, and the level of approved gender mixing in public spaces were real and extensive (Ebrahim 2022; The Economist 2023a, 2023b). Affirming this, an article subtitled 'Hedonism in the Gulf' in the February 2023 issue of *The Economist* began by referencing the mixed-gender music raves being organized in the desert (The Economist 2023a). It went on to emphasize how the Saudi state, once associated with the most socially restrictive form of Islam and regarded as the home of a highly conservative and tribal society, is today being transformed in ways that no one would have predicted five years ago (The Economist 2023a). Throughout 2023, the publication of such articles had become a regular occurrence in prominent Western newspapers and magazines known for credible reporting.[2] Yet, among many at home and abroad, the extent and speed of this change left lingering questions about its permanence. Is a strong backlash, led by marginalized religious figures, in the making? It was a question on the minds not only of external observers of Saudi society, but also, as my interviews suggest, among those who were leading the change. The reasons for this unease were obvious.

Any fast pace of change provokes concerns because when institutions that have enjoyed political backing for as long as the religious establishment in Saudi Arabia have, become marginalized so rapidly, it is natural to expect them to try to marshal support and stage a comeback (Ottaway 2018).[3] Informal institutions, such as social norms, culture, and religious beliefs, are characterized by a particularly strong institutional inertia (North 1990). The complex network of organizations and individuals linked to such institutions ends up creating strong financial and ideological incentives to perpetuate its own survival (Bano 2012). The religious establishment in Saudi Arabia has a sophisticated hierarchical structure, starting at the top with the Council of Senior Scholars (*Hay'at Kibar al-'Ulama'*), the highest religious body in Saudi Arabia with the power to religiously endorse state policies and issue *fatwa*s (religious decrees),[4] extending to the lowest tier, the *imam*s (prayer leaders) in the local mosques. The mosque imams, being based within the local communities, can shape people's beliefs about the right moral conduct, just as do the fatwas and sermons of more renowned scholars serving on the Council of Senior Scholars. At each tier, there is scope for the exercise of individual agency, which can result in outright refusal (or subtle resistance) to follow the orders from the top of the hierarchy if they are seen to be clashing with people's personal religious commitments. To expect the entire religious hierarchy to fall in line with change at such a rapid pace as we have witnessed in Saudi Arabia, due to a shift in state orientation, would appear naive. Being the key partners of the state, actors staffing different tiers of the Wahhabi religious establishment knew its workings very well.

Further, since the 1970s, Saudi religious teachings have also gained a visible following among Muslims worldwide under the banner of Salafism (Bano and Sakurai 2015; Spannaus 2018b; Bano 2018d, 2021), even though they have been highly contentious among adherents of classical Islamic scholarly tradition and within the Shia community (Fouad 2021; Fuller 2000; al-Shihabi 2016). The decision of the Crown Prince and his advisors to turn their backs on the Wahhabi establishment did not mean that its ardent followers, at home or abroad (Bano 2021; Ismail 2021), would give up their religious zeal.

Theoretically, it is well recognized that informal institutions, such as norms, values and beliefs, have a higher level of stickiness because their observation is not entirely conditional on state enforcement mechanisms (North 1990; Greif 2006; Bano 2012). Until the initiation of the recent reforms, Saudi Arabia used *hay'ah* (religious police) to enforce the social puritanism prescribed by the Wahhabi religious establishment; but it was clear that for the majority, the compliance was largely voluntary. The reason why informal institutions persist is that for most adherents there is a strong internal compulsion to obey them, motivated by deep personal conviction in the validity of those religious beliefs or norms – and thus the need for state enforcement is reduced (Coleman 1990; North 1990; Bano 2012). Further, the violation of established religious or social norms normally carries strong social sanctions such as exclusion from the group, losing status in the eyes of the community members, or more direct sanctions enforced by community elders (Coleman 1990; Bicchieri 2006; Opp 2018). Individuals therefore routinely refrain from violating the socio-religious norms, even if they personally might not endorse them (Bursztyn et al. 2020; Nosenzo and Görges 2020).

The difficulty in changing well-established socio-religious norms through state-led policy reforms is well documented in research: one obvious example is that of the practice of female genital mutilation (FGM) prevalent in some African countries. State and donor-led policy reforms aimed at banning this practice have failed because society as a whole remains unconvinced (UNICEF 2023; HRC 2023). The challenges faced in the past by liberal reformers in Muslim societies aiming to engineer support for liberal social norms are also well documented. Turkey under Mustafa Kemal Ataturk (1881–1938), and Ba'athist Syria of the 1970s, are but two obvious examples (Bano 2017, 2018a; Pierret 2013). Ataturk's reforms failed to secularize Turkish society, despite his use of absolute state power, which included the banning of *madrasahs* (Islamic schools) and *tekkes* (Sufi lodges) (Spannaus 2018a; Bano 2018a). Islam survived due to individual commitment to Islamic beliefs, and because the Turkish social fabric was intrinsically shaped by the Islamic ethical and moral framework. The ripping off of Muslim women's headscarves on the streets of Damascus in the 1970s by the Ba'ath regime under its modernization agenda similarly did not make the majority of Syrian women give up their head coverings (Bano 2017). The state-propelled liberalism of Pahlavi Iran faced even stronger resistance, giving way to the establishment of *Vilayat-i-Faqih* (Guardianship of the Islamic Jurist).[5]

Thus, despite the apparent dramatic reversal of the power and fortunes of the religious establishment in Saudi Arabia, as I have found during my fieldwork, there were, and are, on-going debates, even among those who are helping the Crown Prince to shape and roll out the reforms, about what should be the extent of this change and what needs to be done to ensure its durability. In my experience, these debates were particularly intense during the first three years following the initiation of the reforms (Bano 2021). Religious traditions, such as Saudi Salafism, and religious establishments, such as the Saudi Wahhabi elites, have deep roots stemming not just from the power of the preachers but also from the loyalty of the genuine believers (Bano 2021; Ismail 2021). Even if the state can put pressure on the Wahhabi religious elites embedded within the state to stay quiet, as it seems to have managed to do, questions remain about society's acceptance of all these changes. By changing their behaviour in favour of liberal options since the policy announcements have been made, the socio-religious norms of the Saudi public seem to have undergone an actual shift. We are not looking at a situation where a state is merely issuing policy announcements; instead, since the initiation of the social reforms in 2017, we have witnessed an unprecedented rapid shift in social norms.

Finally, in the initial period, the controversial image of the Crown Prince (Kirchgaessner 2021; BBC 2021) also raised questions about a reform agenda strongly associated with his persona. Not only was he, and still is, associated with the use of excessive force to quell any form of dissent (al-Rasheed 2020; HRW 2022; Amnesty International 2023b, 2024a, 2024b); he also represented a major shift in the line of succession in the Saudi royal family (Butt 2017; Macdonald et al. 2023). Political authority has finally been transferred into the hands of a grandson of King Abdulaziz al Saud, instead of one of his many sons (Stenslie 2012).[6] This shift, as scholars had started to note more than a decade ago, was expected to be critical in shaping the future of the royal family (Niblock 2006; Stenslie 2012; Haykel et al. 2015a). The power struggles within the family became very public when the Crown Prince placed some of its members under arrest at the Ritz-Carlton Hotel in Riyadh in 2017, at around the time when initial reforms were announced.[7] These internal factions and rivalries within the ruling dynasty also left lingering suspicion in the minds of sceptics that a possible alliance may be brewing between its aggrieved members and the marginalized Wahhabi scholars.

While these concerns had strong conceptual weight, what makes present-day Saudi Arabia such an interesting case for social science theorizing is that the developments on the ground have largely defied such expectations. While in the initial period, most of my Saudi respondents used to acknowledge that the pace of change is too fast, and that just a few years ago no one could have contemplated such major social shifts (Ebrahim 2022; The Economist 2023a, 2023b), a major share of the public started to take active part in the process of social liberalization almost immediately, and this participation was not limited to the urban centres. Studies of social change almost always record a difference between the sentiments of those in the urban centres, especially the affluent classes living in up-market areas, and those of people in the rural or more remote parts of the country as well as those living on the edge of the cities in economically difficult conditions (Arnosti and Liu 2018; Niskanen Center 2019; Platteau 2000; Luca et al. 2023). The urban centres often lead on the acceptance of such reforms, by virtue of having a concentration of socio-political and economic elites and housing the media outlets, which are normally owned by those very elites (Savat 2020; Luca et al. 2023). Elite adoption of liberal reforms gradually helps to transmit those reforms to the middle- and lower-income social strata, and eventually the acceptance spreads from urban centres to rural areas.

Yet in the case of Saudi Arabia, we have not seen a time lag in winning over a visible number of converts to liberal reforms in remote regions. The acceptance of more radically liberal options, such as participation in mixed-gender desert raves, remains largely confined to the elite segments of the population in Riyadh and Jeddah. However, in terms of participation in basic liberties, such as working in mixed-gender settings or women driving, there was early adoption even in more remote cities. As we will see in this volume, across the country, many Saudi men, women, and families very quickly started availing the new social opportunities promoted by the state, which directly challenged the strict social conservatism and gender segregation that marked Saudi society prior to the introduction of social reforms. This is consistent with the responses of Saudi youth surveyed by Thompson (2019), where 70 per cent viewed social change as being more pronounced in urban areas. However, they did not negate the perception that overall, this change was affecting the entire country.

Failing to recognize the conceptual challenges posed by the rapid acceptance of state-proposed social reforms among visible segments of Saudi society, especially the youth, risks promoting simplistic answers. The most common of these is the assumption that there was never genuine adherence to Wahhabi Salafi teachings among large segments of the Saudi population, and that religious expression was merely a byproduct of state policies. According to this view, once the state reduced its reliance on religious authority and lifted religiously enforced restrictions, the highly conservative nature of society simply vanished. As studies on the growth of Salafi movements across the globe suggest, that is not plausible (Thurston 2016; Bano 2021; Ismail 2021; Rock-Singer 2022). Further, how does such an assertion align with the evidence presented in earlier studies documenting the strong presence of the Wahhabi religious establishment (Mouline 2014) and the popularity of reformist scholars, such as those leading the al-Sahwah movement, among Saudi youth (Ménoret 2020)? Similarly, how does this claim reconcile with the dominant narrative in Western scholarship, which has overwhelmingly portrayed Saudi Arabia as a conservative society, where religion and tribal traditions were the most influential forces in shaping the social and political order (al-Rasheed 2002; Champion 2003)? Were these studies overestimating the influence of religion and tradition to such a degree?

This book unpacks this complex puzzle of rapid norm shifts in a society that, in the view of most observers, manifested an archaic social order and religious devotion – at times even appearing fanatical – and was seen as being incapable of undergoing major social change (Manning 1998; Lippman 2012; Friedman 2015; Whitkaer 2015). In doing so, in line with current theorization on institutional change (North 1990), it presents a fascinating story of how what appears as sudden change is almost always a result of incremental shifts that observers have failed to register.

This book aims primarily to contribute to documenting the rapidly shifting realities on the ground in Saudi Arabia. If the current pace of social liberalization continues, detailed accounts of this transitional period (2017–2025) – which saw extreme orthodoxy give way to relatively liberal social norms almost overnight – will be essential for understanding Saudi society. A close examination of this period is crucial not only to avoid simplistic narratives that overlook the society's historical complexities but also because the trajectory set during moments of profound change shapes the long-term path a society follows. Theories of social change emphasize that the direction taken at critical junctures often determines long-term outcomes due to path dependence (North 1990). Identifying the direction of change set in this initial period is vital because modernity can take many forms – the continuum between a highly orthodox religious society and a secular liberal order is wide. Whether Saudi Arabia evolves into another Dubai – often seen as a crude replication of Western material culture – within the next decade or finds a distinct balance will depend on the power dynamics between the state, religious elites and wider society as they unfold during this initial transition. Accurately predicting the country's future trajectory requires a nuanced analysis of these interactions.

The analysis presented in this book is intended for both academic specialists and general readers seeking to make sense of the profound changes unfolding in Saudi Arabia. Within the specialist audience, the primary group consists of scholars in the field of Islamic Studies who seek to understand the factors behind the sudden decline in the power of the Saudi Wahhabi establishment and its interpretation of Islam, commonly referred to as Salafism. This is a major theme, as Salafism has been the most influential Islamic puritanical movement of the late twentieth-century and early twenty-first century (Commins 2009, 2015; Spannaus 2018a; Bano 2021). From earlier assertions that global Salafism has been fuelled by Saudi money, and that it provides theological fodder to Islamic jihadi groups, the studies that have emerged in recent years on Salafi movements in different country contexts have come to record the role of active local agency in its spread (Eyre 2021; Diwan 2021; Russell 2021). What happens to Salafism in its home base does, however, generate critical questions about the future of Salafism across different contexts.

The sociologists of religion, the second target audience for this volume, are interested in the same issues, but with a view to testing theories of secularization and modernity. The recent evidence of dramatic social liberalization in Saudi Arabia can apparently find support for the secularization thesis, whereby modernity and material prosperity are argued to lead to a decline in religiosity (Taylor 2007; Inglehart 2021). Muslim societies are often presented, especially in anthropological studies, as being averse to processes of secularization (Mahmood 2005; Agrama 2012; Hirschkind 2009).[8] Is the Saudi case proving such an assumption wrong, and if so, then what kind of secularization is under way in Saudi Arabia: a desire to separate church and state, or a much more fundamental shift, whereby there is a decline in belief itself? (Taylor 2007; Inglehart 2021). These developments in Saudi Arabia also provide an opportunity to reconsider the often-posed question: Is Islam going to undergo a reformation as did Christianity in sixteenth-century Europe? (Zubaida 2016; Akyol 2017; Fukuyama 2017a–c).

The third academic audience for which this volume has most critical theoretical and policy relevance consists of scholars, students and practitioners in the field of international development – an interdisciplinary field of inquiry interested in improving human well-being across societies and bridging the gaps that exist between the developed and developing worlds. Among scholars of international development, the earlier focus on studying economic change has now been complemented by a focus on understanding the role of culture and norms in promoting or hindering human flourishing and well-being (North 1990; Klugman et al. 2014). Muslim societies, even the economically affluent Gulf states, are often ranked low on development indicators aimed at measuring human well-being due to receiving negative points due to differences in gender related outcomes (HDR 2019). This is because increasingly the international development institutions attempt to measure societal progress not just by using economic indicators but also by including other variables pertaining to gender equality, democratization, and sexual and civic liberties (GIWPS and PRIO 2017; HDR 2019).

Low performance on such indicators, especially among oil-rich Gulf states, is routinely attributed to Islamic dictates (Klugman et al. 2014; Akeel 2017). Yet the sudden opening up of space for women in Saudi Arabia, a society where they were seen to be denied basic rights due to the influence of Islam, shows how assumptions about the controlling power of norms and religious beliefs in Muslim societies need unpacking. It also shows how our theoretical understanding of the working of the socio-religious norms, why they consolidate or change, and at times very rapidly, is limited. Building an individual-actor approach to the study of social norms (Coleman 1990; North 1990; Bicchieri 2006), as opposed to taking them as a given, this book attempts to refine our theoretical understanding of the working of social norms: why certain social norms come to dictate social order, what gives them stability, what triggers change and why sometimes the change appears so unpredictable and rapid. The policy implications of such an analysis are far reaching in the field of international development. The final chapter of this book will thus particularly focus on theorizing about social norms and making explicit the relevance of these findings for international development policy.

This multi-layered analysis, designed to address various disciplinary interests, may require patience from area specialists who, given the nature of their scholarship, may be primarily interested in the specifics of the Saudi case. While I recognize the value of such a focused approach, my interdisciplinary background and expertise in the comparative study of Muslim societies compel me, as a scholar, to draw broader theoretical and policy insights from any case study I examine. To balance these differing needs, I have structured each chapter to stand independently, allowing readers to directly access their chapter of interest while still following the overall argument. Catering to a mixed audience also means providing, on occasions, broad historical overviews – such as the rise of the Wahhabi Salafi scholarly tradition in Chapter 3 – which are very familiar to scholars specializing in Saudi Arabia but not to those new to the region. At the same time, I hope specialists will uncover new insights in each chapter. Thus, while Chapter 3 devotes much attention to documenting the historical understanding of the rise of the alliance between the House of Saud and the House of Wahhab, its main contribution is to provide key insights into the factors that led to the breakdown of this historic alliance – insights that go beyond what existing scholarship has offered.

It is essential to outline the core argument upfront to ensure that the contribution of each successive chapter in unpacking its components is clear and easy to follow. The first core argument of this volume is empirical: the pace of social change since November 2017 has been rapid by all accounts – whether from observers, Saudis themselves (both youth and adults), or even from the planners' own acknowledgments. The initial part of the volume establishes this argument through fieldwork evidence, tracing shifts in social norms from 2014 to 2025. This provides an objective 'before and after' comparison, marking late 2017 as the key point of transition.

This empirical evidence sets the stage for a conceptual analysis of the forces driving these changes. The story here is complex: while the reforms of this period may appear as sudden shifts orchestrated by the Crown Prince, they are, in fact, the outcome of incremental social changes rooted in investments that began in the 1960s. What seems like abrupt change is a response to gradual shifts – especially among the younger generation – fuelled by development and opportunities that emerged in the 2000s. Moreover, the Crown Prince's influence over the extent and nature of liberal social reforms is not absolute. Throughout this volume, we observe how, if left to his own preferences, he might push further than many segments of society are ready to accept. However, his pursuit of popular legitimacy prevents him from crossing certain lines. With the diminished power of the religious elites, societal sentiment itself acts as a check. As I demonstrate in this volume, wider society favours a middle path – a balance between the extreme conservatism of the Wahhabi establishment and wholesale adoption of Western liberalism.

Thus, we see that the Saudi society's relationship with Islam and tribal traditions is far more nuanced than narratives rooted in either religious essentialism, which allow for no change, or the secularization thesis, which predicts an inevitable decline of religiosity with the spread of education and economic modernization. Simultaneously, the relationship between the Saudi royal family and society is more complex than transactional accounts that reduce it to a mere exchange of rents for loyalty. What stands out during this period of rapid change is the royal family's desire to gain popular legitimacy, particularly among young Saudis. It is my contention that as long as this drive for popular legitimacy persists, the ongoing social transformations are likely to consolidate around a moderate path. The final section of this chapter will outline how individual chapters contribute to unpacking this overarching narrative.

1.1. Saudi social opening

On 26 September 2017, the Crown Prince announced that Saudi women would be allowed to drive, starting in June 2018 (al-Jazeera 2017). The reversal of this ban marked a significant shift in social policy (Le Renard 2014; Ménoret 2014). The ban had been the most frequently quoted reference used by Western media to record concern about the oppression of Saudi women, and it had become a symbol of the Saudi state's unwillingness to yield to external pressures in the shaping of its social norms. Soon, other women-specific restrictions started to disappear. The announcement removing the requirement for women to wear *'abayah* (robe-like dress worn by Muslim women) came in March 2018 (The New Arab 2018; Sanchez 2018). Before long, amendments were also announced to the male guardianship rules (*waliyah*) (al-Hussein 2019), which had long attracted severe criticism from Western human rights groups for restricting female agency in all spheres of life (Beckerle 2016). At the same time, restrictions banning common sources of social entertainment, such as cinemas and concerts, were removed, and a whole array of entertainment options suddenly became available. Simultaneously, the provision and promotion of sports facilities for both men and women became a key priority in a country where this had never previously been encouraged. Further, from being very closed to the outsiders, whereby travel to most parts of the country was restricted even for Muslim travellers coming to the country on pilgrimage, Saudi Arabia opened its doors to tourists from across the globe. To attract Western nationals, who normally have more money to spend, an option of obtaining a visa on arrival was introduced. Former restrictions that had discouraged Western tourists in the past, such as not allowing unmarried couples to check into hotels, were removed (Buckley 2019).

Not just by Western standards but also by the standards of Muslim societies, many of these liberties and social provisions are aspects of basic freedoms. Even in the surrounding Gulf states, including Qatar – the only other state apart from Saudi Arabia that officially subscribes to Wahhabi teachings (Roberts 2014; Dorsey 2017) –women already enjoyed the right to drive.[9] In the United Arab Emirates, the development model has, in fact, taken these liberties as a given. But these shifts are phenomenal in the case of Saudi Arabia, which had held these basic freedoms at bay for most of its history and had done so largely in the name of Islam (Le Renard 2014; Ménoret 2014), and on the basis of Saudi Arabia's stated claim of being the Custodian of the Two Holy Mosques. The state also had funded the required infrastructure to enforce these restrictions: the *hay'ah* police, operating under the directives of the Wahhabi '*ulama*' (Islamic scholars), was responsible for controlling social vice (Mouline 2015). These shifts thus record a major shift in the attitude of the state towards the conception of public sphere and appropriate social norms, and towards the Wahhabi readings of Islam that underpinned it.

Further, since the initial announcements made in September 2017, the social liberalization agenda is not confined to opening up social spaces and giving women freedom: it has gradually come to target specific religious practices themselves. New regulations governing the use of loudspeakers by mosques, announced at the end of May 2021, restricted their use strictly to *adhan* (the call to prayer), and required the volume to be kept low, in a bid to reduce disturbance to the public (al-Jazeera 2021a; Reuters 2021b). The call to prayer, which literally asks believers to 'come to prayer' and to 'come to salvation', before each of the five obligatory prayers that Muslims perform, holds strong significance in Muslim societies. Muslims are advised to listen to it with attention and say *salawat* (to pray for divine blessings on the Prophet Muhammad). A loudspeaker is meant to extend the radius within which individuals can hear the call from a particular mosque. The secular-oriented Muslims often complain that the presence of many mosques in the same area creates noise pollution.

For the majority, such an attitude is disrespectful of adhan. Restricting the use of loudspeakers was thus a contentious decision and a clear statement in favour of secular voices (al-Jazeera 2021a; Reuters 2021b). The policy requiring all shops and businesses to close for prayer was similarly abandoned (al-Kinani 2021; Nasrallah 2021). By implication, Muslim employees in the stores are no longer expected to pray in the mosque, a preferred action for Muslim men than praying at home or at work. While defending these reforms, the Crown Prince went so far as to directly criticize the Wahhabi scholars in interviews given to Western media outlets (BBC 2017a; Chulov 2017; Ottaway 2021a). Since the rise of al-Qaida, which eventually targeted the Saudi state itself, the Saudi government has actively condemned jihadi groups (Maher 2016; al-Saud 2021), but until the Crown Prince made these public critiques, no senior Saudi royal or state official had directly criticized Wahhabi scholarly tradition.

To many Western commentators or media outlets, these changes appeared superficial, and when reporting them, they chose to highlight the continued prohibitions on certain things, instead of focusing on the general significance of the restrictions that have been removed. One such case was the critique of the first Grand Prix held in Saudi Arabia in 2021. The critics mocked the opening by focusing on restrictions such as the requirement of a strict dress code, for women visitors (Marca Monitor 2021) – which was later dropped (The New Arab 2021) – instead of focusing on how an event which would formerly have been labelled un-Islamic was now being held and actively promoted by the very state which previously labelled such events as *haram* (forbidden in Islamic law). The same critical attitude is evident in the engagement of more serious Western organizations with the on-going reforms. For example, Human Rights Watch, which is highly critical of the male guardianship rule in Saudi Arabia and other Gulf states such as Qatar, remains focused on showing how the changes made to the guardianship rules are still highly restrictive (HRW 2023).

Those familiar with the Wahhabi Salafi teachings that underpinned these social restrictions can, however, see that these are major shifts in terms of the social opening up, and also in terms of rolling back the power of the religious elites, and the Saudi state's conscious delinking of itself from Wahhabi readings of Islam (al-Rasheed 2020; Farouk and Brown 2021). Further, those who were frequent visitors to Saudi Arabia before the social reforms can see that a major section of Saudi society has welcomed the changes. The new entertainment venues that have been opened are thronged not only by young Saudi men and women but even more visibly by Saudi families. Western tourists, with men dressed in shorts and women wearing Western attire, are not being shunned. Similarly, many Saudi women have come forward to fill employment opportunities created as a result of the conscious efforts of the state to 'Saudi-ise' the economy and reduce reliance on foreign workers (Akeel 2021). Women are now very visible as saleswomen in shops; they staff the help desks in the malls, and act as guides for many state-funded tourist projects. While some political economists argue that these are low-income jobs, which thus bring limited gains to the employees (Diwan 2019; Hertog 2019), socio-culturally, this development is significant. The fact that these are low-income jobs demonstrates that the gender dynamics are changing – not just among the elite families living in big cities, but even among those in the low- and middle- income brackets, from which women are actively coming forward to fill these roles.

For observers of the Saudi state and society, and for social scientists interested in theorizing about social norms and institutional change, these are fascinating developments. There is also an added dimension that makes the reversal of socially conservative policies, and the curtailed power of the Wahhabi elites, important to study: what happens in Saudi Arabia will have consequences for Islam as we have come to know it on the global stage. The fact that Saudi Arabia encompasses Mecca and Medina lends its interpretation of Islam, even though long contested by classical Islamic schools, a certain degree of legitimacy, especially among the lay public in Muslim countries. Thus, although the thesis that oil money fuels Saudi Salafism across the globe remains contested (Bano and Sakurai 2015; Bano 2021), the legitimacy enjoyed by the Saudi royal family and the Saudi Salafi brand of Islam among large sections of the Muslim population – due to its role as the Custodian of the Two Holy Mosques – cannot be denied. Not just for Westerners, but also for the ordinary Muslim public, the fact that Saudi Arabia controls the *haramayn* ('the two sanctuaries', Mecca and Medina) implies that by default, Saudi readings of Islam represent Islamic orthodoxy. This results in a voluntary deference for imams at the *Ka'bah*, and by default, the royal family – a deference that I have recorded in my work on madrasahs in Pakistan (Bano 2012). It is assumed that Saudi Islam best represents the *sunnah* (practice of the Prophet Muhammad), who founded the first Islamic state in Medina, and the teachings of *sahabah* (Prophet Muhammad's companions) who preserved his practice. Thus, the future of Wahhabism in its home base will have consequences not just for the future of Salafi movements in other countries, but equally for how Islam is presented in the coming decades on the global stage.

1.2. Holding power: Religious legitimacy

Adhering to a highly puritanical strand of Islam was, however, not the only reason why Saudi Arabia often received negative media coverage in the past. The related reason was the lack of democratic governance as understood in the West (al-Rasheed 2015, 2021; HRW 2019). The country is a monarchy. The name 'Saudi Arabia' comes from the very family that founded it, namely the Al-Saud (House of Saud) (Kostiner 1993; Vassiliev 2000; Stenslie 2012). In the Muslim world, while many countries remain under authoritarian rule or are ruled by some form of monarchy, Saudi Arabia was one of the very few to defy pressure to put in place some form of democratic institutions, which could give it a false impression of moving towards electoral democracy (al-Fahad 2004). Most military regimes in the developing world, as well as the ruling royal families in the Gulf and the Middle East, have adopted some kind of institutional or constitutional framework to claim democratic credentials, even if they exercise full control over the parliament, executive, and the judiciary (Brancati 2014; Wright and Escriba-Folch 2012; Ottaway 2021b).

Additionally, it is one of the few Muslim countries that historically did not adopt Western legal systems or related codification of laws (Vogel 2000; Brown 2012; Farouk and Brown 2021; Krell 2025). Most other Muslim nations have done so either because of the legacy of colonial rule or due to competitive pressures from Europe, as was the case with Turkey in the late eighteenth and early nineteenth centuries.[10] Shari'ah remains the basis of the Saudi constitution, and courts are run by Islamic jurists mainly trained in Hanbali *fiqh* (jurisprudence) (Vogel 2000; Krell 2025). Islamic jurists exercise much freedom in deciding a case in the light of their own interpretation of the Quran and Sunnah (Vogel 2000; Krell 2025), while laws are mainly formed by the issuance of royal decrees. Saudi Arabia therefore routinely gets a bad press for enforcing hudud punishments, which include the death penalty, for its failure to move towards electoral democracy, its restriction on civil liberties, and the absence of recourse to justice for political prisoners (HRW 2019). Its suppression of the minority Shia community (ICG 2005; Matthiesen 2015; Coogle 2018), other forms of political dissent by religious actors (Alshamsi 2011; Ménoret 2020), human rights activists (Amnesty International 2024b), and women's rights activists (Amnesty International 2024a; BBC 2024; ISHR 2024), as well as increased surveillance of social media (Diwan 2018; Amnesty International 2023b), is a subject of frequent critique.

Thus, Saudi politics and governance framework remain open to challenge on numerous counts. Within the Muslim world, however, the Saudi monarchy comes under criticism for quite different reasons. Ordinary Muslims, not just members of al-Qaida, remain critical of its alliance with the USA and of the multi-billion-dollar contracts that Saudi Arabia awards to US and European companies in armaments deals. In my experience, such critics don't shy away from labelling these contracts as 'bribes', given to ensure the security of the royal family. The royal family is also criticized for not using its abundant resources to help the Muslim world unite and stand up against Western imperialism – a concern that Ménoret (2020) records as also being shared by young Saudi Islamic activists. Its foreign policy is closely watched, and much hurt is expressed at its failure to use its clout on the international stage to stop the persecution of Muslims in disputed territories, whether in Indian-occupied Kashmir, or north-west China (where Uyghur Muslims are persecuted), or Palestine.[11] After October 7, the Saudi government was heavily criticized for failing to take a bold leadership position against Israel (Cook 2023), leading to significant disapproval among Muslims. Crown Prince Mohammed bin Salman was specifically criticized for engaging in seemingly frivolous activities, such as meeting with footballer Cristiano Ronaldo (Cook 2023), and for Riyadh's decision to proceed with all major planned activities. This included hosting the annual Future Investment Initiative (FII), referred to as 'Davos in the Desert', which welcomed over 6,000 participants from more than 90 countries during mid to late October, as Israel started to bombard Gaza (FII 2024). Social media accounts and international media reports have also noted strong censorship by Saudi police against members of the public displaying symbols of support for Palestine (Dagher 2024; Financial Times 2024). The sense of betrayal arising from this assumed failure of the Saudi royal family to oppose such abuses is most vividly expressed in al-Qaida's targeting of the Saudi royal family for its decision to allow the USA to have airbases on Saudi soil (Miller 2005).

The politics of the Saudi monarchy is thus criticized by both Western observers and more educated members of the public in the Muslim world, although from different perspectives. A monarchy with weak domestic political legitimacy is seen to be using religious legitimacy and oil wealth to assert political power (Champion 2003; al-Shihabi 2016), while simultaneously also guaranteeing armed protection against local revolt by winning support of Western states by offering lucrative contracts to American and European companies. Yet without much ado, the state has restricted the influence of the religious elites, who were previously used to legitimize its rule in the eyes of ordinary Saudis. The once powerful hay'ah police now has highly restricted power (Said-Moorhouse 2016). The state no longer actively seeks to legitimize royal decrees announcing social reforms by obtaining fatwas from the Council of Senior Scholars. Yet, the official Wahhabi establishment has not initiated any mass revolt; there have been no mass resignations or street protests.

These developments demonstrate the need to examine theoretical assumptions about how, and under what conditions, religious elites come to legitimize the power of the political elites. The processes of religious legitimation are much more complex than is, at times, recognized in the scholarship, especially as applied to the study of political and religious authority in the Muslim world. In a steadily expanding body of literature within historical institutionalism, underdevelopment in the Muslim world is being linked to the role of the 'ulama', the religious elites (Rubin 2017; Kuru 2019). It has been contended that the legitimizing power of the religious elites in the Muslim world is particularly strong because Islam, unlike other religions such as Christianity, requires Muslims to defer to the scholars (Rubin 2017). This assertion, based primarily with reference to a verse in the Quran, however, is misleading.[12] What is ignored in the process is that Islam lays down very tough conditions for anyone aspiring to the status of a religious scholar in the eyes of the public. There is no Pope in Sunni Islam; instead, scholars win popular following by demonstrating their individual calibre, which is constantly evaluated by the public against set expectations (Nizami 1983; Robinson 2001).

A scholar is expected to follow the model of the Prophet himself, not just by demonstrating mastery of the core texts but equally by living by the Islamic code of impeccable moral behaviour (Nizami 1983; Bano 2018a). Religious elites can only legitimize political elites if the former have a genuine public following. Once we recognize that the power of religious scholars to endorse political authority in Muslim societies does not simply rest on holding public office – though, as Zeghal (2007) has established in the case of al-Azhar, it can help strengthen the institution by putting state resources at its disposal – but is equally contingent on them living by a complex set of informal checks aimed at measuring their level of knowledge as well as their piety, we start to understand why the legitimizing power of the state-supported Wahhabi establishment has always had its limits. Understanding the sociology of the religious authority of scholars in Muslim societies, which is unpacked in Chapter 3, is also key to understanding the current marginalization of the official Wahhabi establishment in Saudi Arabia.

1.3. Holding power: Oil wealth

In addition to its religiously defined social conservatism and lack of democracy, the third factor that has made Saudi Arabia important in Western discourse on the Muslim world is its oil wealth. While on the one hand, as the second largest producer of oil in the world, Saudi Arabia has exercised much power on the international stage for its ability to influence global oil prices, on the other hand, oil wealth is also argued to be key to preserving monarchical rule and Saudi resistance to socio-political change (Champion 2003; Vitalis 2009). In most other Muslim countries, the West is able to exercise considerable control over socio-economic policies via multilateral and bilateral aid agencies and financial institutions, including the World Bank and International Monetary Fund (IMF), which offer financial bailouts but with major conditions attached (Gould 2006). Saudi Arabia's financial affluence, resulting from its oil wealth accumulated since the 1970s, has saved it from being vulnerable to such external pressures. Instead, it has been in a position to negotiate matters on its own terms. On the other hand, within domestic politics, it has been argued to have the ability to replace public accountability with oil rents, whereby the state offers basic social services and maintains an extended state employment network, to win public loyalty in return for political acquiescence (Vassiliev 2000; Vitalis 2009; Hertog 2010; POMEPS 2019).

In the past, the assertion that the House of Saud has been kept in place by the distribution of oil rents and by religious legitimization routinely led to negative predictions about the future of Saudi Arabia (Manning 1998; Lippman 2012; Whitkaer 2015). Under the Obama administration, the US president himself voiced such concerns about Saudi Arabia, making a serious dent in the decades-old alliance between the two countries. In April 2015, Obama told Thomas Friedman, of *The New York Times*, that Saudi Arabia and its neighbours should recognize that 'The biggest threats that they face may not be coming from Iran invading. It's going to be from dissatisfaction inside their own countries' (Friedman 2015). He listed sources of potential unrest in the following terms:

> populations that, in some cases, are alienated, youth that are underemployed, an ideology that is destructive and nihilistic, and, in some cases, just a belief that there are no legitimate political outlets for grievances. And so part of our job is to work with these states and say, How can we build your defense capabilities against external threats, but also, how can we strengthen the body politic in these countries, so that Sunni youth feel that they've got something other than [the Islamic State, or ISIS] to choose from. (Friedman 2015)

Not surprisingly, senior Saudi royals reacted strongly to Obama's statements; during his April 2016 visit to Riyadh, Obama was publicly snubbed (al-Faisal 2016).[13]

Yet these assumptions of a major revolt waiting to happen, which Western observers have voiced at numerous critical points in Saudi Arabia's history (Manning 1998; Lippman 2012; Whitkaer 2015) – Obama's view being no exception – have never materialized. Instead, the current social opening is marked by active participation and a high level of enthusiasm and support for the Crown Prince's Vision 2030 from many in the public, especially the young (Diwan 2016; Boiler 2018; Thompson 2019). Many of the very Saudi youth that President Obama presumed were highly frustrated, and soon to revolt, appear keen to work with the Crown Prince to achieve the Vision 2030, with its promise of economic diversification, the Saudi-isation of the economy and social liberalization. As my own fieldwork and other recent studies (Thompson 2019) show, a large percentage of young Saudis are keen to take responsibility for their own future and that of the country.[14] The Vision 2030's basic premise, that Saudi Arabia has to wean itself off oil and diversify its economy, has not led to the predicted protests, which had been based on the assumption that Saudi youth were so reliant on state largesse that they are unlikely to be willing to work (Diwan 2019). In initial assessments, the economic diversification plans set out in Vision 2030 were largely deemed unattainable (Diwan 2019; Hertog 2019).

However, as in the case of Saudi society's overall acceptance of the social liberalization process, and the quick reversal of the powers of the religious elites, it is necessary to question the starting assumptions about the Saudi state's capacity to pursue its stated economic reform agenda and the younger generation's willingness to co-operate in the process. Focusing specifically on the tourism industry, one of the three key pillars of the economic diversification plan outlined in Vision 2030 (GoSA 2016), and drawing on ethnographic fieldwork and participant observation conducted at key tourism-promotion programmes launched under Vision 2030, subsequent chapters will demonstrate that on this front, as with the promotion of social liberalization and the curbing of the power of religious elites, the Saudi state has been remarkably effective. In a country that was seen as too hot, too dry (due to its ban on alcohol and social entertainment), and lacking in geographical diversity – and despite the fact that it is largely a desert – an extensive, diverse and highly entertaining tourism infrastructure has evolved in less than four years. This infrastructure, as I found during my fieldwork, is winning the appreciation of Western tourists. Further, young Saudi men and women are actively staffing these projects. These young people have high expectations of the state, but their demands centre on the provision of better education and employment opportunities to build a better society for themselves and future generations, rather than on state largesse.

The state's ability to resist the influence of religious elites, despite drawing on their active support in the very formation of the Saudi state; its ability to convince many young people that the state cannot keep providing free goods funded by oil wealth, and that instead everyone needs to tighten their belts and work hard to contribute to a post-oil future; and, its ability to win significant social support for its liberalization agenda – all these factors demonstrate that the existing conceptions of the state–society relationship, especially those based entirely on rent distribution or oppression, need to be reconsidered (Niblock 2006; Thompson 2019). For the state to win the willing support of visible segments of Saudi society while enforcing a major agenda of socio-economic reform, there has to be some genuine congruence of interest between the two sides, and some level of trust in the state. Trust can only exist when those in power perform adequately by a measure of accountability, such that society views the privileges of the elites as fair compensation for their commitment (Niblock 2006). Further, this trust might be time-bound and conditional on the delivery of promised outcomes. As we will see, it is important to bear these factors in mind when interpreting the enthusiasm of Saudi youth for ongoing reforms.

Thus, we must refine existing assumptions about the nature of the relationship between the Saudi state and society, and we need also to understand the complex dynamics of the three-way relationship between those two elements and the Wahhabi religious establishment. As we will see, the evidence supports existing scholarship that non-Western societies, especially those with strong tribal cultural and religious values, often do have informal mechanisms of accountability that are not immediately visible to outside observers (Fortes and Evans-Pritchard 2015; Baldwin 2016). At the same time, attributing excessive power to religious elites over the shaping of popular perceptions (Rubin 2017; Kuru 2019) has led to a failure to appreciate the limits of religious authority in the Muslim world. People hold the scholars to account on many matters, and only those who meet all expectations can genuinely help to legitimize political authority. A religious establishment propped up by the state will violate some of these expectations sooner or later (Nizami 1983; Bano and Benadi 2017; Bano 2018a).

1.4. Holding Islam responsible: Institutions and development

In contemporary international development theory, the divergent development paths pursued by different societies over time are increasingly being attributed to the quality of their institutions (North 1990; North et al. 2009). A popular definition of institutions is: 'Institutions are the rules of the game in a society, or, more informally, are the humanly devised constraints that shape human interaction' (North 1990). While much earlier work in the field of international development focused on the role of formal institutions in shaping economic growth such as the state, laws, markets, and firms, in the past twenty years the role of informal institutions, such as norms, values and religious beliefs, has come to be recognized as being equally if not more important in shaping the development trajectory of a society (Greif 2006; Bano 2012). These propositions have, in particular, been advanced on the basis of studies that compared societies which were at comparable levels at one point in history, but eventually followed different development trajectories, such as North America versus South America (North 1990), and the Middle East versus Europe (Kuran 2010). Informal institutions are seen to be different from formal institutions because they do not have a formal state enforcement mechanism behind them. Instead, informal institutions shape individual decisions as a result of internal commitment to those beliefs, or the fear of social sanctions. This is argued to give informal institutions a higher degree of stickiness, or 'path dependence', a term that suggests that society often gets locked into certain equilibria due to choices made at an earlier point in time (Liebowitz and Margolis 1995).

Studies tracing what has been referred to as the 'long divergence' (Kuran 2010) at times hold Islamic law responsible for the decline in the economic fortunes of the Middle East compared with Western Europe, starting from the Middle Ages, and at times hold the religious clergy responsible for interpreting texts with the intention of consolidating their authority instead of prioritizing the collective good. Timur Kuran's thesis that Islamic inheritance law and rules relating to *waqf* (religious endowment) properties contributed to economic stagnation in the Middle East has won much traction (Kuran 2010). Drawing inspiration from Kuran's work, Jared Rubin (2017) has attributed this decline to the self-serving behaviour of the 'ulama'. His central thesis is that there are people or organizations in society that, due to their identity or their privileged access to resources, can help rulers to stay in power. He refers to these people as 'propagating agents' (Rubin 2017). Identifying two types of propagating agent – coercive agents and legitimizing agents – he contends that the former propagate rulers through force, and the latter by providing legitimacy. While coercive agents make people obey the rulers by threats of punishment, legitimizing agents do so by bestowing on the rulers the legitimacy and moral authority to rule. Being inexpensive, religious legitimization is highly attractive to the rulers. These propagating agents are clearly beneficial to the rulers, but their co-operation incurs a cost, in that they demand a seat at the bargaining table in return for their support. Rubin's contention is that the law and policies resulting from this bargain reflect the bargaining power of each player and their respective preferences (Rubin 2017).

Rubin uses this framework to contend that the Middle East lost out in economic terms to Europe because the religious scholars exercised a higher degree of legitimizing power in the Middle East than they did in Christian Europe. He attributes the higher legitimizing power of the religious elites in the Middle East to Islamic dictates that, he argues, unlike Christianity, explicitly require believers to obey the imam and the advice of the religious scholars (Rubin 2017: 49–54). The Saudi case helps to demonstrate the limits of such broad-brush historical comparative analysis. In Chapter 3, we will see that while the Quran may advise believers to follow the scholars, the authority of the scholar is not given (Brockopp 2020); it must be earned by demonstrating mastery over the text and living by its dictates. Violation of either expectation results in a highly compromised public following and a weak ability to legitimize the ruler. Thus, the assumption that Islamic scholars could perpetuate highly self-preserving policies and yet retain the public authority to legitimize rulers is not supported by historical or contemporary evidence and is logically inconsistent. Arguments about the Muslim world based on assumptions regarding the working of religious authority in the Christian world are inherently problematic due to the vastly different foundations of religious authority in the two traditions. As we will see in Chapter 3, once we correct for these assumptions, Rubin's thesis, also supported by Kuru (2019), about the role of religious elites in retarding socio-economic progress in Muslim societies, becomes questionable.

These assertions that Islamic law or opportunistic readings of the text by Muslim scholars in order to preserve their authority over the masses have resulted in inferior societal outcomes have not been confined to the domain of the economy. They are even more forcefully expressed in international development discourses about the apparent lag of progress in Muslim societies in terms of internationally developed indicators of female emancipation and civic and political liberties. Islam is perceived as inherently discriminatory against women, based on legal injunctions such as the rules that women receive only half the inheritance their brothers get when a parent dies; that men can have up to four wives at a time, while women can be married to only one man at any given time; or that two female witnesses are needed in matters of commerce, whereas only one male witness is required. Trying to nuance the debates in Western scholarship that judged Islamic law as being unfair, from the 1970s onwards scholars, who are often identified as Islamic feminists whether or not they prefer that label,[15] began to contend that it is not the texts but the male scholars' interpretation of them that leads to these differences (Mernissi 1991; Wadud 2006; Barlas 2019). However, most recent scholarship concerning Islamic women's movements and the propagation of classical Islamic teaching argues for noting the appeal of Islamic gender norms in their own right, rather than measuring them against a Western liberal framework (Mahmood 2005; Bano and Kalmbach 2011; Bano 2017). This line of scholarship argues for recognizing an alternative conception of agency, where the pursuit of piety and moral agency can have active meaning for people, instead of agency always having to be expressed in terms of opposing structures of power (Mahmood 2005). The desire to be close to God does not have to be a product of false consciousness, and in the view of many Muslim women, Islamic gender norms are more likely to create a stable society than the individualistic behaviour promoted by Western feminism (Bano 2017).

Similarly, in the case of democracy, the presence of dictators in many Muslim countries has also been attributed to Islamic texts, making Islam and democracy an actively debated topic (Esposito and Voll 1996). It is argued that Islam does not separate church from state. In Islamic polity, sovereignty rests with God, not the people. By implication, humans can develop laws, but only as long as they do not violate God's word as understood through the Quran and Sunnah. The ultimate vision of a good society is, thus, informed by shariʿah. Similarly, debates about the need to promote respect for pluralism within a religious tradition, for example the need for mutual respect by Sunni and Shia populations, or respect for people from other religious traditions in the Muslim world, often end up holding Islamic texts responsible for a lack of tolerance and support for jihad among some Muslims. Empirically driven studies have, however, shown how the texts or religious reasoning play a secondary role; the primary motives for those joining jihad are often linked to a strong sense of political grievance, or other strategic interests (Gambetta and Hertog 2018; Bano 2021). Such studies thus highlight the need to study the socio-political and economic context of jihadi mobilization, instead of attributing this mobilization exclusively to Islamic texts.

Since Wahhabi Salafi scholarship is also held responsible for fuelling global jihad (al-Shihabi 2016; Maher 2016), the ongoing social changes in Saudi Arabia help demonstrate that assumptions about Islamic law holding back Muslim societies are too simplistic. Officially endorsing the most puritanical and conservative Islamic tradition in the Sunni world, Saudi Arabia was viewed as denying its citizens basic social and civil liberties and promoting an intolerant culture. Yet it has suddenly recorded major reversals. By examining these changes, we can not only refine our theoretical understanding of how and why social norms evolve, consolidate and change; we can also see that it is rare for religion alone to dictate societal outcomes. Further, we see that the beliefs that gain mass adherence are those that provide the best answers in the given context (Bano 2012) and relate to reality as experienced by the individual (Greif 2006). We engage with these theoretical debates in the Conclusion to this book.

1.5. Observing Saudi society: 2014–2025

This book is based on my extended engagement with Saudi Arabia between 2014 and 2025 and is an attempt to record changes in social norms by presenting an ethnography of the evolving norms of appropriate behaviour in the public sphere. These changes affect the behaviour of both genders and encompass individual movement and family decorum in public settings. Le Renard's (2014) study of gender-segregated spaces in Riyadh in the late 2000s, where she studied the decorum expected of women in public spaces to understand gender norms in Saudi Arabia, methodologically comes closest to my approach. She conducted her ethnographic fieldwork with young Saudi women in what she referred to as an 'archipelago of spaces' that she classified into four categories: women's campuses, women's and mixed workplaces, religious spaces and shopping centres. To present a conceptual defence of how these spaces and the observation of behaviour within them provide a powerful lens to study social norms, she drew on three important bodies of literature on the conceptualization of the public sphere. First, literature concerned with defining the public sphere by legal status, whereby a public space belongs to the state or public organizations, including streets, squares, parks, gardens and even public campuses. Second, the conceptualization of the public sphere as a space of debate, exchange and confrontation of points of view, most influentially associated with Jürgen Habermas's (1989[1962]) work, including in-person spaces such as cafés as well as print and online spaces like newspapers and social media. Third, anthropological studies drawing on the work of Erving Goffman, who studied relations in public and behaviours adopted by people unknown to each other in situations of co-presence, leading to a focus on performance (Goffman 1966, 1971). Here, as Le Renard (2014) argues, the public sphere becomes important because observing interactions in it allows for studying societal norms of 'exposition' or 'avoidance' as everyone attempts to control the impression they give to others.

Le Renard (2014) preferred to develop on Goffman's focus on interactions in public spaces to shed light on the appropriate code of gender behaviour and socialization in the gender-segregated spaces she observed in Riyadh. She also documented the strategic manoeuvring of many young women in Riyadh to make those spaces work to their advantage. While sharing her core analytical lens of studying social norms and changes within them by observing what is deemed appropriate modes of interaction in public spaces, I have adopted a broader methodological approach to include a wider range of social spaces than the four she focused on. This expansion is due to the rapidly growing public infrastructure supporting social entertainment and increased mixed-gender activities since the initiation of the reforms in 2017. Additionally, I have actively engaged in monitoring debates on social media, the internet – especially YouTube – and print newspapers to study public attitudes towards ongoing social reforms. This more expansive method was possible due to my much more prolonged time in the field compared to most studies.

Every year, except for 2020 and 2021, when the COVID-19 pandemic limited international travel, I have spent up to three months in Saudi Arabia. My initial visits were tied to a comparative project I led from 2014 to 2019, which examined debates on Islam and modernity within prominent Islamic scholarly traditions, including Saudi Salafism (Bano 2018a, 2018b, 2021). During these early visits, my fieldwork focused primarily on meeting religious scholars and observing religious activities and gender norms that dictated appropriate behaviour in public spaces such as malls, restaurants, parks and mosques, most of which had sections for women. To contextualize the religious debates in the Saudi social milieu, I also interviewed young Saudis, especially young women in universities or in professional roles, to understand their attitudes towards modernity and the restrictions imposed on basic freedoms (Bano 2018e). I found considerable openness in the urban centres of Riyadh and Jeddah, with girls expressing high personal ambitions and often acknowledging the active support of male family members. These girls also introduced me to the active social media scene where Saudi youth shared creative content, which I discuss in detail in Chapter 4, showing their desire for increased social liberties, though largely expressed in humorous rather than rebellious tones. They also encouraged me to visit the trendy food vans becoming popular in the parks, to see how youth are expressing their creative potential.

My host institution, the King Centre for Research and Islamic Studies (KFCRIS), which, until the post-2017 visa reforms, was the main institution facilitating visas for foreign researchers, employed many young Saudi women. Discussions with these women, as well as with other Saudi researchers at the centre, also suggested a dynamic youth. Thus, my initial years of research in Saudi Arabia brought me closer to the work of scholars who argued that, behind the apparent rigidity, Saudi society was changing (Yamani 2009; Haykel et al. 2015b). During these visits, I also spent time in Mecca and Medina, the two holy cities, to study their role in reinforcing the religious legitimacy of the Saudi state in the eyes of Muslim pilgrims from around the world. Over the years, I have interviewed countless pilgrims, especially from South Asia, in these two cities. My time spent in these cities helped me understand their rhythm and its effects on the emotional and religious state of the believers. It also allowed me to assess the management capacity of the Saudi state, as only a robust administrative infrastructure can regulate the multitude of pilgrims crowding into these cities, ensuring the safety of visitors and residents who gravitate toward the two mosques.

It was during my visit in the spring of 2016 that the Crown Prince launched Vision 2030. Widely covered in the Saudi media, the reform agenda was seen to be ambitious but highly desirable. I was particularly interested in the social liberalization promised as part of this agenda, given my on-going research. Each subsequent visit reaffirmed my belief that change is happening. Yet, when the Crown Prince announced major relaxations starting in September 2017, even I was surprised. No one expected such changes to happen, and to happen so fast. Also, as Chapter 2 documents, the government's own actions and statements in the preceding year, while promising change, had argued for the pace to be incremental so that society could absorb it (Arab News 2016). Yet, from September 2017 onwards, the tone and pace of change accelerated dramatically. It was then that I decided to shift my analytical focus to explicitly record the change, both in terms of state-led efforts and societal responses. I therefore expanded the scope of my fieldwork to understand the extent and dynamics of the change by following state policy announcements and plans, and by tracing how the reforms were being implemented and received across different parts of Saudi Arabia. In addition to ethnographic observation of spaces, and informal discussions with participants within them, which is the essence of ethnographic research, I continued to do formal interviews with ordinary Saudis, youth taking the lead in shaping the on-going socio-cultural projects and relevant state officials, especially those in charge of the expanding entertainment and tourism infrastructure. I also held focus group discussions with professional Saudi women in Jeddah.

During my 2019 field visits, I began undertaking short but intensive fieldwork visits to other cities and regions, starting with the two that some of my female informants studying in an elite private university in Riyadh, who came from these cities, argued were preserves of Najdi socio-cultural orthodoxy:[16] Qassim and Hail. Identifying the importance of travel to surrounding Gulf states in changing the sensibilities of Saudi youth, among other factors, led me also to travel down to the oil-rich Eastern Province of Saudi Arabia. Using Dammam as the base, I also travelled to Bahrain, Oman and Kuwait to assess whether these places seemed particularly liberated in social terms when viewed from a puritanical Wahhabi perspective. While changes had already been visible on those 2019 visits, it was my return to Saudi Arabia in early 2022 after two years of COVID restrictions that helped me to record the dramatic extent and pace of change. I now faced a transformed society in terms of social openness. I thus decided to return to my pre-COVID schedule and have been making repeated visits to continue my fieldwork. Short, intense, repeated ethnographic fieldwork at the same sites over long periods brings a unique intensity and ability to observe interactions over time (Bret 2024), which differs from an ethnography conducted over a single concentrated year, giving it a longitudinal dimension (Jeffrey and Troman 2004; O' Reilly 2012). These repeat visits have enabled me to move beyond the major cities to cover all major regions of the country, including the less-developed areas like Jazan in the south. I also made a point of spending time in regions and cities that are sites of major tourist projects that have emerged under Vision 2030: al-Ula, Tabuk, al-Hasa and Abha (see Map 1.1).

During these visits, I have talked to locals, both old and young. Specifically, I focused on having detailed conversations with Saudi youth. This included those studying at leading universities in Jeddah and Riyadh who crowd the expensive malls and sleek restaurants and coffee houses, cinemas and concert halls, as well as those from lower- and middle income families living in the smaller cities, such as the young local male and female guides staffing most of the state tourism projects, and the women I got to interact with and observe in the mosques. Or the young Saudi man whom I met at al-Ula, through my use of the Kaiian app, a local substitute for Uber in the region. As it turned out, he had spent two years in Oxford on an English language programme, funded by a state scholarship. During my time in al-Ula, he became a key local interlocutor. Not only did he provide insights from a local perspective, but he also frequently enriched the analysis by helping me understand how local dynamics were perceived, often through comparisons with how he understood social relations to operate in Oxford.

Similarly, the two young Saudi men leading the popular End of the World Tour into the sand dunes around Riyadh openly shared their views on what was changing, their thoughts on new opportunities being created such as the tour they were leading, and their opinions on the right direction for the future just as many young male and female hotel reception staff and those working in cafés and

Map 1.1 Saudi Arabia: Main cities, fieldwork sites and neighbouring countries

restaurants, even past midnight during Ramadan, also shared their perspectives while working in mixed-gender settings. The analysis presented in this volume is informed by this wide range of interactions and by close to 250 formal and informal interviews. In addition, popular debates and creative content being shared by Saudi youth on social media, the internet, and YouTube, and debates in Saudi newspapers and media channels have been critical complements to my in-country fieldwork. The widespread use of social media in Saudi Arabia, including platforms like Twitter, Facebook and Snapchat, has offered a valuable opportunity to track popular debates and gauge public sentiment, as will become apparent in Chapter 4. Additionally, a regular feature of observing the public discourse and reception of the changes has been regularly following discussions within the Saudi print media.

While the study focuses on observing behaviour in public spaces, it also acknowledges that even seemingly open spaces can have their boundaries, even when not formally enforced. As Le Renard (2014) found in her study, class, income, and education can determine a person's comfort level in accessing or applying to a university, entering an elite mall given the expectations to be slightly dressed up, visiting a posh café or restaurant or applying to an elite private university compared to a state one with subsidized fees. Thus, by covering the above public spaces, I do not claim to have equally covered all segments of the population. My overall responses are higher for bigger cities than remote ones, even though I expanded my research to the remote cities, which few studies on Saudi Arabia do. My respondents are predominantly from the middle and upper income segments of the population, as they are the ones more actively present in big malls, restaurants, cafés, costly entertainment or tourist sites or employed in big multinationals. These include young Saudi entrepreneurs setting up startups and leading social media campaigns, initially on their own and now increasingly supported by Saudi state funds to expand their ventures.

However, I have also made a significant effort to observe spaces targeted toward ordinary Saudis who cannot afford elite entertainments, such as family outings in parks, food festivals, celebrations in old Jeddah during Ramadan and newly created public relaxation areas in old souks, even in remote cities like Tabuk and Jazan. I have ensured coverage of class variations by visiting both state and elite public university campuses and speaking to students in both categories. In the analysis I present, I aim to take the reader to both elite and ordinary spaces, to show that despite the clear differences between the two, there is a shared acceptance and, often a clear celebration of the increased social openness. This volume is essentially an ethnography of what I have observed across these spaces over a decade of fieldwork, which became more formally streamlined between 2017 and 2024. As with all ethnographies, the observational data can be very rich and extensive, so the task of the researcher is to create a convincing narrative from it, drawing together those elements that directly relate to the question at hand and leaving out the rest. What is left out is not wasted but is critical in helping the researcher decide why what is included is important.

It is also important to note the segments of society whose voices are not actively covered in this volume: religious minorities, especially the Shia community, Islamic activists linked to the sahwah movement, and human rights activists (HRW 2022; Amnesty International 2024c), including women's rights activists (al-Jazeera 2021b; Amnesty International 2024b; BBC 2024; ISHR 2024). The Shia population in Saudi Arabia, estimated to be between 10 per cent and 15 per cent of the total population (Adbo 2017), faces significant political and economic inequalities compared to the Sunni majority (Fuller and Francke 2000; ICG 2005; Matthiesen 2015). The Shia community is primarily located in the Eastern Province, specifically in the historical population centres of al-Ahsa and Qatif (Nakash 2006; Matthiesen 2015). Additionally, there is a small Shia community in Medina known as the *nakhawila* (Matthiesen 2015; Abdo 2017). Historically, the Shia have been targeted for conversion to Sunni Wahhabism since the early period of Wahhabism, with prominent Wahhabi religious leaders endorsing their persecution (al-Rasheed, 1996; Ismail 2016). Although the founder of modern-day Saudi Arabia, King Abdulaziz Al-Saud, adopted a less violent approach towards the Shia compared to his predecessors, he still marginalized them politically, economically, religiously, and socially (Ismail 2016). Discrimination against the Shia has been systematic and official. In 1927, a fatwa issued by the 'ulama' declared the Shia as unbelievers, formalizing oppressive state policies against them (Ismail 2016). The Shia are denied the right to practice their religious obligations in public, including calling for prayers and publishing religious texts (Fuller and Francke 2000; ICG 2005).

The construction and renovation of Shia mosques are heavily restricted, with no funding from the Saudi government (Fuller and Francke 2000; ICG 2005). Shia religious and cultural education is also outlawed, with Shia history and traditions excluded from school curricula (Fuller and Francke 2000; ICG 2005). While King Abdullah promoted religious pluralism, he did not significantly improve conditions for the Shia (Matthiesen 2015; Abdo 2017). Ismail (2016) notes that Saudi 'ulama' oppose Shia theology, with their rhetoric influenced by political events such as the Iranian Revolution in 1979 and the subsequent Shia revolt in the Eastern Province. Scholars such as Salman al-Awda, whom she refers to as progressive scholars, have adopted a more conciliatory approach; however, she notes, even they ultimately reinforce the exclusion of Shia from positions of power if they do not convert to 'true Islam' (Ismail 2016).

Furthermore, there are concerns that under the Crown Prince, repression has intensified (al-Jazeera 2020; French 2023; Amnesty International 2024a), and there is increased consolidation of power around him (Reuters 2021a; al-Rasheed 2024). This consolidation is eroding accountability mechanisms within the royal family (Butt 2017; al-Atrush, S. 2022; Gritten 2022), where traditionally, the monarch had to secure the support of senior royal family members who held important government positions (al-Rasheed 2002; Stenslie 2012). The Crown Prince is seen to have cultivated a team of loyalists with highly controversial profiles (Hubbard and Kirkpatrick 2018), who have helped him effectively marginalize other powerful figures within the royal family (Macdonald et al. 2023; al-Rasheed 2024). There is also evidence of increased surveillance of social media and the awarding of harsh punishments for voicing even minor critiques (Diwan 2018; Amnesty International 2023b).

All studies must draw boundaries based on analytical concerns as well as feasibility issues, particularly around access. Covering responses within the Shia community, given its complexity, would require a separate study, while securing access to those in prison is difficult in all contexts, especially in Saudi Arabia. Consequently, this project does not actively seek to cover the perspectives of these groups on ongoing social change, the primary concern of the volume. Further, such access was not essential to understanding the underlying processes leading to the acceptance of social change. The prominent Islamic scholars or women's rights activists in prison are not there for resisting ongoing social liberties. Furthermore, the limited available responses from the Shia community suggest that the social liberalization agenda, while not removing the recorded official restrictions on the observation of Shia religious practices in public spaces in Saudi Arabia (Coogle 2018), has been positively received by the community. The curbing of the Wahhabi 'ulama's power to dictate the religious sphere indirectly reduces their ability to promote anti-Shia rhetoric (Coogle 2018). Similarly, some reports argue that the ending of the war in Yemen and efforts at rapprochement between Saudi Arabia and Iran have created a more conducive environment for Saudi Shias to relate to ongoing changes in Saudi Arabia (The Economist 2018). Referring to the symbolic gestures made by the Crown Prince to win over the Shia community, such as appointing Saudi Arabia's first Shia cabinet minister and including Shia members in significant projects like the Neom city board and the national football team, a report in The Economist (2018) noted how the Crown Prince hopes to win over some of the young Shia Arabs through promoting Saudi nationalism and economic development.

Thus, the arguments I advance in this volume do not actively include the voices of these actors, but they have not been deliberately excluded either. Among the spaces I observed and the people I talked to, there were ordinary Shia families and youth, as well as social activists or women's rights activists. More importantly, I have actively monitored news items and reports by human rights organizations, as referenced in this volume, which have written about or given voice to these actors since the 2017 reforms. For the analytical objective of this project, which focuses on the societal shift from conservative to liberal social norms, the repression of political activists and Islamists is relevant primarily to the extent that it arguably keeps many Wahhabi scholars in check due to the threat of facing similar repression if they openly protest against the ongoing reforms – a subject covered in some detail in Chapter 3.

Overall, as ethnographies do, I have actively drawn on my observations of the selected public spaces and interactions within them over a prolonged period to provide an intelligent and coherent explanation of the complex phenomenon of ongoing social change in a complex society. Here, I see a dynamic society keen to evolve and a state eager to lead. It is also critical to appreciate that while in the past, scholars and observers often assumed the Saudi state and society to be too rigid – thereby failing to notice change – they now risk ignoring the significance of what remains unchanged. A society that changes so much as to lose its primary identity cannot be deemed to be successful (Ober 2008). The ability to transmit one's traditions and values to the next generation, in a way that preserves the core identity while adjusting to forces of change, is key to the self-preservation of a society while ensuring progress (Ober 2008). The contribution of this book rests not in merely recording change but more importantly in documenting what is remaining unchanged. Only by analysing both dimensions of the situation can we fully grasp the central analytical concerns explored in this volume.

1.6. Book structure

The volume findings are presented in three parts. Part 1 (Chapters 2–4) documents the extent of change and the forces propelling it. Part 2 (Chapters 5 and 6) documents what remains unchanged and explains why this is important for understanding the real dynamics of the ongoing change. Part 3 (Chapters 7 and 8) draws on the evidence from these two parts to refine existing theoretical debates about the state–society relationship in Saudi Arabia, and the working of social norms.

Chapter 2 establishes why it is argued that the Saudi social opening has resulted in a major and rapid shift in social norms. It highlights that the liberties granted, although they may appear basic when compared to the Western liberal framework, represent a significant push-back against Wahhabi readings of Islam. The chapter presents rich evidence not only from the urban centres of Riyadh and Jeddah, which are most exposed to change due to the concentration of elites, but also from remote cities. Focusing on three central areas, namely increased liberties for women, the nature of gender mixing and social entertainment and the nature of tourism projects – all of which are central pillars of the ongoing state reforms under Vision 2030 – the chapter records substantial change in social norms. It also demonstrates how this change in norms reflects not only a push-back from the state but also from society itself on key aspects of Wahhabi teachings, which lead to a highly restrictive social sphere due to placing significant emphasis on avoiding minor sins to prevent committing major sins. By presenting evidence of significant shifts in what the public considers appropriate social behaviour, this chapter demonstrates that the phenomenon at hand goes beyond the state announcing liberal policies and reflects a deeper social transformation marked by an actual change in social norms. It reveals how the society has rapidly changed its expectations of what constitutes the right code of behaviour.

Chapter 3 documents how, as part of the ongoing process of social liberalization discussed in the previous chapter, the power of the official religious establishment in Saudi Arabia has been explicitly curtailed. The chapter traces the rise of Wahhabism and the key principles guiding its historic alliance with the Saudi state. It then explains why the Wahhabi religious establishment has been unable to resist the push-back from the Saudi state. The chapter shows how historically the House of Saud played a crucial role in embedding Wahhabi Islam in the Arabian Peninsula. While state support provided resources that helped the religious establishment gain influence in society, its close proximity to political authority also compromised its legitimacy in the eyes of the public, especially in the Hejaz region, where the cities of Mecca and Medina have historically hosted rich Islamic scholarly networks from classical scholarly traditions. In explaining why the Wahhabi establishment has not openly resisted the state's curtailment of its authority, the chapter identifies three important factors.

First, the weakening of the authority of Wahhabi 'ulama' within the public due to the rise of the political Islam, the al-sahwah movement, which emerged as a rival force during the 1970s (Alshamsi 2011; Lacroix 2011). While the movement had been largely contained by the 1990s, some of its prominent figures, such as Salman al-Awda, who continued to command a large following (al-Rasheed 2015; Ménoret 2020), once again ruffled the state by endorsing the protests that marked the Arab Spring (al-Rasheed 2015; al-Azami 2021). Second, the demand for secular and democratically liberal institutions by Arab youth during the Arab Spring (Robbins 2015). And most critically, the weakened position of the official Wahhabi establishment among the youth, who perceive it as too closely aligned with the state (Thompson 2019), and unable to relate to changing modern realities (Le Renard 2014; Ménoret 2014). The chapter also notes how the association of

Wahhabi teachings with global jihadi groups eventually played a key role in the state's decision to curb the authority of the religious establishment. The Wahhabi emphasis on *takfir* (excommunication of fellow Muslims), which was highly beneficial to the House of Saud during its conflicts with rival factions to establish control over the Arabian Peninsula, had increasingly become a source of negative publicity post-September 11.

Chapter 4, the final chapter in Part 1, explains the factors that have enabled Saudi society to embrace the fast pace of ongoing social change. It establishes that this change has not been imposed from the top but is a carefully planned response to the evolving social attitudes and demands of Saudi youth in favour of social openness. The chapter identifies three key factors that have contributed to a major shift in the attitudes of the younger generation: access to education, regional and international travel opportunities, and widespread internet and social media access. The chapter highlights the significant role of social media in cultivating liberal attitudes among the young and enabling them to share ideas and shape a consensus around the desired characteristics of a liberal social sphere. By tracing a timeline of these changes, the chapter reveals that what may appear as rapid change is actually the result of incremental shifts that have been occurring in response to the opportunities systematically provided by the Saudi state to its citizens. Moreover, the chapter provides an in-depth analysis of the content of videos, music and films widely circulated among Saudi youth between 2010 and 2016. It illustrates a growing consensus among the youth, during this period, for increased social liberties and captures the creative energy found in this material. The chapter, however, also reveals that while demanding change, the youth expressed a desire for moderate transformation, where conservative religious and social values are adapted to allow for greater individual freedom without abandoning them entirely. Thus, the chapter goes beyond examining the factors that triggered the demand for change and starts to provide insights into the nature of the desired transformation.

Complementing the analysis of factors facilitating change, Chapter 5, the first chapter in Part 2, complicates the story by showing that while the appeal of liberal norms cultivated by access to modern education, social media and ease of travel has played a key role in ensuring the fast pace of societal change, it is only half of the story. The rapid pace of change in Saudi Arabia would not have been possible without the fact that these changes, while curbing the socially restrictive interpretations of Islam by the Wahhabi establishment, are still within the framework of interpretations provided by scholars trained in classical Islamic scholarly tradition. This illustrates the willingness of Saudi society to move away from restrictive Wahhabi interpretations, but not from what are viewed as core Islamic values. Thus, while the opening of the social space has been largely welcomed, there are active concerns among the public about observing limits. Consequently, so far, there is an active emphasis on ensuring that the projects being designed retain a strong Saudi cultural identity while also taking pride in the country's pre-Islamic heritage and unique geographical characteristics. By examining the actual design of projects aimed at facilitating gender mixing, increased women's mobility, improved social entertainment and tourism promotion, the chapter reveals that the state has taken cues from the content that was circulating on social media between 2010 and 2016.

This has ensured that, at least in the initial stages, the state has been seen as promoting a moderate course whereby increased social freedoms align with liberal thinking, but the shaping of the social space is heavily influenced by Saudi religious and cultural aesthetics rather than simply replicating Western tastes. Thus, while introducing desert raves and Grand Prix events that are modelled on Western aesthetics, there is an equal emphasis on renovating old *souk*s (markets) and setting up appealing stalls around them to make them pleasant family destinations in the evenings. There is also a focus on promoting the pre-Islamic trade routes to showcase Saudi Arabia's rich history. Additionally, my fieldwork shows that an equally important factor in gaining widespread support for the reform agenda is the success of the Crown Prince in getting the Saudi state to develop an efficient infrastructure to implement these changes. The social entertainment facilities provided are extensive and of high quality, while the tourism projects are highly sophisticated and attract an increasing number of Western tourists who leave with a positive experience.

Building further on the theme of continuity, Chapter 6 emphasizes that despite the push-back against the Wahhabi establishment's authority by both the state, and to some extent also by the society, this should not be interpreted as a decline in faith in Islam or the royal family's relinquishing its claim as the leader of the Muslim world. The Saudi monarchs have traditionally exercised religious legitimacy not only for domestic power consolidation but also for the soft power derived from their status as Custodian of the Two Holy Mosques. The chapter demonstrates how the Saudi state's re-repositioning of Saudi society as a socially liberal space does not equate to relinquishing its claim to religious leadership in the Muslim world. By focusing on pilgrims' experiences in Mecca and Medina, it highlights the state's equal investment in improving conditions for worshippers in these cities, alongside launching mega tourist projects. Drawing extensively on fieldwork with Muslim pilgrims in Mecca and Medina, Chapter 6 begins by examining the teachings of a state-appointed female preacher in a *halaqah* (study circle) in Masjid-i-Nabawi, the mosque of Prophet Muhammad in Medina, teaching to pilgrims from South Asia. It shows the relative effectiveness of the extensive teaching infrastructure within Masjid-i-Nabwi in disseminating basic Wahhabi teachings on *'aqidah* (Islamic creed) to visiting pilgrims. The content of the study circles observed helps identify why Salafi teachings continue to attract followers despite criticisms of excessive zeal.

Furthermore, the chapter underscores the seriousness with which the Saudi royal family maintains its role as the Custodian of the Two Holy Mosques. It documents the significant investments the Saudi state continues to make in developing and ensuring the satisfaction of pilgrims visiting these mosques to bolster its legitimacy as the rightful Custodian of the Two Holy Mosques, a title that the Saudi monarchs actively assert both at home and abroad. Additionally, it shows that by allowing the Wahhabi establishment to manage the mosques, including the Two Holy Mosques, the Crown Prince has not attempted to alter religious authority as he has asserted in interviews with Western media (Hammond 2021) or as leaders in other Muslim countries have often done to sideline existing religious elites (Bano and Benadi 2017; Bano 2018a; Wehrey 2021). This indicates that the preference of the Saudi state and the public is to pressure the Wahhabi establishment to adopt a more moderate religious discourse rather than working towards its disbandment.

Moreover, the chapter suggests that there is a growing possibility that Wahhabi scholarship might undergo internal reform and come to endorse a more liberal social sphere despite its reputation for rigidity. This potential shift is influenced by the global nature of Salafi networks, with active connections between Saudi Salafi scholars and those based in other countries (Bano 2021; Ismail 2021). The Saudi state's establishment of the International University of Medina, explicitly aimed at training foreign students in Islamic sciences (Farquhar 2017), has directly contributed to this global spread. One significant impact of the increasing number of foreign graduates is that while many have brought basic Salafi teachings back to their home countries, they have often adapted these teachings to fit their societies' social realities (Thurston 2016; Farquhar 2017). Notably, some graduates who spent years studying classical Wahhabi texts at al-Medina University and then returned to the West to become respected scholars, such as Yasir Qadhi, now command a global following with hundreds of thousands of followers on social media platforms (Razavian 2018a, 2018b). These scholars have done much work to defend many of the social liberties now permitted by the Saudi state, while adhering to Salafi methods of reasoning in response to the realities of their communities. In the growing literature on global Salafism, this trend is increasingly being referred to as 'post-Salafism' (Razavian 2018a, 2018b). With the Saudi state not disbanding the Wahhabi hierarchy but pressuring it to endorse its social liberalization agenda, it is possible that some of the reasoning used by scholars like Yasir Qadhi to justify basic social liberties, and who today have a much more critical relationship with more rigid forms of Wahhabi teachings, will gradually make its way into Salafi scholarship in Saudi Arabia due to interconnections within global Salafi scholarly networks.

The chapters in the final part (Part 3) draw on the evidence presented in the preceding chapters to refine existing theoretical debates about the state–society relations in Saudi Arabia, and the working of social norms. Chapter 7 engages with existing literature that has informed the understanding of state–society relationships in Saudi Arabia, whether through the lens of religion (Mouline 2014; Le Renard 2014; Ménoret 2014), tribes (al-Qassemi 2012; Samin 2015; Yizraeli 2016), or the distribution of oil rents (Beblawi and Luciani 1987; Chaudhry 1997; Hertog 2010; Gray 2011). While recording the importance of these sources of legitimization, especially oil, the chapter contends that the Crown Prince's success – despite being critiqued for a highly authoritarian style of governance – in mobilizing a large support base, particularly among the young, cannot be understood without considering that the royal family has historically managed to meet certain expectations of moral behaviour required by Saudi culture and tradition. Drawing on insights from political anthropology about sources of political legitimacy in tribal cultures, this chapter maps how the sense of family legacy, religious or moral commitments and individual charisma can be powerful forces in shaping political culture. The chapter argues that these traditional sources of legitimacy enjoyed by the royal family are still at play and being utilized even by the Crown Prince. As the reform agenda progresses, these traditional sources of legitimacy are likely to slowly erode, necessitating new forms of legitimization through delivering on Vision 2030 economic promises – a fact also noted by other observers (al-Rasheed 2020). The chapter argues that the Crown Prince, however, might also strategically try to nurture the traditional sources of legitimacy instead of entirely abandoning them.

The final chapter expands its analytical scope from a close examination of the Saudi case to connect with a much broader, theoretically sophisticated literature on the evolution of social norms (Coleman 1990; Bicchieri 2006, 2017; Bursztyn et al. 2020; Nosenzo and Görges 2020), as well as policy-oriented studies geared towards the engineering of social change, including those specially focused on Muslim societies (Young 2007; Davin 2019; UNICEF 2020). It illustrates how the developments in Saudi Arabia make it a perfect case for studying a key theoretical concern that is of interest to social scientists but equally to policy makers and planners in international development agencies: what factors and processes can help to facilitate rapid change in social norms, especially if the existing norms are viewed to be operating at a sub-optimal institutional equilibrium? Drawing on the evidence presented on the Saudi case, this chapter demonstrates how social norms, even if apparently dictated by religious beliefs, are in reality a product of wider societal developments: all stable equilibria are a product of interactions between multiple institutions, what Douglas North (1990) refers to as the given 'institutional matrix'. Thus, development interventions aimed at engineering change in social attitudes that are perceived as producing inferior outcomes for society as a whole or for a particular constituency, such as women or minorities, need to recognize that social norms can only change gradually and when the underlying institutional arrangements incentivizing individuals to make choices that reinforce those norms change. Holding Islam, or the 'ulama', primarily responsible for failures within Muslim societies to evolve efficient socio-political and economic institutions (Kuran 2010; Rubin 2017; Kuru 2019) – a problematic contention to begin with – is particularly challenged by the on-going social awakening in Saudi Arabia. As we will see, Islam, or the 'ulama', is just one part – though admittedly an important part – of a much more complex story.

Part 1

DOCUMENTING CHANGE

Chapter 2

SHIFTING SOCIETAL NORMS

It was New Year's Eve in Riyadh. As the clock started ticking to welcome 2023, long queues of slowly moving cars tried to enter Boulevard World. The most opulent and popular entertainment zone in Riyadh at the time (Saudi Scoop 2023), it had developed at an astonishingly rapid pace, as one of the projects aimed at promoting social entertainment under Vision 2030.[1] Tonight, it was also to host the New Year fireworks. In the Ferrari on my left, there were two young Saudi girls with their heads uncovered and dressed in smartly styled shirts. There were also many other female drivers, some still wearing the ʿabayah and others not, some in up-market cars but many also in ordinary ones. I had previously attended New Year's Eve in Riyadh in December 2019. By then, some of the main social liberalization policies, including women being granted the right to drive, had already been in place for over a year. But if there was any doubt about the likely take-up of these newfound liberties, the visibility of female drivers in Saudi cities by late 2023 and the bustling entertainment sites told a different story. While many Saudi observers, not only outsiders, observed these developments with a certain degree of disbelief; a visible shift in Saudi social norms demonstrated the widespread participation of Saudis from different socio-economic strata, and in urban centres as well as smaller cities, in the spaces that were opening up.

The active take-up by many Saudis, especially the under-thirties who constitute 63 per cent of the total population (Abueish 2023; al-Ghalayini 2023), of the opportunities being made available by the state for women's participation in public spaces for social entertainment and employment showed that the changes constitute more than mere policy announcements. Instead, we were witnessing a clear shift in societal attitudes concerning the observance of long-standing social norms. This smooth transition appeared contrary to the largely negative predictions that were often made by Western journalists and politicians. As outlined in the volume introduction, these forecasts routinely warned of a violent uprising by disenchanted youth who had been raised in an environment of religious extremism and political repression (Manning 1998; Lippman 2012; Friedman 2015; Whitkaer 2015). The core objective of this chapter is to show that what we are seeing in Saudi Arabia is not just a case of top-down enforcement of a collection of policies aimed at social liberalization; rather, we are witnessing a major change in prevalent social norms at a speed, which is only possible with the active participation of a large segment of society. This is puzzling because societies, especially those assumed to be highly conservative, do not abruptly abandon social norms that were synonymous with their core identity (Ober 2008).

Further, as public-policy experts will tell us, policies do not automatically lead to action. The two most obvious reasons for this are a lack of commitment on the part of the initiators and the absence of an enforcement mechanism (Moran et al. 2006; Kerwin and Furlong 2018). Policies are often tokenistic in nature, aimed at pleasing either internal or external constituencies whose tacit support has a bearing on the interests of the political elites. This explains the initial cynicism in the Western press about the Crown Prince's motives behind these reforms in Saudi Arabia. Even where political elites are committed to reforms, for the behaviour of individuals to change, the state must have an efficient enforcement mechanism to ensure compliance, either through the offer of incentives or through the threat of punishment (Moran et al. 2006; Kerwin and Furlong 2018). Especially when policies aim to change long-standing social norms in traditional and religiously conservative societies, success is never assured (Rosenberg 2008). Deeply engrained socio-cultural or religious practices, such as female genital mutilation (FGM) (HRC 2023; UNICEF 2023) or foot binding (Hunt 2017), can be made unlawful, but that does not mean that the community as a whole will desist from those practices. Even in the most conducive circumstances, change is expected to be slow and incremental. Informal institutions, such as norms and values, as North (1990) argues, are expected to show extra levels of 'stickiness' (persistence), mainly because individuals adhere to them not only due to threats of state punishment but because of some level of internal conviction, which thereby guarantees a certain degree of compliance. In the absence of internal conviction, social sanctioning in response to violations of prevalent social norms is argued to act as a deterrent (Coleman 1990; Bicchieri 2006; Opp 2018).

For Saudi society, where rigidly strict social conservatism was associated with deep religious beliefs theoretically informed predictions would have aligned with initial commentaries: namely, the opening up by the state would not result in immediate behavioural change. Resistance by the religious establishment, the threat of sanctions by society and internal commitment to Islamic beliefs were expected to continue to dictate individual adherence to socially conservative norms. Yet by 2023, it was possible to trace enough change in the collective behaviour of Saudi society, as visible in public spaces before and after the reforms, that it can be confidently asserted that social norms are rapidly changing in response to policies announced just five years ago (Slobodian 2023; The Economist 2023a, 2023b). It is thus important to record the changes that help to demonstrate that this period witnessed a process of norm change, not simply policy change, in Saudi Arabia. Equally it is important to record the evidence that Saudi society's absorption of basic social reforms, such as giving women the right to drive or allowing mixing of gender in public spaces, was even faster than the state had expected thereby again showing that while an attempt to engineer a liberal social sphere has facilitated the current change, its speed has been determined by active participation by many segments of the population. At the time of the launch of the Vision 2030 in the spring of 2016, the Crown Prince had contended that policy changes such as granting women the right to drive would need time as they require a gradual shift in societal attitudes (Arab News 2016). However, these very changes were expedited and announced just a year later, with the policy permitting women to drive being unveiled as early as September 2017.

Vision 2030 put forward a daring concept of socio-economic change, but the planned steps towards the promised social opening were accelerated, and expanded, faster than the Vision planners had expected in light of the positive responses to the initial announcements. This rapid absorption of on-going social reforms is what makes the Saudi case particularly useful in refining our understanding of a key theoretical concern in social science: What factors can trigger rapid change in social norms (Coleman 1990; North 1990)? The dominant equilibrium is their persistence, so what triggers change poses a real puzzle for theorists, given that cases of path dependence or persistence are the norm (Sewell 1996; Liebowitz and Margolis 1995). Saudi society's acceptance of Vision 2030 and associated social liberties also raises important theoretical questions about the nature of the relationship between the Saudi state and society. It indicates a much more complex relationship, whereby there is a certain degree of consensus on future goals and a level of mutual trust that exists despite the authoritarian nature of the state – a subject to which we will return in detail in Chapter 7. This chapter focuses on establishing the extent and pace of the change, and Saudi society's absorption of it, by considering policy changes and related behaviour changes across three areas of reform: social liberties enjoyed by women; gender mixing and entertainment; and tourism.

These three areas were particularly representative of Saudi social conservatism. What women were allowed or not allowed to do by Saudi law; the heavy restrictions on gender mixing and its enforcement by the religious police; and the ban on very basic forms of social entertainment – public cinemas, concerts, etc. – were regulated by the Saudi state and Wahhabi religious establishment (Mouline 2014). This excessive zeal for social puritanism was the product of three features of Wahhabi teachings: first, the emphasis on the state's responsibility to establish orthopraxy as part of the Wahhabi creed, instead of leaving it to the conscience of the individual, as operationalized by Muhammad ibn Abd al-Wahhab; second, a strong emphasis on trying to stop *fitna* (civil strife) by punishing minor transgressions that could lead to major sins (such as restricting gender mixing in order to reduce the temptation of adultery); and, third, the commitment to live in accordance with the model of the *salaf* (pious forbears, referring to the first three generations of Muslims).[2] Although such teachings are shared across Islamic scholarly traditions, the Wahhabi Salafi tradition is exceptional in its excessive zeal in enforcing such measures through the apparatus of the state (Commin 2009; Spannaus 2018a). The next chapter will analyse these three aspects of Wahhabi thinking to show how the social restrictions that are now being reversed were strongly embedded within these teachings. The focus of this chapter is on showing significant transformation in all these areas. More importantly, it explores how a large number of Saudi men and women seem largely at ease engaging in this new social milieu. Saudi women interacting with men in their new roles, such as saleswomen in stores, do not seem uneasy in their dealings; women who are choosing not to wear ʿabayah are not facing male harassment, nor are they being stared at by women whose heads are still covered. Similarly, Saudi families move comfortably in these new social spaces where some are now choosing to adopt liberal styles of dress. This evident tolerance in Saudi society today for the right of individuals to behave as they choose, instead of being obliged to adhere to a very strict and conservative code of conduct in public spaces, as recorded by Le Renard (2014) for her female respondents in pre-reform public culture in Riyadh, is reflective of a major change in societal norms.

2.1. Norms of respectability for women

Anyone who had boarded a plane from London, or any other Western capital, to a Saudi city before 2019 would recall the rustling noises that used to erupt once the pilot announced the start of descent. Not only foreigners but even some Saudi women who until then were clad in regular jeans or dresses would reach for their ʿabayahs and headscarves, until then lying packed in their handbags, to meet the dress code required for entry to Saudi Arabia. Enforcing the observation of proper covering by women was one of the key tasks of the *mutawwiʿ* (religious police). Being reprimanded if part of one's hair was showing from below the slipping head scarf was a possibility as soon as one left the plane. In my post-COVID trips starting from early 2022, I have been reminded of the change in Saudi Arabia during the flight itself: the pilot's announcement no longer triggers the old reaction. Saudi Arabia removed the legal requirement for women to wear a headscarf or ʿabayah starting in March 2018 (Sanchez 2018; The New Arab 2018). The queues at the immigration desks now include many women with bare heads and in modern dress. This is a big change, not only because the image of women dressed in black ʿabayah is strongly linked to Saudi identity, but because it is also representative of the major push back delivered to the Wahhabi establishment by the state.

The requirement for women to cover all parts of their body, and be modest in their style of dress is shared across the classical Islamic legal schools in both the Sunni and the Shia traditions (Alkiek 2023). What exactly should be covered is debatable. The very socially conservative Islamic traditions, such as Wahhabi Salafism, can require women to cover even hands and feet, in addition to wearing the facial *niqab* (face veil), ʿabayah, and *hijab* (head covering) (Inge 2017) – although there is always a degree of variation in rulings within a tradition. The shared emphasis on women dressing modestly and ideally covering their heads comes from the verse in the Quran which commands the wives of the Prophet Muhammad to cover their heads.[3] A few progressive Islamic scholars contend that the requirement to cover one's head was specific to the Prophet's wives, who were at that time being targeted by his enemies (Jahangir 2017). In their reasoning, what Islam requires is not necessarily the wearing of *hijab* (head covering) or *niqab* (face veil) but the expression of female modesty whereby a woman does not deliberately provoke male attention with unlawful intent.[4] The dominant approach within the classical schools of Islamic law, however, remains to advise women to wear hijab (Alkiek 2023).[5] Modest styles of dress and restrictions on gender mixing are seen as preventative measures to avert the temptation for both genders to commit adultery, a major sin, which is argued to lead to fitna (Inge 2017; Alkiek 2023). Thus, in requiring women to wear hijab or ʿabayah, the Wahhabi school is not an exception to general Muslim practice (Bano and Kalmbach 2011; Bano 2017; Alkiek 2023); what is exceptional is its zeal to enforce this practice on all women and by the apparatus of the state, instead of treating it as a matter of individual choice. The Saudi state's removal of this core restriction on female dress is thus a major shift away from what Wahhabi teachings and culture had long deemed appropriate behaviour by women in public spaces. The fact that this change has been accepted by Saudi society, and many women are now choosing not to wear ʿabayah or the headscarf and are not being harassed in the malls or public spaces,[6] and the fact that people have a very matter-of-fact attitude to it all, is reflective of a major social change. During my pre-2016 visits, it was not just the fear of the hay'ah police but also a strong sense that Saudi society expected me as a woman to cover myself that guided my own style of dress. Now, that strong sense of being required to conform is gone.

The ban on women driving was a result of similar reasoning. At numerous points, leading Wahhabi scholars had conceded that the act of a woman driving a car is not in itself un-Islamic; the problem in their view was that it opens the door for women to pursue activities which do contravene religious teaching (al-Saadi 2008). Thus, the concern has been that if women drive cars themselves that will enhance their mobility and time spent out of the house on their own, leading to an increased possibility of gender mixing, and opening doors for promiscuous behaviour and at the same time reducing the time spent at home with the family (al-Saadi 2008). Part of this resistance was also couched in the language of ensuring women's security. Moving around alone was argued to expose women to the risk of male harassment, especially in big cities, where people do not know each other. According to this reasoning, it was deemed appropriate for women to drive if they were based in rural areas where communities are small and people know each other (al-Saadi 2008). The reversal of this ban was thus another major move towards guaranteeing freedom of movement to women and a direct push back against Wahhabi teachings on how to regulate the social sphere. The fact that many Saudi women immediately took advantage of this liberty and were not being socially persecuted for it again demonstrates a shift in societal norms.

The two examples cited above were the two most visible limitations on basic female agency. The one that was less visible but more fundamental to everyday life choices in all areas of women's life was the male guardianship system (*wilayah*) that exists not only in Saudi Arabia but also in Qatar (Beckerle 2016). Representative of the classical Islamic understanding of gender roles, whereby the man is seen as the guardian of the family, and thereby responsible for providing its economic and social security, and women in return have to show their submission, the Saudi guardianships laws, have been seen to be highly restrictive and exploitative of women by Western development agencies and think tanks (Beckerle 2016; Amnesty International 2022). Not prevalent in most Muslim countries, due to the adoption of Western legal systems under colonial rule, whereby elements of shari'ah law remain restricted to matters of marriage and inheritance, the male guardianship laws in Saudi Arabia not only regulate many more areas of women's lives, but they also restrict their access to legal documents about their own status as well as that of their children (al-Hussein 2019).

Women are required to seek permission from their male guardian, who might be the father, the brother or the husband, before embarking on international travel, starting a business or seeking employment. In April 2019, a royal decree announced many changes to this system, promising women greater mobility and freedom over their choices: Women over the age of 21 could apply for a passport and travel internationally without seeking permission from a male relative; they can now register the births of their children, access other legal documents related to their status, and register as co-head of the family (al-Hussein 2019). They can also start a business without needing the approval of a male guardian. The passing of the Guardianship Law in 2023, which codifies some of these changes, has been criticized by Western observers for formalizing the continuation of the guardianship system instead of totally abandoning it (Amnesty International 2022; HRW 2023). But, given the starting position, the liberties available to women today are much greater than those they enjoyed five years ago.

Even under the original set of laws constituting the male guardianship system, it must be acknowledged that women did exercise a high level of agency, despite what is often assumed. In my pre-2017 interviews with women from all circles of life, most of them noted the active support that they received from their husbands, fathers and brothers to pursue higher education, seek employment, and travel internationally (Bano 2018e). In a focus-group discussion that I held in 2017 with female executives working at an international corporation in Jeddah, the same kind of agency was on display: While dressed in 'abayahs, which was compulsory at the time, these women were confident of their roles, were articulate and did not view themselves as being suppressed within their households. Similarly, women entrepreneurs existed in this period too. One of the female entrepreneurs in Jeddah with whom I was in touch during this time was leading a research and social policy centre, while also running a private business (Akeel 2004). Having named her centre after Kadijah bint Khuwaylid, the first wife of the Prophet Muhammad, who was also a businesswoman, she explicitly attributed her success to the inspiration that she found in her model.

However, most of those women with whom I spent time during pre-2017 visits were from better-off socio-economic strata of Saudi society. Since the initiation of the reforms under Vision 2030, however, women's participation in economic activity has greatly increased, even in lower-middle-income groups and in smaller towns. The change is very visible. Women are actively employed in shops as salespersons, and they staff offices and hotel reception desks and information desks at the malls. Women are also very actively being engaged in government-sponsored tourism projects. In al-Ula, which is the site of a very successful Saudi tourism project, the extensive network of tourism activities is co-ordinated through a team based at Al-Ula Winter Park, which acts as the main information centre and ticket sales point. The centre is entirely staffed by young Saudi girls, some fluent in English and others still learning, but both sets of girls make major efforts to engage with the tourists and explain to them what is on offer.

These are positions occupied by women from low- and middle-income families, unlike the women whom I used to meet in the past in the elite circles in Riyadh and Jeddah. This growing participation of women in economic activity is reflected in the official figures: from being just 20 per cent in 2018, the female participation rate increased to 37 per cent in 2022 (Akeel 2021). Young girls and women, even in smaller cities, are filling jobs being created, in particular, in the rapidly developing tourism sector. These girls and women are getting opportunities for work that they did not have before, and they are actively taking them up. I came across many young women who were acting as guides on the various walking trails on offer in al-Ula. The young woman who was leading the al-Ula Oasis trail I participated in was from al-Ula and had studied locally in state educational institutions, spoke fluent English and was of the view that traditional Saudi families, like her own family, are happy with the changes as they are creating good employment opportunities for women. Thus, if the space for women to come out and take a more active part in the economy has been created, it is evident that it is being used. Even if many of these jobs are low-skilled, the fact that women are coming out in large numbers to fill them shows that the society, which was long viewed to be confining its women primarily inside their homes, has undergone a significant shift in attitudes.

2.2. Norms concerning gender mixing and social entertainment

For Western researchers wanting to understand gender dynamics in pre-2016 Saudi Arabia, the malls were popular fieldwork sites (Le Renard 2014, 2015; Bano 2018e). The food courts provided one of the sites that were ideal for observing gender dynamics. The other such sites, in the case of bigger cities such as Riyadh, Jeddah, Khobar and Dammam, were restaurants and cafés, especially since many expensive international food and coffee chains are located there. In addition, and in particular in smaller cities, the main entertainment sites apart from malls were the parks. Arriving just before sunset and staying until late continues to be a popular family activity among Saudis. This tradition is well-suited to both the local culture and the extreme weather conditions – unbearably hot summer days give way to relatively pleasant evenings. Families come prepared: Rugs and carpets are rolled out, Saudi tea and coffee pots come out of the picnic baskets, and many Saudi homemade dishes are laid out. Occasional visits to national museums, historical sites such as a fortress or local museums which preserve regional histories were the other main forms of entertainment. Some examples were the National Museum and the al-Masmuk Fort in old Riyadh, and the Regional Museum in Hail. Last but not least, it was also popular to drive out to the desert in the evenings or at night, to sit around a fire cooking and telling stories or reciting poetry. Some families maintained second houses in the desert, and the ownership of camels, as some of my respondents were keen to highlight, was seen as a sign of social status.

Most of these forms of entertainment involved the entire family travelling together, thereby minimizing contact with outsiders. In settings where mixed-sex interactions could occur, such as malls, restaurants and cafés, seating areas were traditionally segregated by gender. A young man and a woman found alone in a public space could be required to produce a marriage certificate or risk being fined by the hay'ah police. Common forms of entertainment, such as music, dance, drama or watching movies, which were discouraged in all Islamic scholarly traditions, were highly restricted in public spaces. This, however, was not always the case. Cinemas did operate in Saudi Arabia in the 1970s (al-Arabiya 2020). They were closed after the violent Mecca revolt (al-Sarhan 2015), which the Saudi royal family quelled but, in return, felt obliged to pursue many puritanical policies in order to win religious legitimacy in the context of the growing threat of militant or political Islamists.[7] In recent memory, among locals as well as visitors, there was thus little recollection of cinemas having ever existed on Saudi soil. This is not to say that Saudi Arabia did not have an indigenous art and entertainment culture consisting of various art forms, in particular poetry but also folk dance and traditional music. When presented in public, these folk dances or other performances involved only men, and the music consisted mainly of the playing of a single instrument, or singing poetic verses praising local traditions and values (Telfaz11 2023b).

By 2023, the transformation was dramatic. In just under five years, the state had developed an extensive infrastructure to support an elaborate network of social entertainment opportunities. People are now presented with an abundance of options when determining which event to attend in big cities like Riyadh and Jeddah, but the other cities have not been ignored either. Cinemas have opened across the country, showing Hollywood movies as well as Arab and regional films. Saudi Arabia is also keen to boost its own nascent film industry. During my December 2022 visit, *Sattar*, one of the first Saudi big-screen movies, was released. I chose to watch it at the Vox Cinema at the Kingdom Centre in Riyadh, which was in the 'Gold Class' category. As one of my respondents had explained, 'while all cinemas here are on a par with the cinema houses in the UK, or in fact are slightly better, the Gold Class is worth paying for at least once for the experience'. It did turn out to be the most lavish of cinema settings. Separating the elegant ticket counter and the cinema screens was a luxurious lounge designed in the spirit of a sophisticated Parisian café with its lush red sofas and stylish ambiance. On one side was a stylish restaurant counter, where smartly dressed waiters took orders. The movie itself turned out to be pleasantly entertaining. Revolving around an ordinary young Saudi who harbours dreams of becoming a famous wrestler, the film, on the one hand, gave touching insights into Saudi family values and culture, while also promoting transnational Muslim brotherhood; but on the other hand, it also provided straightforward fun to the audience by providing high-quality visuals and a good soundtrack. Thus, although by the admission of its director, the movie was deliberately aimed at engaging with the sensibilities of ordinary Saudis, as opposed to focusing on a quirky idea to please Western audiences or elites in Riyadh and Jeddah (al-Turki 2022), it ends up impressing for the honesty of its characters as well as the quality of production. For one of the first Saudi cinema productions, Sattar showed talent and an ambition to develop a more active film-production industry (Arab News 2023; Vivarelli 2023).

In addition to cinemas, an active culture of concerts has evolved. Prominent singers from the Gulf and the Middle East, as well as international bands, are routinely being invited to play in Saudi cities. Hiba Tawaji, a prominent Lebanese singer, was the first female singer to perform in Riyadh (Hussain and Smith 2017). Since then, many major international singers and bands have played in Riyadh and Jeddah, as well as in other cities such as al-Ula, Dammam and Khobar. In the on-going renovation and expansion work in Old Jeddah (Jeddah *al-Balad*) to create a popular entertainment site for locals as well as foreigners, an opera house was also being developed, along with a museum. The *Winter in Tantora* festival, which, since its successful initial launch in December 2018, has become an annual event (Hirwani 2019), similarly features prominent singers from the region as well as from afar at its glamorous concert hall, named *Maraya*, with its striking glass architecture, which makes it appear like a mirage in the desert.[8] These concerts welcome mixed audiences, and some turn into raves, just as the Soundstorm Music Festival, held in the desert outside Riyadh, which has also become an annual feature (Ebrahim 2022), where mixed-gender dancing is allowed.[9] Equally highlighted is the fact that some of the leading DJs associated with it are young Saudi girls (al-Hamawi 2021).[10] Though acknowledged as an extreme case and catering primarily to a small elite,[11] the festival has become part of the diverse palette of activities available.

At the same time, elaborate theme parks have been developed. Some offer regular joy rides for children, such as the Winter Wonderland in Riyadh, which was developed in 2019. Others, however, are much more glamorous and contentious in terms of what is on offer. The Boulevard World, a highly popular theme park in Saudi Arabia during 2023, was one good example. Situated on a vast tract of land at the northern edge of Riyadh, near Diriyyah, where the 1744 pact between Ibn Abd al-Wahhab and Muhammad al-Saud was forged (Commins 2009) – an alliance that laid the foundation for the emergence of present-day Saudi Arabia. Designed to offer high-class entertainment (Saudi Scoop 2023), it featured an artificial lagoon where visitors could ride in all forms of water boats, including Italian-style gondolas. Around the lagoon were grand, ornate cultural representations from different parts of the world. Thus, grand stalls are set up to represent countries and cultures from around the world, including France, the USA, Morocco, Italy, China and India. Some also featured live entertainment by artists and performers from those countries. American music played loudly in most areas. Weekends were deemed the best time to visit, as all sections host live performances. In the American section, the stall dedicated to Marvel film productions drew particularly large crowds. Marvel characters were on display all the time, but at weekends, they also gave live performances. American acrobats, including male and female performers, depicted the popular Marvel heroes and displayed highly impressive, sophisticated acrobatic skills, accompanied by tunes from the soundtracks of the Marvel films in tightly clad garments. Other regions had their own performers.

What is particularly striking was that this elaborate theme park was developed in just eighty-two days as part of the Riyadh Seasons, which is an umbrella programme under which numerous activities were being planned (Riyadh Season 2021). It involved setting up a distinct set of activities in different parts of the city for a couple of weeks or months, to attract visitors to the area in question (Riyadh Season 2021). These festivals were varied in focus: Some promoted local cuisine, some featured performances by local artists, and some promoted exhibitions. The key was that these festivals kept offering people a variety of choices. Given its grand scale, I only came to realize that Boulevard World was also set up as part of Riyadh Season activities and was to be dismantled once the season ended, with the possibility of returning the next year, when I interviewed one of the organizers. It presented such high-quality stalls and entertainment that I assumed it was a permanent theme park. Setting it up and dismantling it on an on-going basis would be costly and also require administrative efficiency.

It is also worth noting here that Boulevard World was not the only entertainment project with this name. When I tried to get there for the first time, Uber picked the wrong location, and the driver took me to the Winter Wonderland, which, as noted above, is an entertainment park primarily offering rides for children. Unable to identify the correct address on Google Maps, I asked two Saudi girls who were walking by the roadside if they knew the best way to get to the Boulevard. Their response was 'Which Boulevard?' As it turned out, there were in fact three new projects that have emerged over the last four years with a similar name. The active ones were Boulevard City and Boulevard World. When I explained that I was trying to get to the one that is supposedly quite grand and popular, they named it as Boulevard World and told me that it was indeed the most popular place right now and that was where I should go. Until it had opened, the most popular site was Boulevard City. The latter was also developed just three years ago, in 2019, and was quite grand for its time. It also featured many entertainment features, restaurants, grand neon signs and good music; but its charm paled quickly once the Boulevard World was opened. I ended up visiting both with a view to comparing them. Looking at these two projects, which developed close to each other, one could note not only the fast pace of the state's development of entertainment infrastructure, but also how the plans are improving dramatically in scope and quality.

Al-Ula is another city where the idea of festivals was being promoted very actively. From the first festival held in December 2018, by early 2023, al-Ula already featured an annual calendar of events aimed at attracting local as well as foreign tourists. Its most famous festival is referred to as *Winter at Tantora*, which takes place between December and early March. Making use of the good weather during this period, the al-Ula tourism authority promotes a whole host of activities, including organized tours to different historical sites, walking trails, guided walks, star-gazing in the desert, and yoga and meditation retreats. During

Ramadan people are encouraged to come to enjoy special *iftar* (evening meal marking opening of the fast) and *suhur* (pre-dawn meal consumed at the start of Muslim fast); and during September a one-week well-being festival aimed at foreign tourists offers multiple sessions including yoga, meditation, and other relaxing forms of exercise, including Pilates, at the Five-Senses Sanctuary – a retreat centre constructed in an orange and lemon orchard in al-Ula (Experience al-Ula 2023).

Furthermore, the café culture, which was already quite elaborate in big cities like Riyadh, Jeddah and Dammam, has now taken on a strongly indigenous flavour. Previously, the foreign coffee chains, such as Dunkin' Donuts, Starbucks and Costa, dominated the scene. Now local coffee houses are opening, with their own menus, and many are housed in very artistically designed spaces. Local coffee-house chains are also emerging. Half Million, also advertised as '½ Million', is one such local chain. Set up by two young Saudis with the ambition to compete with the international coffee chains operating in Saudi Arabia, while having a starting capital of only SAR 500,000 ($133,280), (Half Million 2023), this domestic Saudi coffee chain has been very successful. It has acquired a large following; its cafés are normally very full. Similarly, as discussed in some detail in Chapter 5, private as well as state-supported art galleries are actively coming up (Time Out 2023).

While most of these avenues of entertainment have a clearly Western feel to them, there is also a parallel effort afoot to improvise in the old parts of the cities and develop them into popular entertainment sites. Here, the renovations are done in a way that makes them seem more consonant with Saudi culture and traditions. Diriyyah in Riyadh, Old Jeddah, the al-Qaisaryah market in the capital city of al-Hofuf in al-Hasa, the old town in al-Ula and old areas of other cities such as Tabuk and Jazan are being renovated – but in a way that preserves their traditional culture. Old buildings are being worked on, the entire areas are being beautified by adding visually pleasing decorations, and nicely decorated food and coffee stalls are erected to complement the restaurants. In particular, good use is made of lights, especially illuminations hanging from trees or between poles and buildings, to create a calming and relaxing atmosphere. Across these different cities, the renovated old town areas draw large numbers, especially in the late evening and during the night.

Another related area receiving much attention is that of sport. In big private universities, gyms and swimming pools are now being provided. For ordinary members of the public, the Ministry of Sports is promoting a number of opportunities. It is also keen to host major sports events. The Saudi Arabian Grand Prix, hosted for the first time in 2020, has now become an annual feature. The Saudi soccer team made a notable appearance at the World Cup in Doha in 2022. A few months later, the Saudi professional football team, al-Nasser, signed Cristiano Ronaldo, the premier Portuguese footballer. Since then, Saudi Arabia has entered into more such agreements, to the extent of shifting global soccer dynamics (Woodyatt et al. 2023). The nation has faced accusations of sports washing. Yet, the Crown Prince and his team have remained unapologetic in adopting these strategies (BBC 2023). In interviews with Western media, his team has emphasized that investment in sports is a crucial economic diversification strategy under Vision 2030, with significant funding allocated to sports events and players under the Saudi sovereign wealth fund, known as the Public Investment Fund.[12]

The Crown Prince and his advisors anticipate that these investments will augment the nation's GDP, while many analysts in leading Western media outlets viewed these strategies favourably (Blinder 2023; Woodyatt et al. 2023). In 2023, Saudi Arabia garnered significant attention by relocating major international golf competitions to its land (Blinder 2023). While these endeavours primarily target benefits from the global sports economy, it's imperative to acknowledge how, under Vision 2030, sports are also being promoted within Saudi society as a way to lead a more enriching life and maintain a healthier populace. Moreover, fostering a sports culture isn't limited to physical activities: board games are also being encouraged as forms of social entertainment and relaxation. In Old Jeddah, which hosts an array of social activities throughout Ramadan, there's a dedicated area with comfortable floor seating where young men, as well as women and families, gather to play board games. During my visits, I observed individuals engaged in games like Carrom board, chess and cards, among others.

For a country where, until five years ago, most of these entertainment options were non-existent, the change in terms of what is on offer is dramatic. Until 2020, all shops and businesses closed for prayer to allow employees to pray in the mosque. Now, not only are these kinds of restrictions gone, but the entertainment options made available also directly clash with what was formerly seen as proper social conduct. Viewed through a puritanical Wahhabi lens, performances by male and female acrobats in tight dresses outside the Marvel Studio outlet in Boulevard World, which is regularly visited by Saudi families and not just the youth, the loud Western music playing in many places, and the increasing mixing of sexes across these multiple spaces are all major violations. Yet not only has the state pushed ahead with developing an infrastructure to promote these activities at a very fast pace, but society in general has welcomed it. A large segment of the Saudi public is actively participating in these activities and opportunities. Boulevard World is packed on weekends. The restaurants and cafés are full. Cinema houses are drawing large crowds, and the attendance at festivals is high. Foreign tourists have certainly begun to arrive, but the majority of people occupying these spaces are the Saudis. More importantly, this sudden opening up has not led to much awkwardness or discomfort. As visible through their presence in these spaces, many Saudi men and women seemed at perfect ease with being in these new spaces, which allow active gender mixing, as soon as they opened. It is the ease with which visible segments of Saudi society have embraced a move towards liberal social norms that makes the Saudi experience so worthy of study. From the religious police fining women for showing their hair or charging unmarried couples for being together as recently as 2017, these restrictions now seem part of such a distant past when one is sitting in cafés in Riyadh or Jeddah or taking part in the host of tourism activities being promoted under Vision 2030. Moreover, people are taking many additional social liberties for granted.

2.3. Norms around accepting outsiders

If many social spaces were traditionally closed to the Saudi public due to Wahhabi teachings on social mixing and entertainment, Saudi Arabia as a country was also largely closed to outsiders for similar reasons. The two holy cities of Mecca and Medina, the former housing the Ka'bah (the cube-like structure that Muslims refer to as the House of God), have traditionally been closed to non-Muslims. They are referred to as *haramayn* (Munt 2014), and non-Muslims were restricted from visiting them. Further, tourism was not encouraged, as part of efforts to restrict Western influence and regulate non-Muslim presence on Saudi land. Now, while Mecca still remains closed to non-Muslims, in a surprising move, as part of its efforts to promote tourism, Saudi Arabia has already opened Medina to non-Muslims. Among the promoted attractions, the London-style Hop On and Hop Off bus offers bus tours in Medina. The sightseeing bus takes tourists to a total of eight sites in Medina, including the external areas of Masjid-i-Nawabi. The bus runs throughout the day, every thirty minutes.

The opening of Medina so quickly to non-Muslim tourists represents another major shift away from Wahhabi conservatism, but so are most of the other concessions that are being made to foreign tourists. At al-Ula airport, which, in a bid to attract Western tourists, is planning more direct flights from European cities, one sees women wearing shorts and blouses with bikini straps. The luxury resorts in al-Ula are expensive, but those who can afford them are more or less free to live by Western norms. Habitat and Banyan Tree, the two most exclusive resorts, offer mixed open-air swimming pools. The former restriction on hotels to exclude unmarried couples has now been removed. During my visit in the winter of 2022, many young unmarried European couples were freely travelling in al-Ula and journeying by car to other destinations. Many were excited to be among the first ones to venture out. One middle-aged couple, based in London (although one partner was from New Zealand and the other from Eastern Europe), explained that they were planning to write a travel blog based on their experience of travelling in Saudi Arabia, something which they normally would not do, to encourage other Westerners to come and reconsider their biased views about Saudi Arabia.

Within Riyadh, in addition to Boulevard World and other social entertainment sites, an extensive restoration programme has been carried out at Diriyyah, turning that old historical site into a major tourist attraction (Chilton 2023; Witherspoon 2023). Divided between Bujairi Terrace and Turaif Terrace, the site opened to visitors in 2022. Bujairi terrace offers an extensive array of expensive restaurants, including one run by a Michelin chef and another by Cova, a high-end Italian coffee chain. Turaif terrace features the actual mud building structure that housed the Al-Saud, and also features the mosque. Other projects under development in Riyadh include the construction of a shopping mall resembling a cube, which, to its critics, represents a crude commercial use of the image of Ka'bah.[13] In other places, such as the seaside cities of Jeddah, Khobar and Dammam, the Cornish culture that was already fairly prominent is being further developed and encouraged. In

Jeddah, the key project aimed at attracting foreign tourists is the reconstruction of Old Jeddah with its Ottoman-style houses and nicely planned spaces.[14] During Ramadan, it becomes particularly lively, offering a wide array of activities ranging from an artists' corner to pleasant seating areas, and attractively decorated stalls and cafés. Similarly, other cities and towns are being promoted and actively advertised for certain distinctive features. Al-Hofuf, the capital city of al-Hasa province that hosts the largest oasis in Saudi Arabia, is just a two-hour train ride from Riyadh and is being promoted as a major tourist site for its old and architecturally beautiful souq, Souq al-Qaisariya. A tranquil town rich with historical significance, al-Hofuf also boasts an opulent branch of the Intercontinental Hotel, which serves as a comfortable base for foreign tourists with money to spend. On the west side, in addition to al-Ula, the mountains of Abha in the south and coffee plantations in Jazan, which borders Yemen, are being promoted as popular tourist destinations. In the northwest, Tabuk and the surrounding islands have already started to attract domestic tourists. Neom, the most ambitious and costly project under way – and also the one that seems most likely to fall short of its promised potential – is located on the Red Sea coast, approximately two hours' drive from Tabuk, where an entire futuristic city is being developed.

Promoting tourist attractions in the desert is also a key part of the strategy to attract foreign tourists. *The Edge of the World*, a five-hour organized tour that takes one into the desert area outside Riyadh, where volcanic mountains make shapes that create sharp edges (CNN Travel 2023), has already become highly popular.[15] On my flight from London to Riyadh, I had heard an American woman who currently works in Dubai highly recommend this tour to the passenger sitting next to her. I joined one of these tours, which was well attended; all participants were foreigners, some were based in other parts of the Gulf and were visiting Saudi Arabia for the weekend, and others had come all the way for a one-week or ten-day holiday. Starting at 2 p.m., the tour ended with Saudi tea and coffee, and food cooked over a campfire before participants were driven back to Riyadh around 9 p.m. Participants were very pleased with the experience, in addition to what they had visited and experienced during their visits to other cities.

Meanwhile, the Saudi government is actively encouraging more people to come for *'umrah* (optional pilgrimage to Mecca) by facilitating the granting of entry visas. Previously a highly prized acquisition, often secured through special connections, an 'umrah visa can now be obtained on arrival by Muslims who are nationals of certain countries. Even young single Muslim women can now enter Saudi Arabia alone for 'umrah if they are from one of those countries that are eligible for visas on arrival, or if they have active visas for the USA, Europe or the UK and have entered these countries at least once. This is in stark opposition to the former restrictions whereby a woman could only secure an 'umrah or *hajj* visa if she was travelling with a mahram (unmarriageable kin) or in a group. Saudi Airlines is actively promoting stopovers for 'umrah on its website. Tempting packages are being offered, including a free stopover visa, which allows travel to all parts of the country, including Mecca and Medina. Earlier, the 'umrah visa allowed pilgrims to travel to only Jeddah, Mecca and Medina.

In less than five years, from discouraging travel in Saudi Arabia by Westerners and regulating the movements of Muslim pilgrims, Saudi Arabia has developed a grand infrastructure to attract tourists from both categories. Not all of these policies contravene Wahhabi Salafi teachings, such as allowing Muslims entry to other parts of the country, but many certainly do: for example, major policy reversals that allow single Muslim women under the age of 45 to enter without a mahram if they meet visa requirements; permit unmarried couples to check into hotels; allow Western women to arrive at al-Ula airport in revealing Western attire; and sanction mixed-gender swimming pools within resorts in al-Ula, where diners seated in surrounding areas, including lounges and main restaurants, can view female swimmers in bikinis and men in standard Western swimwear.

The striking aspect of these changed norms concerning the presence of women in public spaces and gender mixing is not the fact that the state is promoting them, but the ease with which society seems to have accepted them. None of the foreigners whom I met expressed any concerns about being made uncomfortable by the locals. One British visitor, for instance, mentioned being cautious in the beginning not to wear shorts. After a couple of days of travel in Saudi Arabia, he, however, started to feel at ease, finding the society to be quite relaxed. When he did wear shorts, no one objected.

I frequently encountered similar evidence when conducting fieldwork at major tourist sites, suggesting the ease with which Saudi society appears to have adapted to a more liberal social atmosphere. The main restaurant at the luxurious Habitat Resort in al-Ula, extensively promoted by the Winter at Tantora Festival and highly popular among affluent Western tourists, offers great views of the al-Ula rock formations, complete with a central open-air swimming pool. I was mildly surprised to see here four middle-aged Saudi men donned in *thawb* (traditional Saudi white gown worn by men) and headgear (*ghutrah*). These men, seemingly distinct from the Western-influenced younger Saudis of Riyadh and Jeddah, chatted leisurely over an extended meal. They seemed entirely undisturbed by the sight of Western women in bikinis and men in trunks. Observing the stark contrast between their dress and the environment, one might instinctively feel they'd be out of place. Yet, they seemed perfectly at ease. Similarly, as a female researcher, I feel no judgment from locals, whether in personal interactions or public spaces, now that I often don't wear an ʻabayah.

Conversations with Western academics working in Saudi institutions have led to similar conclusions. An Italian academic, who had been teaching at King Abdullah University of Science and Technology (KAUST) for several years, observed how he had very similar experiences since the initiation of the social reforms, in these words: 'Initially, the campus was the social epicentre. As the sole co-educational facility, it fostered a more open social atmosphere. Now, with Jeddah's bustling nightlife and myriad events, the campus feels deserted.' He was particularly impressed by how, on his recent visit to Medina, which was formerly closed to non-Muslims, he was warmly welcomed and even escorted into the courtyard of the Masjid-i-Nabawi, which he described as a 'beautiful experience'. Likewise, a colleague who had guided Stanford students on a study tour to

Mecca, Medina and Jeddah during the month of Ramadan emphasized the tour's positive aspects, highlighting the societal openness compared to American media portrayals. Recounting the group's midnight visit to Old Jeddah during Ramadan, he commented, 'It was exhilarating. The area was so nicely done up. The ambiance was tranquil, yet full of joy and laughter. People mingled comfortably. This isn't the Saudi Arabia often depicted in the media.'

Conclusion

In order to explain the nature and drivers of ongoing change in Saudi Arabia, it is important to first establish the validity of the claim that social norms have rapidly shifted in Saudi Arabia over the past five years. This chapter has therefore recorded the level of change in social behaviour and expected codes of conduct in public spaces since the announcement of the initial reforms by the Crown Prince in September 2017. Behaviour as expressed in styles of dress, participation in social activities and gender mixing, which was deemed socially inappropriate only five years ago, is today widely accepted; there is no public expression of condemnation of those who are opting out of the conservative norms that regulated Saudi society for nearly a century. There have been a few reports of female harassment during desert dance raves (Usher 2021), but spaces such as dance floors or crowded concerts do not represent everyday interactions in any culture, including Western ones. Overall, we see women taking advantage of newfound liberties, and a wide array of social entertainment options has become available to both genders, some of which are explicitly Western-inspired. Tourism is being promoted by allowing social concessions that were previously deemed highly inappropriate. The ban on alcohol is the main lingering restriction. Even here, the local observers contend that once the Neom city is ready, then, in order to attract more foreign tourists, the state will rationalize the sale of alcohol to non-Muslim tourists, as other Gulf states already do.

Saudi society has demonstrated an unexpected level of adaptability to rapid changes, surprising those who previously viewed it as rigidly conservative, both socially and religiously. What has propelled this rapid change in social norms? If this social opening is not being forcefully imposed from the top by an ambitious Crown Prince, but major segments of the Saudi society are an active and willing participant in this process, does it mean that there was no genuine loyalty to the Wahhabi tradition on the part of the public? Further, were these then purely religiously informed norms and the local tribal culture and traditions had no bearing? Given that the restrictions on enjoying these basic liberties were a product of Wahhabi teachings, the rapid acceptance of those liberties when they became available may indicate a lack of internal commitment to them. Plausible though such an explanation is, it is not the reality. The mechanisms driving this rapid change in social norms are, in fact, quite complex. The subsequent chapters in this book will unpack those mechanisms, with the next chapter providing an insight into the factors that have contributed to the decline of the authority of the Wahhabi establishment.

Chapter 3

UNRAVELLING OF A HISTORIC ALLIANCE

The rise of Wahhabism is a well-documented historical development. In a small oasis settlement north of Riyadh, in eighteenth-century central Arabia, emerged a radical Islamic preacher who was to exert a decisive influence on how Islam would be perceived globally in the late twentieth and early twenty-first centuries. He was not a great scholar of Islamic jurisprudence, knowledge of which earns the traditional stamp of Islamic authority in Islam, but a *daʿi* (someone who proselytises) (Commins 2009; Spannaus 2018a). His most referenced publication is a slim book on ʿaqidah, unlike the extensive treatises authored by prominent Islamic scholars over the centuries. Yet he would successfully challenge locally reputed scholars in the surrounding oasis settlements, and gradually those in the entire Najd region, as well as the scholarly classes at the most influential centres of Islamic civilisation and learning in the Muslim world. At the time, three Muslim empires – Ottomans in the West (1324–1922), Mughals in the East (1526–1857), and Safavids in Iran (1501–1736) – controlled Muslim lands (Dale 2010). Despite lacking the right scholarly credentials, and promoting a highly restrictive reading of the Islamic creed, not only did this preacher, located on the geographical margins of the Islamic civilisation, stamp his reading of Islamic dictates firmly on the Arabian peninsula, but in the late twentieth century this strand of Islam – referred to by its critics as Wahhabism (Commins 2009) – won large numbers of followers, not only in the Muslim-majority countries but also within Muslim communities in the Western diaspora.

The Kingdom of Saudi Arabia, which was imprinted as a nation state on the world map in 1932, is a product of the pact formed between this radical preacher, Muhammad ibn Abd al-Wahhab (1703–1792), and Muhammad ibn Saud al-Muqrin (1710–1765). The pact was formed in 1744 in Diriyyah, an oasis settlement on the northern edge of Riyadh, which was the base of the Al-Saud family. Today, opened to domestic and international visitors (after extensive restoration work in recent years) as a major historic and touristic site, al-Diriyyah preserves the original mud structures featuring the family quarters, the public meeting spaces, and a mosque. The basis of this mutually beneficial pact was simple: al-Saud, who had taken a liking to Wahhabi teachings, would help promote them on Najdi soil against rival sects, and Ibn Abd al-Wahhab would pledge allegiance to the Saud clan and provide its rule with religious legitimacy (Commins 2009). Over the next century, this alliance fought to defend the First Saudi State (1727) and succeeded in establishing the Second Saudi State (1824). Both proved short lived, as the Ottomans, who at the time ruled over the Hejaz region, suppressed these successes with the support of Egyptian forces and the Sharif family of Hejaz (Commins 2009).[1] The Al-Saud clan, however, finally emerged victorious, under the leadership of Abdulaziz al-Saud (1880–1953), when, after defeating the rival clans and tribes in Najd and eventually also Hejaz, it took control of Jeddah, the last stronghold of the Sharifs (Commins 2009). The country was founded in the very name of the Al-Saud family in 1932.

During these war-waging years, the alliance between the Saud family and the Wahhabi 'ulama' proved mutually beneficial. The Al-Saud family helped to embed Wahhabi teachings in settlements where it established political authority, while Wahhabi scholars helped to legitimize the waging of wars on fellow Muslims clans or tribes by declaring them to be non-Muslims as measured against the Wahhabi creed and its prescribed levels of piety (Commins 2009). Once the Saudi state was formed, however, the Al-Saud clan, now in charge of running the newly formed country, was keen to be pragmatic and establish a certain degree of harmony; but the Wahhabi 'ulama' and also the Ikhwans, the Bedouin fighters recruited by King Abdulaziz on account of their religious zeal, were less accommodating (Commins 2009; Mouline 2014). The result was the forceful crushing of the Ikhwan fighters by the emerging Saudi state, combined with on-going negotiations and tactful adjustments made with the Wahhabi scholars over time (al-Fahad 2004; Commins 2009; Mouline 2014). Gradually, a consensus emerged whereby authority, to a certain degree, was divided between the two sides, to give each side control over specific domains of public life. The Wahhabi 'ulama' came to define and enforce the social norms shaping everyday life and the expected code of conduct in public spaces; this led to control over the spheres of public education and the judiciary (Commins 2009; Mouline 2014). In return, the economic policies, political governance, and strategies of national defence were left almost entirely in the hands of members of the House of Saud, with 'ulama' playing at best a consultative role. Beginning in the 1920s, the Wahhabi establishment also managed to have an official enforcement mechanism, in the form of the hay'ah police (religious police represented by the Committee for the Promotion of Virtue and the Prevention of Vice),[2] at its disposal. This enabled it to enforce its socially puritanical agenda in cases of weak voluntary compliance. In return, the Wahhabi elites justified the Al-Saud family's right to rule by contending that respect for a ruler is necessary in order to prevent fitna and chaos. The only condition under which the ruler's authority can be questioned is if he becomes a danger to Islam itself.

If this close to three-century-old alliance has suddenly and very publicly unravelled starting in 2016, the question is what explains the Saudi state's decision to end the alliance and push back on Wahhabi teachings? Equally importantly, why has such a dramatic and sudden reversal not provoked popular resistance? If the Wahhabi establishment had indeed been able to help legitimize the rule of the Saud family, then by implication it enjoyed loyalty among the public, because a religious authority wins genuine following only by voluntary compliance. Why then have those Saudi citizens who genuinely adhered to the Wahhabi establishment not come out in its defence? Could it be that the Wahhabi establishment, which was labelled as heretical by the earlier scholars, even in Najd and not just in the wider Sunni world (Spannaus 2018a), failed to cultivate a strong sense of loyalty to its teachings, despite the financial and administrative support from the state that it has enjoyed to spread its teachings? If that was the case, then why would the royal family have given in to the pressures of the Wahhabi establishment on many occasions to make the alliance survive (Mouline 2014)? Or is the explanation for the unravelling of this alliance much more complex?

Arguing the latter, the analysis presented in this book shows how the current erosion of the authority of the official Wahhabi establishment is indeed a product of a combination of many factors, including the dramatic social changes that re-shaped what young Saudis, including the younger generation of Saudi royals (Bano 2018e), want for their country. But an equally important role has been played by factors specific to the Wahhabi teachings, most noticeably their focus on *takfir* (declaring someone non-Muslim). The takfiri sentiment within Wahhabi Islam, invoked by most contemporary global jihad networks, including al-Qaida and ISIS, since the events of September 11, 2001 (Maher 2016), has become a huge reputational concern for the Saudi state and an insurmountable hurdle in any attempt to reposition itself as a progressive state on the global stage (al-Saud 2021). A tool that at one point was extremely useful for establishing and promoting the interests of the royal family has now become a major burden in terms of global reputation and a threat to its survival, thus creating incentives for the Saudi state to question its usefulness. Combined with a growing recognition among the Saudi royals that many young Saudis want a more liberal social sphere than that prescribed by the Wahhabi establishment, curbing the powers of the religious elites has become politically viable – although not without its risks.

This chapter focuses on analysing in detail the factors that facilitated the initial establishment of this alliance and its consolidation over time, and it will then identify the logic behind its apparently sudden unravelling. We will see that political scientists make a serious error when they ascribe to the 'ulama' too much binding power over public actions in Muslim societies (Rubin 2017; Kuru 2019). Because Sunni Islam has no central authority like the Vatican, an individual scholar, or a scholarly establishment, has to build legitimacy in the public eye through their own deeds and actions: the authority is thus constructed from the bottom up, rather than bestowed from the top down (Nizami 1983; Robinson 2001; Bano 2018c). Core to the construction of this bottom-up authority is the ability to demonstrate high levels of textual knowledge, but also personal piety and integrity, as the model of Islamic authority for Muslims lies in the life of the Prophet Muhammad himself (Nizami 1983; Robinson 2001; Bano 2018c). For Islamic scholars, winning a mass following is thus contingent on demonstrating that they are trying to emulate the standards that he set. Historically, we have seen those Islamic scholars, who become too close to the state, suffer in terms of popular legitimacy (Nizami 1983; Bano 2018a); closeness to wealth and power leads to questioning of their piety. Moral uprightness and distance from political power are key to winning popular legitimacy (Mernissi 1995).

It is important to acknowledge the rich body of literature on the forms of religious authority in Islam, with many scholars exploring the question of 'who can speak for Islam', (Krämer and Schmidtke 2006; Bano 2018c; Sunier 2024). This scholarship has highlighted not only the historical distinction between the Sufi and spiritually oriented nature of religious authority versus the formal textual authority asserted by the 'ulama', but also how the rise of political Islamists and modernists in the twentieth century has posed challenges to traditional forms of authority (Krämer and Schmidtke 2006; Bano 2018c; Sunier 2024). Additionally, recent research on religious authority in Sunni as well as Shia tradition, including my own research, has explored the emergence of female preachers in traditionally male-dominated spheres of authority, such as mosques and madrasas (Mahmood 2005; Bano and Kalmbach 2011; Bano 2017; Künkler and Stewart 2018). The dynamics of religious authority in Shia Islam are different from those in Sunni Islam due to a greater centralization of authority, though this does not necessarily change followers' expectations for scholars to adhere to an Islamically pious code (Künkler and Stewart 2018). This chapter focuses specifically on the conceptions of the authority exercised by 'ulama', the scholarly classes within the Sunni tradition, who are the subject of critique in the recent political economy studies attributing socio-economic decline in Muslim societies to religious authorities (Rubin 2017; Kuru 2019). Furthermore, for a study focused on changing role of religious authority in Saudi Arabia, Wahhabi 'ulama' become the natural focus, considering the state's requirements for the invisibility of Sufi tariqahs (Sedgwick 1997), the suppression of public displays of Shia religious authority (Matthiesen 2015; Ismail 2016), and state's systematic suppression of the Islamists (al-Rasheed 2015; Ménoret 2020).

The recent political economy studies looking at the relationship between religious authority and lack of development in Muslim societies often fail to recognize the intricate foundation of religious authority in Islam. There is an implicit assumption in these works (Rubin 2017; Kuru 2019) that Muslims unquestioningly follow scholars simply because these scholars assert knowledge of foundational texts. In fact, 'ulama' are constantly being judged against a complex model of knowledge acquisition and pietistic behaviour, based on inherited knowledge in Muslim societies of what to expect from a genuine Islamic scholar (Nizami 1983; Robinson 2001; Bano 2018a). Maintaining popular legitimacy is an ongoing challenge for Islamic scholars and scholarly institutions, as evidenced by the evolving relationship between the Wahhabi 'ulama' and both the Saudi state and society. To understand the importance of this argument, it is important to start by identifying the actual mechanisms that helped the royal family and the Wahhabi establishment to strengthen each other's authority in the early period, and then to examine when and why differences started to emerge, and why the negotiations and mutual concessions that preserved the alliance for most of the twentieth century are no longer effective. As we will see, the alliance with the political authority, while consolidating the authority of the Wahhabi establishment in earlier periods, also consistently compromised its credibility in the eyes of many members of the public.

3.1. The emergence and consolidation of Wahhabism

The emergence of Wahhabism from a minor tradition to a global Islamic reform movement is a fascinating story, but not necessarily unique, when compared with findings in the wider literature on why new religious traditions or strands become influential in certain geographical areas at a particular point in time. Studies of the spread of Islam in new regions in early Islamic history (Hodgson 1977), like the spread of other religious traditions such as Protestantism in sixteenth-century Europe (Fukuyama 2017a, 2017b), document how the conversion of local rulers or kings to the new faith often helped its spread and consolidation. The state bureaucracy helps to embed the religious dictates by incorporating them in law. At the same time, being part of the official apparatus puts the financial and administrative resources of the state at the disposal of the religious actors, increasing their capacity to spread their teachings: access to better religious spaces, improved financial incentives for teachers and students which help to attract talented students, and enhanced administrative capacity for expanding educational services across the country are some of the established benefits.[3] In the 1730s, Ibn Abd al-Wahhab was a lone preacher who, having travelled to Hejaz and Basra, important centres of Islamic learning at the time, returned to preach Islam in his home village in al-'Uyayna, seventy kilometres from present-day Riyadh (Commins 2009; Spannaus 2018a). Critical of many local religious practices, Ibn Abd al-Wahhab pursued a highly puritanical reform agenda, arguing for a return to the Quran and Sunnah. He wanted to cleanse Muslim societies of the state of *jahiliyyah* (a term normally used to refer to the polytheistic beliefs and practices observed by Arabs at the time of the arrival of the Prophet Muhammad) (Commins 2009; Spannaus 2018a). Wahhab's puritanical zeal made him label many popular practices, such as paying visits to the graves of the saints, or the use of amulets, which other Muslim scholars treated as minor digressions, as *shirk* (associating partners with God – the ultimate sin in Islam). His strong condemnation of such acts raised concerns among established scholars. Yet his ability to convince Muhammad ibn Saud, head of one of the settlements in the Najd region based in Diriyyah, of the power of his message transformed his fortunes and those of mainstream Sunni Islam.

Wahhab's primary concern was to promote a strict notion of tawhid. His most popular work thus remains *Kitab-al-Tawhid*, in which he draws on verses from the Quran and hadith to establish the importance of tawhid and explain what it entails. The idea of tawhid is the central pillar of Islam, expressed in the basic declaration of Islamic faith (*shahadah*): 'There is no god but God, and Muhammad is his last Messenger.' Focusing on it was thus not unique, but what was distinctive was the way in which Ibn Abd al-Wahhab operationalized this idea. Ibn Abd al-Wahhab argued that tawhid demands that faith in the oneness of

God should not be treated as merely a matter of inner belief: it must be matched by action (Commins 2009; Spannaus 2018a). Such a notion of tawhid, whereby observable actions and not just inner belief determine one's conviction in tawhid, in the long term, had practical implications for the role of the state in regulating personal piety. Under this extended conception of creed, which moved beyond the expression of an inner conviction to include actual practice of core Islamic rituals, the state gradually acquired the authority to punish those who were seen as not observing their religious obligations, such as reciting the five daily prayers or giving *zakah* (obligatory giving), or those who were viewed to be indulging in practices that he argued violate the oneness of God, such as venerating saints. It reduced the individual freedom of the believer by giving the state the responsibility for regulating individual piety. At the same time, by making the state responsible for enforcing religious piety, it encouraged political quietism, as the state-supporting Islamic framework was to be respected unless it clearly deviated from this responsibility (al-Azami 2021). Thus, a ruler's commitment to establishing an Islamic order superseded other concerns (Spannaus 2018a; al-Saud 2021).

Recent scholarship (Crawford 2014; Bunzel 2023) examining the writings of Ibn Abd al-Wahhab shows that he did not explicitly intend to grant the state the power to enforce and regulate individual religious behaviour. Crawford (2014) highlights that although Ibn Abd al-Wahhab was an advocate of interventionism in the public sphere, he never discussed how best to organize communal enforcement in practice. He did not argue for the state to enforce righteous behaviour. Instead, he viewed it as an individual duty of every believing member of society, irrespective of rank, to command right and forbid wrong. Crawford (2014) shows that Ibn Abd al-Wahhab was conscious that excessive zeal among self-appointed guardians of morality could undermine the unity of the local community. Furthermore, Crawford (2014) notes that in his time, the Arabic word for 'state' (*dawla*) did not invoke an image of a modern state, and that it was only in the final phase of the First Saudi State that the term dawla began to appear in Wahhabi writings with reference to the growing Saudi empire in Dirriyah. It was towards the end of the First Saudi State that formal references to the state in Wahhabi scholarship became visible, coinciding with the increasing formalization of the Wahhabi religious establishment (Crawfold 2014).

Thus, in the long term, Ibn Abd al-Wahhab's strict and widely encompassing notion of tawhid had important implications, not just for notions of individual piety, but for shaping the relationship between state and society, and defining what freedom a Muslim had in pursuing his relationship with God. On the one hand, it curtailed individual freedom in the practice of one's religion; on the other hand, religion became an active part of the public sphere and also a major source of political legitimacy. Further, such a restrictive idea of tawhid made it possible to call other Muslims non-Muslims – a process referred to as takfir. This is what caused most concern among existing scholars (Commins 2009; Maher 2016; Spannaus 2018a). Thus, Shias were declared to be non-Muslims (Ismail 2016), and those Sunnis not adhering to Wahhabi teachings became at risk of similar treatment. This aspect of its teachings, as has been documented in the literature, facilitated the earlier rise of the Wahhabi establishment, as it enabled them to legitimize the Al-Saud family's war against fellow Muslim clans and tribes (Ismail 2016). However, as we will see in this chapter, it has also contributed to its current downfall. Also, as an extension of the same austere notion of tawhid, Wahhabi teachings placed heavy emphasis on the Islamic concept of al-wala' wa-l-bara', which argues for loyalty to Muslims and enmity to non-Muslims (Wagemakers 2012; Mouline 2014; Maher 2016).

The defence for these policies has often rested on the reasoning that preventing people from indulging in minor sins is the best way to prevent the committing of major sins (al-Saadi 2008). It is this aspect of Wahhabi teaching that resulted in establishing a highly restrictive social sphere: banning women from driving cars (not a sin in its own right) became a way of preventing major sins such as adultery that may result from increased gender mixing and unregulated female mobility (al-Saadi 2008). Other measures included the banning of cinemas, most forms of performing arts, and professional music for their capacity to provoke hedonistic desires. Finally, endorsing literalist readings of the Quran and hadith, and actively discrediting more mystical and philosophical trends in Islamic thought, the Wahhabi establishment, not only undertook the active destruction of major Islamic sites in Medina to reduce their chances of becoming sites of veneration; it also promoted everyday habits and lifestyles that aimed to emulate the life of the Prophet and his companions in every action. Rather than helping believers to live honourable lives in current times by following the underlying principles that we learn from the Prophet's life, the focus here, as Islamic scholars critical of the Wahhabi tradition argue, became the requirement to behave as if one were still living at the time of the Prophet (Maher 2016; Fouad 2021).

To convert even Najdi 'ulama', who largely followed Hanbali law, let alone those trained in Hejaz, or the wider Muslim world, where the other three schools of Islamic law – Shafi, Hanafi, Malaki – were followed (Commins 2009; al-Sarhan 2016; Spannaus 2018a), was thus a daunting undertaking. Even Ibn Abd ul-Wahhab's own brother and father, who were respected scholars in the local settlements, labelled him a heretic (Spannaus 2018a). The support received from the political authority that the Al-Saud established in the lands that it conquered was thus key to the gradual embedding of Wahhabi teachings across Najd and Hejaz. The support of political authority helped to promote the Wahhabi teachings while eradicating competition by a number of mechanisms: scholars occupying important religious positions were replaced by Wahhabi 'ulama'; conditions were made difficult for those scholars to teach in their settlements, forcing them to emigrate to other areas; and bureaucratic and financial support was simultaneously provided to Wahhabi scholars so that they could preach freely and win over willing converts (Commins 2009, 2015; Spannaus 2018a). This targeted displacement of scholars from non-Wahhabi schools of thought was key to gradually embedding Wahhabi religious thought and practice across most of Najd. As Commins (2009) records, by the mid-1800s, the Wahhabi 'ulama' had thus successfully formed a regional religious culture with its own doctrine, canon of law, leadership, cadre of 'ulama', and centres of learning, and they were in a strong position to legitimize the Al-Saud family's political authority. Gradually, due to the systematic marginalization of scholars from other traditions and heavy investment in the Wahhabi teachings, Wahhabism became in effect the only doctrine in Najd (Commins 2009). It also made successful inroads in Hejaz; but expelling other Islamic scholarly traditions from Mecca and Medina was not as easy as it had been in Najd. Thus, in Hejaz, the other Islamic scholarly traditions, including the Sufi tariqahs, continued to operate with the knowledge of the Saudi state as long as they did not make their presence actively known.

Across the Muslim world, however, Wahhabism retained a negative connotation among most Islamic scholarly classes (Commins 2015; Fouad 2021). The very use of the term 'Wahhabi', which was developed by its critics, implied that Muhammad Ibn Abd al-Wahhab had introduced a new school of Islamic law and, thus, was a *mubtadi'* (innovator) (Commins 2015). In the eyes of the Wahhabi scholars, 'Wahhabism' thus to date remains a derogatory term. Instead, they have preferred to refer to themselves by other names, such as *muwahhidun* (unitarians) or *Ahl al-Sunnah wa al-Jama'a* (the people of sunnah and the community). Globally, the movement is more commonly referred to as Salafism: a title that the Wahhabi establishment actively self-appropriated from the 1970s onwards (Commins 2015; Spannaus 2018a). The term 'Salafism' had become popular in Islamic circles in the Middle East between 1940 and the 1970s as part of a reformist current which argued for emulating the *Salaf* (the first three generations of pious Muslims). This focus on following the first three generations of pious Muslims had a wide appeal for Muslims of differing orientations. In fact, the scholars initially associated with promoting Salafism were Islamic modernists, such as the famous Egyptian scholar Rashid Rida, who were critical of the traditional Islamic scholarly classes for their failure to rival the Western influence that extended to the Muslim lands under colonial rule (Spannaus 2018a). Instead of following the extensive scholarship produced by scholars within different Islamic schools of law, the modernist Salafis argued for going back to the Quran and Sunnah and interpreting them in accordance with the needs of the time.

Within Saudi Arabia, some of the modernist Salafi scholars from other Arab countries, such as Egypt and Syria, gained a stronghold in the 1960s (Lacroix 2011). Initially welcomed by the Saudi rulers, these scholars ultimately became a concern as their ideas became mixed with those of the Muslim Brotherhood and acquired a political undertone (Lacroix 2011). Partly driven by an impulse to displace the power of the political Islamists, and partly to gain greater legitimacy among the Muslim *ummah* (global Muslim community), from the late 1960s onwards, the Wahhabi establishment labelled itself as Salafi. It did so successfully by publishing writings that presented Wahhabi beliefs and practices as being in accordance with the Salaf (Spannaus 2018a). Wahhabi 'ulama' were included among the biographies of the Salafs (Spannaus 2018a). Primary religious texts were re-edited to highlight a historical link between the Salafi tradition and Wahhabism. Foreign authors who wrote Salafi works with a pro-Wahhabi perspective were patronized (Commins 2015; Spannaus 2018a). It is due to this success that today, Salafism is synonymous with Wahhabism and not with the work of the Islamic modernists or political Islamists. Today, the terms Wahhabism and Salafism are thus invoked interchangeably in writings about the Saudi religious sphere, even though the term Salafism was initially associated with Islamic modernists (Commins 2015; Spannaus 2018a; Bano 2021).

In return for the support that they received for consolidating their religious authority at different points in time, the Wahhabi scholars used this authority to legitimize the rule of the House of Saud and endorse the policies of the Saudi state. In the early periods, they helped to mobilize the Ikhwan, who became key to King Abdulaziz's ultimate victory (Commins 2009). However, as the Al-Saud came close to formation of a formal state, it was clear that the royal family and the Wahhabi scholars have slightly diverging preferences (al-Fahad 2004; Mouline 2014) Recognizing the need to forge unity across the tribes and across Najd and Hejaz, having already disbanded the Ikhwan by late 1930, once Saudi Arabia was established in 1932, King Abdulaziz adopted a more pragmatic approach of reconciliation and a certain degree of tolerance (al-Fahad 2004; Mouline 2014). The Al-Saud clan thus tried to rein in the enthusiasm of Wahhabi scholars by means of direct and indirect checks. In Hejaz, for example, they filled many senior posts with local figures, instead of deploying Wahhabi 'ulama' (Commins 2009). The degree to which the Saudi royals could resist the pressures of the religious elites in subsequent decades depended partly on their individual character (Niblock 2006; Mouline 2014). King Faisal, whose mother came from a family of Wahhabi 'ulama', and who was personally perceived as being very pious (Commins 2009; Mouline 2014), thus was most able to exercise greater control over the Wahhabi establishment by bringing it under the control of central state institutions (Mouline 2014, 2015; Commins 2015). Functionally, the Saudi state, over time, came to exercise overriding powers. Especially after King Faisal's administrative reforms, the royal family gained the upper hand, rendering the religious establishment more subservient to their political authority (Mouline 2014, 2015). After Faisal's death, however, the royal family again had to allow greater concessions to the religious establishment, as subsequent Saudi monarchs lacked Faisal's charisma and authority (Mouline 2014). Also, the legal system being based on shari'ah left much power in the hands of the *qadi*s (judges) who are part of the religious establishment (Vogel 2000; Krell 2025). However, during King Abdullah's reign (2005–2015), especially in the context of post–September 11 pressures, the state did start to pressure the Wahhabi establishment to curb readings of religious texts that could be seen as endorsing global jihad (Razavian 2018a).

The relationship between the Wahhabi establishment and the Saudi royal family has thus evolved according to the needs of the time and has been a product of constant negotiations and mutual concessions made by the two sides. What then has recently disrupted this balance of power between the two sides? What has made the Saudi state abandon the Wahhabi religious establishment and deprive it of the infrastructure that it had formerly put at its disposal, to enforce highly restrictive social norms? In order to understand this, we need to understand the factors influencing the current actions of the Saudi royal family, as well as those of the religious establishment.

3.2. Causes of the state's abandonment of Wahhabism

Observation of recent developments in Saudi Arabia, analysis of statements by the state actors, especially the Crown Prince, and my own interviews with the actors involved in on-going reforms suggest that three major factors have convinced the Saudi state to break away from its old alliance with Wahhabism. This parting of the ways has also been symbolized by the Saudi state's decision in 2022 to celebrate 'Saudi Founding Day' on 22 February, a date that marks the 1727 establishment of the Emirate of Diriyyah by Muhammad ibn Saud, rather than tracing the origin of Saudi Arabia to the 1744 pact between him and Ibn Abd al-Wahhab, which was formerly the case (Alamer 2022). The three key factors are the perception of Wahhabi creedal debates justifying takfir becoming a burden rather than an asset; the growing threat posed by political Islamists, reinforced by the Arab Spring; and declining tolerance for Wahhabi puritanism on social issues among the young, who have grown up in a very different and globally connected Saudi Arabia than that experienced by previous generations.

The rising cost of takfiri ideas

As noted above, a key implication of the strict conception of tawhid promoted by Ibn Abd al-Wahhab was that it made excommunication of fellow Muslims easier. This had directly benefited the Al-Saud clan in the earlier period. The Wahhabi use of takfir enabled the Wahhabi scholars to endorse the wars that the Al-Saud waged against other tribes and clans for almost two centuries before the Kingdom of Saudi Arabia was established (Commins 2009). After the establishment of Saudi Arabia, the Saudi state, as well as the Wahhabi 'ulama', became cautious about the use of takfir to legitimize war in order to gain authority in the eyes of Muslims from different Islamic traditions (Mouline 2014). But these ideals were invoked for strategic purposes when needed: the Saudi state used them again, for instance, when it allied with the USA against the USSR and helped to recruit jihadis to fight a war in Afghanistan in the 1980s (Maher 2016).

What is little appreciated, however, is that the same ideals became a major concern for the Saudi state when the rise of global jihad, especially after September 11, saw the jihadi networks, such as al-Qaida, deploy the same Wahhabi teachings of tawhid and takfir to justify their actions (Maher 2016). These groups actively legitimized jihad against Muslims and non-Muslim targets alike by drawing on the related Wahhabi ideal of al-wala' wa-l-bara', which implies that one is a friend of those who are pious Muslims and against all those who are non-Muslims or Muslims who do not follow the strict ideal of tawhid as operationalized by Ibn Abd al-Wahhab (Commins 2009; Maher 2016; Qadhi 2019). The concept of al-wala' wa-l-bara' operates in a similar fashion to takfir, as a tool of 'in-group' control which draws a line against those deemed to be outsiders; it forms a distinct delineation between the Salafi-Jihadi constructions of Islam and everything else (Maher 2016). Providing a historical overview of the concept from its pre-Islamic beginnings to its reinterpretation in nineteenth-century Wahhabi discourse, with special attention to Abu Muhammad al-Maqdisi's rediscovery of the Wahhabi version of this notion and its further development by Saudi-Wahhabi scholars and activists, Wagemakers (2012) notes that it is unclear whether wala' and bara' were initially connected or only later came to be seen as two sides of the same coin. Both terms entered the Islamic lexicon meaning 'loyalty' and 'disavowal'. As Wagemakers (2012: 149) notes, both terms 'indicate a desire to enhance solidarity among and maintain the homogeneity of the "in-group" on one hand and create a clear distinction with the "out-group" on the other'. Wagemakers (2012) argues that this provided an effective defence of the strictness and purity that Salafi scholars associated with their doctrine. It makes it easier to separate right from wrong, and insiders from outsiders, reducing the chances of committing bida, kufr, or shirk by avoiding people who are viewed as promoting sinful ideas, while increasing loyalty to Salafi 'aqidah (Wagemakers 2012).

The increasing attribution of global jihad to teachings of Saudi Salafism by scholars and Western governments alike placed indirect responsibility for religious extremism at the door of the Saudi state (Maher 2016; al-Saud 2021). This had costs in terms of Saudi Arabia's image on the global stage. This is despite the fact that after the Iraq War, al-Qaida had started to target the Saudi state itself for its compliance with the Western states, especially the USA, to whom Saudis had conceded military bases on Saudi soil (al-Saud 2021). Once takfiri ideas began to pose a threat to the Saudi state itself, the Wahhabi scholarly establishment came under growing pressure to repudiate such interpretations. King Abdullah directly challenged senior scholars for having indirectly nurtured strands of radical thought (Razavian 2018a). In the past decade, the Saudi state has thus made the Wahhabi establishment change the religious discourse on jihad; Saudi school curricula have also been revised to ensure that the education system condemns global Islamic militancy (al-Otaibi 2020) – an effort which has been further accelerated now (Gold & al-Lawati 2023).[4]

Yet, even within the Saudi royal family and among Western observers, there were continuing concerns about elements of Wahhabi Salafi thinking contributing to global jihad and anti-royalist sentiments. As noted by one of my respondents in Riyadh, commenting on the on-going changes, 'there is a realization that we don't want to be contributing, whether knowingly or unknowingly, towards producing another *Da'ish* (Islamic State of Iraq and the Levant, ISIS)'. Thus, Wahhabi ideals, which at one point in history helped to establish the political authority of the Saudi royal family on the Arabian peninsula, had now become a source of negative publicity around the globe, and a threat to the royal family itself. This dramatic shift in the use of ideals associated with Wahhabi teachings has played an important part in making the royal family increasingly question the value of this partnership. This became particularly the case when the Crown Prince presented Vision 2030, which requires the re-positioning of Saudi Arabia as a progressive modern state on the global stage.

The power of political Islamists

In addition to the weakened use of the Wahhabi establishment in legitimizing the royal family in the eyes of the global jihadis, the Wahhabi scholars had also not been particularly effective in countering the popular appeal of the political Islamists who emerged from among the Wahhabi Salafi ranks from the 1970s onwards and became a powerful force on Saudi university campuses in particular (Lacroix 2011). Recent scholarship has established how by the 1980s the influence of Muslim Brotherhood members who had come from Egypt and Syria mostly to work as the staff in newly established Saudi universities had led to the first major Islamic political resistance (*al-sahwah al-Islamiyyah*) in opposition to the Saudi state (Lacroix 2011). The prominent scholars within this movement have faced repression from the Saudi state from time to time (al-Rasheed 2015), and continue to do so today (Qiblawi 2019; al-Rasheed 2021), but a dynamic domestic discourse on political liberties defended from within an Islamic framework has evolved due to the existence of these actors (al-Rasheed 2015).

These actors were also vocal during the Arab Spring. Scholars, such as Salman al-Awda, associated with the al-Sahwah movement and other Islamic activists, legitimized the notion of political rebellion from within a Salafi framework during this time (al-Rasheed 2015; al-Azami 2021). These scholars countered the traditional position of the official Wahhabi establishment, which argues for obedience to the ruler at all costs, in order to avoid the risk of fitna. Instead, using the same Islamic sources as those used by the official Saudi Salafi establishment, they defended the public's right to engage in political protests against unrepresentative regimes (al-Rasheed 2015; al-Azami 2021). Young Saudis' following of these scholars, as visible in their social media profiles and the signing of the petitions that they have initiated (al-Rasheed 2015),[5] has been a source of concern for the Saudi royal family, which helped to suppress the Arab Spring across the region. The royal family actively supported President al-Sisi against the Muslim Brotherhood in Egypt (Lippman 2013; Riedel 2013), who came to power after staging a coup against the Muslim Brotherhood-led government, to curb the growing power of political Islamists in the region.

Thus, the Wahhabi establishment has proved to be ineffective in recent times, in terms of countering global jihadism, which is increasingly costly to Saudi Arabia's global image and also poses a threat to the Saudi royal family, and also in terms of the challenge posed by the political Islamists at home who despite systematic repression by the state (al-Rasheed 2015; Ménoret 2020) have been building a case for greater political freedoms in the Kingdom (Alshamsi 2011; Lacroix 2011). Unlike the earlier period of the alliance, when Wahhabi scholars had come to command an overriding influence on matters of religion, the emergence of rival religious forces since the 1960s, and their persistence over time despite state oppression, has motivated the royal family to question the usefulness of this alliance. This became particularly so with the attitudinal shifts that had started to become visible among Saudi youth in recent years. As we will see in subsequent chapters, this factor is key to the breaking up of the alliance.

Young Saudis' changed sensibilities

The extent to which Saudi youth were ready for social opening became apparent to the Saudi state only after the initial reforms announced in 2017 were so warmly received. However, there were enough signs of young people wanting a more open social sphere before the announcement of the initial reforms that the Crown Prince felt confident to embark on his reform programme. A key platform from which the state could observe these attitudinal shifts and preferences was provided by social media, which, as the evidence suggests (Diwan 2018; al-Rasheed 2021), and as I also found in my interviews, the royal family monitors closely. The curtailing of powers of the hay'ah police in 2016, which pre-dated the announcement of any social reform policies, was triggered directly in response to a video that went viral on social media, showing the hay'ah police dragging two Saudi girls to their vehicle from a shopping mall (Said-Moorhouse 2016; Bano 2018e). The government's ruling to restrict the powers of mutawwiʿ to take people into custody was, however, not a response to this single event but a result of the slowly growing pressure from the public and the more progressive members of the royal family to remove such forced restrictions on individual behaviour. My own interviews with young Saudi girls during this period had revealed similarly modern sensibilities: equipped with expensive mobile phones and the latest social media apps (Chaudhary 2016), they were aware of global lifestyles and were expressing very modern sensibilities associated with Western culture (Bano 2018e). The Saudi royal family was witnessing similar intergenerational changes in values and taste. Elaborating on how change is bound to come, one of the female royals had mentioned to me in an interview in 2015: 'When we were young, our governesses used to recite the verses from the Quran to lull us to sleep as they combed through our hair; now my daughter falls asleep watching television. I tell her this is not right, but that is how this young generation is growing up.'

Vision 2030 was developed after widespread consultations had been held with the Saudi public, and especially with young people across the different regions of the country (GoSA 2016). The Crown Prince himself, unlike many Saudi royals, had studied at King Saud University in Riyadh, rather than going overseas to study. He was thus seen to have developed a good sense of what Saudi youth want (DW 2018) – although, as we shall see, he himself has been surprised by the extent of the positive reception given to the social reforms, thereby expediting their pace compared with what was initially planned. The sense that the younger generation needs a different social milieu from the one that has been promoted by the Wahhabi establishment was, however, the third key factor in the Saudi state's recent detachment from the Wahhabi establishment. As in the case of the takfiri ideals, the over-puritanical zeal of the Wahhabi establishment, limiting gender mixing and social entertainment, which in the early period had helped to establish a certain degree of social order and control, was now a burden on the state, as young people had limited appreciation for it. Equally, such teachings could not allow for the development of a large tourism sector, which under Vision 2030 is one of the key strategies for economic diversification away from a dependence on oil.

Finally, it is also important to remember that underneath the Wahhabi-dominated religious sphere, the Saudi public, especially in the Hejaz region, continued to nurture different Islamic sensibilities (Yamani 2009). In my own fieldwork prior to the 2017 reforms, I had found many subtle instances illustrative of this tolerance: for example, Muslim scholars from other countries who are vocal critics of Saudi Salafism yet could secure access to the important religious sites, such as the house that is marked as the birthplace of the Prophet Muhammad, to which the Saudi government restricts access. This reflected the connections of these scholars to those members of the royal family (or senior Saudi officials) who themselves are of Sufi orientation and have respect for their scholarship. Further, while the first and the third Saudi states might have destroyed tombs and important Islamic remains dating from the Prophet's time, it was possible for a prominent Saudi scholar to work on developing an app that maps all the important sites from the Prophet's time, giving the visitor immediate (virtual) access to them. As this scholar argued: 'Our idea is that the buildings might be gone, but the location is most important and it can still be visited and cherished.' He was not at odds with the Saudi authorities; in fact, he was a respected member of the official establishment, but he could develop an app to record the locations of graves and monuments with the explicit intention of making them accessible to other Muslims – even though such a project counters the Saudi government's attempts to restrict veneration of those sites. Furthermore, despite Saudi Salafism's aversion to Sufism (especially the practice of shrine visits), *tasawuf* (Islamic mysticism) remains important to many Saudis and also to some influential members of the royal family; appreciation for Moroccan Sufis, Turkish mysticism and current scholarly revival, and the contributions of Muslim converts such as Humza Yusuf and Tim Winter – who defend a strong mystical and philosophical approach of Islam (Bano 2020) – were some surprising findings of my interviews with a senior member of the royal family.

Given the above observations, it appears that the legitimizing power of the Wahhabi establishment had been steadily eroded in past decades, firstly due to the rise of rival religious actors, with which it could not effectively compete, and more recently due to changed social attitudes among young people in favour of Western-style social liberties (Yamani 2000; Thompson 2019). Why the attitudes of Saudi youth have changed so dramatically from those of their parents' generation will be discussed in the next chapter, while a more extensive analysis of these changed attitudes will be presented in Chapter 5. For now, this analysis has focused on registering how this change influenced the Saudi royal family to review the pact with the Wahhabi establishment.

3.3. Understanding scholars' acquiescence

If it is important to understand the reasons that made the royal family risk breaking up the old alliance, it is equally important to examine why the Wahhabi establishment, or its sympathizers among the public, have not responded aggressively. There has been no large-scale revolt by members of the Wahhabi establishment, either in the form of resignations, staging of street protests or leading media campaigns against the Saudi regime.[6] The threat of state repression, to which political Islamists are already exposed (al-Rasheed 2015; Ménoret 2020), is indeed one of the main explanations. There are, however, also a complex set of related factors dictating this outcome: pragmatism for the sake of survival; a genuine commitment to the Wahhabi ideal of respecting the state to avoid fitna; and, arguably more importantly, the Wahhabi establishment's own awareness of its weakened position within Saudi society due to changed attitudes of the younger generation.

Being pragmatic has been key to the survival of the Wahhabi establishment since the foundation of Saudi Arabia. Despite the historical rigidity associated with Wahhabism, since the establishment of the Saudi state, the Wahhabi scholarly classes have, in practice, as noted earlier in this chapter, demonstrated a high degree of pragmatism and flexibility (al-Fahad 2004; Mouline 2014). Especially since the late 1960s, when King Faisal curtailed the authority of the religious establishment, the scholars have had to exercise a certain degree of responsiveness to the changing demands of the state and society (al-Fahad 2004; Mouline 2014). When the pressure has come from the state or society (whether due to internal changes or to global pressures), the Saudi scholars have adjusted their established consensus in the light of the realities of the time, be it in the area of politics, economics, or social change (al-Fahad 2004; Mouline 2014). Even before the current on-going reforms, the Saudi religious establishment routinely offered pragmatic responses to help defend the political authority of the royal family. It allowed the government to form economic policies even if those policies might be violating the Islamic prohibition of *riba* (interest on financial loans), as in the case of Saudi policy on mortgages (Mouline 2014; Spannaus 2018a); and more recently, under King Abdullah, when the state pushed forward certain gender-based reforms, such as opening a co-educational university for the study of science and technology, the religious establishment, despite its apprehensions, had largely tagged along. Only one scholar from the Senior Council of 'Ulama' protested against the establishment of a co-educational university setting and was duly dismissed (Dawn 2009; Hoteit and Radsch 2009). But, more importantly, as noted above, even on matters of 'aqidah and the subject of takfir, the Wahhabi establishment has in practice shown much more flexibility since the formation of the Saudi state (al-Fahad 2004; Commins 2009; Mouline 2014; Spannaus 2018a).

Although neglected, other madhhabs, plus Sufi tariqahs, to which Wahhabi ideology is strictly opposed, were not actively persecuted (Sedgwick 1997); they have been allowed to operate as long as they do not pose any opposition to the state. The twenty-two-member Council of Senior Scholars has only one representative from the other three madhhabs (Hanafi, Maliki, Shafi'i) (Mouline 2014); yet, given the original Wahhabi emphasis on takfir, the mere survival of these groups in Saudi Arabia illustrated a certain level of tolerance and pragmatism. Further, compared with the hostility shown by the first and second Saudi states towards Sufism, whereby the holy shrines and sites in Mecca and Medina were destroyed

(Commins 2009), the modern Saudi state, from the start, allowed Sufi groups to operate in Mecca and Medina. Many transnational Sufi orders have managed to maintain a strong presence in these Muslim holy cities for a number of years. The Saudi royal family is aware of their existence but allows them to operate as long as they don't make themselves visible to the public or hold public gatherings (Sedgwick 1997).

The same sense of pragmatism is at play now, whereby it is deemed best to go along with the changes, rather than try to resist them. This is particularly so when the Saudi state has shown its willingness to use oppression if need be. As also noted in the volume's introductory chapter, many political Islamists from the sahwah movement, who do not abide by the political quietism supported by the Wahhabi establishment, have been imprisoned (al-Jazeera 2019). Salman al Awda, who, as noted earlier, is a prominent senior leader of the sahwah movement, has been in prison since 2017 (Bruton 2018), and in 2019 came close to facing public execution (Qiblawi 2019). Some of the other Islamist scholars imprisoned during this period are Safar bin Abdulrahman al-Hawali, Nasser al-Omar, Ali al-Omar and Awad al-Qarni (al-Jazeera 2019). They have been kept in harsh conditions, including solitary confinement, and many have reported deteriorating health (al-Jazeera 2019). Thus, fear of repression is indeed a key factor keeping the Wahhabi 'ulama' from openly resisting the ongoing reforms. However, in adopting such pragmatism, the Wahhabi establishment is also being loyal to its teaching about the need to accept the power of the ruler to avoid civil unrest. During my fieldwork, many Saudis from different backgrounds have acknowledged to me that the chaos that ensued after the Arab Spring in other Arab countries led even the critics of the Saudi regime to support this reasoning, as they could appreciate the value of political stability. Thus, my interviews suggest, the post-Arab Spring political developments in the Middle East in fact created a wider support base among Saudis for Wahhabi-style quietism towards political authority.

However, it is also important to note that not all of this pragmatism on the part of Wahhabi scholars is about their own strategic survival: even if marginalized, they retain their well-paid posts in the state bureaucracy. The fact that the Wahhabi scholars still have control over the teaching of the creed in mosques and study circles, provided that they refrain from promoting jihadi sentiments, has been an important factor in their acceptance of the social changes. This point was repeatedly emphasized to me during my engagement with the religious scholars and those who are closely aligned with them. Despite making assertive claims like 'I will return Saudi Arabia to Moderate Islam' (Chulov 2017), indicating a commitment to overhauling the religious establishment in Saudi Arabia (BBC 2017a; Chulov 2017), the Crown Prince has not attempted to establish an alternative religious authority to replace them – a topic explored in depth in Chapter 6. The Wahhabi establishment has thus accepted its loss of control over the regulation of public and social spaces, gender norms, and acceptable modes of entertainment, as long as the control over the core teachings concerning an individual's relationship with God is still left in their hands. Although the Crown Prince has publicly critiqued the rigidity of Wahhabi teachings and called for a return to moderate Islam (BBC

2017a; Chulov 2017), he has not directly intervened in the Wahhabi 'ulama's instruction of Islamic creed. Neither has he tried to replace them with scholars from other Islamic traditions (Hammond 2021).

We have enough historical evidence that, when under pressure, Islamic scholars can strategize to focus their energies on teaching what to them is the core of the faith; the rise of the socially conservative and inward-looking Deobandi movement in British India is a classic example (Metcalf 1982). Finding themselves in a challenging political and social context, Wahhabi 'ulama' are thus strategizing to focus their energy on preserving individual piety through direct religious teachings, whereas previously they could get it enforced by means of the apparatus of the state. Thus, what appears as pragmatism on the part of the Islamic scholars is often not motivated merely by the preservation of material comfort or status: there is often built in within it an ideological agenda of preserving what is viewed as being core to the faith, creed, and compulsory rituals, while letting go of concerns which are deemed important but secondary to core issues. Studies that attribute socio-economic decline or stagnation in Muslim societies to Islam or to religious scholars (Rubin 2017; Kuru 2019), thus often fail to recognize how pragmatism shown by 'ulama' is normally as much about preserving what to them is core to the faith as it is about preserving their material comfort or status.

Last but not least, the other reason why Wahhabi 'ulama' have not actively resisted the state's modernizing reforms is that they themselves are aware of their compromised following among the younger Saudi generation. The Wahhabi establishment has failed to produce a charismatic figure such as the late Abdulaziz ibn Baz (d. 1998), who is often identified as one of the last prominent scholars within the official Wahhabi establishment to command a high degree of respect among the public for his knowledge (Haykel et al. 2015a). Scholars appointed to such senior positions since his death have asserted their legitimacy as being descendants of Muhammad ibn Abd al-Wahhab, rather than by impressing the public with their own scholarly credentials (Haykel et al. 2015a). The current scholars can also clearly see the changed attitudes of young Saudis, especially in the way they have warmly welcomed the reforms. In my own interviews with young Saudi men and women, I found little respect for the official religious establishment, which was seen as being too close to the state and too motivated by the desire for material comfort. Further, many, especially in the Hejaz area, never fully accepted Wahhabi teachings: my respondents in the 2017 focus groups that I held with Saudi women working in senior positions in a multinational company in Riyadh expressed concerns about Wahhabi teachings in state curricula, as some of them belonged to long-established Hejazi families who never fully absorbed Wahhabi teachings (Yamani 2009); others mentioned following scholars from different traditions who were based overseas.

Thompson (2019) records similar ambivalence about the Wahhabi establishment among young Saudi men whom he interviewed across the country. His discussions with them show that Islam is very important to them (Thompson 2019: 33–4), but many have reservations about the official Wahhabi establishment: respondents noted concerns about scholars who have 'strong ties to the government', religion being used as a 'powerful political tool to control the masses', and for being told that there is only '"one way to do things religiously"' (Thompson 2019: 32). Some of these respondents were particularly critical of the hay'ah police, with some of them asserting that it is well-known that many members of this force were formerly petty criminals (Thompson 2019: 32). Further, in recent years the power of the Wahhabi establishment over the religious sphere has also been compromised by a trend among some of the scholars from within the Wahhabi Salafi tradition towards more liberal readings of the creed, which allows for more individual freedom in matters of religious belief, and more flexibility in adjusting to the needs of modern times. The work of some of these scholars will be considered in Chapter 6.

Conclusion

Not only in the current Saudi context, but also studies examining socio-economic stagnation in Muslim societies, often identify Islam as a powerful force in shaping socio-economic and political realities in Muslim societies, based on the assumption that religious elites enjoy almost unquestioned authority to legitimize political actors in the eyes of the public, which they then use to prevent the political elites from embarking on progressive reforms (Rubin 2017; Kuru 2019). Such a framework is based on two assumptions, which, as this chapter has tried to demonstrate, are in need of more nuanced analysis: first, that the Muslim public follows Islamic scholars blindly, thus enabling the religious scholars to promote self-serving ideas, even if they result in suboptimal societal outcomes, without losing public following; and second that the religious elites are ultimately pragmatic and self-serving, in that they prioritize the consolidation of their own authority over loyalty to the Islamic dictates. This chapter has shown that both these assumptions are simplistic. As we see in the Saudi case, the religious elites did dictate much of the social conservatism that restricted women's liberties, gender mixing, and basic forms of entertainment that had the potential to enrich human life, but they were able to do so only because the political and social contexts of twentieth-century Arabia were conducive to those restrictions. What was sustaining the power of such conservatism was not Islam or the Wahhabi 'ulama', but the specific mix of socio-political, economic, and even cultural institutions that was being invoked in the name of Islam.

As we will see in the next chapter, with the change in social, economic, and political contexts, due to increased education, travel, and global connectivity, the 'ulama' are no longer able to enforce the traditional socially conservative framework. Similarly, political elites embraced religious ideas championed by religious authorities, motivated in part by religious commitment but only as long as these ideas posed no threat to their political survival. Once those ideas jeopardize their position, these same religious concepts are publicly disavowed. As is often the case, this is being done by asserting that they were extreme interpretations propagated by religious elites and not fundamental to the tradition itself. It is highly unlikely that the religious elites in the Muslim world ever actually exercised the unchecked authority over the interpretation of religious texts that some political scientists, who are not specialists in Islamic Studies but are writing influential studies on causes of wider socio-economic shifts in Muslim societies over many centuries, end up attributing to them (Rubin 2017; Kuru 2019). Similarly, any political legitimizing power enjoyed by religious elites in Muslim societies has been strongly linked to their personal calibre and demonstrated moral behaviour, and not exclusively to their religious office (Nizami 1983; Robinson 2001; Hallaq 2009; Bano 2018a). The authority of the religious scholars in Muslim countries is not a given condition but is always open to question.

The closeness of Wahhabi 'ulama' to the state, and the failure of the Wahhabi official establishment to produce prominent scholars who can command authority and relate Islamic dictates to present reality – a requirement which was key to establishing authority of a scholar in early Islamic history (Bano 2018c) – have contributed to the erosion of popular respect in recent years. It is because of this that religious scholars in Muslim countries cannot act too opportunistically, as they know that they are being constantly judged by the public in terms of their knowledge, but also in terms of their levels of demonstrated piety. Even when being pragmatic in engaging with political elites to preserve their own status and material comfort, they have to show some commitment to the core tenets of the faith, because their ability to influence the masses relies on the latter (Nizami 1983; Bano 2018a). This, in turn, is what makes them useful as a legitimizing force in the eyes of the political authority.

Thus, revisiting the thesis advanced by Rubin (2017), which is based on comparing divergent socio-economic and political developments in Europe and the Middle East over many centuries, we see that while his theoretical conceptualization of the bargaining power of the religious and political authority is relevant and useful, and religion can be an important force in the legitimizing of political authority, the mechanisms of this legitimization, and the ways in which religious elites in Muslim societies build their authority, are much more complex than is assumed by the scholars who take religious authority in Christianity as their starting point. Recognizing the limits of religious authority in Muslim societies helps us appreciate the complexity behind claims that Muslim scholars hinder societal progress.

Chapter 4

INTERGENERATIONAL SHIFTS

Back in Saudi Arabia for a month in early 2019 for fieldwork, I was puzzled by the visibly growing popularity of the Crown Prince. Women were known to be carrying keychains stating, 'We love the Crown Prince,' and were running campaigns in his favour on social media. He seemed extremely popular among young Saudi men, too. His popularity was acknowledged even by members of the royal family whom I met. My questions about potential threats to the Crown Prince from the rival factions within the royal family normally generated a calculated response to the effect that any rival faction has to be careful, as his popularity among young Saudis is very obvious. In the words of one respondent, 'the excitement among the crowd, when he turns up is palpable'. Only a year and a half on from the announcement of initial reforms in September 2017, the steady growth in his popularity that I was witnessing in each successive visit puzzled me. I felt perplexed not just by the complete lack of visible resistance by the Wahhabi elites, and their possible public sympathizers, despite the steadily growing scope and speed of reforms, but also because this visit had come soon after the murder of Jamal Khashoggi, in October 2018 (BBC 2021), which had severely tarnished the image of the Crown Prince on the global stage (Kirchgaessner 2021). I had expected him to be exposed to a similar level of critical scrutiny at home, especially given the understanding that the popularity of his reforms among the young was a sign of the growing appeal of liberal socio-political norms.

Puzzled by this, I consulted a senior researcher at the King Faisal Centre for Research and Islamic Studies (KFCRIS), the main institution hosting Western scholars writing on Saudi Arabia prior to recent changes. His answer was straightforward: I need to recognize the major intergenerational divide in attitudes. Himself in his late-forties, he was of the view that, while the Khashoggi murder was a concern for people in his age group and above, for the under-thirties such concerns were marginal, compared with the appeal of the vision of the new Saudi Arabia and a new Saudi identity that the Crown Prince was offering to the younger generation – an identity that is much more historically rooted and dynamic rather than being narrowly tied to religious identity. During the same conversation, he noted how, even regarding gender roles, the attitudes of the younger generation differ from those of the older generations, and that this is the case not just in the urban centres but even in smaller cities. The idea that there is a clear generational divide in Saudi Arabia and that the attitudes of the young towards religion and society are different from those of their parents and grandparents is widely discussed in the media (DW 2018) as well as by state agencies (Obeid 2022; al-Ghalayini 2023). Thompson (2019), who, as noted earlier, helps capture voices of young Saudi men from across the country, on issues of on-going reforms, Saudi identity and aspirations for the future, similarly notes how, while discussing any of these issues, 'A common refrain is "older generations do not understand us . . . " (Thompson 2019: 40).

The fact that young Saudis are developing fairly liberal sensibilities concerning social liberties, associated with the globalization of Western values, had become clear to me even on my initial visits starting in 2014, when I conducted interviews with women in private universities in Riyadh and Jeddah. The sensibilities of these young Saudi girls, their future career aspirations and their confidence levels were no different from those of the girls in urban centres whom I met in cosmopolitan cities of other Muslim societies, such as Cairo or Islamabad. In those initial visits, my fieldwork was largely confined to the well-off segments of society in these two major cities. Conscious that these findings are not generalizable, given the socio-economic and cultural variations across the country, during this visit I started to expand the scope of my fieldwork to other cities. This was particularly evident as other scholars had been recording similar shifts, to some extent, across the country.

Shifts in this direction were recorded as early as the turn of the current century in Yamani's (2000) *Changed Identities: The Challenge of the New Generation in Saudi Arabia*. She noted how television, cable networks and internet access were influencing the attitudes of younger generations, exposing them to socially liberal values associated with Western culture. Similarly, based on the focus group discussions he held with Saudi youth, Thompson (2019) notes that young generations are affected by Western cultural influences through social media, cinema and television programmes, with shows like *Game of Thrones* being widely popular among the youth. His respondents acknowledge that younger generations are more comfortable with Western social norms, even though they know their parents do not accept these norms. Further, they attributed this difference to the limited exposure their parents had to Western entertainment compared to themselves (Thompson 2019). Other studies have recorded similar influences of social media within Saudi Arabia and the wider Arab world (Chaudhary 2016; Gunter 2016).

I initially chose to do additional fieldwork in Hail and Qassim, which are north of Riyadh, and Khobar and Dammam in the Eastern Province. Such a selection enabled exposure to two directly opposed segments of the Saudi population spectrum: As highlighted by my respondents, the first two regions are perceived as being more traditionally conservative, while the Eastern Province, which is rich in oil reserves and is home to both Aramco and Saudi Arabia's Shia population, is seen to have more liberal and cosmopolitan tendencies. Dammam is also the gateway to Bahrain, which is connected to Saudi Arabia by a causeway bridge barely 25 km long, and was a popular weekend destination for Saudis seeking a relaxing getaway, enjoying Western-style entertainment in malls, bars or cinemas in the pre-reform Saudi Arabia. Thus, while the core fieldwork in Riyadh and Jeddah helped to identify the dominant social trends, extending the fieldwork to Hail and Qassim helped me to cover the more orthodox and traditional belts, while Dammam and Khobar gave me a sense of the most liberal social settings and spaces in Saudi Arabia prior to the on-going social reforms.

My arrival in Buraydah, the capital city of Qassim province, by a morning train from Riyadh was from the very beginning a highly illuminating experience. My local assistant, a young Saudi woman, came to meet me at the train station in her small but flashy red car with a female friend – both visibly excited about being free to drive around, and proud to explain to me that my research assistant was among the first women in town to exercise this newly found freedom: women were allowed to drive starting in June 2018 (al-Jazeera 2017; Hubbard 2017). In the process of establishing and running her own travel agency, she 'loved' the Crown Prince for the freedom that he has offered her and other women. During my time in Qassim, she and her friend remained my main facilitators. They exposed me to many spaces where women were visible: in the traditional souq running food stalls, as leaders of an NGO which was promoting products of female craftsmen, and also those engaged in regular home routines. A divorcée, she was of the view that the restrictions being eased were in need of removal as they represented the psyche of the Wahhabi establishment, and not that of Islam in general.

Similarly, in Hail, staying with the family who had facilitated my visit, I was exposed to three generations of Saudi women. The differences in personalities as well as concepts of what makes for a happy life varied across the three generations. Contrary to assumptions that young women in Riyadh and Jeddah are exceptions, in terms of absorbing global tastes and liberal attitudes, the teenage granddaughter in this family had very different sensibilities and aspirations for her future life from those of her mother, aunts and grandmother. While clearly not opposed to getting married and having a family, which was the primary concern of the women in the other two generations, she was keen also to pursue further education and have a career. More importantly, she felt that both the male and female members of the family were supportive of her desire to strike such a balance. She also had a very good command of English, which prompted me to ask her where she had acquired knowledge of the language. Her answer was straightforward: 'my local state school'. We exchanged phone numbers and agreed to stay in touch on WhatsApp. Two years later, I received a WhatsApp message from her, updating me that she was now in Washington, DC, pursuing a master's degree at Johns Hopkins University.

The quality of education provided in state schools in Saudi Arabia has often been found lacking (al-Otaibi 2020; OBG 2022). Not just on international assessment tests (OECD 2023), which, as their critics highlight, have a Western-centric bias (Young 2013), but even by domestic assessments (al-Otaibi 2020), Saudi students are recorded as performing poorly. Yet the young women whom I had met in these two conservative cities were full of optimistic agency and quite capable of taking on professional opportunities or pursuing a higher degree in an American university – and they were products of Saudi state schools. Further, I could not detect a major difference between their sensibilities and those of the female students whom I had interviewed in the elite universities in Riyadh and Jeddah. Just as the realities of women in elite neighbourhoods of Riyadh and Jeddah differ from those residing in less affluent ones, so is there a variation in the life experiences and aspirations of the women in these other cities, based particularly on their socio-economic class. What, however, was shared across all cities was the clear presence of a constituency of young women who wholeheartedly welcomed the on-going reforms. The girls in elite universities in Riyadh and Jeddah might have more refined English accents or more modern styles of dress, as was also the case for the university students whom I engaged with in Khobar and Dammam, but what would be referred to as a modern feminist sensibility of wanting education, having a career and feeling confident to pursue one's choices was equally demonstrated by the girls whom I met in Qassim and Hail.

Since then, expanding my fieldwork to other important regions of Saudi Arabia, including Tabuk, Jizan, al-Ahsa, al-Ula and Abha, I have consistently come to the same conclusions. Further, in my fieldwork across all these cities I found that while wanting to exercise increased liberties to make decisions about their lives, these women did not sound frustrated by, or opposed to, the male segment of their society, unlike the expectations of the Western feminist framework. Just as I noted above for the granddaughter in Hail, most of the young girls I have interviewed across Saudi Arabia have always acknowledged that men in their family are very supportive of their educational activities or their desire to pursue a career. This finding is also supported by other studies: Thompson (2019) records support for female employment among young Saudi men, and a recent paper aimed at studying the attitudes of Saudi men to female employment shows how most of the men surveyed expressed the view that their wives should be able to work (Bursztyn et al. 2020). I have also often heard young girls note how their mothers are not keen for them to drive and be away from home alone – while in contrast, the fathers want them to learn to drive and be mobile. Thus, while there was clear evidence of a shift in attitudes among young Saudi women towards wanting more freedom and economic empowerment, I did not find among them the kind of strong anti-patriarchy discourse that has historically underscored Western feminist thought (Rendall 1985).

More importantly, as I have expanded my fieldwork across multiple cities in Saudi Arabia, I have come to identify the significance of the same three factors that I had initially found to be important in explaining the causes of these intergenerational shifts in attitudes towards women's economic empowerment and changing gender norms. Firstly, the steadily expanding access to education for both men and women since the 1960s but most noticeably since the early 2000s, when opportunities for pursuing higher education at home but also abroad on generously funded state scholarships were made available both to Saudi women and men; secondly, the material affluence that enables international travel for the upper income classes but also enables a major segment of the ordinary Saudi public to undertake regional travel; and thirdly, access to high-quality internet connections, exposing young Saudis to global discourses and tastes, combined with the ability to afford smartphones, resulting in a generation of young Saudis who are highly connected via social media (al-Saggaf 2004; Chaudhary 2016; Diwan 2018). Overall, one can see that the policy of social opening and the state push back against Wahhabi social conservatism have paid off because the time is right: Saudi society is now ready for it. The evidence presented in this chapter thus demonstrates that institutions do not shift overnight: behind the story of sudden change apparently engineered by a strategic reformer lies the power of incremental change.

4.1 Saudi Arabia: Geography and demography

Before the on-going reforms, Saudi Arabia was largely presented in the popular media in the West (but also in much of the Muslim world) as a religiously orthodox and static society, resistant to change and the influences of modernity. Yet, when we look at the facts, underlying the apparent stagnation was a story of rapid modernization, especially after the 1960s, when oil revenues started to come. What is often forgotten is that when Saudi Arabia became a nation-state in 1932, the majority of its population was still living in the desert, either as Bedouins (nomads) or as hadar (sedentary population). While each group had distinct characteristics, both shared a lack of exposure to modern educational institutions, namely schools and universities, and the absence of basic urban development, be it roads, modern housing, modern sanitation or health facilities. Writing in the late 1950s, Wilfred Thesiger, a British traveller who spent a number of years traversing the Arabian desert on camels and on foot with the Bedouins, captured the scarcity of material comfort marking their lives, while simultaneously recording a culture of deep comradeship, honour and generosity – values that these Bedouins strongly credited to Islam (Thesiger 2007). Being there at a time when the oil wealth was just starting to trickle in, he lamented the loss of this traditional culture. Once the process of modernization started, roads got built, replacing reliance on camels with four-wheel drives, and gradually the state applied pressure on the Bedouin population to make them adopt a settled life in the name of modernity. This, its critics argue, was coupled with the desire of the central state to assert its authority, in the process eroding much of the sense of comradeship that marked the tribal culture (Thesiger 2007; al-Fahad 2015a). While not disregarding the cost of the erosion of the traditional culture, it is important to recognize that, in terms of material comfort and modern living, Saudi society has been undergoing rapid transformation since the 1960s.

It is also important to recognize that this development has affected all regions of the country, and not just the major cities. Thus, there are indeed major socio-economic variations across the country, with the southern region historically characterized by the lowest development indicators (Hertog 2010; 2015), but even there, the basic living conditions have been transformed to meet the requirements of urban living, as opposed to the traditional structures that marked life in the 1960s. Thus, it is only over a period of almost sixty years that most regions of the country have been transformed from observing a pre-modern social order, with people living in small groups in tents or mud-built structures in oasis settlements, to a modern state where dispersed groups come to recognize a central state authority and enjoy some of the facilities associated with urban life. In just over three generations, Saudi citizens have seen a dramatic shift in lifestyles, material comfort and access to future life opportunities. It is therefore not surprising that among Thompson's (2019) respondents, many allude to the advice that they routinely receive from their grandparents: to work hard to preserve what they have and avert the hardships that were common in their generation. If declining oil wealth necessitates a strategy of diversification, then, in the view of the younger generation, they need to co-operate to avert a decline in living standards.

With steady developments in the socio-economic domain marking three generations, it is not surprising if we see Saudi society record a corresponding shift in social attitudes in response to these changes. What, however, is more critical is to recognize the distinct point in time when any additional modernization efforts by the state began to lead to attitudinal changes that have culminated in the current shifts in social norms. It was between the 1960s and the mid-1990s that the Saudi state made a major investment in infrastructural development and the provision of basic education and health facilities (al-Rasheed 2002; Vasil'ev 2000; Peterson 2018). But it was the additional investments made between the mid-1990s and 2015 that led to attitudinal changes in favour of the on-going reforms. This period witnessed the societal developments that led to a tipping point in 2017 with the initiation of the on-going social reforms by the Crown Prince. The initial investments intended to modernize Saudi society did not put much pressure on the conservative social norms, as they were aimed at establishing very basic levels of modern living, given the low starting point: They consisted largely of making Bedouins who were used to living in camps in the open desert with bare essentials settle into city housing schemes, and putting in place basic primary and secondary school infrastructure, and gradually expanding its access to girls – a development for which King Faisal had to take a strong position against the Wahhabi scholars. Nor did the move towards the establishment of universities from the late 1950s onwards immediately lead to calls for social liberalization.

By the late 1990s, a critical juncture was reached in Saudi Arabia. At this point, the majority of Saudi children were enrolled in schools, half of the eligible population was attending university and the country had a highly developed road and air travel infrastructure (Yamani 2000; Peterson 2018). Additionally, access to television channels had become widespread (Yamani 2000; Thompson 2019). This set the stage for the next wave of investments to significantly impact people's social attitudes. It is the twenty-year period from 1995 to 2015 that is significant in this respect, especially the period between 2005 and 2015 under King Abdullah, who began investing in areas that enabled the changes in social attitudes witnessed after 2017. The state's focus moved from the provision of basic education to providing good-quality higher education, marked by the establishment of the King Abdullah University of Science and Technology (KAUST) (Jones 2015) and the introduction of a generous international scholarship scheme by King Abdullah (Alotaibi 2022;

Western University 2023). It was also in this period that internet connections became available across the country, and so did mobile phone technology (Yamani 2000; Thompson 2019). Travel also became more affordable. In the case of the Saudi elites, the taste for travel has resulted in a strong tradition of holidaymaking in European capitals, but it is also visible in the popularity among ordinary Saudis of regional travel within the neighbouring Gulf Co-operation Council (GCC) countries. As my respondents often noted, these countries are accessible by road and offer Western-style entertainment, such as cinemas, bars and entertainment zones offering live music and gender-mixed spaces.

The apparently dramatic shift in social norms is thus a result of incremental shifts in attitudes in response to the steadily changing socio-economic context, particularly over the past two decades. But, equally importantly, there was a clear point in time when the basic groundwork in terms of establishing a modern state with a central authority structure and a well-developed urban infrastructure can be seen to have been completed, and from that point onwards further investments, 'the second-tier investments', had a rapid impact in terms of changing attitudes in favour of liberal social norms. But the Saudi case also helps us to identify the importance of unexpected factors in triggering norm change. The fact that this period also coincided with the events of September 11, 2001, after which Saudi Arabia and Wahhabism became increasingly implicated in cases of global jihad (Maher 2016), meant that the young Saudis, who were now more globally connected than the previous generations, were also experiencing much negativity and hostility in the global context. This negativity has gradually forced not just the royal family to question its association with the Wahhabi establishment, as recorded in the previous chapter, but, as I have found in my interviews with young Saudis and as was visible in the creative content that was being shared on social media during my visits in 2015 and 2016 (discussed below), it also made the younger generation want to counter this negative image of themselves and Saudi society. It is this wider global context that has made the promise of cultivating a new progressive Saudi identity so appealing to young Saudis.

4.2 Education

Access to primary and secondary education spread across the country from the 1960s to the 1980s (Yamani 2000; Peterson 2018), and university education became more accessible for women from the 1980s onwards, but it was in the mid-1990s, under the reign of King Abdullah, that investment in providing good-quality higher education to improve the country's human capital became more pronounced (Jones 2015). He launched the KAUST university as a flagship initiative to promote technological and societal advancement (Jones 2015). This university was not only an expression of commitment to educational and economic development but also signalled the need to challenge existing gender norms, as it was the first co-educational university campus in Saudi Arabia. The second major move in the education sector during this period was the introduction of

King Abdullah's Scholarship Programme (KASP) in the early 2000s (Alotaibi 2022; Western University 2023). By 2015, over 100,000 young Saudis were estimated to have benefited from the programme, most of them receiving full scholarships (Thompson 2019). This access to university-level education, especially in private universities in Riyadh and Jeddah, was key to changing women's aspirations about their own future, but also the expectations of the male members of their families.

During my visits to leading Saudi universities in 2015 and 2016, I found young Saudi women no less cosmopolitan than the girls I have interviewed across a range of Muslim countries and among Muslim-diaspora communities in the West. In fact, the benefits of Saudi economic affluence have ensured that women are in fact more globally connected, travel overseas and have highly Westernized tastes in terms of their sense of style, modes of entertainment and increasingly even their professional aspirations. On the campus, with the ʿabayahs off, the student culture was no different from what one would find in institutions such as the American University of Cairo or Lahore University of Management Sciences (LUMS) – both offering co-education and known for promoting very Western and socially progressive values. These girls were pursuing degrees in a wide range of areas, such as law, economics and sociology. Girls spoke fluent English, thanks to the mushrooming of private English-language tuition centres where they could take lessons from native English speakers in addition to pursuing their university education. The girls were confident, vibrant and extremely well conversant with the latest apps and social media technology such as Facebook, Twitter and WhatsApp. Many mentioned travelling overseas during the summer. Most were single, but also among the students were many who were married and a few who were divorced.

Already at that time, there was a general recognition among the faculty, as well as among the students, that the attitudes and aspirations of Saudi girls were changing. One of the expatriate teachers who had been working within the university for over ten years made the following observation:

> The culture is changing rapidly. This is visible in small as well as big matters. When they enter the classroom today, students say *hello* or *good morning* instead of *salam*. They are excellent with the use of modern apps. They in fact taught me how to use Twitter, which I now find very useful to follow individuals or institutions whose reports and publications are relevant to my field. They also are very mobile; it is very normal for them to go out and socialize in groups at cafés. In recent years, much is changing. I don't personally see how life in Riyadh is that different from Dubai. I think these girls are enjoying being part of the global culture as much as girls in other Muslim societies do.

Girls themselves acknowledged that it is now normal to take pride in speaking good English and 'broken Arabic'. Most shared inspiring plans for higher studies; some also planned to study overseas. All appreciated opportunities for overseas travel: Most importantly, not all were keen to rush to the West, as often imagined; some instead shared details of family trips to Indonesia, Malaysia and Japan, and with great enthusiasm, some expressed a desire to explore alternative cultures. But some also expressed concern that the Western influences were going too far, threatening to erode the moral values of society:

> I am different; I still like to socialize with the girls from my extended family network. I have a big family network, so when we get together, we have 10–12 girls in the family, and we were taught this is the best form of socialization. But now many girls instead want to socialize outside. Girls in the university routinely make group plans to go out to restaurants. When I will have a child, I will want to self-teach that child, because it is today so difficult to control the different influences that are affecting the young children in schools.

This concern that the attitudes of young educated girls are changing, and perhaps too fast, was also reflected in a video on the Human Rights Commission website which showed a mother on her mobile phone, stepping out of a car and extending her arms to welcome the child, while the child instead runs into the arms of the maid accompanying her (Bano 2018e). The change in gender norms was also visible in increasing divorce rates, which by default indicate a decline in the practice of polygamy – the trend has continued to grow (Fatima 2022; Nasrallah 2022). As divorces become more prevalent, there is less pressure on a woman to stay with a man against her will in case he decides to take on a second wife. Discussions with girls and teachers also revealed how, in many cases, their divorced peers had in fact often themselves initiated the divorce – and at times for purely subjective reasons. As one teacher noted:

> One of my students took a divorce because she found her husband to be too lazy. She told me that her husband says what is the problem when I am keeping you financially comfortable? But she argued that she wants a husband who does something productive, she does not want to be with someone sleeping late into the morning, having no purpose.

These cases also showed that many of these young women had support from their parents and brothers in initiating divorce; instances of many married girls pursuing higher education, on the other hand, showed how they had the support of their husbands.

Similarly, even in this period, which was pre-2017 reforms, regularly expressed concerns about the highly restricted mobility of Saudi women were not in fact upheld for women from this stratum of society: taxis were very easy to order and were widely used by these girls, who were very comfortable ordering a cab using Uber (or another app, named Careem). Whenever I finished a meeting, someone would offer to get me a taxi, using one of the two mobile apps. The state had also clearly intensified its efforts to signal to outside observers its commitment to respecting the United Nations human rights mandate: the Human Rights Commission had only recently been established (GoSA 2023c). This Commission had a separate (and quite extensive) unit dedicated to protecting the rights of women and children, which was led by Saudi women. This unit worked in close association with the main Commission but exercised a high level of independence. During my interviews in the Commission, apart from being briefed about the various educational, economic and legal provisions made available to Saudi women, I was also enabled to meet one of the young Saudi interns who had been based in the United States for the last ten years, pursuing her education. Very progressive and liberal (in her dress as well as her ideas), she was advocated by Commission members as a model for Saudi girls.

All of this was happening in 2015 and 2016, before the announcement of the social reforms initiated mainly from September 2017 onwards. This indicates that the Crown Prince's decision to introduce social reforms was based on growing evidence of changed subjectivities among young Saudis in favour of liberal gender norms and social mixing, and it was a response to bottom-up demands rather than being entirely a product of a top-down reform agenda. As we will see in the final section of this chapter, this change of attitudes in favour of more liberal social values was also discernible in the content of creative material being circulated on social media by young Saudis in the period preceding the announcement of Vision 2030 and the related social reforms. Further, despite some voicing concerns that the changes might be going too far, as was also noted above, there were no real signs of any desire to rebel against religion or tradition among the girls with whom I interacted. Instead, there was a confidence about Saudi society's ability to move forward at a moderate pace, retaining much of the national tradition, yet adapting to modern realities and cashing in on new opportunities.

The same expatriate teacher who noted the shift in morning greetings from salam to good morning also recorded the girls' response to any mention of Mecca or Medina: 'If I ever tell them that I am going to Mecca or Medina or need to take any of my visitors to these cities, they go out of the way to help me. You can see how their heart melts at the reference to these cities. Few care when I announce my travel to some other city.' The changes were thus in moderation prior to state initiation of reforms formally. These young Saudi girls were not losing respect for their religious tradition; they were opting for a little bit of flexibility in its interpretation.

4.3. Travel and exposure

My fieldwork suggests that, along with education, travel has played a key role in raising awareness about global cultural norms and in changing attitudes in their favour. As recognized by many of the university students whom I interviewed, the opportunity for travel had played an important role in triggering on-going changes in social norms. This travel has been for the purposes of entertainment and relaxation, but from the 1980s onwards, much of it has been linked to securing education overseas (Commins 2009; Yamani 2000). Although the scholarship programme started by King Abdullah has had an impact on changing of social attitudes due to its sponsoring of young Saudi men and women from across the country to pursue education in leading universities in the West, during the 1970s and 1980s, the Saudi state had already routinely sent young Saudi bureaucrats to seek higher education or professional training overseas (Commins 2009). The time spent at Western educational institutions influenced tastes in favour of more liberal social norms. At this stage, it was mainly the men who received this exposure, yet it also had an influence on wider gender norms: on return home, these men wanted to have wives who could share their tastes and sensibilities (Commins 2009). Thus, a significant proportion of these Saudi men married women from other Arab countries, who favoured more liberal social norms (Commins 2009).

At the same time, the material affluence enjoyed by Saudi society since the discovery of oil, even though not equally spread across the country, has enabled a large segment of the Saudi public to undertake travel for pleasure. Thus, in my own interviews, while the women from elite families attending elite universities mentioned the importance of international travel to Europe or other popular holiday destinations such as Malaysia to gain exposure, women from more ordinary backgrounds, such as my informants in Qassim and Hail, mentioned the importance of travel to GCC countries. The government data shows that close to 50 per cent of Saudi outbound travel is to those countries (Arab News 2022a). Much of this travel was to pursue entertainment options not available in Saudi Arabia prior to the on-going reforms. As reflected in my interviews, the UAE was the preferred destination in this respect, but even Bahrain, Oman, Kuwait and Qatar offered more entertainment options and more relaxed regulations on gender mixing than did Saudi Arabia. My respondents routinely mentioned how a holiday weekend away in any of these countries was a popular phenomenon. Exposure to all these modern forms of entertainments – cinemas, concert halls and clubs, close to home in the neighbouring GCC countries – has ensured that none of these modes of entertainment is entirely new for the Saudi population. As many of my respondents noted, this frequent exposure to different cultural contexts and entertainment options, whether within Western countries or in other Muslim contexts, has played an important role in leading the Saudi population to accept the changes with relative ease. As one respondent explained, 'We [Saudis] had been seeing these things abroad, so there is no surprise and no awkwardness about it'. Similarly, one reason many Saudi women have easily taken to driving was argued to be their prior experience of driving in other countries during their travels or periods of education abroad.

It was a recognition of the expenditure of large volumes of Saudi money on frequent overseas travel, especially to neighbouring GCC countries, that made the promotion of tourism and social entertainment options at home an important goal of the diversification strategy under Vision 2030 (GoSA 2016). While the heavy investment in promoting a vibrant tourism sector is clearly aimed at attracting international tourists both from the West (to destinations such as al-Ula and the upcoming beach resorts) and from the Muslim-majority countries (by ensuring easy access to visas to visit Mecca and Medina), Vision 2030 is very explicit about the related ambition of retaining Saudi money in Saudi Arabia by giving Saudis ample entertainment options at home, thus reducing the attraction of crossing over into the GCC countries for entertainment-fuelled weekends (GoSA 2016). The Crown Prince himself has strongly emphasized the importance of retaining Saudi money at home, instead of it being spent on entertainment pursuits overseas. The opportunity for travel, both for education and for entertainment, has thus played a key role in giving exposure to liberal social norms. Even more importantly, because it provides first-hand experience, as opposed to just viewing something on social media, the ability to travel has helped to internalize liberal social norms as normal. This is key to understanding why men and women, who until recently were only allowed highly restricted social contact, seem very comfortable dealing with mixed-gender settings, which have suddenly become the norm. Given that a core argument in defence of co-education is that it enables both sexes to develop a comfort level by early exposure to each other in institutionalized settings, the lack of expected awkwardness on suddenly being allowed to enter gender-mixed spaces results from the fact that most Saudis had routine exposure to such spaces in neighbouring Muslim GCC states, if not beyond.

4.4. Media, connectivity and attitude formation

The third factor that has played a major role in triggering a change in attitudes towards more liberal social norms among the young is the access to high-speed internet services, starting in the late 1990s and followed by access to good-quality wireless connectivity and smartphones (Yamani 2000; Thompson 2019). Television was introduced in Saudi Arabia in the mid-1960s under King Faisal's reign, and satellite channels were accessible from the early 1990s. Starting from the late 2000s, social media apps including Twitter (now X), Instagram, Snapchat and WhatsApp have also become extremely popular.[1] Ask a young Saudi man or woman in any city in Saudi Arabia where they learned about a particular event, or ask them for advice on finding out what is on in the city, and it would be highly unusual not to be enthusiastically advised to search for related hashtags on Twitter/X, Instagram or Facebook. The widespread access to the internet, wireless and smartphones in Saudi Arabia since the turn of this century, especially under King Abdullah, has played a critical role in changing attitudes in favour of liberal social norms in two distinct but connected ways.

At a basic level, access to the internet and social media apps made the young generation of Saudis even more easily connected to the global culture, but as per the accounts of my respondents, equally to trends in surrounding Muslim countries, than travel alone could provide. Internet connectivity extended such access even to those who could not undertake international travel, and it provided this access on a continuous on-going basis. More specifically, the extensive use of social media apps in Saudi Arabia mobilized a high level of social connectivity among young people across social classes and across the different regions of the country, resulting in the emergence of shared online spaces where the young began to express their changing tastes, mostly through creative content produced on YouTube, which I analyse below. While the internet exposed them to global culture, the social apps connected young people and enabled them to share their desire for change. The links to the YouTube videos presenting creative content were widely shared through social media apps, which in turn helped to build consensus around these ideas. Further, the popularity of these online platforms could be monitored by the number of hits that they receive, as well as the nature of comments that followers leave on these platforms. Tapping into these online sources enabled the Crown Prince, and his team of advisors, to be confident about the likely positive reception of his reforms among a major segment of the younger generation.

In my 2017 interviews in the newly established General Entertainment Authority, which since then has become a major implementation arm for the on-going social liberalization agenda (GoSA 2023b), the staff acknowledged closely monitoring the public responses on social media apps to their announcements of forthcoming social events; they also noted the importance of monitoring the online chatter post-event. This, they explained, helped them to test the limits to which they can push the existing boundaries when planning the next event. At the time of the interview, they were planning the first concert to be held since the announcement of the reforms, and the limits of what would be acceptable to the public were being tested by a proposal to host gender-segregated concerts in the first instance. The staff at the Entertainment Authority acknowledged closely monitoring public reactions to these proposals on social media before finalizing their plans. At that time, they reported receiving many positive responses but also witnessing certain pockets of resistance, which emphasized the need to move cautiously. Yet, only a few months later, they were able to start hosting concerts with the first concert by a Lebanese female singer, Hiba Tawaji, taking place in December 2017 (Hussain and Smith 2017; O'Malley 2017). This suggests that the number of those expressing enthusiasm surpassed those recording discontent with on-going reforms.

Just as some travelled around the world and others gained their exposure to more liberal social norms mainly through travel in the GCC area, the nature of exposure through the internet and social media also varied according to people's social and economic profiles. Elites in Riyadh and Jeddah mainly sought Western media content; but among many women whom I interviewed in other cities, social apps were a popular way of seeking insights into the daily lives of women in the neighbouring GCC countries. Many of my respondents reported comparing their lives with those of women in the surrounding Gulf countries by means of social media. In my interviews with women in Hail or Qassim, I often heard them referring to watching videos of female influencers based in another GCC country. The liberties that they saw these fellow Arab Muslim women enjoy resonated more with them than the feminist ideals and calls for complete sexual freedom or recognition of fluid sexual identities that they encountered in Western media content. These apps have thus facilitated access not only to Western culture but also to alternative lifestyles adopted in neighbouring Muslim countries, which, while offering a comparatively more liberal social sphere than was enjoyed by Saudi women before the on-going reforms, still operate within an Islamic framework. The liberties exercised in those contexts were thus more critical in changing the tastes of young Saudis, given that those societies were also Muslim but did not live under the rigid social conditions prescribed by Wahhabi scholars.

During my visits in 2015 and 2016, already many of the young girls I was meeting in universities in Jeddah and Riyadh had started to introduce me to a wide range of creative content being produced by young Saudis, which either challenged traditional social norms or parodied the negative image associated with Saudi Arabia's extreme religious conservatism. The YouTube videos produced were circulated widely by means of social media apps. Common themes covered in these videos related to restrictions on women's mobility, romantic relationships, globalization, religion and wider social restrictions. A demand for the adoption and toleration of global and more liberal tastes marked all this creative content. Yet, as noted in the case of the young girls interviewed in elite universities in Riyadh and Jeddah, while arguing for and embracing change, the producers of this creative content did not seem to be proposing a major rebellion against Saudi culture or Islam. Nor did they seem in need of venting the excessive frustration or discontent that many Western observers attributed to them (Manning 1998; Lippman 2012; Friedman 2015; Whitkaer 2015). Instead, while questioning religious or cultural conservatism, they showed a high degree of confidence in the ability of Saudi young people to engineer change and move to a more moderate path.

There was a clearly articulated desire expressed in these videos to preserve a Saudi cultural and religious identity while relaxing the prevailing rigidity and adapting to modern tastes. In the following section, I share some of the material that was being circulated widely during my 2015 and 2016 fieldwork, to which I was introduced by my female respondents in Riyadh. Most of the platforms listed below have, since the initiation of the social reforms, been adopted by commercial outlets such as Netflix and are now actively receiving support from the Ministry of Culture – a fact which again supports the contention that the Crown Prince's social liberalization agenda has been popular because it is attempting to build on what young Saudis were asking for; it is not an agenda entirely enforced from the top. When sharing links to this content, my respondents also used to highlight how, in their experience, this material, because of being widely shared on social media, is helping to create a growing sense of connectivity among young Saudis and a consensus around the need to allow for a more liberal social sphere. The creative content circulating at the time could be divided into three distinct forms: films, music and visual arts.

YouTube videos and music

One of the media through which a consensus in favour of a more liberal social sphere became increasingly vocalized by young Saudis between 2010 and 2016 is YouTube. A number of private YouTube channels, some operated by companies and others by individual artists, were launched during this period and developed large followings for their trendy videos, which addressed conservative social norms in critical but highly humorous ways. Most noticeable of these channels was Telfaz11 (Telfaz11 2023a). Set up in 2011, to date it hosts and helps to produce creative content generated by young Saudis. Affiliated with C3 Film Company, the channel identifies itself as being 'an initiative to stimulate creative culture, which is based on extending a helping hand to every creative, persistent, ambitious and passionate individual who deserves praise and encouragement for his dedication to serving his goal' (Telfaz11 2023a). The people behind the channel, however, also had a stated goal of serving Saudi society, as mentioned in its mission statement: 'We seek to serve our society by searching for and appreciating the creative abilities of its members and hopeful youth. Although the site is simple in its role as an electronic viewing platform, the site will be dedicated to celebrating human talent based on imagination, ambition and creativity' (Telfaz11 2023a).

With more than 3.41 million subscribers and a combined 630,493,987 views, Telfaz11 (Telfaz11 2023a), whose creative content is mostly in Arabic, features a network of independent filmmakers whose work both challenges and expresses great pride in Saudi culture. Currently also very active, it has been running two popular video series: *Folklore 101* and *Naas* (People). Videos produced in the Folklore 101 series have a vintage feel, while the latter have a more contemporary look. Now also supported by the Saudi Cultural Fund, the films in its Folklore 101 series cover themes relating to Saudi ancient arts, stories, and myths, as well as featuring traditional games and music videos mostly featuring the work of artists playing stringed and wind instruments or singing folksongs (Telfaz11 2023b). The large number of comments left by viewers express praise for a shift towards celebrating Saudi heritage in its entirety, instead of associating it narrowly with a Saudi-Salafi worldview. At the same time, many comments recorded nostalgia and pride in Saudi history and criticized the trends in contemporary music seen to be too heavily influenced by Western popular music. Thus, both in the creative content and in the comments section, there was an emphasis on the need to allow greater social freedom, but also a recognition of the importance of retaining Saudi religious and cultural heritage.

The video produced under the *Naas* series highlighted and showcased people engaging in creative and sporting pursuits not normally associated with Saudi society, such as skateboarders in Jeddah or cyclists enjoying a ride and comedians approaching traditional themes in creative ways, challenging the negative stereotypes. Comments, particularly regarding the comedians' video entitled 'Axis of Laughter', oscillated between praise for the creativity displayed by Saudis and finding humour in the religiously regulated environment. One user, for example, added in a humorous tone, 'I hope you don't put music in your videos, because it will become a constant sin for you. Thank you ♥.' Some episodes also highlighted changes in Saudi culture through the adoption not only of Western cultural influences but also of global ones, such as anime (Japanese animation) and manga (Japanese comic books), which are very popular in some sections of the younger generation in Saudi Arabia.

The channel also promotes other YouTube channels, as well as featuring independent videos not part of these two series. It also promotes trailers for Saudi films being produced for cinema or commercial networks such as Netflix, which, since the opening of the social sphere in Saudi Arabia, has started to actively feature work by Saudi artists. A highly popular comedy channel distributed by Telfaz11 was Khambalah. Launched in May 2012, it remained very active between 2012 and 2016, acquiring 2.34 million subscribers and 303,039,133 views of its comedy videos (Khambalah 2023). These videos continue to receive comments even now, with many viewers remembering the impact they had on them upon first release. One comedy sketch video entitled 'Filter of a Nation' (Khambalah 2015) showed various parts of society coping with the advent of the app Snapchat in Saudi Arabia, which today is widely used. In the montage of initial brainstorms about how to use it, a group of women suggest they might use it to show the world that they can drive, but the mother in the group resists this idea. A group of scholars suggest using it to showcase the Quran. It then shows the chaos and mania that ensue when Snapchat is widely used: young people engaged in synchronized dancing while on their phones, a woman in niqab hula-hooping, men showing displays of wealth and young people trying to create viral trends. The playful and lighthearted tone of the video stood in stark contrast to the serious and sombre attitudes often associated with Wahhabi Salafi teachings and Saudi society, effectively challenging these perceptions. The video showed a Saudi Arabia that is aligned to global norms and behaviours, and a society which is marked by no single ideology but by a plurality of responses to modern life.

In addition to channels like Telfaz11 and Khambalah, which promoted the work of multiple actors, many artists launched their own YouTube channels. Meshal Al-Jaser, a dark and surreal comedian, is one of these highly popular figures. His satirical sketches mostly touched upon restrictive social norms and religious dictates. He was actively posting content on his YouTube channel between 2012 and 2018 that addressed restrictive social norms in deeply satirical but also humorous ways. His YouTube channel has 1.03 million subscribers and more than 94 million views. One of his popular pre-2017 videos, entitled 'Can I Go Out?', focused on recording the social mobility problems that daughters face when they wish to go out or visit friends. The role of parents as overbearing guardians enforcing arbitrary rules, and the efforts that daughters have to make to engage in normal social activities, are wittily explored. The Saudi guardianship rules are targeted by showing how the daughter is left to seek her brother's help if she wants to go out: a responsibility that he is not keen to shoulder. Left with the sole option of engaging a taxi, she finds herself in a situation where a *tasbih* (rosary) with the name of Allah emblazoned on it hangs from the rear-view mirror used by the driver, yet a shot of the driver clearly shows that he has not so noble intentions. The video cuts with her pulling out a gun in readiness for what is to come. The video shows in a darkly comedic way the challenges and dangers of the guardianship system and the restrictions on women's movement.

Similarly, Majed Alesa is a Saudi music-video director belonging to 8ies Studios, whose videos have become viral hits for addressing social issues with a creative and humorous approach and high-quality production values. One of his viral hits was 'Barbs' (Alesa 2015), which is a hip-hop song released in 2015. The video displays a mixture of Arabic influences (Arabic writing, duff playing) and African American hip-hop influences (breakdancing in high top sneakers). The

Figure 4.1. *Barbs* (Alesa, 2015): Viral Saudi Hip-Hop Video

song enjoyed viral status, with people making videos of themselves dancing to the music. The hit is still circulating on the newer platform, TikTok. Comments on the video express surprise that it is a Saudi-produced song.

Majed Alesa also directed 'Hawages' ('Concerns') (Alesa 2016), released in 2016 (64 million views), a song sung by an unknown female trio. The song is very catchy and upbeat, with a mix of traditional Saudi and Western music influences. Visually highly appealing, the video shows how, despite the restrictions, Saudi women have great creativity and agency and have fun. The video starts with views of Saudi women wearing colourful clothes and sneakers, skateboarding skilfully while dressed in their ʿabayah and niqab. It goes on to show them skating, playing basketball and having fun at a fair, while in between displaying funny shots of their male family members trying to restrict them and images of Donald Trump dismissing Hilary Clinton. The singing by the women is very upbeat until suddenly the visuals shift to more traditional images, and more sombre singing is accompanied by traditional drumbeats. Its striking visual criticism of Donald Trump and its critical but light-touch lyrics (including lines such as 'May men go extinct, they cause us to have mental illnesses') won it much acclaim. It also attracted attention in Western media (Atassi 2017) and won positive reviews in publications such as the feminist online magazine *Jezebel* (Jezebel 2017). Local music productions such as this one were entirely new to Saudi Arabia and captured the desire among the young generation of Saudis for greater social freedom, demonstrating their ability to engage with change confidently.

Films

Efforts to challenge restrictive social and religious norms, while also showing the energy, enthusiasm, and creativity of young Saudis and also of Saudi society in general, also found expression in the form of local films produced during this period. *Barakah Meets Barakah*, released in 2016 (TIFF Trailers 2015), was one of these films. Written, produced and directed by Mahmoud Sabbagh, a prominent independent filmmaker in Saudi Arabia who founded Elhoush Productions in 2015, *Barakah Meets Barakah* was Saudi Arabia's first romantic comedy. Focusing on a romance that develops between two individuals representing very different segments of Saudi society – Barakah, a middle-class man (who is played by Hisham Fageeh, who also stars in some Khambalah sketches) and a successful female Instagram influencer – the film, by exploring the difficulty of pursuing a romantic union outside marriage, is a commentary on many important social themes. It addresses the social restrictions on individual choices imposed due to religious policing, and the politics of these restrictions when Barakah begins comparing today's Saudi culture with that of his uncle's generation, and, looking at old slides, he recounts how men and women used to be able to socialize in public, and there were cultural heroes besides imams.

The film also records the generational difference in attitudes towards relationships between men and women. Barakah's aunt, for example, argues that he needs a wife to wash his clothes and take care of the house, while Bibi, the female lead, being from the elite class and more exposed to Western values, guides him towards modern forms of courtship, advising him how to wow a girl with gifts and how to communicate during the early stages of the relationship. The movie thus beautifully captures the opposing pulls felt by Saudi individuals, with a view to presenting a case for the acceptance of more individualistic notions of romance. Widely popular among young Saudis, the film was chosen to be part of the Toronto International Film Festival and has gained critical success as a film in its own right, but also for the social and political messages that it conveys. One reviewer noted: 'Rather than break down barriers and throw bombs at taboos, *Barakah Meets Barakah* chooses a humor of clever restraint, rare for any first feature' (D'arcy 2016). As noted for the other productions reviewed in the previous section, this ability to demonstrate 'a humour of clever restraint' is a striking feature of all the popular productions dating from the pre-social reform period of 2010–2016.

Wasati bila Wasatiah (A Moderate Without a Middle-Ground) was the second film to receive major acclaim for similarly taking on Saudi religious hardliners with an appeal for moderation (IMDb 2016). The film was an attempt to capture the tension between the two ideological extremes influencing Saudi society: the liberals who want to fully absorb Western cultural norms, abandoning their own culture and religion and the religious extremists carrying out destruction in the name of religion and resisting any progressive change. The film's message is to show how 'the majority in the middle' aspires to adopt a moderate course. Released in 2017, the film was based on true events during the performance of a play in Riyadh ten years ago. In al-Yamamah University, students established a cultural week and performed a play with the title of this film. A group of students attacked the theatre, and the play was shut down. The film shows the lead-up to the play, the increasing anxiety of the actors faced with the presence of students with extreme views, and the innocent moral themes that it covers. The shift from the initial backlash to this play by extremist student groups, to it becoming a film popular in Saudi Arabia within one decade, is in itself indicative of the major cultural change in attitudes that Saudi Arabia has experienced in this period. The film won many international awards and also features in Netflix's *Six Windows in the Desert* series, which includes six films from Saudi Arabia that are selected for their high production quality and commentaries on important socio-political themes (Netflix 2020).

Visual arts

Between 2010 and 2016, another creative medium that became popular was the visual arts. The promotion of art, especially figurative art, is discouraged by Wahhabi and Salafi teachings. Thus, the promotion of art studios or major art exhibitions was rare in Saudi Arabia. Yet, during this period, some impressive projects evolved, and, as in the case of the other media discussed above, they focused not merely on good-quality production but equally on making a strong social commentary. Gharem Studio, run by Ajlan Gharem, a Saudi artist, to provide a space in which to nurture the local artistic community, was one such effort that won attention (Gharem Studio 2023a; 2023b). Having set up the studio to provide a space in which to nurture the art community, on his website, he has stated: 'Operating as an alternative space for people to meet each other, Gharem Studio's main goal is to cultivate natural and organic growth in the local art community, without any outside influence' (Gharem 2023). Openly critical of the unnecessary restrictions on individual agency, he has noted how in his youth he suffered from 'what I call being *a double dealer*, where in front of society you are a certain person and behind closed doors you are someone else' (Gharem 2023).

His painting entitled 'Paradise Has Many Gates', which shows a glass-built mosque (Gharem 2023) in an open space, has won attention at home and abroad. Commenting on the piece, which was installed at the Vancouver Biennale in 2018, he explained that in his view the older generation of Saudis has 'more beliefs than knowledge, and our generation has more knowledge than beliefs, so we're trying to find beliefs that can be harmonized with our knowledge' (Gharem 2023). He adds, 'In the Quran, it is said that there are eight gates to paradise . . . in our respective societies, we all can find the gates that will lead us to paradise'. Like the artists reviewed above, he has thus been keen to challenge Wahhabi religious rigidity in order to allow for more individual freedom in religious and social spheres of life. He has toured the USA with several other artists and exhibited *Parallel Kingdom: Contemporary Art from Saudi Arabia*, which featured work of twelve established and emerging Saudi artists (Guardian Cultures 2016). Ahmed Mater, a Saudi artist who co-founded the initiative 'Edge of Arabia', which showcases Saudi art globally, is another artist who has been promoting local Saudi artists globally (Jones 2018).

Thus, between 2010 and 2016 there was much creative expression demonstrated by young Saudis through the three media analysed in this section, whereby they expressed their desire for a more open socio-religious sphere, and also

Figure 4.2. 'Paradise Has Many Gates' (Gharem 2023)

demonstrated their ability and desire to opt for a moderate course, whereby the excessive religious zeal of the Wahhabi establishment is reined in without abandoning confidence in Islam or one's cultural traditions to blindly adopt Western cultural tastes and moral reasoning.

Here, it is also important to refer to the work of Sean Foley (2019), who has undertaken focused research on the visible flourishing of artistic activity in Saudi Arabia since the early 2000s, examining multiple domains including the visual arts, stand-up comedy, online YouTube content and feature-length films. Many of the cases he documents overlap with those discussed in this chapter, and his overall analysis is closely aligned with the argument I have developed on the basis of my analysis of social media content. However, by virtue of his primary focus on the artistic domain, his work is more directly concerned with the artists themselves and their platforms, including the nature of their patronage base. For my analytical purposes, these artists and their platforms were important primarily in terms of how they were received by Saudi youth, who themselves introduced these networks to me. Thus, while our work reinforces a shared argument about the creative energy visible within the Saudi artistic sphere since the 2000s, I have primarily focused on demonstrating the reception of these ideas among youth, whereas those interested in the backgrounds and profiles of the artists themselves can turn to Foley's work.

Conclusion

This chapter has demonstrated how the apparent sudden change in Saudi social norms is in fact a product of incremental shifts whereby attitudes have gradually evolved in favour of a more liberal socio-religious sphere and individual freedom, in response to socio-economic developments. The investments made in the education sector, the ease of international and regional travel, and access to high-quality internet and wireless communications via mobile apps and social media have played a critical role in promoting these values among the young generation of Saudis. Yet, analysing the creative content shared on social media which challenged the socio-religious rigidity of pre-2017 Saudi society, we also see that, although cognisant of the stifling aspects of Wahhabi teachings and related social restrictions, the younger generation were not up in arms preparing for rebellion against the Saudi monarchy, as was often predicted by Western observers (Manning 1998; Lippman 2012; Friedman 2015; Whitkaer 2015), including leaders such as President Obama as noted in the volume introduction (Freidman 2015). Instead, while addressing the prevailing societal rigidity, the producers of this creative content always demonstrated a light-heartedness in approaching the topic, an ability to laugh at themselves and record a need for change without appearing frustrated and desperate. Just as importantly, this creative content displayed a strong sense of pride in Saudi culture and traditions, both those deeply rooted in Islam and those predating the Islamic era. The content also conveyed confidence that Saudi society can steer a moderate path – one that preserves belief and tradition while avoiding both the rigid extremes of Wahhabi doctrine and the excesses often associated with secular, liberal Western lifestyles.

As we will see in the next chapter, the reason the social reforms have been quickly absorbed, leading to rapid norm shifts, is that the state has been very effective in tapping into these sentiments of young Saudis as part of the Vision 2030 development process: it is building on the work of those artists and is thereby maintaining the consensus on developing a moderate social sphere, instead of one simply trying to replicate Western cultural tastes. As we will see, all these independent initiatives arguing for change are now enjoying active support from the numerous institutions established under the Ministry of Culture. This support is at times financial, and at other times it takes the form of active promotion of these young artists at home and abroad. This suggests the success of these reforms is due to their being in line with a new vision of Saudi society that young Saudis themselves had started to actively vocalize.

Thus, what appears like top-down reform is actually a skilfully designed response by the state to the changing sensibilities of the younger generation. The state's investment in societal development, as recorded in this chapter, which has led to demands for change, as well as the on-going efforts by the state to ensure that the change is in line with the desires of young Saudis, suggests that the royal family is keen to expand its sources of legitimacy beyond religious authority and distribution of oil rents – a focus of analysis in Chapter 7. Such a focus aligns with recent studies on other Gulf countries, which highlight the importance of understanding how globalization and changing socio-economic conditions, both domestically and abroad, are prompting states in this region to expand their sources of legitimization beyond the distribution of oil rents (Gray 2011; Jones

2017). Meanwhile, in the next chapter, we will see how studying the actual content of change is key to appreciating why social reforms at times lead to rapid change in social norms, while in most cases, such efforts fail. We will also see how studying the actual content of change is key to predicting the long-term development trajectory of that change.

Part 2

THE DIRECTION OF CHANGE

Chapter 5

CONTINUITY WITHIN CHANGE

When studying norm change, a critical conceptual concern is how to assess its stability and likely future course. On the one hand, this is a question of numbers; on the other hand, it is about the actual substance of change. The purpose of the analysis presented in Chapter 2 was to demonstrate that enough has changed in Saudi Arabia in terms of societal behaviour in public spaces concerning women's liberties, gender mixing and opportunities for entertainment and tourism since the social reforms were initiated in late 2017 for us to refer to it as a process of shift in social norms rather than a set of policy prescriptions. That chapter deliberately did not pursue the next-level analysis, which is to examine the depth of change. If highly conservative social norms are giving way to more liberal norms, then in order to assess the durability of this shift, as well as the likely long-term trajectory of societal development, we need to examine the ratio between those who are actively adopting the new behaviour and those who are taking part in the new social spaces but not necessarily changing their own behaviour. We also need to examine the substantive nature of change – that is, what values underpinning the conservative norms have been displaced, and what new values are being adopted. The former requires enumeration; the latter requires close examination of the actual content of the reforms and the new opportunities that are being made available as a result.

Thus, on the one hand we need to remain mindful of the need to assess the ratio of women who have taken off their ʿabayah versus the proportion of women who are comfortably participating in the mixed-gender social spaces but are still choosing to wear their ʿabayah; or the ratio of Saudi youth who are participating in the desert raves versus those who are appreciating the increased entertainment opportunities and social opening but find such raves too drastic a break from their moral and religious framework and culture to be endorsed. On the other hand, we need to examine whether, across the diverse set of entertainment options and tourist projects being made available to the Saudi public, there are any signs of lingering Islamic and traditional values and cultural influences – or are they simply a replication of what is on offer in the West? Together, these two elements will help us to assess the likely future trajectory of norm development in Saudi society. They will also give us insights into why the on-going social reforms have been sufficiently well received to record a visible change in social norms in the first place. Equally, such an analysis is key to conducting a more objective discussion on what can be deemed desirable change. When studying the success of Athenian democracy, Ober (2008) notes how no society can be deemed a success if it loses its core identity: innovation and adaptation make for a vibrant society, but in the past, societies have equally valued preserving their values and traditions.

There is, thus, an element of value judgement involved when assessing what is a desirable trajectory of social norm change in Saudi society now that it is experiencing a move away from the rigid orthodoxy associated with Wahhabi Islam. Is Saudi Arabia now treading an inevitable course towards adopting Western liberal social mores with little scope for retaining loyalty to local traditions and values, as many argue is the case with the United Arab Emirates? Or can it carve out its own moderate course, blending the two value systems and cultural influences? Western observers, assessing on-going social reforms against the liberal feminist framework and more general social liberalism, are concerned that the liberties being allowed still do not meet Western standards; Human Rights Watch (HRW), for instance, finds the changes to the Saudi guardianship laws superficial (HRW 2023). The sceptics at home and within the wider Muslim world, however, are concerned that the change could result in uncritical replication of Western modernity, with its focus on consumerism and indulgent pleasures.

In line with the analysis presented in the previous chapter, the evidence presented in this chapter will demonstrate that social reforms announced by the Crown Prince have from the start received a positive response from many because the change, while appearing dramatic, as exemplified by events such as the Saudi Grand Prix and the elaborate music and dance raves being held in the desert (Ebrahim 2022), which appear too big a break from Saudi religious and traditional values, is on the whole moderate and retains a strong organic flavour. As was visible in the content of the creative material produced by Saudi artists, film directors and musicians, analysed in the preceding chapter, the initiatives led by the state demonstrate a strong desire to retain a Saudi cultural identity, which in turn is closely interwoven with Islamic values (but not necessarily the Wahhabi Salafi teachings). A closer examination of the initiatives being led by the state illustrates a move away from rigid Islamic teachings, not Islam *per se*. Similarly, in the design of actual activities, we see an appreciation for Western aesthetics, designs, music and cinematography, but equally a desire to blend them with aspects of Saudi culture. The secret to the success of these reforms to initiate a rapid norm change, as we will see in this chapter, rests on the conscious efforts being made by the Saudi state to offer this balance to the public. That is not to say that the Crown Prince himself necessarily favours a moderate course. There is nothing to suggest that he is uncomfortable with making Riyadh another Dubai: he is as proud of hosting the desert raves and Grand Prix as he is of promoting festivals featuring Saudi cuisine, coffee or music. The evidence, however, suggests that both he and other royal family members close to him are strategic and realistic enough to recognize that Saudi society is complex. While the majority of Saudis seem in favour of some degree of social liberalization and improvements to the quality of life, they are not in favour of abandoning Islam or their pride in Saudi cultural identity, which is closely interwoven with Islamic moral values and Arab tribal culture.

The ability of Saudi society to carve a moderate course was, however, not obvious to me during my initial years of fieldwork in Saudi Arabia. I often used to think that, although criticized even by many Muslims for its religious and cultural orthodoxy, this very rigidity puts Saudi society in a unique position to give Islam a genuine opportunity to engage with modernity. It is one of the very few Muslim-majority countries where this engagement could take place unmitigated by the Western colonial experience. While media coverage of Islam in Saudi Arabia focused on the restrictions on women's lives, or the mandatory closing of stores at the call for prayer, in my experience the less noted aspects of Islamically informed practices in Saudi Arabia were more striking: for example, the fact that it still officially uses the Islamic Hijri calendar, which, as I found in my fieldwork, still remains the dominant mode of organizing the year in the minds of most Saudis living outside the big cities,[1] instead of the Gregorian calendar. Another example was the organization of the National Museum in Riyadh around the conception of the universe as manifest in the verses of the Quran. A land never colonized by European powers, and the state of its institutions being too basic at the time of European ascendency to absorb indirect influences, as did those of Ottoman Turkey (Spannaus 2018b), Saudi Arabia did offer a fertile ground for innovative mixing of tradition and modernity if a social opening was to take place. It is this very aspect of Saudi Arabia that made it popular with Islamic modernists such as Rashid Rida (1865–1935), who supported the House of Saud (Spannaus 2018a), at a time when many socialist-minded rulers were emerging in the post-colonial Muslim countries, even though these Islamic modernists' methodological emphasis on interpreting Islamic texts to relate to the needs of the time was in conflict with the textual rigidity of Wahhabi scholars.

Yet while conscious of this potential, I, like other observers, had little confidence in the ability of the Saudi state or society to realize it. By recording the creative agency marking the on-going reforms, this chapter highlights the need to question assumptions about the docile nature of Saudi citizenry. The chapter equally demonstrates that the rapid shift in the behaviour of individuals, which collectively led to changes in social norms, is equally a product of the state's ability to put in place, at an exceptionally fast pace, an extensive infrastructure required to make the exercise of alternative choices possible. Also important is the fact that the new infrastructure, from users' perspectives, is of high quality and is being managed very efficiently. Overall, the Saudi case demonstrates how changes that build on prevailing values, instead of offering a dramatic rupture, could find rapid social acceptance, especially if the related infrastructure required to exercise new choices is made available. Thus, as the theories of institutional change also suggest (North 1990; Greif 2006; Bano 2012), behaviour underpinning existing norms does not change simply by informing people of alternative options; it changes when the practical mechanisms and incentives to support the adoption of new tastes become available.

5.1. The organic nature of change

A review of the developments in Saudi Arabia shows a strong continuity of religious and cultural values and aesthetics in the events and mega projects being developed, whether in the domain of tourism or social entertainment or the exercise of increased freedoms available to women. Most of the state-led activities and projects carry explicit references to the ethos of Islam and its cultural symbols, and they express pride in Arab history and the complex geography of the Arabian desert.

A strong Islamic ethos

The continued importance of Islam to Saudi society, even when the appeal of the highly conservative readings of Wahhabi Islam dictating the social sphere is disappearing, is obvious. Unless one chooses to focus exclusively on events such as the desert raves or the design of grand projects such as the Neom city being built on the Red Sea Coast (Ebrahim and al-Masri 2023), where the Saudi state is expected to further relax religious restrictions on modes of social entertainment by legalizing the consumption of alcohol, one can see that the state as well as Saudi society is treading a moderate course. Most people are actively participating in the new spaces that are becoming available for entertainment, tourism and the employment of women, but participation in these spaces does not necessarily mean changing one's own lifestyle to exercise all the newly granted freedoms. This delicate balance between people's desire for greater social freedom and the desire to enjoy this freedom according to their own understanding of religious dictates is best demonstrated in the arena of increased liberties for women. The fact that women from all income levels, and not only the elites, are active in the new social spaces, both with their families but also on their own or in the company of their female friends, is undisputed. Whether in the cafés and restaurants, or entertainment spaces like the Boulevard World, or the Old Jeddah, or cinemas or shopping malls, the presence of women is as evident as that of men.

Similarly, women's presence in the formal employment sector has rapidly increased. From 2015 onwards, it became common to see increasing numbers of Saudi women in the role of saleswomen in major stores, and since the introduction of the reforms, the visible presence of women in the tourism and hospitality sectors is striking. Young women serve in cafés and restaurants, at cash desks and at the reception desk in hotels. Even more striking is the fact that in all these settings, they are working in close contact with male colleagues. When checking into hotels, I would routinely find male and female members of staff jointly managing the reception desk; in cafés and restaurants, one would find waitresses working alongside male waiters. In all these contexts, they all seemed perfectly at ease working together. When they were not busy serving the clients, one could see them chatting with each other, laughing at jokes and enjoying each other's company. Such staffing combinations and interactions were not confined to morning hours;

the same staffing arrangements marked the night shift cover in the hotels and in the cafés and restaurants, which often operate until midnight and during the month of Ramadan often stay open almost until dawn. In a society where before the social reforms single men and women could not sit together in a restaurant or a café (Le Renard 2014), the high level of mixing among staff members, and their ease of interactions, are indicative of a genuine shift in social norms, especially given that such mixing on a daily basis can lead to opportunities to have affairs and indulge in sexual transgression: behaviour which is still not accepted by Saudi society and is also still checked by law. This illustrates the major shift in social norms governing women's presence in public spaces, their economic independence and the approved levels of gender mixing. However, it is also important to note what has not changed: only a fraction of the Saudi women participating in these spaces have chosen to remove their ʿabayah.

While the mandatory wearing of the ʿabayah was relaxed in 2018, in my observation across the multiple sites, no more than 30 per cent of Saudi women, even in the large cities, have chosen to remove their ʿabayah or niqab, while the number who do so in the remote cities is almost negligible. Despite strong evidence that Muslim women's decision to cover themselves is not a product of male pressure or a sign that women buy into sub-optimal life choices due to social pressures (Mahmood 2005, Bano and Kalmbach 2011; Bano 2017), it is difficult for many Western observers to see the element of agency in it (Abu-Lughod 2013). Yet neither discussions with Saudi women, nor the active agency of those young girls whom I have already profiled, have led me to deduce different conclusions from what I myself and other scholars have recorded about Muslim women's conscious choice to wear the hijab (Mahmood 2005, Bano and Kalmbach 2011; Bano 2017). The fact that society in general has accepted the broader norm shift allowing for gender mixing while women are still choosing to retain the ʿabayah and niqab demonstrates that Saudi society's acceptance of provisions being made available by the state is selective. There are active debates within families and among individuals about the limits of legitimate reform. The requirement for women to dress modestly and cover their hair is emphasized by the four main Sunni madhhabs (Alkiek 2023); the Quranic injunctions on the Prophet's wives to dress modestly compel believing Muslim women to observe this as a core principle of Islamic piety (Alkiek 2023). By contrast, the act of participation in a mixed-gender setting to undertake economic activity or partake in social activities in public spaces has generated more nuanced debates within the Islamic legal tradition. Women used to have direct access to the Prophet Muhammad when they wanted to ask him any question. Khadija, his first wife, did business and Aisha, his youngest wife, remained engaged in shaping the political landscape in Medina after the death of the Prophet and engaged with male scholars in the process of compiling hadith (Mernissi 1991). Thus, it is not surprising that contemporary Saudi society can view the strict rulings on gender segregation as a product of Wahhabi rigidity, rather than viewing it as one of the non-negotiable principles of Islam, even while applying a different interpretation to the requirement for women to cover themselves.

The same tendency to modernize but remain loyal to core Islamic principles is visible in more general social behaviour. One good example of this is the continued emphasis on the preservation of prayer areas in all public spaces: hotels, restaurants, airports, train stations, Boulevard World, al-Ula old town, etc. This ensures that men as well as women can easily perform the five obligatory prayers when they are away from home, even though the earlier requirement for businesses and shops to close for prayer has been relaxed. The continued provision of these spaces to ensure the observation of the obligatory five prayers when one is away from home remains an important demand by members of the public. This is reflected in the design of even the new projects, such as the Boulevard World, which, although it offers an explicitly Western form of entertainment, provides mosque areas for men and women and proper facilities for people to undertake *wudu* (ablution). Such systematic provision of these facilities, which greatly facilitate the performance of obligatory prayers when one is away from home, is rare in other Muslim countries. The Saudi public's expectations concerning the continued provision of these facilities, even in newly designed projects, remain unchanged and so does the state's commitment to ensuring their provision.

Similarly, if the state agencies are involved in planning a rich set of entertainment activities to match the mood of different months and seasons, they are also invested in ensuring that Ramadan retains a celebratory spirit. During this holy month, the daily routine shifts to a night cycle. Most people sleep in the mornings and come out just before iftar. There is much festivity during the entire night, marked by large prayer congregations in mosques for the 'Isha' prayer, socialization in cafés, restaurants and parks, families picnicking or walking along the corniche in the cities that border the sea, or simply strolling through the markets in preparation for Eid shopping. During my visit in December 2022, I found an array of entertainment options available at the Winter at Tantora Festival at al-Ula, which was in its fifth year and has become highly popular with foreign tourists, offering concerts, fine dining, guided tours of the fascinating Nabatean archaeological sites and stargazing in the desert at night. During my visit from March to April 2023, I was similarly spoilt for choice when deciding which mosque to select for the performance of night prayer, followed by tarawih prayers (a set of eight to twenty nafls said daily after 'Isha' prayer during Ramadan, when every night the imam covers one full chapter of the Quran). For Muslims, saying the tarawih prayer during Ramadan is a major commitment, and having access to spacious and clean mosques with good reciters can turn this into a great spiritual treat. Saudi mosques have always offered these services very well, and social liberalization and the promotion of secular entertainment options have not resulted in any loss of emphasis on them, by either the state or society. Rather, additional efforts are being made to develop the areas around old mosques to make them more attractive as tourist sites.

The renovations undertaken in Old Jeddah best illustrated this spirit during the Ramadan month, as the area transforms during this period. The area became particularly alive after iftar, providing numerous entertainment options for families as well as individuals of all ages. The old mosques located inside the area offered tarawih facilities with experienced reciters reciting the Quran in beautiful voices. Despite recent regulations forbidding the use of loudspeakers for prayers (MEM 2023), the sound of tarawih recitation, though faint, was often audible to the passers-by on the nearby streets, while families, young and old, relaxed and enjoyed local food purchased from simple but stylishly decorated stalls; the whole environment felt very pleasant under the decorative lights covering the entire area. There was also an artists' corner where there were regular performances, and a separate games area, where individuals or families sat and played games, including chess, carrom board and cards. While the Ottoman architectural landscape made Old Jeddah a particularly attractive and appropriate site for this night-long festivity during Ramadan, in most cities, as part of the ongoing development of social entertainment options, the Ministry of Culture has tried to promote a similar culture in old markets. In al-Ahsa, the streets in front of the old souq were similarly beautifully decorated with lights, so that sitting out in the café post-iftar or simply walking in the area, felt a bit reminiscent of eras gone by; the same treatment had been applied to the old district in Yanbu, where the old houses, including that of Lawrence of Arabia, who lived there for two years (Lawrence 2015), have been nicely renovated and a very aesthetically pleasing seating area with food stalls has been developed next to it for public use.

Similarly, while even in other months one often finds recordings of Quranic recitation playing in cars booked through Uber, Careem or other car-sharing apps, during the month of Ramadan it becomes the norm. The possibility of someone listening to music during Ramadan is extremely low: mostly one gets to hear Quranic recitation, or in a few cases Islamic sermons, or there is silence. This reverence for the Quran, which in the Muslim faith is the untouched word of God, manifests itself in unusual places: such as a young woman with a melodious voice reciting passages from it from memory in a low voice, sitting next to her husband in a restaurant while waiting for the food to be served, or the woman sitting reading the Quran on the seat behind mine on a five-hour-long SAPTCO bus journey from Tabuk to Umluj. In the same way, the reverence for Mecca and the deep emotional attachment to Medina, as the city of the Prophet, come across clearly. Whenever I would mention that I have been to Mecca or Medina or am heading there, I received approving nods from local Saudis, and it is very rare for them not to say with a beaming face, 'Medina is "*kuways*" (good)'.

Even when promoting tourism, while the focus is on ensuring services that will appeal to Western tastes, such as the mixed open-air swimming pools in al-Ula resorts, there is a very active emphasis on celebrating the rich Islamic history of the Arabian Peninsula pre-dating the emergence of Wahhabism. A more holistic narrative of Islam in Saudi Arabia is being developed, which is not confined to discussions about the teachings of the Wahhabi doctrine or the deeds or habits of the Salaf but also proudly includes the monuments from the Ottoman period. Whether it is Old Jeddah, with its rich Ottoman architecture, or the countless small castles that can be found particularly in the Hejaz region from that period, or the legendary Hejaz railway that Ottomans built in the early twentieth century to facilitate pilgrimage to Mecca by connecting Damascus to Medina and offering stops on the way in key cities such as Tabuk and al-Ula, all these historical sites are now owned by Saudis and actively presented to the visitors with a great sense of pride as part of the country's rich Islamic heritage. A visitor to these tourist sites, unaware of the resistance of the Saudi-Wahhabi alliance to the Ottoman Empire in the struggle to establish control over the Arab Peninsula (when Ibn Abd al-Wahhab declared the Ottoman Empire as 'kufr') (Bsheer 2020), would get no inkling of this deep historical hostility.

The opening up of social spaces in ways that are a direct push back against Wahhabi teachings is thus not a sign of a decline in conviction in Islam itself; Islam remains very important to Saudi society. While Saudis have welcomed the social opening, the majority are changing their own behaviour only to the point at which they feel that, in accordance with their individual understanding, they are not violating the core Islamic principles. This choice to respect what most view as core Islamic dictates is also reflected in the continued social and legal prohibition on dating. Despite widespread use of social-media apps, dating apps have limited uptake in Saudi Arabia (Bruton 2017). This low usage is partly due to the fact that the act of dating is still illegal, but it is equally an outcome of society's low tolerance for changes in sexual mores, given that sex outside marriage is classified as a major sin in the Quran itself for both men and women – thus making it, for the majority, one of the non-negotiable principles of Islam (Ali 2016). One of my respondents in al-Ula, who, as mentioned in Chapter 2, had spent two years studying in an English-language institute in Oxford, gave a good insight into the low tolerance for such changes with the sudden intensity with which he reacted to one of my observations. While visiting the remains of the Hejaz railway station in al-Ula, which was in a slightly isolated part of town, I was struck by the fact that the small park next to it was well populated, though mainly by men sitting in pairs and chatting. I commented that it seemed to me that Saudis really like to meet friends in parks. In a contemplative tone, he said, 'Yes, they do', but immediately followed up in a more assertive tone, which also carried a slight sense of distaste, adding, 'but remember it is not a place for the meeting of men and women'. Given that much of our conversation was in the context of his time in Oxford, his immediate instinct was to make it clear to me that the meeting of friends in parks has very different significance in the two places – given that in Oxford, a university town, it is common to see couples lying on the ground relaxing together.

In my interviews, most respondents were very conscious of the need to retain this balance between respecting core Islamic dictates while enjoying increased social freedom. Respondents frequently made reference to what they viewed as the UAE's uncritical adoption of Western cultural values, observing that following a similar course would be undesirable for Saudi Arabia. As one respondent remarked, 'We in Saudi Arabia have been joking about the UAE's recent move to change the weekend to Saturday and Sunday; such a move would be unthinkable in Saudi Arabia'. The argument was that devoting Friday to Jum'ah (Friday congregational prayer) and spending time with the family after that is such an integral part of the Saudi culture that to deviate from it would be unthinkable. Ultimately, one cannot predict whether this reservation will persist, given that many of the current changes, such as women's right to drive or the creation of mixed-gendered working conditions, could not have been predicted before 2016. The tendency to compare Saudi Arabia with the UAE, however, does show that people are very conscious of the need to identify boundaries, which, if crossed, would generate fear of the loss of one's identity.

A strong cultural imprint

A key feature of the state's discourse concerning on-going social reforms is to highlight its commitment to 'cultural revival'. The adoption of more liberal social attitudes and Western cultural tastes is not being forced on the public, unlike what was attempted in Kemalist Turkey (Bano 2018b; Spannaus 2018b) or Ba'athist Syria (Pierret 2013; Bano 2017). Instead, the focus is on reviving the rich cultural heritage, which, as per the narrative promoted by the Crown Prince, was suppressed in recent decades due to the pressure that the state had to accommodate from competing Islamist groups (Chulov 2017; al-Rahseed 2020). Vision 2030 identifies culture as being 'indispensable to our quality of life' and pledges to increase both the quality and quantity of cultural activities in the country (GoSA 2016). It states three objectives: promoting culture as a way of life; enabling culture to contribute to economic growth; and creating opportunities for international cultural exchange. To advance these objectives, the Ministry of Culture has identified sixteen priority sub-sectors, which have been organized under eleven commissions: Heritage; Architecture and Design; Culinary Arts; Music; Libraries; Theatre and Performing Arts; Museums; Visual Arts; Film; Fashion; and Literature, Publishing and Translation.

All these commissions plan their own activities, but they also co-ordinate projects among themselves or with other ministries or departments. The result, as mapped in the preceding section, is that an array of cultural activities is being planned to cater to varied tastes, so that if some activities directly borrow from Western entertainment culture, others clearly build on local tastes. Further, even in the design of activities strongly shaped by Western aesthetics or tastes, there is often an attempt to add a Saudi cultural touch. It is also very clear that the targeted audiences for these two sets of activities are different: the former is aimed at catering to the tastes of elites in big cities, while the latter is meant for mass consumption. This strategy – to diversify and offer something to everyone – is also reflected in the price of the entry tickets. While entry to spaces and events like the Boulevard World and Soundstorm Music Festival can cost around $50 per person, and big sporting events such as the Grand Prix can start at $400, admission to seasonal festivals, decorated souks and places like Old Jeddah is free. Also, the former normally house the most expensive food chains and international restaurants, including those owned by Michelin-star chefs, to ensure that while the Saudis who can afford it can taste the best of flavours while remaining in Saudi Arabia instead of flying out to European destinations, the latter offer nicely decorated small food stalls where a family or a group of teenage friends can buy tasty local food and enjoy soft beverages whose price starts from SAR 30 (US$8) per head. Thus, the festivity marking the annual camel festival, held outside of

Riyadh every year and recorded in a February 2023 issue of *The Economist* as a sign of things being the same outside the capital city (The Economist 2023a), is in my assessment, actually part of a planned strategy to ensure that, while introducing global entertainment culture, the local cultural festivals and activities are also nurtured. This is due to a continued sense of pride in these traditional events, but it is also a conscious strategic choice on the part of the planners to ensure that all segments of the population have access to the types of social entertainment activities that they want.

Thus, in addition to all the high-value entertainment and tourism projects that have been introduced since 2017, a few of which were discussed in some detail in Chapter 2, a systematic effort is afoot to further enrich and facilitate the provision of traditional festivals and activities that are in line with local cultural tastes. In addition to the investment made in decorating the old souq areas and creating attractive seating areas and food halls around them, there is also a concentrated effort to make the corniche areas and parks more entertaining for families. In the coastal towns of Umluj and Yanbu, which are attracting tourists with their beautiful beaches and views of untouched coral reefs, it is common for families to enjoy the seaside area by bringing their picnics and spreading out large rugs and carpets where they sit for hours. Under the auspices of the cultural and tourism departments, the areas around the corniche are being developed to provide better playing areas for children and shaded resting spaces, too, but public swimming is not allowed, as that would negatively affect the family-outing culture in that area. There is much talk of promoting luxury beaches on the Red Sea coast and even along its southern coastline as international tourist destinations, which would require provisions for public swimming and sunbathing areas (Hodgetts 2024). The shortlisted islands for these projects suggest that the government does not plan to select the beaches or corniche areas close to established cities (Hodgetts 2024). This would enable Saudi families to continue enjoying them in the traditional style, reducing the chances of protests.

Similarly, the design of the major tourism projects often includes an effort to give international visitors a taste of Saudi hospitality, which is central to the country's culture and tradition. Thus, the paid tours to Hegra, the main Nabatean archaeological sites in al-Ula (Visit Saudi 2023e), include not just the coach ride to the multiple stops on the route, but also a taste of Saudi hospitality and local foods. On arrival at the main stop, visitors are served freshly squeezed juices, locally dried fruits and tiny pieces of locally baked wheat desserts, packed for individual consumption. The culture of hospitality is reflected not just in the free serving of these items but also in the etiquette with which the young Saudi men and women, assigned to this role, serve them. Further, the selection of items served is designed to spark interest in Saudi cuisine as the diverse selection of refreshments on offer represents local produce and flavours. If participating in the night visit to Hegra, visitors are offered light blankets to keep them warm in the desert wind. Thus, whether on the morning tour or the night tour, visitors are made to feel like guests rather than customers, in order to impress on them the Saudi traditional emphasis on hospitality.

At the same time, the Ministry of Culture is making dedicated efforts to promote Saudi cuisine by actively hosting food festivals in a range of cities (Riyadh Season 2021). The annual food festival held in Riyadh as part of Riyadh Season offers cuisine from all regions of Saudi Arabia and attracts locals as well as visitors. The most significant set of activities under this head is, however, linked to the promotion of Saudi coffee production. In addition to hosting an extensive network of Western coffee chains, which are extremely popular, there is a strong tradition of local coffee in Saudi Arabia (Charles 2023). Saudi coffee uses very different cultivation and production methods from those used in the West; there are also clear etiquettes prescribing how it is to be served and consumed. As part of the Saudi cultural revival, the government is making a very serious effort, with the active engagement of the Ministry of Culture, to enhance Saudi coffee production and to adopt treatment methods that may lead to its usage for the production of Western-style coffees (Charles 2023). This promotion has been very effective: the big cities such as Riyadh and Jeddah offer an array of independent cafés. Located next to international coffee chains such as Starbucks and Dunkin' Donuts, these local cafés offer high-quality espressos and Americanos as well as the usual lattes and cappuccinos. Often established by trendy young Saudis, these coffee outlets normally place a great emphasis on creating an attractive ambience by blending Western aesthetics with local tastes. The outlets of the popular Saudi coffee chain, Half Million, which, as noted in Chapter 3, is the product of a bet between two friends that they could match the sales of international coffee chains in Saudi Arabia, are always full (Half Million 2023). I have found Western visitors quite impressed with the quality of coffee on offer in the independent café, as Saudis have a taste for strong brews. The rich experimentation going on in cafés in Saudi Arabia creates a sense of a genuine cultural renaissance in the making.

Similarly, all art forms are being actively promoted by the state in the form of local films and the hosting of large-scale art exhibitions. *Sattar*, which, as noted in Chapter 2, is one of the first local films to hit the screens in December 2022, has been actively promoted by the Ministry of Culture and its relevant institutions (Vivarelli 2023). A comedy, but aiming to cover serious themes, the film revolves around a young Saudi who, facing professional and personal challenges, tries to pursue his childhood dream of becoming a wrestler. In pursuit of this dream, he is confronted with serious setbacks, but he persists. The movie proved a hit and reportedly grossed $2.2 million within the early weeks of its launch (Vivarelli 2023). Having watched it in a cinema in Riyadh, it was easy for me to appreciate why. The main character, of humble origins and limited talent, is someone ordinary to whom Saudis could relate, but at the same time, the quality of production, the soundtrack, and the storyline (which rewards truthfulness, loyalty, and innocence in the face of treachery) make for a very engaging drama, even for outsiders. The movie offers insights into how, despite modernization and growing commercialization in society, the integrity of human behaviour is highly valued by Saudis. By giving a prominent role to a Pakistani actor, who, out of a strong sense of Muslim brotherhood, leads the main character to victory against a rival with no morals, the movie also affirms that Islam remains an important lens through which ordinary Saudis relate to other nationalities.

Highlighting the importance of comedy in Saudi culture, Alshehri, the film's director, noted in an interview, 'We are a society that loves comedy. We love to laugh and joke around, and that's our goal with this' (al-Turki 2022). The film was produced by al-Telfaz, which, as noted in the previous chapter, aired much of the creative content produced by young Saudis before the reforms of 2017. The al-Telfaz team involved in the production of *Sattar* has stated its ambition to cultivate more serious genres of films in the future. *Sattar*, they have argued, was deliberately designed to attract audiences by drawing on Saudis' love of comedy, with the aim of encouraging them in the future to engage also with Saudi films focusing on more serious themes. As Alkhairallah, the producer of the film and one of the actors, explained in one interview, 'Let's give the audience what they want now and then give them what we want after. It's a strategy. Let's not shock them from the beginning' (al-Turki 2022). The production team has emphasized how its members made a very serious effort to ensure that all the film's details – the sets, the location, the costumes and the manner of interaction among the characters – are true to Saudi culture. They also mentioned listening to Saudi music played at wrestling matches when deciding on the music for the film. This led them to discover the Sheilat genre of music, which is influenced by Saudi oral poetry. Similarly, the team engaged with the Saudi Pro Wrestling Society alongside the top Saudi wrestler, Naif Al-Mutairi, to ensure that the fight scenes reflect local wrestling practices (al-Turki 2022; Arab News 2023).

This commitment by independent actors, but so far also by the state, to draw upon and promote Saudi culture while pushing back against Wahhabi restrictions on basic modes of social entertainment is key to explaining the rapid acceptance of spaces made available by the reforms. That the state is trying to build on local culture and traditions, rather than exclusively enforcing notions of modernity borrowed entirely from the West, is also clear from the fact that most of the actors, directors, producers, and musicians who were producing content (analysed in the previous chapter) before the 2016 reforms are now receiving patronage from the state, either through receipt of funds for developing bigger productions or through promotion of their works at home and abroad. The same is true for artists, who now have opportunities to advance their work through important local and international exhibitions promoted by the state. The most high-profile effort in this regard is the founding of the Saudi Arts Biennale, an art exhibition curated by leading international and local promoters and artists to showcase the art and artistic culture of Saudi Arabia. Rotating between contemporary and Islamic Art Biennale on an annual basis (Bari 2023), the exhibits feature some of the best collections in the field. Its first Islamic Arts Biennale took place in Jeddah between March and April 2023, attracting large numbers of Saudis as well as international visitors. It was sponsored by the Diriyyah Biennale Foundation (DBF 2023), which receives support from the royal family. Hosting this large annual exhibition places Saudi Arabia prominently on the global art scene.

Another good example of the state's attempts to promote art, but with a strong local flavour, is the establishment of the MiSK Art Institute (MAI) (MAI 2023). Directed by Ahmed Mater (Jones 2018), the artist who led the exhibition of twelve Saudi artists to the USA that was mentioned in the previous chapter, MIA is part of Mohammed bin Salman's non-profit MiSK Foundation. Keen to promote Saudi art forms and artists, the Institute encourages the promotion of traditional art forms such as geometric art, while promoting exchanges with European institutions. The focus thus is on experimenting with and developing the local art forms, rather than abandoning them in favour of Western art techniques or aesthetics. Consequently, very few images of people are visible on its website or in the art on display. This is consistent with the preference within Islamic artistic tradition to avoid drawing the human form, due to the consensus among leading Islamic scholars that it is prohibited. The institute offers residencies to existing artists and training to nurture the talent of future artists. This Saudi approach to promoting local talent and art forms is distinct from the way in which other Gulf states developed their art scene, as noted in an article published by Sotheby's (Zand 2018):

> The Saudi cultural landscape however has some differences from its Gulf counterparts. Where countries like the UAE and Qatar have relatively small, young populations with recent cultural infrastructure, a grassroots artist-led scene has existed in the Kingdom. As formal institutional support is instigated for the first time in Saudi Arabia, its existing creative communities are mobilized. The nascent scene is therefore both established and new.

The fact that Saudi Arabia has a much larger population – 36 million, compared with just a few million in the other Gulf states[2] – does give local society more weight. Different regions have their own rich traditions and practices, which are strongly rooted in the local culture.

Cultivating pride in history and geography

Just as there is a conscious effort to acknowledge the mixed influences from the pre-Wahhabi Islamic period, there is also a conscious effort to create a sense of Saudi history that acknowledges the pre-Islamic influences on the Arabian Peninsula. There is an attempt to claim a rich historical past when social life was quite advanced (Chulov 2017), particularly in the region around Hejaz, even before the early Christian era (Visit Saudi 2023d). In developing this narrative, the most explicit emphasis is placed on the presence of Nabateans and the fascinating archaeological remains that they left in the city of Hegra in al-Ula. Hegra houses more than 100 Nabatean tombs and is being promoted by the Saudis as a rival to Petra in Jordan (Visit Saudi 2023e). In addition, other sites from the time of Moses are being identified and promoted as tourist destinations. One such site is referred to as the Well of Moses (Viator 2023). It is believed to be the well where he met the daughter of Prophet Sohaib, who became his wife. The well is a two-hour drive from Tabuk. Most significant in developing this grand historical narrative is the skilful use of references to old trade routes that operated through the Arabian desert. Saudi promotional material, as well as the guided tours conducted in al-Ula, which was an important city on these routes, emphasizes their almost mythical glamour, as illustrated by this example (Visit Saudi 2023e):

> For centuries, camel caravans laden with frankincense, myrrh, spices, silk and precious stones traversed ancient Arabia, skirting the desert sands of the unforgiving Empty Quarter, on gruelling, months-long expeditions. Using an established network of waypoint towns and caravanserais, this trade traffic brought prosperity to the blossoming cities along the Arabian Peninsula's western coast, and these routes fostered the exchange of goods and ideas across continents. Still today, relics and reminders of these important journeys can be seen in Saudi Arabia.

This emphasis on promoting early historical sites in Saudi Arabia directly aligns with Crown Prince Mohammed bin Salman's effort to foster a new Saudi identity (England and Omran 2019), which al-Rasheed (2020) refers to as an 'aggressive national rebranding'. This identity is being promoted through various platforms, such as the celebration of Saudi Founding Day on 22 February (Alamar 2022) and the promotion of the Saudi national anthem (Bing 2024). Al-Rasheed (2020) argues that this is the third attempt by the Saudi state to develop a national identity, with the first being religious nationalism immediately after the creation of the state in 1932 and the second being pan-Islamic transnationalism in the 1960s. Al-Rasheed argues that in this current attempt, the Crown Prince is promoting a shift towards a narrower Saudi nationalism, emphasizing a strong local identity. This is represented in online campaigns and hashtags such as 'Saudi Arabia for Saudis' and 'Saudi Arabia is Great'. She notes that the newly celebrated citizen is no longer one who obeys religious clerics and is rewarded with state-sponsored prizes for religious observance and zeal, but rather the eclectic and creative young entrepreneur who is expected to celebrate and swear allegiance to the Crown Prince, rejoicing in the promise of future economic opportunities (al-Rasheed 2020). This new identity also draws on pride in ancient archaeological sites like Madain Saleh and Al-Ula, which were previously neglected as icons of blasphemy from the pre-Islamic era but are now sources of national pride (al-Rasheed 2020). The development of tourism at these ancient sites is now seen as integral to the new Saudi national project, and al-Rasheed (2020) contends that Saudis are expected to celebrate the listing of some of these ancient sites as UNESCO World Heritage sites.

The greatest emphasis has been placed on highlighting the importance of 'The Incense Route', which is believed to be one of the world's oldest trade routes, originating four thousand years ago. The narrative promoted runs as follows. Covering two thousand kilometres, it was one of the main routes for the transportation of frankincense and myrrh to the Mediterranean from south of the Arabian desert (Visit Saudi 2023e). These items were in high demand in Egypt for the embalming of mummies, as ingredients in medicine and cosmetics, and for the performance of religious ceremonies in Roman and Jewish temples and Christian churches – to the extent that on occasions they fetched a price higher than gold. Running parallel to the Red Sea along Saudi Arabia's west coast, the route is believed to have benefitted the Nabateans, who traded with the passing merchants. The Nabataean funerary symbols that were carved on tombs are argued to have been borrowed extensively from the Romans and the Greeks, which the Saudi narrative contends was a direct result of cultural exchange along this trade route. When the ancient Romans conquered southern Arabia in the first century CE, they named the region Arabia Felix, meaning 'Happy Arabia', because of the extraordinary wealth accumulated from this trade route (Visit Saudi 2023e). However, according to the information provided to the Saudi visitors, the Romans gradually moved towards the development of a boat-based trade route, which was easier to navigate than the Arabian desert and could be under their control. Emphasis is also placed on the importance of Saudi coastlines, which linked up sea routes with land-based offshoots from the Silk Road, running between China and Europe (Visit Saudi 2023e). Both the Red Sea in the west and the Arabian Gulf in the east were part of these trade routes, through which cardamom, cinnamon, ginger, nutmeg, pepper, turmeric and other spices were transported from Asia to Europe. The ships docked in ports around the peninsula, and spice shipments from Southeast Asia and India were transferred to other boats in Jeddah, which won it the title of 'the bride of the Red Sea'. By emphasizing the centrality of Saudi Arabia to these old trade routes, the aim is to establish that Saudi identity is much more complex than that which is narrowly equated with radical Islam (Visit Saudi 2023e).

Finally, there is also a conscious effort to inculcate a strong sense of pride in the geographical complexity of the Arabian Peninsula, highlighting the beauty of its various rock formations and the oasis settlements filled with date-palm treats and the distinctive lifestyle that desert living promotes and the human virtues that it inculcates. The government, as well as private companies, are organizing events in the desert, celebrating the natural beauty of the land (CNN Travel 2023). The hosting of the largest annual musical rave in the desert area just outside Riyadh has proved very popular. The Edge of the World tour, which was mentioned in Chapter 2, expresses a similar sense of pride in the natural beauty of sand dunes and different desert rock formations. Many one-day tours are available in most cities, taking tourists into the desert areas in a couple of hours. Similarly, al-Ula is being presented not just as a rich archaeological site but as one that demonstrates the richness and diversity of Saudi desert rock formations. Promotional material about al-Ula refers to it as the 'world's largest living museum' due to its striking rock formations reminiscent of the fairy chimneys in the Cappadocia region in Turkey, covering a large area of land (Experience al-Ula 2023). The beauty and peculiarities of oasis life are also being highlighted through the organization of tours to large oases such as the one in al-Asha. There is equally much promotion of centuries-old rock carvings that can be found across most regions of Saudi Arabia.

Visitors are particularly encouraged to spend days exploring such carvings outside the cities of Hail and Tabuk. At the same time, visitors are presented with tantalizing information about the Sarwat mountain, which is a green mountain range that emerges on the southwest border of Saudi Arabia and which on most days is surrounded by mist. The city of Abha, located in this area, along with the hanging villages and stunning mountain views, is becoming popular with tourists. At the same time, the existence of pristine beaches and untouched islands along the Red Sea coast, as well as on the southern coast, features prominently in the Saudi publicity material aimed at encouraging tourism but also at boasting Saudis' pride in the richness and diversity of their land (Visit Saudi 2023c). This diverse geographical landscape, and the resilience developed through desert living, are being actively promoted to nurture a sense of national pride and to convince Saudis that they do not have to escape to the West for relaxation and entertainment when such richness of experiences can be enjoyed at home.

The reason why the on-going social reforms have thus won rapid popular support is that they have pushed back on Wahhabi conservatism while trying to respect principles that are viewed as core to the Islamic faith by most Sunni schools of law. Reforms have been accepted because most of them are attempting to build on Saudi cultural identity in creative ways, rather than abandoning it. In my 2022 and 2023 visits to Saudi Arabia, it was difficult not to feel a sense of cultural flourishing, and not to find that most of the young respondents agree with that sentiment. This positive and creative energy was best captured in my meeting with coffee producers in the city of Jazan, where people have traditionally cultivated coffee plants for commercial purposes but also for everyday consumption. As part of the state's effort to enhance local coffee cultivation and improve the coffee-bean roasting techniques to cater to an international market, Jazan is one of the cities where, in partnership with Aramco, the Ministry of Culture and the Ministry of Agriculture are supporting local farmers to improve the quality and yield of their crops and consider new production procedures. Emphasizing how pleased the local people were with this programme, one of the respondents noted, 'The people here have grown coffee for ever, but now they feel a sense of pride in their tradition, as it is being valued by outsiders and we are having international visitors who are keen to engage with our practices'. He noted that the involvement of the Ministry of Culture in this process was very important, because while Aramco and the Ministry of Agriculture helped with technical and marketing skills, it was the Ministry of Culture that enthused the public to take pride in a practice that has been so central to their tradition but for which they never received any credit: 'It was like the programme gave new life to a body that was almost dead.'

5.2. Supporting infrastructure and efficient management

While the Saudi experience has on the one hand demonstrated the importance of ensuring a degree of continuity while engineering social change, on the other hand, it shows that the success of such reforms is equally contingent on the state's ability to develop at a fast pace the infrastructure that allows for the exercise of alternative choices. The pace with which the Saudi state has developed the social entertainment and tourism facilities has been very rapid on all counts. Elaborate projects, such as the Boulevard World in Riyadh, suddenly emerged on the north side of Riyadh in a matter of eight to ten months. During my interviews, respondents always commented on how quickly these facilities had been developed. Moreover, not only did the state manage to develop the facilities, but it also proved effective in training young Saudis to fill many of the positions in these projects: organizing capacity-building training in-country while also sending some candidates overseas for the acquisition of certain skills. Commenting on how the public is happy with the employment opportunities that these projects have generated for the locals, my female guide on a tour to an oasis in al-Ula noted that on the initial announcement of Vision 2030, most had expected the projects to progress slowly. Yet the fast pace with which al-Ula was developed as a tourist destination and opened many employment and income-generating opportunities for the locals surprised everyone and built confidence in the state's ability to implement the proposed plans.

In assessing the success of these reforms, it is equally important to note that the rapid pace of development of this supporting infrastructure in the fields of social entertainment and tourism did not come at the cost of quality. Whether it is the decoration of the traditional souks, the development of large tourism or entertainment projects, such as al-Ula or Riyadh Boulevard or the renovation of old districts such as Old Jeddah, the quality of what is on offer in terms of aesthetic appeal and product output is consistently very high. Thus, the young Saudi female yoga instructor whose session I observed in the Five Senses Sanctuary in al-Ula, which hosts an annual well-being retreat promoting holistic lifestyles, met the standards that, in my experience, are displayed by young instructors in the leading studios in the West. Locally trained in a tradition that has no indigenous roots, she had received all of her Yoga training in Saudi Arabia. Similarly, I repeatedly found Western tourists speaking highly of their experiences. The Hegra night tour, where the visitors get to see the Nabatean sites in the dark, combines a walk along centuries-old desert paths illuminated by beautiful lamps, a ride in horse-driven carriages from one location to the next, and guides dressed in traditional attire spinning out local folk tales. Based on my observations of the reactions of the foreign tourists, such a combination leaves the visitors little to complain about. When we add to this the strong sense of physical security that the Saudi state offers to its citizens (whereby visitors are repeatedly told with great confidence by Saudi men and women of all ages and orientations that the country is very safe), it becomes easier to appreciate why a large number of Saudi families have readily ventured out to explore the newly created social spaces.

In conservative societies, one of the main factors restricting women's mobility is the fear of their being harassed when they are out alone, especially at night. This, as was noted by many of my respondents, also puts pressure on the men who might accompany them, as they become responsible for their protection. In Saudi Arabia, the state's relative effectiveness at ensuring security is key to ensuring that more and more women are being allowed to engage in mixed-gender settings on their own. The young female receptionist at my hotel in Tabuk, while confirming that it was perfectly safe for me to walk out at midnight and enjoy coffee at a nearby café, said with a big smile: 'It is Saudi Arabia. Just have your phone and camera with you and you don't have anything to fear.' I kept repeating this question to the reception staff in every city where I stayed, and whether they are local or expatriates, the answer is always the same: it is perfectly safe to go out or take a taxi as a single woman late at night. This strong sense of security that the Saudi state provides to its citizens, while partly attributable to the application of hudud punishments, which remain controversial from a human rights perspective (Amnesty International 2024a), is part of the wider infrastructure required to ensure that even men in conservative families feel secure taking their families out and letting their young daughters, sisters or wives take part in the social and economic opportunities that are now becoming available. As we will see in Chapter 7, the Saudi state's provision of a strong sense of security for life and property is quite central to understanding the foundation of the Saudi state–society relationship.

Finally, it is also important to note that ensuring the success of these reforms requires the state not just to develop the required infrastructure but also to demonstrate the ability to run it efficiently. This efficiency needs to manifest itself in the management of the technical aspects of the projects but also in the level of ease with which the public feels able to utilize these facilities. Thus, the social entertainment and tourism projects are not just offering good entertainment: they are doing so efficiently. The buses in al-Ula that take visitors on Hegra tours all provide charging facilities enabling visitors to recharge their mobiles while on the move. Further, the buses are running on electric engines in order to ensure that they are environmentally friendly – a feature the state takes active pride in for all the tourism projects. The facilities for purchase or cancellation of tickets, in my experience, are also very efficient. Sales are encouraged online, and the most important aspect of the sale is that in case an event is cancelled, the cost of the booking is automatically reimbursed on the customer's card without the need to file a request. I did not necessarily trust that information when, on arriving at the closed entrance to a newly created entertainment park in Riyadh, I was told by two Saudi girls who happened to be walking past that the park had been closed due to rain and that I should not worry about the ticket as I would be automatically reimbursed.

It was a park featuring rides for children that I had meant to explore as part of my effort to form a good sense of the range of entertainment projects that the state had developed within the past two years. Catering to ordinary Saudi families, the cost of an entry ticket for an adult was only SAR 25 ($6.5), compared with SAR 100 ($26) for Boulevard World during weekdays and SAR 150 ($40) at weekends. I thus did not expect the government to put in place an elaborate ticket-monitoring system for entrance to this park. Yet the two girls' trust in the system was valid: a few days later, I did indeed find the money credited back to my account without my having to do anything. Similarly, the online information that the Saudi government is providing on its constantly expanding list of tourist destinations is also very efficient. The 'Visit Saudi' website presents extremely useful information on all the tourist destinations, with very useful advice on where to stay, what to eat and what to do. In the absence of reliable tourist guides, given the evolving nature of these tourist facilities, this website becomes critical for tour planning. It also offers visitors ideas on possible travel itineraries across the country and provides up-to-date information on the festivals or special activities taking place during different months in different cities (Visit Saudi 2023c).

Conclusion

In line with the findings from the previous chapter, we have seen that the social norms concerning women's participation in public spaces, gender mixing, and the importance of social entertainment for individual and societal well-being have changed rapidly because the changes build on prevailing values and traditions in creative ways, instead of abandoning them. Further, the state has developed an extensive infrastructure to support this change and is running it efficiently to make it possible for the people to make alternative choices in favour of new social norms. Responding to religious and cultural cues has given the message a stickiness; if the idiom of change were entirely Western or foreign, the change would have appealed only to a few. Such an approach has been particularly appealing to the younger generation, who are now enabled to assert a much richer sense of national identity, one that draws on the pre-Islamic past as well as the grandeur of Islamic civilisation, instead of being narrowly tied to a form of Islam that they see globally associated with militant tendencies and highly restrictive of individual agency. The change has also made them part of a society that feels much more dynamic and fuller of initiative than in the past.

The evidence presented in this chapter thus does testify to the limited ability of highly restrictive religious movements to retain their hold in the modern age. At the same time, by recording the importance of Islam and traditional culture for Saudi society, the chapter has demonstrated the ability of the wider Islamic tradition to adapt to retain the loyalty of believers. It is also clear that this preference for a moderate way forward is the result of the particular composition of Saudi society. Having a much larger population than other Gulf states and enjoying a diverse culture and local traditions across different regions make it impractical for the state to force alien ideas on its people from the top. Thus, the potentially controversial entertainment options, such as the desert raves, have been aimed at the liberal elites in the big cities, and large international tourism projects, whether the development of beach resorts or futuristic cities, such as Neom (Ebrahim and al-Masri 2023), where Western cultural norms are likely to supersede any remaining Islamic prohibitions, are being developed in areas where there is not settled Saudi population. These locations are likely to remain pockets of entertainment that are largely closed off from the wider society. The state's overall respect for people's preference for a moderate way forward, rather than enforcing a liberalization agenda that does not reflect public sentiments, suggests that the initial success we have seen is partly a product of this responsiveness.

What the nature of the on-going change, and its management, tells us about the dynamic of state–society relationship in Saudi Arabia is an issue that we will address in detail in Chapter 7. Before that, it is important to note that despite the state's pushback against Wahhabi rigidity and its attempt to reposition itself as a modern progressive nation, there are no signs of the Crown Prince wanting to relinquish the royal family's claim to being the leader of the Muslim world and the associated soft power it enjoys on the international stage. In the next chapter, I explore how promoting the social liberalization agenda at home does not diminish the Saudi state's use of Mecca and Medina as sites for reinforcing the Saudi royal family's claim as the rightful guardians of these sites and, by extension, as rightful leaders of the Muslim world and promoters of the most authentic teachings of Islam. Asserting religious legitimacy, despite curtailing the power of the religious establishment at home, will, in my assessment, remain a key feature of the Saudi state's survival strategy, including that of the Crown Prince. This is evident, as we will see in the next chapter, in the on-going expansion work in Mecca and Medina under his leadership, alongside the promotion of tourism and social entertainment in the rest of the country.

Chapter 6

ISLAM'S ENDURING INFLUENCE

The large number of South Asian pilgrims in the women's sections of Masjid-i-Nabawi (the Prophet's Mosque, in Medina) makes their presence noticeable, as it does in the Masjid-i-Haram (the Great Mosque, in Mecca). A visit to the *rawdah* (the green carpeted area between the *minbar*, pulpit and the chamber of Prophet Muhammad in the Masjid al-Nabawi, which is next to his grave; it is also referred to as the *Riyad al-Jannah* and is believed to be a part of heaven), though optional, is for most pilgrims an essential part of ʻumrah and hajj. Most spend at least seven days in Medina, either before or after performing the obligatory rituals in Mecca. During the days in Medina, on at least one morning, if not all, these women are exposed to the halaqah led by a fiery female preacher of Pakistani origin. Appointed as one of the official preachers by the Saudi authorities responsible for managing the educational programmes inside Masjid-i-Nabawi, she preaches to the women as they wait for an opportunity to enter the rawdah. Having a strong voice, and frequently slipping into Punjabi, a provincial language which sounds like an uncouth version of Urdu, although she mainly teaches in the latter, her halaqahs command attention. Unlike the sobriety or strict decorum that one expects from the Wahhabi or Salafi female preachers, she demonstrates the energy and wit of the common people, frequently drawing on popular vocabulary from Punjabi culture, which hooks her audience, which primarily consists of Pakistani, Indian and Bangladeshi women from low- and middle-income backgrounds – although women from other income groups are also present. Her halaqahs adopt a different structure from those led by other female preachers, who are mostly of Arab or African origin and are assigned to teach a set course to a fixed group of enrolled students, mostly locals or long-term residents in Medina. Instead, her halaqah is designed to fill the time as these women wait after *Ishraq* (an optional prayer to be performed just after sunrise) to enter the rawdah – a wait which, until a recent change of rules, was long and unpredictable. This unpredictability had consequences for the mood of the listeners and their assessment of the Saudi government's management of the haramayn.

The process of seeking entry to the rawdah in the women's section has improved since the end of the COVID pandemic, due to the introduction of an app for mandatory booking of a fixed time slot. In the pre-COVID period, the management of Masjid-i-Nabawi used a set of arbitrary rules, including wilful deception, to manage the large crowds of female pilgrims, who in their zeal to gain access to the rawdah would push and pull with a fervour that would result in loud screams violating the decorum that is expected of pilgrims: one should approach the rawdah respectfully in silence, while sending *salawat* (to pray for divine blessing on Prophet Muhammad), and say two *nafl*s (a type of optional prayer, which is not obligatory but promises reward), and then exit. The resulting chaos was, and still is, a result of excessive zeal, but it was also a product of the unpredictability that marked the management of the process.

Entry to the rawdah, in the pre-COVID period, required moving through a number of barriers at the right time, while the cut-off time remained unspecified. Entry doors opened, for an hour or slightly more, three times during the day: after Ishraq, *Zuhr* (obligatory noon prayer), and *'Isha'*. To visit the rawdah after Ishraq prayer, normally performed around 6.30 a.m., one had to ensure arrival at the mosque at least an hour and a half before the *Fajr* (obligatory dawn prayer) in order to occupy a place in the front-most section, doors to which closed as soon as it became full. Having made it to this section, however, did not guarantee access, for the front section was further divided into three parallel sections, each with a door that led to the rawdah. Women were assigned to these three sections, which were divided by barriers, according to their nationality. The cause of panic, however, was that on any given day it was not obvious which of the three gates the management would open first; and, at times, only two gates were opened, so that those waiting behind the third door would not gain access at all. Thus, women who might have come to the mosque at 3 a.m. at night to ensure access to the rawdah after Ishraq prayer still risked not securing entry after waiting for more than four or five hours.

It was during this wait that most women ended up joining the halaqah of this preacher. They thus comprised a critical audience. Most were tired, due to the long wait. Many would normally come to sit down next to women sitting around the preacher, not realizing that someone was delivering a sermon. Further, in every halaqah that I have attended, a few in the audience were always of the Barelvi orientation, a South Asian Islamic tradition with a strong emphasis on the worship of saints, who openly expressed their reservations about Wahhabi teachings. Yet, over the seven years in which I have repeatedly joined this halaqah and observed the women engage with this preacher, I have found her highly effective in winning over those who did not have a prior attachment to a particular school of thought or Sufi tariqah. After sitting there for a few minutes, most women started to listen attentively to the preacher, and they followed up with active questions addressed to her, primarily aimed at seeking clarification on various issues. By the end of the halaqah, the majority of the women present requested the preacher to add them to her WhatsApp group, through which she circulates regular messages. During these visits, I also routinely came across women who had previously visited Masjid-i-Nabawi and expressed gratitude to her for her on-going guidance. The affection that they showed always appeared genuine. While the messages that she sends on WhatsApp may help to enrich the knowledge of a few, more striking was the impact that she could have during the one and a half hours of her halaqah.

By addressing a set of loosely structured themes, this preacher was able to engage many women with Salafi teachings. Part of the credit was due to her engaging style and powerful personality, but it was also evident that the clarity and appeal of her message played a significant role. Despite its being explicitly framed within a Wahhabi framework, it was difficult to identify anything contentious in her teaching.

By devoting the early part of this chapter to documenting the existence of this halaqah, which is part of the extensive teaching infrastructure supported by the state inside the Masjid-i-Nabawi and remains intact after ongoing reforms, I aim to first demonstrate how the state's ambition to utilize Mecca and Medina as sites for asserting Saudi Arabia's leadership in the Muslim world and its role as the most authentic interpreter of Islamic teachings remains undeterred. Further, by analysing what was compelling about her teaching, I will try to provide an insight into why the teaching of 'aqidah using the Wahhabi methodological approach, when checked for its excessive zeal, mainly its propensity to declare takfir on fellow Muslims for presumed transgressions such as visiting the shrines, can be so compelling. In doing so, I will connect my own findings with the growing literature on Salafi networks and movements as they operate in different Muslim-majority contexts (Thurston 2016; Eyre 2021; Diwan 2021; Russell 2021; Rock-Singer 2022) and among Muslim-diaspora communities (Inge 2017). By mapping the organic nature of these movements, these studies question the popular perception that the global spread of Salafism over the past five decades can primarily be attributed to the Saudi state's financing of the necessary infrastructure for its spread. These studies have established the role of local socio-political dynamics in the evolution of Salafi movements in different contexts, and explained their appeal in terms of the religious certainty that it offers, and its methodological emphasis on quoting directly from the Quran and Sunnah to support its positions. In this chapter, I will examine in detail those aspects of Wahhabi teachings that make it so compelling for lay Muslims who are not strongly attached to a particular school of thought.

The chapter, in addition, demonstrates that the Saudi state has continued to entrust the teaching of 'aqidah to the Wahhabi establishment by leaving responsibility for managing the mosques in its hands. Just as the social sphere, despite opening up, is retaining Saudi religious and cultural influences, the power of the religious establishment is being curtailed and its excesses checked, but there is no attempt afoot to replace the Wahhabi establishment with the promotion of an alternative religious authority. Unlike Muhammad al-Sisi of Egypt, who actively courted al-Azhari scholars in the aftermath of the 2013 coup in order to undermine the religious legitimacy of the Muslim Brotherhood (Bano and Benadi 2017), or unlike Sheikh Mohammed bin Rashid Al Maktoum, Prime Minister and Ruler of Dubai, who is actively promoting scholars associated with more mystical or philosophical approaches to Islam, including influential teachers such as Shaykh Bin Bayyah and Hamza Yusuf, in order to enhance his image as a liberal Islamic reformer, the Crown Prince of Saudi Arabia has not tried to actively promote an alternative network of religious scholars to side-line the Wahhabi establishment. Given the bold announcements made by the Crown Prince pledging to 'return

Saudi Arabia to moderate Islam', a similar strategy to visibly replace the Wahhabi scholarly elite could have been adopted (BBC 2017a; Chulov 2017).

Hammond (2021) notes how under the Crown Prince, the Saudi state has sought to disseminate the trope of Saudi Arabia entering 'post-Wahhabi era' in Western media and policy circles utilizing a large network of public relations firms, Gulf-funded think tanks and even academics. Instead, the Saudi state is choosing to focus only on reining in the excesses of Wahhabi teachings. This, in my assessment, has been an effective strategy in winning legitimacy within the public for reforms aimed at social liberalization, especially the more conservative segments, as this approach is more consistent with the public's preference for a moderate approach to reform recorded in the preceding chapters. Curtailing the excesses of Wahhabi teachings is much less controversial and, as analysed in previous chapters, is a shift actively welcomed by the young but to replace the sobriety of the Wahhabi establishment with scholars who are seen as too liberal or lax in their approach to interpreting Islamic rulings in order to conform with modern reality can make many young Saudis uncomfortable given Saudi society's preference for social reform to stay moderate (Thompson 2019). Allowing the Wahhabi establishment continued control over the teaching of basic principles of Islam to the next generations of Saudis also reduces the chances of the emergence of resistance from within the Wahhabi establishment. Thus, being an effective strategy from the perspective of the Crown Prince and his close advisors.

The important question, then, is how realistic it is to leave the teaching of 'aqidah in the hands of the Wahhabi establishment while expecting it not to indulge in its excesses. This question requires observation of the debates within the Salafi scholarly sphere in Saudi Arabia over the next few years. However, in this chapter, I demonstrate how, within the global Salafi scholarly milieu, where like-minded scholars are interconnected (Isamil 2021), particularly due to many of them having studied at the International University of Medina (Farquhar 2017), ongoing debates already allow for the exercise of increased social liberties. This is evident in the work of Yasir Qadhi (Razavian 2018b), who, upon returning to the USA after his years in Medina, had to provide meaningful responses to young Muslims wanting to be active participants in socially liberal spaces in the West. I draw on the growing scholarship on his contributions, which is leading to debates on post-Salafism (Razavian 2018b). I also highlight how the existence of scholars such as Hatim al-Awni within Saudi Arabia, whom Qadhi views as a like-minded scholar (Qadhi 2018), indicates the possibility of similar discourses gaining traction within the Saudi Wahhabi and Salafi scholarly spheres. However, I consciously choose not to draw on the work of Salman al-Awda or other scholars associated with the al-sahwah movement, as their primary focus has been on demands for political liberties and is well recorded (Lacroix 2011; al-Rasheed 2015). Given the analytical focus of this volume, I aim to exclusively show how some scholars trained within the Wahhabi Salafi tradition are today also presenting arguments in favour of increased social and religious liberties.

Whether the appeal of such scholars will grow within Saudi society, or the state will find them useful partners to legitimize its social liberalization agenda, will need to be studied over time. The purpose of the analysis presented here is to highlight that this is one possibility. Such a development could potentially offer a win-win situation for the Saudi state, society and the clerics. It helps to mitigate the risk of two extreme outcomes: the Saudi state actively working to side-line Wahhabi preachers by promoting scholars from other traditions, or some members of the Wahhabi religious elite leading a vocal or violent resistance against the on-going reforms. The clerics retain their hold over the transmission of basic Islamic knowledge to the next generation and promotion of individual piety with a continued emphasis on teaching about the purity of ʿaqidah, and society continues to benefit from the services of a well-trained religious clergy that offers high-quality spiritual services in well-run mosques, while people can enjoy a greater degree of freedom than before to decide their own religious actions, and, the Saudi state continues to assert its claim to being the guardian of authentic Islam, thus retaining legitimacy in the eyes of Muslim believers for its claim to the title of Custodian of the Two Holy Mosques, while at the same time actively repositioning itself as a modernizing force.

Finally, by mapping the state's continued commitment to managing the two holy mosques and its ongoing investment in their expansion, this chapter demonstrates how the Crown Prince, like his predecessors, is eager to assert the religious legitimacy and claim to leadership of the Muslim world that come with overseeing Mecca and Medina. At the same time, he is positioning Saudi Arabia as a modernizing force. In line with the findings in previous chapters, this chapter shows that, based on developments to date, the Crown Prince is skilfully manoeuvring to maintain this balance. In the previous chapters, we saw that the state's commitment to opening up Saudi society is genuine, but there is a conscious effort to inform the social sphere with Saudi religious and cultural values. This chapter similarly shows that while the state is committed to curbing the excessive zeal of Wahhabi teachings, this does not mean that either the Saudi state or Saudi society is questioning its commitment to Islam itself.

6.1. Ordinary believers and the appeal of Wahhabi teachings

The basis of Islamic faith is the expression of tawhid, *la ilaha illa Allah* (there is no god but Allah). The teaching of tawhid is thus at the core of Islamic teaching. However, while making a Muslim child or a convert memorize this basic principle is easy, building an understanding of what this belief entails and how to develop real conviction in it is a highly complex process. What are the characteristics of this God that we believe in? What does He expect from the believer? What is the best way to approach Him? These are but a few of the complex questions that mark the natural progression in the thought of a believer who takes religion seriously. While they are discussed in great depth by early Islamic theologians and philosophers (Walbridge 2010; Bano 2020), in contemporary times, most Islamic scholarly traditions avoid addressing these complex questions in their teachings to the lay public.

Instead of addressing the complexity of these questions, the focus mostly is on instilling belief in one God through building conviction in the idea of an omnipotent God, and the teaching itself focuses mainly on the importance of establishing daily five time prayers (*salah*), imparting knowledge about how to perform core ritual obligations, teaching basic moral principles, and addressing the issues of what is *halal* (legitimate) and what is *haram* (forbidden in Islamic law) in everyday life (Bano 2012). More sophisticated audiences move towards discussions about operationalizing core principles of shariʿah to apply to present-day realities (Bano 2017). On the other hand, there are the Sufi tariqahs: Instead of engaging with Islamic legal debates, here the emphasis is on cultivating one's spiritual relationship with God by focusing on purifying the *qalb* (heart) through ritualized practices, the most important of which is the daily *dhikr* (remembrance of God). Drawing on a closer examination of the teachings of the female preacher profiled above, in this section we will see that the appeal of Wahhabi teaching is very much determined by the same issue, which has also historically led to its excesses: its explicit focus on discussing complicated questions concerning ʿaqidah with lay Muslims and giving very clear guidelines on how to seek closeness to God.

Ibn Abd al-Wahhab wrote as many as eighteen books, but the one most alluded to Kitab is -al-Tawhid (Book of Unity). In this short book, he spelt out his understanding of ʿaqidah. A preacher rather than an erudite scholar, in his books, Ibn Abd al-Wahhab did not attempt to present a complex intellectual analysis of the theme at hand; instead, his books are noticeable for their analytical simplicity. Consistent with this approach, Kitab-al-Tawhid makes no attempt to present a complex analysis of the subject by considering the nuances of meaning of an Arabic word, or referring to the complexity of Arabic grammar or trying to interpret a verse in the light of other verses – methods that Islamic scholars belonging to different madhhabs deploy to ensure that individual verses of the Quran are not taken out of context (Hallaq 2009). Instead, the short book, divided into sixty-seven chapters, follows a very simple method and structure: each chapter heading introduces one aspect of tawhid and is directly followed by presentations of Quranic verses that relate to it. The subsequent section lists related hadiths, or narrations by Companions of the Prophet. Only in the final section, entitled 'Important Issues of the Chapter', does Ibn Abd al-Wahhab express his views by listing in bullet points the key lessons that he asserts must be drawn from the above.

There is no attempt to complicate the debates, unlike the complexity reflected in the methodological evolution of the four key Sunni madhhabs or in the tense and intellectually intense exchanges between *the al-muʿtazilites* (those representing a distinct school of speculative Islamic theology) and the traditionalists on this subject in the thirteenth century (Hallaq 2009). Instead, the simplicity of his method and the assertive tone of his conclusions suggest that each individual verse of the Quran can be studied in isolation, and its meaning can be interpreted easily without contention and with any remaining need for clarity being secured by reference to the hadith. It is this very methodological approach that today underpins the Salafi method of reasoning, whereby works of earlier scholars are set aside, and emphasis is placed on direct engagement with the Quran and

Sunnah (Haykel 2015; Commins 2009). Combined with the Hanbalis' preference for textual literalism, inherited by the Wahhabi 'ulama', such a methodological approach leads to the assertion of absolutist claims about what is right and what is wrong. Thus, across the sixty-seven chapters, Ibn Abd al-Wahhab is quick to declare even basic acts of bid'ah a shirk. His judgement on what is right or wrong is absolute.

While this absolutist approach to interpreting texts is viewed as resulting in the excesses associated with Wahhabi teachings, closer examination of the discussions between the women pilgrims and the female preacher at Masjid-i-Nabawi shows why this simplicity of message and the clarity of focus can often be very compelling when preaching to a lay audience. In her one-and-a-half-hour session, she would talk with great certainty and simplicity about the core aspects of the 'aqidah. She raised questions related to one's faith in God. Many in her audience were vaguely familiar with the concerns that she raised, but those were not the central focus of the basic Islamic education that they received when growing up. In the repeated halaqahs that I have attended with her, I have seen her follow a similar flow of arguments, given that she was addressing a new audience each day. The core of her teachings could be divided into three parts: explaining the demands of 'aqidah to establish a direct connection with God without any intermediaries; the related demand to have unlimited faith in destiny, 'God's will'; and guidance on the correct way to approach God and win closeness to Him, by performing the rituals correctly. By addressing these issues, she was able to leave the audience with a vision of a God who is entirely self-sufficient and in control of an individual's destiny, while at the same time so directly accessible to the believer that even His favourite subject, Muhammad, is always described as a 'messenger' and not as an intermediary.

Further, like the writings of Ibn Abd al-Wahhab, in an attempt to convince her audience of these demands, she relied on only two sources, the Quran and Sunnah, and on occasions she also drew on examples from the lives of the companions of the Prophet. In order to assert the authenticity of her message, she carried a set of laminated A4-sized coloured sheets which were loosely bound together at the end of a two-foot-long wooden stick that she held firmly against the ground. Each sheet carried a Quranic verse or a *sahih hadith* (authentic saying of the Prophet) with exact references to which she constantly referred when building an argument. This had the expected impact on her audience, who then began to show attentiveness. Even those who could initially be seen whispering to each other about her Wahhabi orientation, or were directly challenging her, started to pay attention and ask her questions, rather than voicing their disagreement. It was the ability of the Wahhabi approach to teaching 'aqidah to establish the beauty of developing a direct connection with God, giving very clear guidelines on how to do so and supporting the arguments by extensively quoting from the Quran and Sunnah, that, in my observation, helped this preacher to convince women of the authenticity of her teachings.

Her halaqahs normally began by addressing the importance of understanding God's demands of the human being, as part of the Islamic 'aqidah. Often starting by reminding the women of their good fortune in being invited by God to visit Mecca and Medina, she would smoothly transition to highlighting that in return, they were obliged to be grateful to Him and live according to the guidelines that He has provided in the Quran. Spending some time discussing the Quranic verse, 'I did not create jinn and humans except to worship me' (51:56), she would emphasize to the woman, 'Allah says, I created you only to worship me'. She took time to highlight how the primary purpose of life is to worship God and seek closeness to Him. Arguing that the Quran states that true human intellect requires listening not only to one's powers of reason but equally to the heart, she would advise the women of the need to seek God's guidance and follow one's heart, in response to which God will guide one to the right way of worshipping Him. In between, she also kept reminding these women how their time on this earth is transitory and that real happiness rests in cultivating a direct connection with God, which requires following His dictates as stated in the Quran and Sunnah.

Guiding the women on the practical details of how to worship God correctly, she did not immediately move to a focus on the performance of obligatory rituals, such as the five daily prayers or the giving of zakat. Instead, she focused on the broader principle of belief, whereby true 'aqidah requires one not just to perform the ritual but to do every action with a view to winning the love of God. Thus, she would tell the women in her audience how even the simple act of meeting a friend can be an act of worship if one goes to that friend because she loves Allah; but that, devoid of that intention, the act is a waste of one's time. Noting that 'Allah does not want attachment and enjoyment for its own sake, He wants attachment only to Him', she continued: 'I love my mother not because she is my mother, I do it because Allah said be good to your parents. I love my children not because I bore them for nine months, I love them because they are Allah's *amanat* (trust). God does not want that you develop an attachment with anyone more than with him.' Emphasizing that every action should be for God, she advised the women to even ask for blessings from Allah with the intention that they will help bring them closer to God. Ask Allah in these terms, she advised her audience: 'Give me a son so that I can teach him to work in the way of Allah; give me long life so that I can do things that bring me close to God.'

The second issue that she would routinely highlight in explaining how to worship God correctly was the need to follow the example of the Prophet. She would make this point repeatedly by referring to Quranic texts which urge Muslims to follow the Quran and the example of the Prophet if they want to be on the right path. She would also quote examples from the Prophet's life and quote hadith in support of the points that she was making. But it was in this very context that she would also keep highlighting the need not to think of anyone as a mediator in shaping one's relationship with God. She would keep emphasizing how prophets are to be followed, but it is critical that neither they nor any pious men be treated as mediators, given that the Quran makes it clear that even the Prophet Muhammad is just a messenger, who, as she would always elaborate, 'has no power to influence any individual's *qadr* (predestination), which is entirely in the hands of God'.

This emphasis on cultivating a direct connection with God and believing in qadr as part of the core aspects of Islamic ʻaqidah was the second key theme in her teachings. Repeatedly, she would highlight that we must face with forbearance the challenges that we confront and put our trust entirely in God. She would go on to elaborate how individuals who we think are the cause of our pain have in reality no power to harm us 'if Allah had not written that test in our destiny'. In every halaqah, she chose to elaborate on this point by giving examples of issues that affected most of the women in her audience, who were mainly traditional housewives. Teaching the women that God expects them to be patient, given that in the Quran He has promised rewards to those who are patient, she would repeatedly advise the women, 'If your husband is angry, go to him with a smile, as it is his right. If he is cheating, don't cry. Pray for him to be guided to the right path. Allah says cover the faults of others, don't publicise and disclose.' She always emphasized that the fact that the other party is doing wrong does not absolve you from the responsibility that God has placed on you to follow the right path.

Thus, she taught that believing in qadr did not absolve one of the responsibility to do the right deeds. Instead, the essence of the message was that the idea of tawhid required us to believe that both good and bad comes from God, and therefore one has to remain moral and righteous in the face of adversity by observing the righteous behaviour as prescribed in the Quran and Sunnah. In this vein, she would continue to advise these women, 'Still do your wifely roles, still be pleasant to him [your husband], as God asks that of a wife. If he does not improve, then he is the one deprived of God's blessing. He is the oppressor in this context. But if you do the right things, then you become closer to God in the process, and he [the husband] becomes the one who has failed, the one actually oppressed.'

I repeatedly found that this example proved very effective in engaging the women in her audience, most of whom lived in economically difficult conditions and households where gender norms were still largely patriarchal. Many asked follow-up questions regarding what is the right way to cope with specific challenges of marital life. Here she also made the argument more compelling for these women by sharing her experience of Saudi women, who, she would argue, have much stronger faith in qadr and thus deal with hardship with more resilience. This, in turn, she credited to their better understanding of ʻaqidah. A story that she narrated with great enthusiasm and compelling power in almost every halaqah was that of her female Saudi neighbour who had a difficult husband. Whenever the preacher tried to console her by trying to talk to her about her domestic troubles, her neighbour would say, 'Should I complain to you about my Allah, who has put me in this test? This was written in my qadr five hundred thousand years ago.'

For most of the South Asian women in the audience, whose exposure to Islamic teachings is normally quite basic and revolves around the performance of obligatory rituals (Bano 2017), this emphasis on looking at every action in life through the lens of one's belief in God, and how each action can bring one closer to God, when stated with absolute clarity becomes compelling. Not only do these women get the message that by putting one in a difficult position, 'Allah has given her an opportunity for earning *thawab* (reward) by observing correct moral behaviour in face of adversity', they also find the message liberating due to its emphasis on recognizing that no human being has the ability to harm another unless Allah has allowed for that. It is not that these women did not know that the Islamic faith expects them to believe that everything is in the hands of God; what the preacher does is to engage with this idea in depth and make it real for them by giving examples of issues from their own lives.

The certainty with which she talks also helps to build conviction among the listeners. This ability to make believers actively think and reflect about the demands of 'aqidah, rather than just focusing on the performance of rituals, is what makes Wahhabi teachings very compelling to such a lay audience. It is also important to note that in her teachings, while explicitly shunning the idea of intercession and related practices of saint or shrine worship, she does not go into the issues that have made Wahhabi teachings contentious: the declaration of takfir on fellow Muslims, or the idea of enforcing religious virtue through state action. This distinction is key to understanding why Wahhabi Salafi teachings can appeal to many ordinary Muslims: Minus their excesses, these teachings are very compelling in directing believers how to cultivate a strong 'aqidah.

In addition to addressing these more foundational questions of belief, she also allowed time for addressing questions that asked for clarity on some of the issues discussed above or asked about the correct ways of performing rituals. One of the themes that she emphasized a lot in this regard was the best way to say the *du'a'* (supplication). Quoting from the practice of the Prophet, she emphasized to the women that the best way to perform du'a' is to say it when one is in sujud. She noted how the South Asian way of saying the prayer by holding one's hands together in front of oneself is not the preferred way, due to ample evidence that the Prophet preferred otherwise. In every halaqah, when she said that, one would see many women whispering to each other that they did not know that important fact. The reason why they found this convincing was that it is well known in the Muslim tradition that being in sujud is a posture dear to God, as it shows man's complete submission.

She would advise the women, 'Ask God for favours, always when you are in sujud not by holding up your hands. In sujud say Allah, guide me, teach me and he will guide you.' In between, she would also touch on lighter subjects such as reminding the audience that one should eat with the right hand and make dhikr, and with the left hand one should make wudu'; or the need to ensure that whenever one starts something, one must say *Bismillah* (in the name of God). 'If you don't start with His name, He will take the blessing away,' she would emphasize. She would also remind them of the etiquette of visiting the two mosques, giving advice such as 'Whenever you come into Allah's house, make du'a' for the house'; or that on entering the rawdah, one should act with calm and only say two nafls and then leave, to allow space for women waiting behind, instead of attempting to say many nafls. Women raised many questions seeking further clarity on these issues.

Thus, a halaqah that most women joined unconsciously, routinely, had a highly engaged audience by the end of it. The majority of listeners went up to the preacher at the end, asking for private advice on their personal circumstances, most of which revolved around challenges that they faced at home; others requested advice on how to continue to enhance their knowledge of Islam. Many ended up requesting her to add them to her WhatsApp group, on which she regularly circulates religious material that takes the form of five-minute videos that she prepares on a topic, with photos of key Quranic verses or hadith with translations, recommendations about Islamic publications to read and links to speeches or sermons of prominent scholars of Salafi orientation. It is this very aspect of Wahhabi teachings, its ability to focus on establishing the purity of Islamic ʿaqidah and direct connection with God which, despite the excesses associated with Wahhabism, historically helped the Wahhabi establishment to develop a degree of voluntary following in the Najd region (Commins 2009; Spannaus 2018a), despite its being embedded by means of political force in the initial period.

This factor is also core to explaining the continued resilience of strong Salafi movements across many Muslim countries, as well as among the Muslim diaspora, even when the Saudi state has reduced its support for global Salafi daʿwah (Bano 2021; Mandaville 2022). Yet it is also very important to remember that these discourses become more sophisticated according to the background of the audience. Thus, the scholarship of Salafi movements, due to their often being focused on discourses of the Salafi preachers and their active followers or those of Salafi jihadi groups, ends up highlighting the polarizing aspects of the Salafi teaching by focusing on theologically more complicated concepts such as takfir (Maher 2016). As demonstrated here for the ordinary lay Muslims, the basic appeal of Salafi teachings rests in helping them to build their own relationship with God, rather than regulating the behaviour of others. Recognizing this, as we will see in the next sections, is important in order to appreciate why a slightly reformed Wahhabi Salafi movement might prove effective in retaining a local and global following.

6.2. Demanding moderation: The approach of the Saudi state

If the clarity of the Wahhabi teachings about basic ʿaqidah and rituals works for the pilgrims, they continue to work for the Saudi royal family and Saudi society in general, too. Despite the clear reversal of support for the Wahhabi establishment's excessive zeal to regulate individual religious behaviour, and especially in the social sphere, as documented in this volume, it is clear that the state and society are happy to leave the teaching about the fundamentals of ʿaqidah, and basic Islamic teachings and performance of religious rituals, in the hands of the Wahhabi establishment, which continues to regulate the provision of basic Islamic education and ritual services in the mosques. The social endorsement of these services is evident in the full attendance at the mosques, with packed congregation halls for Jumʿah (Friday congregational prayer) and also for special prayers such as the daily *tarawih* prayer (special prayers said after ʿIshaʾ prayer during Ramadan, often involving reading large portions of the Quran) and the Eid prayers. It is also evident in the continuity of imams from within the Wahhabi establishment in the religious leadership at the two holy mosques in Mecca and Medina,[1] where services are still of very high quality, and unchanged from the way in which they were conducted before 2016. It is clear that the royal family remains keen to demonstrate its ability to be the legitimate bearer of the title of the Custodian of the Two Holy Mosques and trusts the ability of the Wahhabi religious establishment to provide religious services of a quality that leaves the pilgrims spiritually satisfied.

It is well-established that the Al-Saud family, upon taking control of Mecca, undertook highly controversial measures, such as destroying many historical remains from the time of the Prophet and his companions, as well as deliberately eroding the remnants of the Ottoman legacy in the area (Bsheer 2020). However, to gain legitimacy, it also ensured it performed well on certain core expectations. Ensuring the safety and comfort of the pilgrims en route to Mecca has historically been critical for any Muslim ruler who wished to win popular legitimacy as the rightful guardian of the two holy mosques (al-Sarhan 2016). On acquiring control over Hejaz, King Abdulaziz took responsibility for ensuring the security of the pilgrim routes seriously (al-Sarhan 2016). He also showed commitment to improving the services available to the pilgrims at the two mosques and to investing in the development of their physical infrastructure, with the aim of increasing the size of the prayer area but also of improving the safety of the existing structures. The expansion of these two revered mosques started in the time of the early caliphs to meet the need of the steadily growing Muslim community: Umar ibn al-Khattib, for instance, built a wall around the Ka'bah in the year 638. The developments continued under different Muslim dynasties that controlled the Hejaz region over the centuries (Macaulay 2015). The Abbasid Caliph al-Mahdi (775–785) rebuilt damaged areas of the Masjid-i-Haram, just as in 1571, Ottoman Sultan Selim II directed the court architect Sinan to make improvements to the building (Macaulay 2015). The expansion of the two mosques under the Saudi royal family was, however, on a totally different scale (Macaulay 2015). This was the product of three related factors: improved technology facilitating rapid and more complicated construction; the introduction of commercial flights, which resulted in a dramatic increase in the number of pilgrims to Mecca from the 1970s onwards; and the Saudi oil wealth, which made it possible for the royal family to commit large funds to support the expansion plans.

The first Saudi expansion of Masjid-i-Haram began in 1955 during the reign of King Saud, and when it was completed in 1973 the total constructed areas of the mosque had been extended from about 290,000 square feet (27,000 square metres) to about 1,630,000 square feet (152,000 square metres) (Arab News 2020), and the mosque could accommodate 500,000 worshippers. The second expansion project started under King Fahd in 1984, raising the mosque capacity to accommodate a million worshippers. King Abdullah, who took the throne in 2005, initiated the third major expansion. Still on-going, under this plan the capacity of the *mataf* area (the area immediate around the Ka'bah where tawaf takes place), where Muslims perform seven rounds of *tawaf*) was increased three times: it now accommodates 130,000 people an hour, compared with 50,000 people prior to the third expansion (Arab News 2020). In 2015, King Salman further launched five additional projects designed to allow the mosque to accommodate nearly two million worshippers (Arab News 2020). Neighbouring properties worth billions of dollars have been acquired to allow for continued expansion of the mosque area. Similar expansions have happened in Masjid-i-Nawabi under Saudi rule, so that today the mosque has the capacity to accommodate over 600,000 worshippers at one time. These expansion projects have equally focused on ensuring fine aesthetics, so that the two mosques offer visually very appealing spaces to the worshippers, while being very comfortable. They are fully air-conditioned, keeping the internal prayer areas very cool and comfortable, even while there is simmering heat outside. In the case of Masjid-i-Nabawi, even the outside prayer areas are covered with canopies (very aesthetically designed and strongly built). When fully open, these canopies do not merely provide the worshippers with very effective protection from rays of the scorching sun when they are performing the mid-day prayer, especially during the summer months: They also make the courtyard look very pleasing.

While this chapter opened with a description of the chaos that marks the process of female pilgrims securing access to the rawdah, it is important to recognize that this happens in a context of overall fairly effective management of the two mosques by the responsible state authorities. Controlling large zealous crowds intent on gaining access to the Ka'bah or to the rawdah at any given time is not an easy feat for any regulatory authority. While there is scope for improvement in the management of access to the rawdah, the Saudi management of the two mosques leaves most pilgrims overall satisfied. They appreciate the focus on maintaining a high level of cleanliness in the two mosques, which are crowded with worshippers around the clock. Masjid-i-Haram, in particular, is never without large crowds at any given moment during the day or night. Ensuring this level of cleanliness requires an efficient oversight of the whole process, which involves a large team of cleaners and senior managers, playing their roles efficiently around the clock. The large number of cleaners can be seen constantly cleaning different parts of the mosques, while also having to manage the movement of worshippers from one section to the other. They have to make large crowds move swiftly from one area to another in order to ensure that all parts of the mosques are vacated for 10–15 minutes during the day for proper cleaning. A combination of cleaning techniques, some involving heavy machinery, is used to ensure proper cleaning of carpeted areas, bare floors and areas that get wet.

The constant supply of Zamzam water inside the two mosques for two or three million pilgrims on a daily basis is another major management project in its own right. In the simmering heat, constant free supplies of any kind of clean drinking water are to be valued, but to have free and non-stop access to Zamzam water is such a privilege for a believing Muslim that it cannot go unnoticed. Again, a large team of workers, with distinct roles, can be seen at work around the clock, replacing empty water barrels with fresh ones, replacing used plastic cups with clean ones, and constantly cleaning the surrounding areas, which get wet when pilgrims try to walk around with water cups or pass them on to fellow pilgrims. While the physical labour is provided by thousands of South Asian workers employed by the management authorities, senior Saudi officials can be seen actively overseeing the process to guarantee quality. Managing the public toilet facilities that cater to millions of pilgrims on a daily basis is another key service, which the management of the two mosques executes with high levels of efficiency. Given the large numbers and the very mixed profiles of the pilgrims, the level of cleanliness maintained in the toilets is often appreciated by the pilgrims. The need to be in wudu all the time means that most pilgrims have to use these public toilets even if they are staying in hotels immediately around Masjid-i-Haram.

In all these administrative areas, the teams act in a highly disciplined way and follow a set routine which is clearly a product of complex planning and learning through experience over the years. The development of extensive commercial areas, featuring malls, stores, restaurants, and international hotels around Masjid-i-Haram since the 1970s often provokes criticism that such commercialization clashes with the spiritual ethos of the haramayn (Bsheer 2020). It is, however, also true that the proximity of hotels, restaurants, cafés and stores makes access to these facilities easy for the worshippers, most of whom are keen to fulfil these basic needs promptly in order to spend most of their time inside the mosque. The on-going expansion plans for the mosque, however, involve the deconstruction of parts of this commercial infrastructure so that, as the prayer area is expanded to allow for more worshippers, the access to these facilities is pushed a bit further away. The area immediately around the current boundaries of Masjid-i-Haram is thus constantly being reshaped.

In addition to offering good infrastructure and services within the two mosques, the Saudi government has historically placed much emphasis, and it still does, on ensuring that the pilgrims have a good spiritual experience: imams who are known to be the best Quranic reciters are appointed to lead the prayers at the two mosques. The role of the imams becomes particularly important during the month of Ramadan, when, during the final *'ashrah* (the last ten days of Ramadan), the number of pilgrims is as high as it is during hajj. The requirement to perform the tarawih prayers during Ramadan makes the role of the Quranic reciters very important for the spiritual experience of the pilgrims. While hajj follows a fixed set of rituals which are physically taxing, performing the 'umrah during Ramadan is an act of optional worship, but one which confers very high merit. The performance of tarawih prayers, which consist of twenty *rak'ah* (a 'unit' of ritual prayer in Islam consisting of a combination of certain prayers and actions). A full prayer, salah, is composed of multiple rak'ahs, involves the imam completing recitation of one full chapter of the Quran each night, so that the full Quran has been recited by the end of the month. The daily tarawih prayer thus lasts for up to an hour. Further, in the last ten days of Ramadan, the two mosques also host *kayam-i-leil* (night vigil), which takes place after midnight and lasts for over an hour. During this prayer, different sections of the Quran are recited. The beauty of the Quranic recitation by the reciters at the two mosques routinely makes men and women, including on occasion even the imam himself, start to weep.

Furthermore, the most convincing evidence that the Saudi royal family, including the Crown Prince, views efficient management of the haramayn as a crucial source of winning moral legitimacy in the eyes of the wider Muslim community is the hospitality offered to pilgrims during iftar. In my assessment, this hospitality has been further enhanced post-reforms. Iftar is an extremely joyous occasion in both mosques. Due to conscious efforts made by the Saudi state and the public, the crowds of worshippers opening the fast during Ramadan in each of the two mosques receive, as a minimum, a portion of dates and water, and many get additional food items, ranging from small snacks to proper meals, as different groups distribute items in different sections of the two mosques. Keeping these large and complex systems working, with a high degree of predictability and efficiency, requires a competent bureaucracy on the part of the management authority responsible for each mosque and indicates to the pilgrims that the royal family is committed to ensuring effective management of these two holy mosques.

Having done fieldwork in the two mosques during 2015 and 2016 and then again in 2022 and 2023, I could see that the social opening and push back on the religious excesses of the Wahhabi reading of the texts had not led to any shift in the Saudi royal family's commitment to retaining its status as the rightful Custodian of the Two Holy Mosques. In fact, it was clear that during the COVID pandemic, the managers of the two mosques did much experimentation to figure out how to allow regulated access. This experimentation led to the introduction of an app with which pilgrims had to pre-book slots to secure entry to the Ka'bah in Mecca and to the rawdah in Medina. While the use of this app has largely been abandoned in Mecca, due to pressure from the pilgrims to secure repeated entrance to the Ka'bah during their stay in Mecca, the app-based entry system developed during the COVID period has, as documented at the outset of this chapter, led to permanent changes in securing access to the rawdah. A visitor could now enter the rawdah only once per visit, as only one entry permit per person can be issued in a month. By my early 2024 visit, access had been reduced to one permit per individual per year to further rein in the crowds. This, as noted above, has relieved, though not fully resolved, the challenges that marked the process of securing access to the rawdah area. The Crown Prince's claim to modernizing infrastructure and introducing efficient management, visible at the new social and entertainment sites, is also evident here.

Similarly, despite the discontinuation of the permit-based entry system for Ka'bah, during my 2023 visit it was clear that because of the experimentation done during the COVID period the management had worked out a slightly more effective system of regulating entry and exit through the multiple doors of the Masjid-i-Haram, so that pilgrims were forced to exit the tawaf area on completing the tawaf by making it impossible for them to sit in the areas around the exit. This helped to ensure a continuous flow of movement, allowing other pilgrims to enter. Before COVID, the main tactic used to regulate numbers inside the Masjid-i-Haram was to deny entry at certain points during the day, when the internal areas were full. Since these closures were random and unpredictable, they used to frustrate pilgrims, although under this system, it was easier to stay inside for longer periods of time. The new system, by controlling the entry and exit routes in ways that make sitting inside for long periods impossible, allows for more predictable access, as it has minimized the need for closing the entry doors.

Even the distribution of dates, water and other food items at iftar time seemed to have improved during my 2023 visit. Historically, the process of distributing goods for iftar was more systematic in Masjid-i-Nabawi, as the people of Medina have historically taken active responsibility for providing the food items. During my 2023 visit, the system was quite elaborate even in Mecca and much of it was overseen by the staff of the management authority.

The management authorities at the two mosques also invest in other activities to enrich the experience of the pilgrims, such as curating exhibitions about the Islamic heritage. Particular emphasis is placed on providing such additional services at Masjid-i-Nabawi. This is because the pilgrims have more free time in Medina than they do in Mecca, where most are keen to maximize their time inside the Ka'bah, whether performing tawaf or 'umrah, saying compulsory or optional prayers, or just sitting looking at Ka'bah and making du'a'. In Medina, on the other hand, once the pilgrims have visited the rawdah they can relax. In Masjid-i-Nabawi two permanent exhibitions have thus been very popular among the pilgrims for many years: the Quran Exhibition and the Life of the Prophet Muhammad Exhibition. During my 2023 visit, the Prophet Muhammad exhibition had been expanded further and provided extensive information on the life of the Prophet. The guided tours, offered in multiple languages, were heavily subscribed and their touch-screen displays enabled further exploration of the themes that interested individual pilgrims most. In the enthusiasm with which the tour guides talked about the whole exhibition and the continued efforts made by the management to expand it further and also export it to other countries, there was no sign of a declining commitment by the state or the royal family to promoting such flagship Islamic projects.

Overall, these services serve as powerful signals to pilgrims of the Saudi royal family's commitment to promoting and preserving the Islamic faith. Also, even for those pilgrims who are critical of Wahhabi tradition, Saudis' command of the Arabic language, especially *fus-haa* (Classical Arabic), gives the Wahhabi establishment a great deal of legitimacy. Many, by the end of their time in Mecca or Medina, come to identify their favourite reciters from among the imams whom they had heard during the prayers. They can be seen in the Islamic bookstores that abound around the two mosques, buying DVDs of the entire recitation of the Quran by their favourite reciter. Since the imams in the two mosques do not preach from the pulpit, apart from giving the twenty-minute Friday sermon, it reduces the chances of pilgrims belonging to the other school of thought leaving the two mosques frustrated. Any teaching that takes place happens in the halaqahs held in the two mosques, especially in Masjid-i-Nabawi, attendance at which, as explained in the case of the halaqah run by the Pakistani woman preacher, is entirely optional. For the ordinary pilgrim, the Wahhabi establishment mainly plays the role of providing highly trained imams and reciters, and on these counts, they leave most pilgrims highly satisfied. It is also worth noting that before the Saudi takeover of the management of the Masjid-i-Haram, the imams from the four schools of Sunni law used to lead their individual prayer congregations in turns (al-Sarhan 2016). Under the rule of Al-Saud, this system was abandoned to make all worshippers, irrespective of which school of law they belonged to, perform behind one imam (al-Sarhan 2016). The system of all worshippers performing behind one imam is today so well entrenched, and logically so convincing in the eyes of most Muslims, that, in my experience, the idea of having four imams lead their separate congregations in parallel or one by one seems needlessly divisive, even to Wahhabi critics.

Thus, it is important to understand how followers assess state legitimacy through multiple lenses. While Western scholars, or even many Muslim scholars, view the Al-Saud family's destruction of historical sites and deliberate erosion of the Ottoman legacy as a significant loss and evidence of their incompetence in regulating the haramayn, this concern is not a primary consideration for most poor pilgrims that I have encountered in Mecca. For those who are aware of these issues, they often balance them against the practical challenges of managing the haramayn and its large crowds. While many remain critical, blaming the Saudi state for admitting too many pilgrims for financial gain, others deeply appreciate the opportunity to return. Therefore, while historical critiques remain valid, so does the argument that the Saudi royal family invests heavily in improving the system's efficiency, earning the respect of many overseas pilgrims.

Further, the continued control of the Wahhabi-trained religious hierarchy over the mosques, including the two holy mosques, shows that it is important not to read too much into the Crown Prince's open critique of Wahhabi excesses in his interviews with Western media (BBC 2017a; Chulov 2017). The state is pushing the Wahhabi establishment to adopt a more moderate discourse; it is not trying to threaten its very existence by promoting a counter-religious authority to take control of the basic religious duties. This approach could prove effective, given the evidence presented above about the appeal of the core of the Wahhabi teachings, when cleansed of its excesses and Saudi society's preference for a moderate way forward. The likelihood that the Wahhabi establishment would under the current circumstances retain control but in the process move towards the adoption of a more moderate discourse on exercise of basic social and religious liberties becomes even more plausible when we move beyond looking at assumed strategic interests of the Wahhabi establishment and start to examine the increasingly pluralistic nature of debates occurring within the global Wahhabi Salafi scholarly sphere.

6.3. *Internal reform within the Wahhabi Salafi school of thought*

In Chapter 3, we reviewed the reasons why the Wahhabi establishment has not mounted a strong resistance to the steady scaling back of its official authority by the state since 2016. Among numerous factors mentioned, the chapter alluded to the increasingly vocal voices for reform coming from within the Wahhabi Salafi tradition. It is now pertinent to unpack this issue in some detail, as it helps to explain why the possibility of a violent backlash from the official establishment remains slim. No theological or intellectual sphere shaped by a major religious tradition is ever monolithic, and the same has been true for the Wahhabi Salafi sphere, which has seen increasing polarization from within, especially since the 1960s. While the official Wahhabi establishment has always supported political quietism, the rise of the Saudi al-Sahwah movement, initially inspired by the influence of Muslim Brotherhood members from other Arab states, had by late 1970s led to demands for political freedoms by some prominent scholars trained within the Wahhabi scholarly tradition (Lacroix 2011; al-Rasheed 2015). The emergence and impact of the al-sahwah movement on the Saudi religious and political spheres is by now well recorded (Lacroix 2011; al-Rasheed 2015). What is less well understood is that in recent years some scholars trained within the Wahhabi Salafi tradition have also started to argue for greater social freedoms, as well as freedom of conscience. While the al-sahwah movement, by arguing for greater political freedoms from within an Islamic discourse, posed a threat to the political legitimacy of the Saudi royal family and to date its members remain the target of state oppression (al-Jazeera 2019; Amnesty International 2024a), the scholars within the Wahhabi Salafi circles who are asking for increased individual freedom in making religious and social choices are providing the discourse from within the tradition that can support the on-going social reforms.

Examining the scholarly debates within the tradition, we can see that, just as the attitudes of the state and society towards social space and modern living changed over time in response to the process of modernization and globalization, the 'ulama' as a group have also not been entirely impervious to these changes. The evidence that in the past the Wahhabi establishment has acted pragmatically when it comes to ensuring the survival of its alliance with the Saudi royal family has diverted attention from the fact that processes of modernization, and exposure to its related opportunities and challenges, can lead to a genuine evolution of thought even among scholars belonging to most conservative religious traditions. This aspect of internal reform has in particular been underestimated for the Wahhabi Salafi scholarly sphere. Especially in the past ten years, prominent scholars trained in the Wahhabi Salafi tradition at the International Islamic University of Medina have reopened debates concerning issues that were previously considered to be settled for good (Razavian 2018b). The willingness to question some of the foundational beliefs within the Wahhabi Salafi tradition has led some to argue for labelling the work of these religious scholars as post-Salafism (Razavian 2018b). Yasir Qadhi is one Islamic scholar whose own evolution of thought epitomizes this process. He has an established following among young conservative Muslims in the West but also in the Muslim-majority countries, and he has also written extensively to document this process of internal reform within the Wahhabi Salafi tradition.

Based in the USA, Qadhi maintains the reputation of an erudite scholar who is loyal to the Islamic textual tradition. He is, however, often subjected to criticism by radical Salafi youth because he has made a very public shift from actively preaching from within the Wahhabi Salafi tradition, starting from when he was a young student at the International University of Medina, to now openly criticizing the divisive nature of Ibn Abd al-Wahhab's original teachings. A closer examination of the defence that he provides for this major shift in his own intellectual reasoning helps to illustrate how there are major reformist currents within the Wahhabi Salafi scholarly sphere, involving individuals who do not belong to the al-sahwah movement or to jihadi networks, and instead are focused on defending greater individual freedom in the area of individual belief and practice, and the organization of social life. In a recent interview (Qadhi 2019), while defending his intellectual evolution, Qadhi noted how he is not the only scholar within the Wahhabi Salafi sphere who has come to recognize the excesses of Ibn Wahhab's original teachings, which he refers to as the 'Najdi da'wah'. Elaborating on how scholars in successive generations have come to recognize the inherent challenges posed by Ibn Abd al-Wahhab's conception of takfir, whereby actions which fall into the category of bid'ah came to be labelled as kufr (Qadhi 2019), he explained how over his twenty-six-year intellectual journey, which began when he was a student at the International University of Medina and progressed to preaching widely and later also researching for a PhD at Yale, he has come to identify three stages of Salafi da'wah. The first phase consists of the work of Ibn Abd al-Wahhab and his sons and grandsons; the second stage began when King Abdulaziz realized the need to quell the excesses of the original teachings by placing a check on the demand of the Wahhabi scholars to continue waging war against fellow Muslims.

In the interview, Qadhi noted how, with the help of Mufti Ibrahim, King Abdulaziz tamed some of the excessive zeal of the original Wahhabi teachings. He explained that the third phase, which he associates with the scholars who came to influence the Wahhabi networks during the 1960s, further expunged most of the more radical elements of Nadji da'wah. Noting that this was the phase to which he was introduced when he started as a student at al-Medina, he describes how he fell in love with it. However, the more he read as he progressed on his intellectual journey, the more he realized that the teachings of this third phase of Najdi da'wah were very different from those of the first phase. He explains that he had repeatedly found that the scholars in the third wave had made the teachings of the original Wahhabi da'wah palatable by qualifying many of Ibn Abd al-Wahhab's extreme positions by arguing that he could not have actually meant it.[2] They had to do this partly because the scholars of this generation realized that one cannot live in the modern world with such fanaticism, and even the second Najdi da'wah was too much for the modern world by the 1960s. Thus, the third wave had to start. Gradually, however, Qadhi came to realize that such qualifications used by scholars in the third phase to justify extreme aspects of Wahhabi teachings were not valid, given that Ibn Wahhab's life history made clear that his actions supported the extreme positions.

Qadhi goes on to explain how Ibn Abd al-Wahhab fought decades of war in his life, a war which he referred to as jihad, and all this time, he was fighting the fellow Muslims on whom he was declaring takfir, not non-Muslims. Noting that Ibn Abd al-Wahhab declared the Ottoman Empire in its entirety as being *kafir* (unbeliever) and declared jihad against it, he explains how he came to realize the negative repercussions of Ibn Abd al-Wahhab's teaching that there was only one right way of being Muslim and that, in Ibn Abd al-Wahhab's view, was his way. He notes how the current Wahhabi Salafi clerics, whose writings are used by jihadi groups such as ISIS, invoke Ibn Abd al-Wahhab's reading of the concept of *al-wala' wa-l-bara'*, whereby anyone who is not seen to accept the Wahhabi Salafi creed is declared a kafir. Noting other Sunni scholars – such as the famous Yemeni scholar Muhmmad al-Shawkani – Qadhi contended that they have undergone shifts in their approach to Wahhabi teachings similar to his own. Qadhi therefore argues that we should not study the writings of Ibn Abd al- Wahhab without considering his actions: what he did to his fellow Muslims, how he justified attacking fellow villagers, and how he justified attacking Ottoman Empire.[3]

Qadhi further notes that even though Ibn Abd al-Wahhab claimed allegiance to Ibn Tamiyyah positions, he was not loyal to them. Ibn Tamiyyah, he argued, never declared takfir on other people for actions which would be considered bid'ah rather than *kufr*, unlike Ibn Wahhab. He contended in the interview that currently a fourth wave of Salafi da'wah is in the making, and although he does not place himself within this fourth wave, others have noted his on-going scholarship to be a classic example of further internal reforms in the Wahhabi Salafi tradition – a body of scholarship that is also being referred to as 'Post-Salafism' (Razavian 2018a, 2018b).

Highly sought after for his lectures and sermons, in person and online, his own scholarly contributions are noticeable for helping Muslims, especially those living in the West, to answer everyday questions that present a challenge to their faith. Qadhi has tried to address many critical questions concerning living in a liberal social sphere, such as how to approach the issue of same-sex marriage laws in the USA, approaches to liberal citizenship and respect for the law of the state when Muslims are in a minority. To support arguments in favour of adapting to modern reality from within classical Islamic scholarship, Qadhi often draws on conservative historical fatwas to show how they led to a negative socio-political or economic outcome for Muslim societies. He wrote his PhD thesis on Ibn Taymiyyah's attempt to reconcile reason and revelation (Qadhi 2013). While Ibn Taymiyyah is viewed by most as being opposed to rational inquiry, Qadhi presents him as a scholar 'who redeems *'aql* (reason) while keeping *naql* (text) supreme' (Razavian 2018a, 2018b; Qadhi 2019). Defending such an approach, whereby text remains supreme but allows space for rational analysis, Qadhi's approach to addressing contemporary legal questions advocates retaining unchanging loyalty to what he views as being clear in the text (for example, a complete Islamic ban on homosexuality), while allowing for debate on other issues (such as participation in democracy and Western democratic institutions).

Challenging traditional Wahhabi Salafi conservatism as being reluctant to bring change in Islamic law even when it provides the scholars with the tools for reasoning and adapting the laws to contemporary needs, in his own writings he has addressed questions and issues that pose a challenge to traditional conservative views, such as how to recognize evolution as a scientific truth but at the same time justifying God's intervention; how to obey laws of the secular state that might clash with Islamic rulings; or how to participate actively in modern democracies despite their Western origin (Razavian 2018b). The most recent example of the balance that he attempts to strike is evident in how he has worked with other scholars in a bid to defend Muslims' religious beliefs regarding LGBTQ+ practices when faced with social expectations in the West to conform. Supporting Muslim parents' concerns about efforts by Western states and societal actors to promote these values in children, irrespective of parental consent or opportunities to express conscientious objections, Qadhi has been a prominent signatory to the petition by Muslim scholars in the USA and the UK that has received much attention in 2023 (Public Statement 2023). Entitled *Navigating Differences: Clarifying Sexual and Gender Ethics in Islam* (Public Statement 2023), the petition argues for noting that moral disagreement does not amount to intolerance or incitement of violence, and that Muslims need to be given the right to express their beliefs while simultaneously recognizing their constitutional obligation to exist peacefully with those whose beliefs differ from theirs. The petition further notes that Islam means submission to God, and that submission requires that the ultimate source and basis of morality is divine guidance, not just reason or social trends and that while Islamic jurisprudence allows for diverse perspectives and accommodates various cultural norms, there are particular principles that are explicitly stated in revelation, known to be necessary elements of Islam, and unanimously agreed upon by qualified scholars and thus are deemed immutable and not open to revision by any person or entity, including the highest religious authority.

Arguing that a ban on homosexuality is one of these non-negotiable principles in Islam, the petition requests liberal Muslim figures not to make erroneous pronouncements on behalf of Islam and appeals to the wider Western society not to judge Muslims for this choice, which is an integral component of their faith. To fellow Muslims arguing for this freedom, the cleric's response is that curbing one's propensity for things that are forbidden is a difficult test, but the tougher the test, the greater the reward. Thus, Qadhi continues to position himself within the conservative religious circles. His open critique of Wahhab's original daw'ah does not mean that he is working to brand himself as a liberal. The growing emergence of scholars like these who defend the conservative positions consistent with Wahhabi Salafi teachings but also are keen to expose its excesses illustrates how internal reform is on-going.

Another prominent scholar in the Wahhabi Salafi scholarly sphere who has received much attention for his arguments for increased theological freedom is Hatim al-Awni (Qadhi 2018). Like Qadhi, he is initiating debates on issues that were long viewed to be part of the established consensus; these include the foundation of the Wahhabi conception of 'aqidah. Al-Awni is important because of being based in Saudi Arabia and also due to his family lineage, age and educational background (Qadhi 2018). Representing an older generation than Yasir Qadhi, he was a student of the famous Salafi scholar, Nasir al-Din al-Albani (1914–1999). He has taught in a number of Saudi universities and has also written extensively on hadith science and law. al-Awni's critique of dominant Wahhabi Salafi teachings about 'adiqah is particularly important because it does not come from an external opponent, and like Qadhi he also remains an admirer of Ibn Taymiyyah, but challenges Wahhabi teachings (Qadhi 2018; Razavian 2018a).

Al-Awni's main focus is on establishing the importance of tolerance and deliberation within the domain of 'aqidah and exposing the limits of Wahhabi thought from within. He argues for allowing space for more open dialogue and discourse, and for freedom of conscience. In doing so, he critically engages with the Wahhabi concepts of takfir and al-wala' wa-l-bara'. In his writings, he tries to demonstrate how key Wahhabi texts end up endorsing the use of takfir and thus play into the hands of the jihadis. A Wahhabi text that he has analysed in great detail is *al-Durar al-Sanīyah fī al-Ajwibah al-Najdiyah* (The Glittering Pearls of the Najdi Response), which is a collection of the writings of Wahhabi scholars from the time of Ibn Abd al-Wahhab until the mid-twentieth century. This book, considered an essential reference in Saudi religious scholarship (Razavian 2018a), is known to have inspired influential jihadis, but its potential to inspire jihadism is normally denied by Wahhabi scholars. Challenging this approach, al-Awni accuses them of complacency concerning the agenda of the jihadis. He goes so far as to refer to them as dormant members of ISIS (*al-da'ishiyun al-qa'dah*) who are waiting for an opportunity to implement their vision of takfir (Razavian 2018a). Noting that the subject of takfir is central to this text, he contends that the scholars' denial is deliberate. Al-Awni's two influential works on the subject of takfir are *Takfir Ahl al-Shahadatayn* (Excommunicating the People of Two Witnesses), which presents an analysis of the permissibility and possibility of excommunicating other Muslims; the other is called *al-'Ibadah: Bawabat al-Tawhid wa Bawabat al-Takfir* (Worship: The Gate of Tawhid and the Gate of Takfir) (Razavian 2018a).

Apart from presenting a detailed critique of the Wahhabi reading of tawhid, al-Awni has also criticized Wahhabi readings of the concept of al-wala' wa-l-bara'. As explained in Chapter 3, the notion of al-wala' wa-l-bara' requires that Muslims must be loyal to those who defend tawhid and must disown those who do not. Al-Awni acknowledges the importance of this concept but places strong emphasis on the use of moderation, tolerance and mercy in its application. This means that in practice he checks many of the potential applications of al-wala' wa-l-bara' by the jihadi groups: 'Muslims cannot force non-Muslims to believe in Islam; Muslims are bound to honour any contracts or deals that they have with non-Muslims; and, that it is haram for Muslims to kill any non-Muslims who are abiding by their contracts and the conditions of *dhimmah (treaty)*.' His view is that Muslims have to protect the basic human rights of non-Muslims and treat people of all religions, not just fellow Muslims, with justice and kindness. Further, al-Awni argues that an action that might contravene the concept of al- al-wala' wa-l-bara' would indeed be a sin, but it does not make the doer of that action a non-believer. This is so because the concept of al-wala' wa-l-bara' is based on one's beliefs, and only God knows what is within a person's heart; thus, actions do not reveal actual levels of inner belief. Such a position poses a fundamental challenge to the Wahhabi notion of tawhid, which, as explained in Chapter 3, made action central to showing commitment to tawhid. By advancing these arguments, al-Awni is questioning the very foundation of the Wahhabi doctrine of 'aqidah.

The existence of such scholars from within the Wahhabi Salafi tradition shows that mainstreaming these debates, instead of trying to establish a parallel reformist religious hierarchy, could be one plausible strategy for the Crown Prince to continue to get religious endorsement for his social liberalization agenda. During my visit in the spring of 2023, in my interviews with some British Muslim students due to complete their degrees at the International University of Medina, suggestions were made to this effect. The students had found their time at the university intellectually rewarding. They appreciated the fact that the shari'ah programme covers comparative law, instead of just teaching the Hanbali madhhab. One of the students explained how the comparative approach exposed them to a diverse range of earlier scholars, even some from the rationalist tradition: he gave the example of Ibn Rushd's book on fiqh, *Bidayat al-Mujtahid: Distinguished Jurist's Primer*, which he had covered as part of the curriculum and found most intellectually stimulating. They were also of the view that scholars at the university are starting to be open to engaging in debate, and one can ask them critical questions. The teaching of 'aqidah, however, remained in the hands of the Wahhabi scholarly establishment – but even here they noted an increasing tolerance of debate among the scholars.

Conclusion

By focusing on the teachings of one of the female preachers in Masjid-i-Nabawi to her lay audience from South Asia, this chapter has illustrated how using Mecca and Medina remains, for the royal family, including the Crown Prince, an important source of winning religious legitimacy in the eyes of the wider Muslim public. Additionally, it shows how the simplicity and clarity of the Wahhabi Salafi teachings on complex theological questions strengthen their appeal to ordinary Muslims. Its methodological focus on drawing on verses from the Quran and extensive use of hadith gives it a uniquely convincing power. It is therefore not surprising that we see extensive Salafi networks across the world in Muslim-majority countries, as well as in the West, where they were never exclusively reliant on Saudi financial support, or the support played a facilitating role in their emergence and growth, instead of being the primary propeller (Thurston 2016; Inge 2017; Eyre 2021; Diwan 2021; Russell 2021; Rock-Singer 2022). The teachings of the principles of creed as taught in the Wahhabi Salafi circles, when curbed for its excesses, particularly its tendency to declare takfir on fellow Muslims, are in common with classical Sunni tradition, and thus, when taught with the focus and clarity that marks the Wahhabi Salafi method of teaching, they become particularly compelling. A strong 'aqidah is the foundation of the Islamic faith, and if the Wahhabi Salafi tradition remains focused on teaching that, without straying into more polarizing interpretations which argue for enforcing righteous behaviour on others, it can, as I have tried to illustrate in this chapter, ensure a continuity of strong individual faith in Muslim societies while allowing for secularization of the social sphere. The Saudi experience of social opening is thus recording patterns similar to those observed in other Muslim societies: Islam seems particularly effective at preserving individual belief (Inglehart 2021). Even when these societies open up in social terms, the calls for modernization and secularization remain limited to the separation of religion and politics, instead of resulting in a decline in faith itself, unlike the evidence from the West (Inglehart 2021).

Further, while the previous chapter demonstrated that the pushback against the Wahhabi Salafi establishment does not reflect a decline in Islamic conviction within Saudi society, this chapter has shown that it also does not mean a reduced emphasis by the royal family or the Crown Prince on asserting their claim as the legitimate leaders of the Muslim world or their stated commitment to teaching the most authentic Islam. Instead, the state continues to expand and develop facilities at the two Holy Mosques to ensure that pilgrims, as well as the local public, view it as committed to providing a comfortable and spiritually enriching experience expected of the Custodian of the Two Holy Mosques. This chapter also recorded similar efforts in the form of the generosity that marks the services provided at the two mosques, especially during the month of Ramadan. Similarly, we have seen that the royal family has curtailed the power of the Wahhabi religious establishment, but it has not abandoned it nor has it attempted to create a parallel religious hierarchy. The focus is on putting pressure on the religious establishment to rein in its excesses.

In the final part of this chapter, we have seen how some prominent scholars from within the Wahhabi Salafi tradition are exposing the polarizing nature of Ibn Abd al-Wahhab's teachings. These scholars are keen to demonstrate the excessive nature of Ibn Abd al-Wahhab's teachings whereby minor sins (bi'dah) are routinely raised to the level of major sin (shirk) in order to declare takfir on fellow Muslims. While the emergence and implications of the Saudi al-sahwah movement that challenged traditional Wahhabi teachings in defence of the ruler to argue for greater political freedoms has already been well documented, the analysis of the work of the scholars presented in this chapter shows how there are now increasing numbers of scholars from within the tradition who are arguing for greater social freedoms and individual freedom in the exercise of religion. These scholars are providing the Wahhabi establishment with tools to cope with ongoing social change; whether these tools will be widely absorbed within the official Wahhabi establishment remains a promising area for future study. For now, it is important to review what this continued effort by the state to retain religious legitimacy while pursuing a modernization and reform agenda says about the dynamics of the state-society relationship. Retaining a degree of religious legitimacy is likely to remain central to the Crown Prince's political legitimization strategy, even as his push for Vision 2030 leads many to view his future legitimacy as tied to the delivery of economic promises.

Part 3

THEORIZING CHANGE

Chapter 7

STATE–SOCIETY RELATION IN TRANSITION

The literature on the state–society relationship in Saudi Arabia has attributed the endurance of the rule by the Al-Saud family largely to three main forces: religious legitimacy, effective use of cultural traditions (especially through patronage and consolidation of tribal networks) and, most frequently, the strategic use of oil rents (al-Rasheed 2002; Yamani 2000). Recent studies have delved into these factors in detail. For instance, Mouline (2014) provides an in-depth analysis of how accommodations by both the royal family and the Wahhabi establishment have consolidated their mutual power. Other studies, such as Le Renard (2014) and Ménoret (2014), illustrate how religious framing has enabled the state to regulate ordinary spheres of life. Le Renard (2014) focused on demonstrating this through the expected norms of decency for women in public spaces, while Ménoret (2014) examined the alliance between state and religious establishment to regulate youth culture by creating moral panic around acts of car drifting. Among studies that instead argue for recognizing the Saudi state's active use of tribal identities to consolidate its hold (al-Qassemi 2012; Yizraeli 2016), Samin (2015) presents the most detailed analysis. Examining the work of Ḥamad al-Jasir, a scholar who documented tribal genealogies, and recording how ordinary Saudis are keen to feature within them, Samin (2015) argues that the state's active recreation of tribal identities, rather than religious dictates or oil rents, has played an important role in how it has consolidated its hold.

The most extensive scholarship aimed at understanding the historic dynamics of state–society relationship in Saudi Arabia, and the wider Gulf region, however, approaches the issue through the lens of rentier state theory (Chaudhry 1997; Gray 2011; Malik 2017). A political economy framework that aims to explain the nature of the economy but also of the state and society interaction in states that derive a large portion of their income from rents – externally-derived, unproductively-earned payments (Beblawi 1987; Gray 2011; Malik 2017). The basic premise of the theory is that since the state receives substantial external income and distributes it to society, it can avoid imposing taxes. The resulting lack of a need for transparency, due to reliance on wealth from natural resources as opposed to tax collection, is argued to have major effects across the socio-economic and political spheres (Beblawi 1987; Moore 2004; Ross 2004; Gray 2011). In the economic domain it is argued to lead to the crowding out of other industries, and the domination of the public sector over the private sector with bloated state institutions, and politically a subservient and disengaged citizenry, which trades off political liberties and demands for public accountability in return for welfare services (Beblawi 1987; Beblawi and Luciani 1987; Moore 2004; Ross 2004; Gray 2011).

In the last two decades, the literature on rentier state theory has been enriched by studies that complicate the motives of both the state and its citizens. This growing body of work includes comparative analyses of states that benefit from resource rents, highlighting that natural resource rents do not always lead to authoritarian regimes (Esanov et al. 2004; van der Ploeg 2011; Lashitew and Werker 2020). Additionally, not all authoritarian regimes use oil rents to buy citizens' loyalty through economic and welfare programmes (Dunning 2008; Haber and Menaldo 2011), prompting scholars like Eibl and Hertog (2023) to explore why some oil-rich states provide generous welfare while others do not. This line of inquiry has fuelled a dynamic research agenda, with numerous studies emphasizing the importance of pre-existing institutional structures at the time of natural resource discovery in determining whether resource wealth strengthens or undermines democratic governance. Dunning (2008), for example, analyses the democracies of Venezuela, Norway, and Botswana, arguing that the effect of oil on democracy depends on pre-existing structures and levels of inequality. These factors influence whether elites are incentivized to limit access and protect their rents (leading to more autocratic outcomes) or whether pressure on the state to expropriate is relieved (leading to more democratic outcomes).

Within the literature, there is thus a growing focus on understanding the historical processes and institutional frameworks that shape governance. Crystal (1995) compares Kuwait and Qatar, showing how the pre-existing power and coherence of merchants can influence their involvement in political decision-making institutions after the rise of the oil industry. Kiran Chaudhry (1997) contrasts Saudi Arabia with Yemen, noting that Saudi Arabia did not have a singular moment of nation-building but rather an elite composition, explaining why mass politics has not become a significant element of Saudi political society post-oil. Similarly, Hertog (2010) argues that the frameworks of 'state' and 'society' need to be broken down to capture the complex realities of their interactions, highlighting that the distribution of oil revenues is quite complex. Noting the importance of historical institutional development, al-Rasheed (2002) argues that Saudi Arabia was effectively a rentier state long before oil wealth began flowing, due to the ruling family's reliance on rents from trade and pilgrimage. This income allowed rulers to impose far less taxation on the population. In the early years of the Kingdom, the royal elite had a symbiotic financial relationship with merchants, relying on them for money and goods in exchange for broader freedoms, new business opportunities and other concessions.

This need to contextualize the use and impact of oil rents on state–society relationship within the local cultural and historical context has become particularly attractive with the Gulf states trying to transition away from oil-based economies. Looking at the case of Oman, Valeri (2009), for instance, explores how the state–society dynamics evolve as an oil-rent economy falters, especially with half the population under fifteen years of age and when recently enjoyed privileges may no longer be tenable. These evolving dynamics of state–society relationships in light of changing socio-economic dynamics in the Gulf, such as globalization, new technologies, freer trade and investments, social changes and development imperatives that require a move away from oil to other sectors, have made some scholars argue that we are witnessing 'late rentierism' (Gray 2011). While these regimes do maintain clear 'red lines' on what are acceptable or unacceptable political challenges to state authority, as Gray (2011) notes, it is also clear that the assumption that citizens in these states are completely docile or disengaged is in need of questioning. An increasing number of scholars are thus arguing for empirical studies of precisely how citizens engage with the state under conditions shaped by oil. There is a recognition of the need for empirical study of Gulf citizens' expectations of their governments and of those governments' attempts to shape their citizens (Jones 2019; Louër 2021). As noted by one of the scholars arguing for a reappraisal of how oil affects attitudes towards the state: 'the link between rents, rents distribution and societal quiescence is not nearly so settled' (Mortiz 2019). These scholars are highlighting the need to capture citizens' own views about the state and society by means of interviews or surveys.

Slightly overlapping with the research focus of this volume, in her book *Bedouins into Bourgeois*, Jones (2017) presents a close study of the state's attempts to engineer a modern UAE national identity. Defining 'social engineering' as deliberate efforts by state leaders to influence the minds and behaviours of citizens, Jones (2017) argues that the UAE government has only partially been successful in its agenda of engineering the modern citizen so that in the case of UAE, she finds citizens buying in on social liberties but still demanding government jobs and oil-based economic benefits. Her findings are particularly important because, though her work is focused on interviews with the planners and is not an ethnography of actual change on the ground, she does show that the citizens can welcome the social liberalization agenda but not buy into the government's argument for the need to move away from oil-based economic benefits. In Saudi Arabia, on the other hand, the response, at least in this initial phase, has been more favourable (Diwan 2016; Boiler 2018; Thompson 2019).

The Crown Prince has successfully garnered support among many youth for his Vision 2030 agenda, which focuses on economic diversification, despite its plans to cut back on oil-based subsidies. As Diwan (2016) notes, the vision calls for the youth to be willing to give up many state benefits in the future. Similarly, young people participating in the focus-group discussions conducted by Thompson (2019) voiced clear expectations of the state to build supporting infrastructure for economic diversification under Vision 2030, but they consistently expressed willingness to take an active part in ensuring the success of Vision 2030. Instead of showing laziness and demanding access to unchecked flows of subsidies, his respondents were largely willing to take an active part in building a post-oil future, while having clear expectations that the state has to lead the process and create an enabling environment for change by providing good-quality education and employment opportunities (Thompson 2019: 283–7).

However, in this expanding literature arguing for understanding the more complex basis of state–society relationship in oil-based economies, taking into account historical conditions, ongoing economic changes, and different strategies of state legitimization, there is still a limited debate about the need for moral legitimacy for long-term survival. Addressing the question of moral legitimacy, Abulof (2017) argues that rents can provide provisional, but not sustainable, stability for authoritarian regimes. He distinguishes between negative and positive political legitimacy: the former concerns 'what is legitimate' (liberty vs. security), and the latter 'who is the legitimator' (divine/hereditary right vs. popular sovereignty). Sustainable stability, he argues, requires both types of legitimacy. This argument comes closest to my own argument. In my assessment, the state–society relationship in Saudi Arabia has been grounded in certain expectations of moral behaviour, shaped by religious and traditional values, and the royal family has tried to live by those expectations. These historic sources of moral legitimacy of the Al-Saud family are, in my observation, still working in favour of the Crown Prince. However, to be effective in retaining loyalty in the long term, the Crown Prince has to ensure that he establishes new sources of legitimacy, such as effective delivery of a market-based economy, as promised under Vision 2030, before these old sources of legitimacy completely run out. Equally, he might choose to continue to build on these old sources of legitimacy, as has been documented in the previous chapter, whereby Mecca and Medina are still being used as active sites to reinforce the Saudi state's image as the leader of the Muslim world, while curbing the power of the religious elites.

The core argument of this chapter is that to more accurately predict the future evolution of state–society relationships in Saudi Arabia, we cannot dismiss the importance of oil rents as they still remain critical to the economy and the primary source of financing the diversification agenda, but we must complement the analysis by also weighing in the role of these other more subtle and culturally and religious-informed sources of moral legitimacy that have regulated state–society relationship in Saudi Arabia. This approach enables us to recognize that, despite the apparent consolidation of authority in the persona of the Crown Prince, the state–society relationship in Saudi Arabia is in flux and many factors can shape its future course. It is true that the Crown Prince's political legitimacy has become highly linked to delivering on economic diversification promises through the creation of well-paid and satisfying jobs (Thompson 2019; al-Rasheed 2020) and showing an efficient bureaucracy at work. As Schmidt-Feuerheerd's (2023) study of the Saudi state's active use of an extensive dissemination network drawing on media outlets, government briefs and social media, to promote an image of effective management of COVID-19 shows, under the Crown Prince, the state is keen to develop 'performance legitimation'. However, as demonstrated in the preceding chapter, it is equally likely that the Crown Prince will continue to draw upon the traditional sources of moral legitimacy that have informed state–society relationship in Saudi Arabia. Below, I unpack these arguments.

7.1. Complicating motives of the monarch

A central assumption underpinning the rentier state framework, as discussed above, is the assumption that there can be 'no representation without taxation' (Moore 2004; Ross 2004). State legitimacy in this framework rests on its financial capacity to collect taxes and redistribute them across society (Moore 2004; Gray 2011). It is argued that when any natural resource, such as oil, becomes a source of income for the state, it erodes the need for public accountability, because when the public is not paying taxes, it has no mechanisms available to demand accountability (Moore 2004; Ross 2004). Such a conceptualization, especially about the docile citizenry, intuitively appears particularly applicable in the case of states that are governed by monarchies. To grasp the complex mechanisms that historically shaped the governance of state–society relationships across different societies, we need to examine the public's ability to hold rulers to account beyond the narrow lens of elections and taxation. In trying to develop a theory of power with a view to understanding what leads to accountable governance, Mancur Olson (2000) made the famous distinction between what he referred to as a 'roving bandit' versus a 'stationary bandit': both want to exploit, but the latter, unlike the former, by virtue of commanding control over a fixed community develops long-term stakes in its prosperity. A stationary bandit can only profit in the long term if the community has some degree of prosperity. Noting that in an anarchy not much is produced and thus there is little to steal, a stationary bandit develops incentives to offer a degree of security to the populace in order to ensure that there is production, which in turn enhances his own profits. At the same time, Olson (2000) argued that in understanding how power is exercised in a given context, it is important to remember that human beings are extraordinarily complex and act as a result of a complex set of motives, and that historical outcomes are contingent not just on the incentives and self-interest of the rulers but also on their morals and temperaments. Thus, even when wealth maximization and control over resources is the dominant motive, it can compete with other equally powerful motives, such as a desire to win respect, or to consolidate the family legacy, or to be known as honourable or to earn closeness to God.

Such an analysis reveals how the impact of oil wealth on state–society relationships cannot be studied in isolation. Recognizing this does not mean denying the centrality of self-interest in shaping the actions of both parties. It simply means remaining cognisant of the fact that self-interest can include the pursuit of psycho-social incentives, such as social status or honour (Frey and Oberholzer-Gee 1997), and not just the accumulation of wealth. In most cases, humans try to strike a balance where possible, to optimize both sets of incentives (Frey and Oberholzer-Gee 1997). Consequently, individuals routinely exercise internal checks on the pursuit of material comfort to maximize these other sources of utility. Further, as Tim Niblock, who has also argued for a recognition of the complex dynamics of the contract between the Saudi state and society, notes: 'The claims that the regime makes to legitimacy indicate how the regime seeks to relate to the population and which parts of the population it will turn to for support' (Niblock 2006: 10). It is thus important to examine the discourse and practice through which the Saudi royal family justifies its rule as legitimate, and the mechanisms by which the public holds the royal family to account.

Loyalty to family legacy

An incentive to build or consolidate a legacy can be a powerful driver of human behaviour. In the case of the Saudi royal family, the incentivizing power of such a discourse has been very important. The House of Saud has a strong sense of pride in being the founder of the modern state of Saudi Arabia (Niblock 2006; Thompson 2019). In popular discourse, the Saudi royal family presents itself as 'father of the nation' (Murphy 2013; Thompson 2019). Such a claim is not just based on its provision of many free services to the public. Instead, the narrative has a strong historical grounding, referring to over two centuries of history during which the House of Saud waged wars against rival clans to assert authority across large portions of the Arabian Peninsula. The primary focus is placed on highlighting how the House of Saud brought stability and security to the populace by bringing an end to a culture of inter-tribal wars between rival clans and laying down the foundation of the modern state in 1932. Related emphasis is placed on highlighting the commitment of the subsequent kings to systematic modernization, transforming a society consisting of nomads and small settlements into a modern state over a matter of a few decades. When identifying three main aspects of Saudi national identity, Yamani (2000) ranks the first as the consolidation of the nation around the Al-Saud family. Similarly, al-Rasheed (2002; 2020) notes how the Saudi royal family has relied heavily on legitimizing its rule by crediting itself with the creation of the Saudi state and its steady modernization. Karolak (2016) also highlights the significance of Saudi national history being deeply embedded in founding myths associated with the Saudi royal family. Additionally, studies such as Kattan (2017) demonstrate how the Saudi state has used civic education textbooks to actively shape the idea of Saudi identity and tie it closely to the Al-Saud family.

This narrative, while contested by rival groups (al-Rasheed 2021), in my experience, resonates with many segments of the population. While such a narrative appears paternalistic, for many members of the public, it builds legitimacy, as it shows a state keen to take responsibility for social well-being. Equally, the narrative of a grand family legacy works on the psyche of members of the royal family as well. The desire to retain or further enhance this family legacy binds prominent members of the royal family to live by a certain code of conduct that demonstrates mutual respect and commitment to enhancing collective well-being and to curbing the blind pursuit of material ambitions. This is not reflected only in the state's emphasis on the provision of social services and subsidies, given the evidence and supporting theoretical assumptions that political elites in many natural resource-rich countries choose not to do so (Bourguignon and Verdier 2000; Acemoglu and Robinson 2006), but also in everyday interactions between leading members of the royal family and the public.

During my fieldwork, I have always found that in gatherings where senior members of the royal family, especially those who hold official positions, are present great emphasis is placed on the upholding of Saudi traditions and explicit expressions of mutual respect. This decorum is reflected at public events when these members of the royal family are attired in graceful traditional dress, reinforcing their image as upholders of Saudi tradition. Further, their gestures and greetings follow a code of behaviour strongly reflective of mutual respect. At one dinner reception hosted by King Faisal Centre for Research and Islamic Studies (KFCRIS) as part of an international awards-giving ceremony, King Salman, who had recently been appointed as the monarch, was to preside and present awards to the winners. In his early 80s, dressed in sophisticated black robes and headgear, the way he stood to greet the large audience, and the humility marking his facial expressions and gestures evinced a keenness to show respect to the audience while asserting an aura of strong authority. The audience, similarly, was keen to show both respect and warmth in the manner in which they received him. Although at the numerous events that I attended of this nature, the audience consisted mainly of the social elite, during my visit to other cities, I also routinely came across expressions of respect for the senior members of the royal family among ordinary members of the public.

In Jazan, a coffee planter from a local mountainous tribe, who had become very popular on social media for experimenting with different techniques of local coffee production as part of the ongoing efforts to promote coffee production in the region, was keen for me to visit his coffee plantation and also meet other planters in his community. My schedule was tight, which led me to propose meeting the next day. He, however, was committed to taking a group of orphaned children to an iftar reception led by a senior member of the royal family. We therefore could not co-ordinate the plan. What, however, was striking for me was the enthusiasm with which he talked about the reception, how it was something that he and the children looked forward to with great excitement, and how the invitation was a great privilege. Again, it is important not to misread this reaction. It was not a sign of submissiveness or unquestioning obedience; instead, it was clear that there was genuine excitement at the idea of being invited by a host whom they genuinely respected and whom they expected to be generous in his hospitality.

I repeatedly came across many such examples that illustrated a harmonious relationship between the royal family and many segments of the ordinary public. This is not to deny that some Saudis are openly critical of the royal family or that people do not distinguish between different members, especially given its extended nature. There is talk about those who are perceived as overspending, indulging or lacking humility in public. However, my observations indicate that the relationship between the public and the monarchy is highly contingent on the public's perception of the actions of the ruling monarch and those who hold prominent offices, both at the centre and in the regions, as exemplified by my respondent in Jazan. At all these occasions, I found the senior members of the royal family keen to appear generous and gracious, and also keen to show a certain degree of humbleness while exuding authority. It is easy to dismiss such a relationship as being paternalistic, but such dismissal without considering its basis and implications results in a failure to understand the complex considerations and incentives that drive the royal family, and the role that commitment to retaining the family legacy plays in shaping the actions of the Saudi state. It also results in a failure to appreciate why we are seeing the Crown Prince enjoy a relatively high level of legitimacy in the eyes of many socially active youth, as profiled in Chapter 5, many of them creative artists, while he is clearly associated with the use of force to suppress political dissent. The family legacy of the royal family does, at least for some Saudis, build confidence in its capacity to rule effectively.

Further, it is to be noted that the idea of a grand family legacy becomes even more powerful when one can also add to it a sense of divine endorsement. For a Muslim leader, the title of being the Custodian of the Two Holy Mosques, in its various variations over the centuries, has been the highest possible honour (al-Sarhan 2016). Retaining control over Hejaz was, for example, crucial for the Ottoman Empire to maintain its legitimacy as the leader of the Muslim ummah (Lawrence 2015). The Ottoman Empire invested in developing the Hejaz railway, connecting Damascus to Medina in the early twentieth century, in an effort to consolidate its political control over Mecca and Medina (Landau 1971). The previous chapter described the religious fervour that marks Mecca and Medina, and the clear commitment that the royal family continues to show to date towards preserving the religious appeal of these two cities. It also recorded how the services provided at iftar during Ramadan develop a sense of the royal family as being generous hosts. Just as in their interactions with the local public, even with the Muslim pilgrims, the royal family is keen to establish a relationship of respect and to be perceived as being generous and committed to living by the Islamic code of conduct. This is particularly so when showing mutual respect (seen as an extension of the Islamic emphasis on everyone being equal) and generosity: two key virtues that Islam expects of a pious ruler (Mernissi 1995; Abdelaal 2015). Again, this is not to argue that the senior royal family members are pious, but to record how they are not free of expectations from the popular public to try to appear so and live by certain standards of moral behaviour.

Islamic governance ideals

Just as the potential role of family legacy in regulating the behaviour of the royal family is often underestimated, the role of Islamic values in shaping the state–society relationship in Saudi Arabia and informing public expectations of how the ruling family should behave is also often underestimated. Saudi Arabia does not have a modern constitution. Instead, it has been regulated by Islamic Shari'ah law, unlike most other Muslim countries, where exposure to colonial rule led to the introduction of Western legal systems and codification of law. In 1992, Saudi Arabia did introduce a Basic Law of Governance, but it again reaffirmed its commitment to governing under Islamic law (GoSA 2023a):

- Chapter 1, Article 1, states: The Kingdom of Saudi Arabia is a sovereign Arab Islamic State. Its religion is Islam. Its constitution is Almighty God's Book, The Holy Quran, and the Sunnah (Traditions) of the Prophet (PBUH).
- Chapter 2, Article 7, states: Government in the Kingdom of Saudi Arabia derives its authority from the Book of God and the Sunnah of the Prophet (PBUH), which are the ultimate sources of reference for this Law and the other laws of the State.
- Chapter, 2, Article 8, similarly notes: Governance in the Kingdom of Saudi Arabia is based on justice, shura (consultation) and equality according to Islamic Shari'ah.

Announcing the 1992 Basic Law of Governance, King Fahd did not use the words 'social contract', but he emphasized the importance of respectful state–society relations:

> The relationship between citizens and state officials is founded on solid and deep-rooted traditions, compassion, mutual respect and loyalty stemming from the sincere and firm convictions in the hearts of this country's people generation. There is no difference between the ruler and the ruled. They are equal before the law of God, and they are all equal in their love of this homeland and in their eagerness to maintain its safety, unity, pride and progress. (GoSA 1992)

The same commitment is reflected in the Vision 2030 policy documents. The Vision 2030 website lists three intrinsic strengths that underpin the vision. The first one is: 'Saudi Arabia is the land of the Two Holy Mosques which positions the Kingdom at the heart of the Arab and Islamic world' (GoSA 2016). Only after this is the country's ability to invest heavily to create a more diverse and sustainable economy mentioned. Even if these pledges are dismissed as mere empty statements, this ranking is reflective of how the Saudi royal family wants to be seen at home and abroad. Being loyal to Islam and regarding one's status as the Custodian of the Two Holy Mosques as a great privilege remains its top stated priority. Similarly, the original Vision 2030 document, which opens with a statement from King Salman, states his title as the Custodian of the Two Holy Mosques, and not as the King of Saudi Arabia (GoSA 2016). Like the Vision 2030 website, it also emphasizes the centrality of Saudi Arabia's Islamic identity above all other things:

> The first pillar of our vision is our status at the heart of the Arab and Islamic worlds. We recognize that Allah the Almighty has bestowed on our land a gift more precious than oil. Our Kingdom is the Land of the Two Holy Mosques, the most sacred sites on earth, and the direction of Kaaba (Qibla) to which more than a billion Muslims turn at prayer. (GoSA 2016: 6)

Just as the desire to build on the family legacy can provide incentives for a ruler to exercise self-restraint and not appear to be outrightly exploitative, religious commitment can place equally powerful checks – at times being even more powerful than state laws – on a ruler's exploitative tendencies. Not only in analysing its interactions with the local public, but even in its role as the Custodian of the Two Holy Mosques, the possibility that members of the royal family might have a genuine allegiance to the Islamic moral code of conduct is rarely taken seriously. This is misleading, given evidence that to many senior members of the royal family, religious commitments have been important. King Abdulaziz's commitment to Islamic beliefs is well recorded, even by those who have noted his pragmatism in dealing with the Wahhabi establishment after the foundation of Saudi Arabia (Asad 1954; Thesiger 2007). Western writers who wrote about their direct or indirect interactions with King Abdulaziz always recorded his commitment to religious ideals (Asad 1954; Thesiger 2007); the seriousness with which he initiated expansion work at the Two Holy Mosques has also been credited to his religious commitment. While King Faisal, whose mother was from a family of Wahhabi ʿulama', commanded great respect across the Muslim world for his visibly pious demeanour, other kings, though lacking the religious charisma of King Faisal, have generally been viewed as being keen to demonstrate commitment to core Islamic values.[1]

The respect for Islamic dictates has also been clear in the royal family's commitment to ruling the country by shariʿah law (Vogel 2000; Krell 2025). Saudi judges, historically embedded within the Wahhabi establishment, have long enjoyed considerable discretion in interpreting Hanbali law (Vogel 2000). As Krell's (2025) study demonstrates, jurists continue to exercise substantial agency despite ongoing institutional and legal reforms. Application of an Islamic legal framework, though often criticized by Western human-rights groups for using hudud punishments, has made the Saudi state relatively effectively on the core responsibility of any state: ensuring law and order (Moore 2004). Saudi Arabia has a very low crime rate, partly attributed to its controversial application of severe punishment justified under shariʿah law, and, as noted in Chapter 5, it is also a relatively safe place for women to travel alone, albeit requiring modest dressing. This trust in the state's ability to offer security has played a critical role in the rapid take-up of the opportunities being made available for female mobility and employment. In my interviews, I have always found the Saudi state's ability to offer law and order to be highly valued by Saudi society. Even those respondents who were lukewarm about the social liberalization efforts qualified their critique of the state by saying that it provides security, and for that, it should be respected. In prioritizing the provision of law and order as the core function of the state, the Saudi public is not an exception; all Western political theorists have historically argued the same (Moore 2004).

Once we allow for even a small degree of religious commitment on the part of members of the royal family, it becomes difficult to ignore the internal checks that such a framework places on the actions of the ruler and the kind of relationship that he builds with society. Islam makes very strict demands on a ruler to act justly (Mernissi 1995; Abdelaal 2015). It is a belief system that spells out the expectations of a ruler in very precise terms and creates active fear of two-fold accountability: to the public and to God (Mernissi 1995; Abdelaal 2015). The virtuous behaviour expected of a Muslim ruler is also very clear because, unlike most other religious traditions, in Prophet Muhammad, whom Muslims are required to follow, there is a model of a just ruler (Mernissi 1995; Abdelaal 2015). Muhammad established the first Islamic city-state in Medina and acted as a spiritual and political leader. After him, the first four caliphs selected from among his companions, who were referred to as the 'Rightly Guided Caliphs' due to their steadfastness, exemplified the high standards of integrity expected of a ruler (Mernissi 1995; Abdelaal 2015). For fear of being held accountable to God for not fulfilling his obligations to the public, Caliph Umar was known for walking on the city streets at night to meet the needs of the poor. It is the strong emphasis that Islam places on social justice and on the ruler's responsibility to act justly that has led many Islamic-inspired political parties across the world to have Justice in their name.[2]

The authority of the political leader in Islam is thus also based on his following a complex set of popular expectations shaped by the Islamic moral and legal framework, as was documented for the authority of the 'ulama' in Chapter 3. The most important of these expectations is that the leader should be pious and just. In the ideal Islamic state, there is equality for all, and even the beggar can hold the imam to account. Islamic historiography is full of such examples (Mernissi 1995; Abdelaal 2015). With this kind of heavy emphasis placed within Islam on accountability to the public and to God, it is problematic to assume that such a powerful mental framework will not inform the actions of the rulers to some degree. As Olson (2000) notes, history is shaped by material interests but equally by the different propensities and moral commitments of the individual leaders. For a state and society where religion has historically been a powerful force, it is therefore problematic not to acknowledge its role when predicting the motives and actions of the ruler. This is particularly the case when studying the incentives and motives shaping actions of the senior members of the Saudi royal family, which, though run as a hereditary monarchy, includes members of different propensities. King Abdulaziz is recorded as having twenty-two wives. These women belonged to different tribal groups and among them bore him almost one hundred children. The Saudi royal family is therefore often argued to be a headless tribe within which several groups make contending claims to leadership (al-Rasheed 2002; Stenslie 2012). Religion remains a powerful force for many of its members. It is thus not possible for a king to behave in ways that entirely negate the Islamic expectations of a good ruler and retain public legitimacy for long. Such an analytical framework suggests that the popularity the Crown Prince has enjoyed among the youth is not unconditional; it will ultimately wane if he is seen to persistently exceed a moderate course, whether in terms of excessive social liberalization or public repression.

Traditional and cultural values

Finally, it is also important to remember that Saudi society inherits centuries-old customs and traditions that evolved in the desert, as both the Bedouins and hadars tried to find some stability and security in the absence of a central state, while surviving in a very harsh environment (Kostiner 1993; al-Rashed 2002).

An elaborate set of rules and the valorization of certain human virtues helped to maintain social order. Egalitarianism was at the heart of this system, whereby everyone was treated equally and where status was acquired not on the basis of wealth, but by shows of bravery or statesmanship (Kostiner 1993; al-Rasheed 2002). Those who were good swordsmen and could fight to defend themselves and their tribes, those who could demonstrate diplomatic negotiation skills in inter-tribe feuds and those who could be trusted to stand by their word rose in status and were rewarded materially as well as through the bestowing of public respect. Odes would be written in their honour. Underpinning this complex code of conduct was the concept of *marjla*, meaning 'manliness' (al-Fahad 2015). It prescribed when it was honourable to fight but also when to withdraw; those who overstepped the limits were punished not just through the institution of vengeance (*thar*) but also by the loss of their reputation. Public opinion was the core enforcement mechanism in this context.

Raids and counter-raids were central to Bedouin survival. Yet, it was also recognized that excessive raiding would lead to a permanent state of insecurity. Thus, raiding was also governed by a strict code of conduct. One could raid in order to acquire material possessions, but not with an intention to kill (al-Fahad 2015). Enemies were treated with respect and as equals. A respected warrior regarded it to be below his status to fight someone below his calibre. Also, killing was never the objective, and it was deemed honourable to give the enemy a chance to flee if one had proved victorious in a duel (al-Fahad 2015). During raids, it was deemed important to respect the weak, including old or sick people, women and children. The Bedouin also had a complex code of conduct for the resolution of disputes. Judges were men of good repute, and it was a position often inherited in a family for many generations. Their role was to apply the customary rules faithfully by drawing on precedents, and their judgements were binding for all parties involved (al-Fahad 2015).

As with raiding, other aspects of collective living were regulated through a complex web of social norms and values. The main possessions of a Bedouin were his camels and his land, which was referred to as *dirah*, pastureland. If this land was on a major trade or pilgrimage route, where large caravans would pass through, it enabled the Bedouin to gather a tribute called *akhawat* (al-Fahad 2015). In return, he had to guarantee the security of the travellers, and failure to deliver would result in great social condemnation. Control over dirah also allowed control over wells. Since water was a scarce commodity, complex rules also evolved to ensure peaceful access to wells, which were controlled at the clan level. Knowing that one might oneself be in need of water in the dry season, it was normal to allow access by other tribes when one's own area received good rain. Other sacred rules in the desert included the institution of offering refuge to the innocent and the offender alike (*dakhil*), as tribal chiefs gained honour by mediating in these matters (al-Fahad 2015). The custom of *jar* is another sacred institution that created mutual obligations for the host and his guest: if a chief gave refuge to a member of another tribe, he would have a responsibility to protect him, and in return, the guest had to contribute to any loss incurred by the host while defending him (al-Fahad 2015). The tradition of *milha*, or sharing salt, required that sharing food or drink creates mutual obligations for the host and guest alike (al-Fahad 2015).

While the basic code of tribal conduct was underpinned by values of honour, bravery and keeping one's word, there was another virtue which was core to the determination of prestige within hadar and the Bedouin population alike, and that was the virtue of generosity (Thesiger 2007; al-Fahad 2015). The standards of hospitality were so high that to outsiders they often appeared reckless. Thesiger (2007), in his account of the years that he spent travelling with a group of Bedouins in the Arabian desert, narrates how he was, on occasions, left puzzled and at other times frustrated by the level of generosity shown by the Bedouins who accompanied him. On occasions, they would share their meagre food supplies with visitors, going without food themselves. As al-Fahad (2015) notes, a 'permanently lit hearth' was a sign of one's generosity, whereby coffee was ready to be served at any time and animals would be slaughtered for special guests.

While these authors, noting the importance ascribed to these virtues and adherence to strict codes of conduct, lamented their disappearance with the rise of the modern state (Thesiger 2007; al-Fahad 2015), the fact is that the collective memory of these customs and traditions has not disappeared. Many recent studies have come to assert the continued importance of tribes in contemporary Saudi Arabia (al-Qassemi 2012; Samin 2015; Yizraeli 2016). I have, similarly, often found in my interviews that Saudis still take pride in their Bedouin ancestry, and the ability to keep a camel in a holiday home in the desert is still mentioned with great pride. Similarly, those from a hadar background take pride in their lineage. In my experience, honour, truthfulness, bravery, standing by one's word, generosity and hospitality are values that are still important to Saudis, especially since these are values that are also emphasized in Islam. As noted in the previous chapters, there are many occasions on which one can see the social reverence for these values. The strong sense of hospitality that marks the iftar organized by the state and the local public for the pilgrims in Mecca and Medina, the serving of fresh fruit juices, dried fruits, and sweets when visitors take tours in al-Ula and the importance of trust and bravery as demonstrated by the characters in the movie *Sattar*, which, as discussed in Chapter 4, aimed to capture the essence of local Saudi culture, all illustrate the lingering emphasis on these values. While modernization did erode the social codes that society had locally evolved over the centuries to regulate collective behaviour, the collective social memory of these traditions and values, in my experience, has not been eroded.

Seen in this historical context, the investment that the Saudi royal family has made in social development is very much aligned with these traditional values, whereby one's standing in the community is shaped not just by wealth but equally by demonstration of one's willingness to share it with others. The investments made by the state in social development or welfare services, in such a historical and cultural context, thus become not a sign of its desire to keep people politically disengaged; instead, they become the foundation for generating communal bonding by demonstrating commitment to traditionally expected behaviour. It becomes a way of winning active political legitimacy, instead of being an attempt to keep the citizenry at a distance. This desire to build an engaged citizenry, which respects the royal family even if it is denied the right to elect the ruler, is also reflected in the way the Saudi state, as analysed in detail in Chapter 4, first invested in the development of urban infrastructure, followed by investment in the development of human capital. The sequencing of the nature of these investments was logical. In the initial period, the focus was on the development of infrastructure and settling the Bedouin population in cities, with an emphasis on the provision of basic education (Yamani 2000; Vassiliev 2000). From the 1980s onwards, investment was also made in expanding higher education (Yamani 2000; Jones 2015). Similarly, while the extensive efforts to settle the Bedouin population into permanent dwellings and invest in modern urban infrastructure before substantial oil revenues began to flow can partly be explained by a desire to control society (Kostiner 1993; Vassiliev 2000; Samin 2015), it is difficult to entirely rule out the possibility that some senior members of the royal family genuinely wanted to advance the society towards becoming a modern state. After all, many resource-rich states have not invested in societal development. This has led to a growing body of literature focused on explaining the conditions under which some resource-rich states, like Saudi Arabia and most Gulf states, invest in welfare provision (Eibl and Hertog 2023).

Further, the state's decision to focus on the provision of education from as early as the 1950s, though initially prompted by external actors (Vitalis 2009), did, over time, clearly acquire a degree of genuine commitment. By the early 1960s, King Faisal personally led the efforts to enrol girls in schools, despite resistance from religious elements. The centrality of education to social development is well established within international development literature. The established benefits of access to education include not just economic development but also the development of a political consciousness about one's rights, and the confidence to demand those rights (Bourguignon and Verdier 2000; Hickey and Hossain 2019). Studies from across developing countries record how political elites often deliberately choose not to invest in education to minimize the risk of increased public accountability (Bourguignon and Verdier 2000; Hickey and Hossain 2019). Yet, the Saudi royal family has systematically invested in education, even if this initiative was initially propelled by external actors (Vitalis 2009; Peterson 2018). As demonstrated in this volume, and also noted by other scholars, widespread access to basic education (Yamani 2000), followed by opportunities for higher education, including scholarships for studying abroad under King Abdullah's scholarship programme (Thompson 2019), has been crucial to the current social transformation.

While the initial investment at the school level could arguably have been influenced by a desire to shape national mentality and ensure obedience to the rulers as done by state in many historical contexts (Ramirez and Boli 1987; Pagayan 2021) – the recent investments, particularly under King Abdullah Scholarship Programme that has enabled Saudi men and women to pursue higher education in leading Western universities (Alotaibi 2022; Western University 2023), cannot be explained in such narrow terms. These recent investments provided young men and women with opportunities to study at leading Western universities, reflecting a broader and more genuine commitment to encouraging academic excellence. The fact that successive members of the royal family consistently invested in education when political elites in many country contexts fail to do so again shows that the royal family's motives for offering social services have involved a degree of genuine commitment to collective social development. The improvement established in the living conditions in Saudi Arabia in just over fifty years is unprecedented compared with most other contexts. During the 1960s, the Saudi population was barely six million people, most of whom lived a nomadic life, and life expectancy was a mere forty-five years (Aldosary et al. 2021). Today, the population has expanded to thirty-six million, is settled in well-developed modern cities and life expectancy has increased to seventy-seven years (Aldosary et al. 2021). Just as with the provision of education, the primary motive for leading this social transformation could have been the consolidation of political power (Kostiner 1993; Vassiliev 2000; Vitalis 2009). However, this does not entirely rule out the possibility that a genuine desire for societal uplift also played a role.

Recognizing these factors underscores the importance of understanding that, as argued in Chapter 3, the 'ulama' must meet certain expectations of moral behaviour to exercise authority. Similarly, the authority of the royal family is informed by a complex moral framework shaped by tribal customs and Islamic teachings. Therefore, the state's motives for engaging with the public cannot be reduced exclusively to wealth maximization if it seeks to maintain at least some degree of popular legitimacy. Human motives are often more complex than the simple pursuit of material interests. Abiding by religious and traditional values offers a powerful source of internal well-being, as does material comfort. As studies in the field of psychology show (Frey and Oberholzer-Gee 1997), there is often a tension between the pursuit of material and psycho-social rewards, and often strong material incentives can crowd out the latter – but that is not the optimal condition, as individuals prefer to maximize different sources of well-being (Frey and Oberholzer-Gee 1997). In a context of dire economic conditions, it might make sense for the ruler to indulge in extremely exploitative behaviour, with an exclusive focus on securing rents, but in the context of financial affluence, such a strategy is not optimal. Winning the voluntary compliance of the public is not only a more cost-effective and sustainable way to rule, given that ruling by force increasingly becomes more costly (Malik 2017), but it is also more rewarding, as it bestows genuine honour and prestige on the ruler (Abulof 2017). Credit to the oil rents, and prior to its discovery, due to other sources of geo-strategic rents (al-Rasheed 2002; Perterson 2018), the Saudi state has never been so desperate as to think only in terms of survival. In addition, the title of the Custodian of the Two Holy Mosques in itself compels the holder of this title to have grand ambitions to lead the Muslim world. My assessment of the basis of state–society relationship in Saudia Arabia is thus more in line with those of Niblock (2006) and Thompson (2014, 2019), who have similarly argued for recognizing the complex nature of the Saudi state–society relationship not to deny the centrality of oil rents in shaping its dynamics, but to highlight that the Saudi royal family has survived not just by meeting public material expectations but also by meeting certain level of moral expectations set by religion and tradition. Only a holistic approach to studying the state–society relationship, one that considers both material and moral expectations that society has of its rulers, can fully explain the survival of the House of Saud. Such an approach is also essential to accurately predict the conditions under which the Crown Prince will secure further legitimacy, as well as those under which support among the youth will diminish. The next section elaborates on this further.

7.2. Accountability beyond taxation

Having questioned assumptions about the motives of the state to engage in welfare provision, it is important to demonstrate why the same moral and religious framework that can contribute to building internal checks on the rulers' actions can also provide guidelines to the public on how to hold the rulers to account: paying taxes is not the only route to inducing the public to demand accountability. The assumed centrality of taxation to the establishment of an accountable state that underpins rentier state theory is again a product of historical developments in the West (Moore 2004). This assumption is based on the understanding that sources of revenue have a major impact on patterns of state formation (Moore 2004). Yet historically, we have seen the relationship between the state and society being shaped by many factors. As early as the 1930s, anthropologists started to gather evidence of this. Fortes and Evans-Pritchard (2015) brought together a collection of essays presenting a detailed study of the political systems of different tribal groups in Africa. Expressing their concern that political philosophy has 'chiefly concerned itself with how men ought to live and what form of government they ought to have, rather than with what are their political habits and institutions' (Fortes and Evans-Pritchard 2015), they emphasized the need to study the diverse state institutions as they exist on the ground across different regions of the world. Being particularly interested in studying the nature of political authority in primitive societies, they focused on studying two types of tribal formation in Africa: primitive states and stateless societies.

The former consisted of those societies which had some level of centralized authority, administrative machinery and judicial institutions, while the latter lacked a centralized government. Studying examples of both types, they argued for recognizing that there is always a balance between power and authority on the one hand and obligations and responsibility on the other; the authority of the ruler, unless exercised entirely on the basis of force, is never really unchecked. In Evans-Pritchard's words: 'A chief or a king has a right to exact tax, tribute and labour service from his subjects; he has the corresponding obligation to dispense justice to them, to ensure their protection from enemies and to safeguard their general welfare by ritual acts and observances' (Fortes and Evans-Pritchard 2015: 16). Though not elected by means of a modern voting system, the structure of an African state, they argued, shows that the kings and chiefs rule by consent. He further contended: 'A ruler's subjects are as fully aware of the duties he owes to them as they are to the duties they owe to him and are able to exert pressure to make him discharge these duties' (Fortes and Evans-Pritchard 2015: 16).

Similarly, Tim Niblock (2006) has argued for recognizing how, despite assumptions of a lack of accountability, the Saudi state survives by delivering on public expectations that help it to meet four critical sources of popular legitimacy.[3] He first of all notes the importance of eudaemonic legitimacy, under which he includes the legitimacy earned by providing welfare services valued by the public, but equally the state's capacity to show that it can promote national dignity and security, for example by promoting foreign policies that have public support. He goes on to demonstrate how, since the 1970s, the royal family has met these expectations by investing in infrastructural development, the provision of free education and health care and an extensive network of welfare services and security. The network of social services available to a Saudi citizen can be rivalled by few other states. Each Saudi is entitled to free education from primary school to university level, with provision of international scholarships for bright candidates to study abroad (Aldosary et al. 2021). Health care is free of charge, including medicines and costly surgical procedures. There is no income tax, and only 15 per cent VAT is applied on some items (Aldosary et al. 2021). Families below a certain income threshold receive monthly allowances for gas and water bills. Saudis who are unemployed receive a monthly support allowance for up to a year until they find a job. Women whose salary is less than 8,000 Saudi riyals get an 80 per cent discount on their daily commute to work; they also get a discount on the fee they have to pay for their children's day care (Aldosary et al. 2021). Saudis who are categorized as earning a low income are eligible to receive loans with zero interest rates to help them establish small businesses and projects, to get married or to buy their first car.

Second, Niblock (2006) highlights the source of a state's democratic and structural legitimacy. In this regard, he emphasizes the importance of recognizing that the Saudi state maintains a structure of law and government which is effective in maintaining law and order on the ground and which, due to being based on the Quran and shari'ah law, is in line with Islamic legal and moral principles and thus has legitimacy among the public. The regime might not have won legitimacy for its actions by winning votes, but it does so by ensuring that it is perceived to be governing according to the dictates of Islamic law. It is due to this that the Saudi state has historically valued its alliance with the Wahhabi establishment and supported its expansion, giving Wahhabi clerics power to enforce Islamic law by controlling the courts and having hay'ah police at their disposal. Further, as Niblock (2006) and other scholars (Matthiesen 2009; Thompson 2019) have noted, the continuity of the traditional practice of holding *majlis* (gathering) on the part of the King and the senior members of the royal family acts as a tribal form of democracy whereby any citizen can approach the ruler or those close to him in order to press their case. Though not a channel for input into major policy issues, the platform does provide an ordinary citizen with the means to seek immediate relief for practical problems (Thompson 2019).

Thirdly, Niblock (2006) notes the importance of traditional legitimacy, which he refers to as a ruler enjoying acceptance on the grounds of inheritance, where this inheritance links him to an established line deemed to hold the right to rule. As above, this source of legitimacy links with the factors that were analysed in the previous section that provide the royal family with internal motivation to build a degree of genuine legitimacy. Niblock also notes that their having ruled areas of the Arabian Peninsula since the early eighteenth century gives the royal family traditional legitimacy. This becomes a particularly powerful source of legitimacy as the family also takes credit for the unification process that led to the birth of Saudi Arabia as a nation-state. The family, he notes, still presents itself as the unifying force holding disparate parts of the country together.

Finally, he also notes the importance of personal legitimacy, which he argues exists when the public believes in a ruler's right to rule due to his exceptional personal qualities. A charismatic leader can win popular legitimacy due to his actions and the relationship that he builds with the citizenry. As noted in the preceding section, Niblock (2006) also highlights how all of the kings from King Abdulaziz onwards have placed emphasis on appearing as capable, morally upright and caring about the public interest. They have focused on presenting themselves as fatherly figures who care for the well-being of all. Noting how the personal charisma of King Abdulaziz and King Faisal was particularly effective in winning popular legitimacy for the rule of the Al-Saud family, Niblock (2006) also notes how its lack, and a reputation for weak moral character, especially in terms of following Islamic dictates, curtailed the rule of King Saud.

The very same religious and moral framework that informs the worldview of the royal family, as analysed in the preceding section, also informs public expectations of how a ruler should rule. There might not be an electoral and taxation-based accountability system in place, but the public still has clear expectations concerning how the ruler should rule, and the ruler also has a clear sense of the obligations he must meet if he is to rule peacefully. Thus, as Fortes and Evans-Pritchard (2015) had argued, considering the primitive stateless societies in Africa, no society or social group can operate in a state of calm unless there is a clear sense of the respective rights and obligations of those who rule and those who are ruled. In the case of Saudi Arabia, the state's ability to provide law and order while officially adhering to an Islamic ethical and legal framework shows to the public that the ruler is subjecting his or her authority to divine power, at least to some degree, and thus accepting the checks that Islam places on political authority. This becomes a powerful source of legitimacy for many members of the public. The extensive system of checks that Islam places on the use of authority by the ruler becomes the barometer against which the public constantly judges the performance of the rulers. In the same vein, family legacy acts as a legitimizing force because it acts as a signal that the family is capable of delivering, based on past evidence. Finally, personal charisma and demonstration of moral uprightness on the part of the kings have been important in winning political legitimacy, because it signals that the ruler is efficient and capable of delivering on his promises and that he has a moral commitment to upholding the public good.

How a society rationalizes the legitimacy of an act by a ruler is thus a complex matter. It is interesting to note that in my interviews, many young respondents dismissed concerns about lavish spending by the Crown Prince on personal items, such as the £450 million mega yacht, which was widely covered in the Western media (Walker 2016), on the grounds that, as the Crown Prince of Saudi Arabia, he can afford to spend like that. Similarly, as discussed earlier, the Crown Prince's controversial actions of detaining members of the royal family (BBC 2017b), while evidently aimed at consolidating his personal power, were perceived by many youth as a genuine commitment to combat corruption (Thompson 2019). Their main concern was whether or not he would deliver on the promises of Vision 2030. The fast-paced delivery on many of the promised projects, such as those covered in Chapter 5, had, in my assessment, made a major contribution to increasing public trust in the Crown Prince's ability to deliver. The female tour guide who led the oasis walk that I had joined in al-Ula, while talking to me about her experience of working as part of the al-Ula tourism development programme, had noted how the local public had been surprised by the fast pace at which the tourism opportunities had developed in the area. 'When the Crown Prince had announced Vision 2030, we had thought these things will take time. However, we saw the opportunities develop in al-Ula at a surprisingly rapid pace. This has really built people's confidence in Vision 2030,' she noted. A respondent in Jazan, who was involved with the coffee-plantation programme, similarly noted how the local public had been highly impressed with the commitment and efficiency with which the state had pushed the programme and was supporting local cultivators. That the Saudi royal family does not claim legitimacy just on the basis of spending a small part of its oil rents on public welfare is also supported by the fact that the most intense political mobilization in Saudi Arabia happened in times of high (1979–80) or rising (1990–4; 2001–5) oil prices, when the state had extra money to appease the public (Guase III 2015). This puts into question the assumed causation between social spending and political quietism. Thus, the increase in studies aimed at understanding citizens' perceptions and expectations of states in the Gulf region (Jones 2019; Mortiz 2019), to test the political docility assumption underpinning the rentier state theory, has genuine merit.

For any state, having an engaged citizenry is a boon, because it is easier to govern people by consent than by force. No regime can effectively rule on the basis of fear and force alone – it is too costly an option to be viable in the long term (Malik 2017). Especially for a state which takes pride in its grand family legacy as the father of the nation, and as the Custodian of the Two Holy Mosques, there is an inbuilt incentive to govern in a way that wins respect and popular legitimacy. The internal checks on excessive expressions of power can, at times, be more powerful than the external ones. When examining the Saudi state's use of force to suppress political dissent (al-Rasheed 2015, 2021; HRW 2019), which, as noted in the introduction to this volume, is indeed a significant aspect of formal governance in Saudi Arabia, it is important to note that the state has generally been careful not to appear completely unchecked. For instance, there have been no incidents akin to the Rab'a mosque massacre in Egypt, where the Egyptian state killed over 800 civilians in a single operation, including many women and children (HRW 2014). The al-sahwah movement, which, since its emergence in the 1970s, has made demands for greater political freedoms using a discourse from within an Islamic framework, has been decisively repressed (Ménoret 2020). However, its leading figures could not have survived if the royal family were completely unchecked in its use of force to quell dissent. Prominent figures of the al-sahwah movement, such as scholars like Salman al-Awda, have experienced systematic state persecution (Bruton 2018; Qiblawi 2019). He was imprisoned in the 1980s and has been in prison again since 2017, despite deteriorating health. Other prominent scholars associated with the al-sahwah movement have faced similar fates (al-Jazeera 2019). However, what prevented the state from eliminating him in the 1980s, or why have the death penalties awarded to him and some other scholars during their current imprisonment been repeatedly postponed (al-Jazeera 2019)? Their continued survival cannot be attributed to any moral reservations by the Crown Prince regarding the use of extreme force, given the treatment of Khashoggi (BBC 2021; Kirchgaessner 2021). Instead, it is primarily due to the recognition that these scholars are widely respected (Mirza 2018), especially by many youths, and eliminating them would seriously erode the Crown Prince's moral legitimacy. While there are reports of solitary confinement and denial of adequate medical treatment, there is no evidence of horrific torture in prisons, as has occurred in Syria (Amnesty International 2023a). In my assessment, this restraint by the Saudi state in avoiding excessive force is a result of the Islamic moral framework that places heavy emphasis on fairness on the part of the ruler. To permanently eliminate those Islamic scholars who are arguing for political freedoms could be highly appealing to the royal family, and especially to the Crown Prince, but they also know that such actions will come at a serious cost to their moral standing in the eyes of the Saudi public. The fact that, despite facing a steady threat from the al-sahwah movement, the state has avoided the exercise of extreme options, reflects the royal family's confidence in the degree of legitimacy that it thinks it enjoys among the public. It recognizes that retaining popular legitimacy is more important for regime stability than eliminating the threat of political Islamists.

Conclusion: The Power of Labels

Why does recognizing the complexity of motives guiding state–society relationships really matter? First of all, the purpose of all social science inquiry ideally is to capture reality as accurately as possible. But, equally, the failure to recognize this complexity leads researchers to draw faulty conclusions that result in misinformed policies. Such conclusions also risk retarding the confidence of the public in their own future. We have seen that relabelling a country's experiences as positive, when they were formerly viewed to be failing, can influence subsequent scholarship. The label of 'developmental state' that evolved in the 1970s to recognize the distinct development trajectory followed by East Asian states, which due to the authoritarian nature of their regimes were formerly presented negatively in the Western scholarly literature, shifted the discourse around them and led to a rich literature highlighting how even states that are not democratic can achieve economic efficiency and invest in human development (Johnson 1999; Wade 2018). The gradual uptake of the label of development state gave legitimacy to the East Asian development model, which now features prominently in Development Studies textbooks. Similarly, the label of welfare state, which was introduced in reference to Britain and the European states as they took on the responsibility to provide basic services to all after the end of the Second World War (Briggs 1961), carries a positive connotation of a state that is accountable to its citizens. The label invokes an image of a state that has reached a high level of social development and prioritizes public welfare.

The central question is why a state's emphasis on providing social services to its citizens in one context wins it the label of a welfare state, while in a different country context, the provision of the same services is seen as a tool of political appeasement. As argued in this chapter, when such a labelling is based on the assumption that voting and taxation are the only sources of political legitimacy (Moore 2004), we fail to recognize the complexity marking state–society relationships in different cultural settings and stages of societal development. This, as we have seen in this volume, has resulted in generating a systematic negative bias in predictions in the Western media as well as among politicians and academics about the future direction of Saudi Arabia. Historically, most predictions made about Saudi Arabia's future have been negative (Manning 1998; Lippman 2012; Friedman 2015; Whitaker 2015), and media reports show the Western observers' relative surprise at the success of many social and economic reforms to date (Gary 2023; Slobodian 2023; Economist 2023b). Consequently, both scholars and Western policymakers largely failed to anticipate the dynamism that has characterized the engagement of Saudi youth with the state reform agenda since 2016.

Responding to accusations of slow change prior to 2016, Prince Turki bin Faisal, a prominent senior member of the royal family, often argued that we must remember Saudi Arabia's short history as a nation-state and engage with it knowing that 'it is a state still in the making' (Bano 2018e). This particularly holds true now, as the state–society relationship in Saudi Arabia has entered a new phase, whereby under the Crown Prince's leadership, the state has pledged to deliver on major targets, and a major share of the young population has come forward to support that effort. Whereas formerly the state drew its legitimacy from the provision of core services and from claiming religious legitimacy, moving legitimacy forward is becoming conditional on the delivery of the promised targets. As the state–society relationship increasingly centres around the pursuit of a shared vision for the future, contingent upon achieving the targets outlined in Vision 2030, the traditional sources of political legitimacy discussed in this chapter are expected to diminish in relevance (al-Rasheed 2020). This risk is inherent in the reform agenda led by the Crown Prince. However, it is in the Crown Prince's favour to bolster multiple sources of legitimacy rather than tie his political survival solely to delivering on economic promises. Therefore, the Crown Prince might strategically continue to harness traditional sources of legitimacy, as discussed in the previous chapter, in addition to establishing new ones. Either way, as society evolves, so will its political institutions. Political scientists who are willing to approach the study of the state–society relationship in Saudi Arabia with an open mind are likely to discover fertile ground for theorizing how the social contract between the state and society transforms when traditional institutions give way to modern forms of governance.

Chapter 8

THE RE-MAKING OF SOCIAL NORMS

The study of social norms, long a focal point for sociologists, has recently become fertile ground for scholarship across a range of disciplines, including economics (Bursztyn et al. 2020; Nosenzo and Görges 2020), public policy (Young 2007; Davin 2019; UNICEF 2020), and philosophy (Bicchieri 2006, 2017). While the idea that social norms influence economic and political outcomes is not new, what distinguishes current research is its grounding in methodological individualism (Swedberg 1990). This differs from traditional sociological approaches, which took social norms as a given until Coleman's (1990) influential study on the *Foundations of Social Theory* established the importance of understanding how social norms actually come about as a product of individual action. Beginning in the 1970s, this methodological shift sparked dynamic debates within and across disciplines (Swedberg 1990). Researchers are exploring not only how social norms affect socio-political and economic outcomes but also the conditions under which these norms emerge, stabilize, or change (Bicchieri 2006 and 2017). The emphasis has shifted from merely examining the impact of social norms to understanding their inner workings. This trend aligns with parallel developments in economic theory over the past three decades, particularly within the New Institutional Economics (NIE) (North 1990; Greif 2006) and, more recently, behavioural economics (Bursztyn et al. 2020; Nosenzo and Görges 2020). These frameworks increasingly recognize the role of informal institutions, such as social norms, values and belief, in shaping societal development trajectories. Studies comparing the divergent development paths of the Middle East and Europe, for example, have highlighted the role of informal institutions like Islamic law (Greif 2006; Kuran 2010). This growing body of work on informal institutions complements research specifically focused on social norms. Although terminology may vary, for instance the concept of 'path dependence' is commonly used in NIE literature to explain the persistence of institutions, the underlying analytical issues remain the same.

This chapter engages with key theoretical debates from two distinct but related bodies of literature: studies on social norms and research on informal institutions within the NIE framework. It integrates these insights with findings from preceding chapters that explore the evolution of conservative social norms in Saudi Arabia, particularly those emerging from the Wahhabi-Saudi alliance and why these norms are now transitioning to more liberal forms. The inductive approach of this chapter complements theoretical models based on pre-designed questionnaires or assumptions, offering instead insights grounded in the open-ended observation of complex realities as they naturally unfold. Much recent theorizing on social norms, particularly in philosophy and economics, relies on game theory (Bicchieri 2006, 2017; Bursztyn et al. 2020; Nosenzo and Görges 2020). These disciplines also frequently utilize surveys and experiments, much like psychologists do. While such methods offer the benefit of precise predictions under specific conditions, the identification of these conditions can be arbitrary and may not fully capture real-world complexities (Bursztyn et al. 2020; Nosenzo and Görges 2020). This limitation is also noted in the previous chapter, which discusses the state-society relationship in Saudi Arabia. This issue becomes especially salient in the field of international development, which focuses on applying learning from the developed world to the developing world. It is widely recognized that many international development interventions fail because they are predicated on assumptions rooted in Western experiences (North et al. 2009). These assumptions often do not apply in societies at different stages of socio-economic or political development, or in countries with divergent socio-religious values.

Qualitative studies, whether based on interviews or ethnographic observations, may lack the predictive precision of tightly framed models. However, when well-executed, they can be far more effective at identifying the intricate web of factors that influence individual actions and collective societal outcomes within specific contexts. The methodological approach adopted in this volume complements on-going efforts to refine theoretical understandings of social norms and informal institutions, particularly those that start with an individual actor approach. Drawing on rich ethnographic data, this approach allows for the close observation of relevant actors and their interactions in natural settings. This is in contrast to relying on assumptions about how people are likely to behave under specific conditions or using evidence generated in artificially created experimental settings. Additionally, by combining interviews with ethnographic observations, this methodology provides insights into the possible motivations guiding the actions of the individuals involved. While interview data may not reveal an absolute truth, interviews do offer a window into how respondents wish to present issues or what they perceive to be socially acceptable responses.

Mapping the on-going societal shift in Saudi Arabia towards liberal social norms not only informs rational choice theories on social norms and informal institutions but also addresses another critical question that has been at the centre of sociology for nearly a century: the relationship between economic modernization, the associated decline in religiosity and the emergence of liberal social norms – a process commonly referred to as secularization (Taylor 2007; Inglehart 2021). This transition from what can broadly be categorized as conservative social norms to liberal norms involves a shift in the relative power of the individual versus the collective. Conservative norms empower the collective to regulate individual social freedom, while liberal norms allow for greater individual choice. This progression is often assumed to be a natural part of societal modernization (Taylor 2007; Inglehart 2021). Economic development is expected to lead to reduced religiosity and consequently diminish the influence of religious elites. In many instances, this shift from conservative to liberal norms has evolved over several centuries. However, the rapid pace of change in Saudi Arabia, where the entire process has unfolded in less than a century, makes it a particularly intriguing case for identifying the mechanisms and processes that facilitate such a shift.

It's important to note that even in the case of the West, the spread of liberal norms, as we recognize them today, is a relatively recent development. For example, women in the West gained the freedom to apply to most colleges at Oxford or Cambridge University only from the 1970s onwards (Malkeil 2018). Similarly, sexual norms in the West began to change after World War I and World War II (Rendall 1985), but the acceptance of single motherhood and LGBT rights took much longer to gain traction; the latter became widely recognized only at the turn of the current century. In contrast, the Saudi case provides an opportunity to examine such a shift in values over a much shorter timeframe. From living in deserts as nomads or in small oasis settlements, commuting on camels with sparse material possessions, Saudi society transformed into a modern state with global influence in approximately seventy years. Furthermore, it underwent a dramatic transition from conservative to liberal norms in just five years. This rapid change offers an illuminating perspective on the interplay between economic development, the increasing desire for individual freedom and the diminishing role of religion in regulating the collective social sphere. Even when the social freedoms being granted may seem basic from a Western liberal viewpoint, such as Saudi women now having the right to drive a car, it's crucial to recognize that the underlying shift is phenomenal. Society is now embracing the basic principle that individuals should have the freedom to choose how they observe their religion. This core change in societal consensus underpins the on-going social liberalization in Saudi Arabia and reflects the central concerns that historically have driven societies towards secularization.

Yet, the Saudi case is also an exemplary study to show that this shift in societal consensus towards greater freedom in religious practice does not necessarily lead to uniform outcomes. The Western model is just one possibility, where secularization has resulted in a decline in religiosity itself (Inglehart 2021; World Values Survey (WVS) 2023). Evidence from other contexts, particularly Muslim societies, shows that it is possible for a society to respect freedom in the exercise of religion – meaning that the state does not enforce religious virtue – while still maintaining strong levels of religious belief (Inglehart 2021; WVS 2023). In such settings, religious tenets continue to shape the social sphere, as society refuses to endorse behaviour that deviates significantly from its core religious traditions. This is what we are also seeing in Saudi Arabia: the on-going social liberalization in Saudi Arabia is not causing a decline in religious belief. The Saudi public is increasingly seeking freedom in social matters, but it is retaining strong convictions in God and Islam. They are also resisting shifts in sexual norms, restrictions which, as discussed in Chapter 5, are seen as core tenets of Islamic doctrine. This pattern aligns with experiences in other Muslim countries, most of which have long permitted the social freedoms that Saudi Arabia is only now embracing. Yet, levels of reported religiosity remain high, not just in comparison to the West, but also in absolute terms (Inglehart 2021). Even second- and third-generation Muslims in Western diasporas consistently report high levels of religiosity, making the declining levels among local Christian populations appear particularly striking (WVS 2023). The Saudi example thus enriches our understanding not only of the mechanisms driving the processes of secularization but also of the various forms that secularization can take. It prompts us to question an often-posed query by some observers in the West: 'Why isn't Islam undergoing a reformation like Christianity did?' (Hasan 2015; Mastracci 2016; Zubaida 2016; Akyol 2017; Fukuyama 2017a, 2017b, 2017c).

Finally, the analysis presented also helps identify why Western aid-funded development programmes aimed at fostering liberal social norms in Muslim-majority countries often fail. Most Muslim-majority countries are categorized as developing nations, and they routinely rely on the economic support of international development agencies. These include the United Nations, the World Bank, the International Monetary Fund (IMF), and a range of bilateral donor agencies such as the British Department for International Development (DfID), now known as the Foreign, Commonwealth and Development Office (FCDO), and the United States Agency for International Development (USAID). While these programmes have historically focused on economic development and poverty alleviation, they have increasingly begun to explicitly target what are viewed as unproductive informal institutions or social norms (Klugman et al. 2014). Aid programmes that actively lobby for the formation of certain laws, the provision of specific services or changes in people's attitudes to support liberal norms are widely implemented under the banner of equality and social justice. This is particularly evident in interventions aimed at empowering women or promoting sexual freedom. Examples include development agencies' support for combating practices like female genital mutilation (UNICEF 2023) and early marriage, while advocating for family planning, sexual freedom and LGBT rights. One reason the individual actor approach to studying social norms and informal institutions has gained popularity is that this methodological framework reveals how it's not just ideology or beliefs, but often practical limitations that inhibit the shift from conservative to liberal norms. Recognizing this is key to designing more effective interventions.

The Saudi case offers compelling evidence for this argument. As modernization processes have opened up avenues for more individual choices, social preferences have shifted. Importantly, belief in Islam has not prevented the rollback of many socially restrictive norms, which were until recently justified on religious grounds. However, the Saudi case also illustrates the pitfalls of assuming that all societies will, or should, gravitate toward Western-style liberalism or fully adopt the principles that underlie liberal moral frameworks. As we have observed, the Saudi public has managed to modify behaviour concerning social norms without showing any decline in their faith in Islam or deviating from core restrictions, such as the prohibition on premarital sex or the acceptance of homosexuality. This suggests that there may always be differences across societies regarding what is perceived as the ideal balance between conservative and liberal stances, particularly on matters of gender and sexuality. This realization challenges the universalist assumptions that certain social norms, such as societal acceptance of premarital sex, children born out of wedlock, or the on-going debates in the West about same-sex partnerships and sexual fluidity, are universally optimal. Consequently, efforts by development agencies aiming to promote liberal social norms in Muslim societies need to account for the practical reasons why conservative norms persist, particularly in societies at lower levels of socio-economic development. At the same time, they must appreciate and respect that genuine differences in societal preferences may exist on certain issues.

8.1. Social norms and informal institutions

While different theories that utilize the individual actor approach define social norms in various ways and differ in the degree to which they attribute their production to strategic forward-looking behaviour versus natural responses to evolutionary forces (Opp 2018), there is a shared understanding across these definitions and approaches: social norms arise to regulate individual self-interest in order to produce a socially valued good. They are thus a product of human efforts, whether conscious or unconscious, to solve a collective action dilemma. James Coleman, who laid the foundation for the individual actor approach in sociology, defines social norms in these terms: 'A norm concerning a specific action exists when the socially defined right to control the action is held not by the actor but by others' (Coleman 1990: 243). He argued that, instead of taking norms as a given, we need to understand under what conditions, and to what extent, individuals cede the right to undertake an action to the collective. To fully comprehend why norms emerge, Coleman maintained that we must explore two related processes: the existence of a 'demand for a norm' and the 'realization of a norm'.

Coleman (1990) attributed the rise in demand for a social norm to the existence of an externality, whereby an action taken by one party has consequences for the other over which the latter has no direct control. The argument is that when the actions of one party have implications for another, and these implications are not regulated by law, the issue is either resolved through individual negotiation between the parties or, if that fails, society over time evolves norms to regulate such behaviour (Coleman 1990). This is particularly true for behaviours that may be individually productive but are collectively sub-optimal. For example, noise created by one's neighbour that causes disturbance, or smoke generated by a smoker in a public space affecting non-smokers (Coleman 1990; Opp 2018), can result in the demand for the emergence of social norms. These norms help mitigate negative externalities or promote positive ones, especially when the consequences of the externality are significant for collective well-being. The social enforcement mechanism can take the form of threats of social sanctions, such as isolation by the community, or the offering of rewards, such as bestowing social recognition or status. Similarly, within the NIE framework, the concept of transaction costs that arise when externalities cannot be resolved between two parties is key to explaining the rise of institutions, whether formal or informal (North 1990: 3). The same dilemma underlies the generation of a social norm, as a norm can only exist if members of the relevant group are willing to enforce sanctions against violators or endorse those who help enforce the norm. In this context, the role of dense social networks and the size of the group (Coleman 1990), which makes each member's actions noticeable, has been recognized as key.

While the explanation above provides a compelling account of the emergence of social norms as an evolutionary response to collective action dilemmas, it is worth noting that another significant source for the creation of social norms has historically been religiously endorsed moral frameworks. Across various societies, dominant social norms have often been products of religious teachings (Taylor 2007; Inglehart 2021). Although in recent history Western societies have moved from religious moral frameworks to secular reasoning (Taylor 2007; Inglehart 2021), ideational commitments, whether religious or secular, remain a key source for the emergence of social norms. Religiously inspired social norms are often more enduring than norms that have evolved as societal responses to collective action problems. This is because they are grounded in complex networks of religious belief systems. Decisions regarding a single social norm are often made based on how well it aligns with a broader, religiously informed moral framework (Coleman 1990; Opp 2018; Inglehart 2021). However, as evident in the rapidly changing socio-religious norms in Saudi Arabia, even religiously informed social norms can change. We, though, have also seen that norms based on core beliefs, those articulated in the Quran and endorsed by the Prophet, remain largely unchanged.

Therefore, when it comes to promoting liberal social norms in Muslim societies, it's crucial to recognize that many social norms are negotiable and can adapt to changing contexts. These are often based on secondary religious concerns. However, norms linked to core religious precepts tend to be very resilient within Islam. This explains why conservative religious communities might opt for liberal choices in one domain but not in another. It also sheds light on why some religiously influenced social norms in Saudi Arabia have undergone significant change, affecting the majority of society, such as women working in mixed-gender settings, while others have been accepted only by minor segments of the population, such as norms related to women wearing headscarves or ʿabayahs. As detailed in Chapter 2, these differences are often linked to how central the issue is in Islamic teachings and how firm the prohibitions are.

In this volume, we have explored three pivotal time periods that mark the emergence, consolidation and transformation of social norms in Saudi Arabia. The first era was characterized by social norms that shaped expectations of collective behaviour in Bedouin communities; the specifics of this period were covered in Chapter 7. By the late eighteenth century, the Wahhabi-Saudi alliance began to challenge these Bedouin norms with Wahhabi socio-religious norms. By the 1960s, these had become the dominant norms, effectively supplanting the Bedouin social norms (as discussed in Chapter 3). Now, another significant shift is underway. Wahhabi socio-religious norms are giving way to liberal social norms, where the individual's right to choose how to express their religiosity and enjoy social freedoms is becoming the dominant paradigm. Analysing the forces that shaped the emergence of specific social norms during these three periods, as well as their consolidation and the factors that triggered changes, offers a fascinating, inductively driven inquiry into how social norms emerge, stabilize and evolve.

Emergence of social norms

In Chapter 7, we explored how, prior to the establishment of modern Saudi Arabia, the Bedouins had a robust framework of social norms that regulated societal order. These norms were designed to ensure security and safety in the absence of a centralized state, as well as to facilitate basic survival in harsh desert conditions where access to water and food was uncertain. Dominant social norms discussed in the preceding chapter, embedded within the overarching norms of manliness and the valorization of bravery, emerged as society's evolutionary response to resolve numerous collective action dilemmas, including the fundamental issue of protecting human life. The norms valorizing warriors and those who demonstrated bravery were critical for maintaining law and order, as these virtues helped tribes defend their members against other tribes. While the emergence of, or demand for, such norms is understandable, their realization was facilitated by strong social networks and the severe consequences of not adhering to them. Tribal groups, as well as settlements around oases, were small and closely knit; individuals' contributions and actions were easily noticeable. The harsh desert conditions also made individuals and tribes wary of breaking commitments, due to a high degree of interdependence. For example, they needed to rely on rainfall in each other's areas, given the unpredictability of supply over time, as well as to prevent a constant state of warfare among and within tribes. In line with existing theories, close social networks, combined with the intensity of the needs outlined, ensured that members of the social group adhered to agreed-upon norms.

This setting also explains why virtues such as bravery, obedience to authority and generosity, which often come at a material cost to oneself, were highly rewarded. In the absence of a central state or formal economic sector, virtues like bravery and skills such as being an effective warrior or negotiator were highly valued. Individuals who demonstrated these qualities contributed to the survival of the tribe. Generosity was similarly valued by society, as it encouraged those with more resources to share, especially in a context where the majority struggled to meet basic survival needs. Precisely because these virtues entailed risks to one's life or the sacrifice of one's material goods, social norms required expressions of great respect and deference for those who demonstrated such behaviour. Good warriors who fought bravely, and those known for their wisdom and negotiation skills, rose to leadership positions. Those who showed generosity received the highest levels of societal respect. Odes were written in honour of warriors and individuals known for their generosity.

Thus, in such a context, a robust system of social norms emerged. Those who were less influential offered tributes by showing respect and bestowing honour on individuals who possessed these virtues, thereby incentivizing them to protect the collective interest. These social norms also created internal checks on those who held these virtues, restraining the excessive use of force and exploitation within their own tribe, which in turn ensured collective survival. Likewise, extensive norms governing what was deemed acceptable behaviour during raiding and what level of killing was considered excessive and dishonourable helped ensure that inter-tribal relationships didn't descend into complete chaos. Since this complex set of social norms, regulating both inter-group and intra-group behaviour, evolved over centuries as a natural but logical societal response to the local context, the evolution of these norms that governed societies in the pre-Wahhabi Arabian desert supports theories favouring the role of evolutionary forces (Opp 2018). According to these theories, the optimal solution emerges when people are free to coordinate their actions in response to incentives offered by the environment (Opp 2018). In such a framework, there is no need for a strategic planner or third-party enforcement, such as a state.

On the other hand, the replacement of these Bedouin social norms with Wahhabi-inspired socio-religious norms, which regulated Saudi Arabia's social sphere until the initiation of recent reforms, was largely a result of strategic efforts by the Al-Saud clan and its ally, the Wahhabi establishment. Studies on the embedding of a new religious movement in any context often highlight the role of the ruling power (Fukuyama 2017a, 2017b), and the Saudi case is no exception. Unlike the Bedouin social norms, which evolved as a logical response to natural conditions rather than being a product of a religiously informed moral framework, the Wahhabi social order was a product of an ideational framework. In this framework, commitment to religious ideals, as interpreted by Wahhabi scholars, shaped social norms. As recorded in Chapter 3, the religious norms promoted aligned with the interests of both the Al-Saud and Al-Wahhab clans. State machinery was actively used to embed these norms. During this phase, a central state evolved to enforce new societal norms, reducing the earlier freedom societies had to self-regulate through tribes and the enforcement of strong social norms. The Al-Saud clan actively helped to embed Wahhabi teachings by crowding out the spaces available to their rivals and by making state resources available for the spread of Wahhabi da'wah, allowing for the gradual conversion of people to Wahhabi ideals. Further, due to the formation of the Saudi state, the support provided by the state persisted long enough to not just introduce but also embed these new norms in society. Thus, in contrast to the Bedouin-era norms, which were largely a product of societal efforts to address collective action dilemmas, the Wahhabi Salafi norms were a product of a religiously guided moral framework, as interpreted by the Wahhabi establishment. While the former were a product of rational responses to evolutionary forces, the latter were a result of strategic design.

Persistence and path dependence

How Wahhabi-inspired socio-religious norms came to dominate the Saudi social sphere for close to a century also provides insights into how social norms consolidate over time. Within the literature on social norms, there is an active debate on the introduction and enforcement of social norms, but questions surrounding norm consolidation and change have received limited attention. Insights from NIE literature are illuminating in this regard. Institutional persistence, within this framework, is explained by the concept of path dependence, which emphasizes resistance to change due to past investments. In the Saudi case, the longevity of the rule helped embed Wahhabi teachings. Over time, the steady spread of Wahhabi da'wah led to genuine conversions to its teachings. Equally important was the state's provision of a formal enforcement mechanism in favour of socio-religious norms. In the absence of voluntary compliance, courts run by Wahhabi-trained judges and the hay'ah police could enforce the adoption of these norms. Whereas in the Bedouin era, main sanctions and rewards came in the form of honour or disgrace, violators now faced legal sanctions and formal punishments.

As Hobsbawm (2012) noted in his influential work on the invention of tradition, states can effectively use their propaganda machines to make certain beliefs part of the national identity by incorporating them into the national curricula. Similar processes marked the embedding of conservative norms by the Saudi state. School curricula came to promote the Wahhabi interpretation of Islamic social norms, and state-sanctioned events boasted the importance of the Saudi-Wahhabi alliance (Spannaus 2018a). These state-led efforts can help cultivate a sense of history, even if the ideals being promoted have only evolved over a couple of generations. Within the path dependence literature, the main on-going debate concerns whether this continuity is a product of habit or of a lack of superior options (Liebowitz and Margolis 1995). The Saudi case lends greater support to the latter. Wahhabi socio-religious norms survived only as long as they served a purpose: they helped legitimize Al-Saud's war on rival tribes and the formation of a central state. Now that society has economically developed and is globally connected, the excessively puritanical aspects of these norms are out of sync with current realities. Consequently, pressure has built up for these norms to give way to more liberal alternatives. Thus, the inertia caused by path dependence is broken when superior alternatives become available (Liebowitz and Margolis 1995; Bano 2012).

What we observe from the Saudi case is thus counterintuitive. It seems that pragmatic norms are often a reaction to evolutionary forces. This means that societal conditions create incentives for the creation and enforcement of social norms. Given the severity of their need, the majority come to contribute to their provision, thereby overcoming the collective action dilemma. Involvement of the state in embedding ideational social norms, whether based on religious or secular moral frameworks, is, however, not unique to the Saudi Arabian case. As we find in many historical contexts, when new religious traditions embedded themselves in a given society, these norms are often a product of strategic effort from the top (Fukuyama 2017a, 2017b, 2017c). Unlike pragmatic social norms, they do not necessarily offer immediate solutions to a problem.

The irony, however, is that once embedded, these norms gradually acquire powerful agency in influencing individual behaviour, more so than pragmatically induced social norms. This is because they offer a more complex set of incentives than those offered by pragmatic norms. Adherence to a socio-religious norm is motivated not just by fear of social repercussions or the pursuit of social recognition, but above all, by the desire to win God's approval. The ability of religious beliefs to inculcate a strong internal compulsion to adhere to prescribed behaviour acts as a powerful check on free-riding, making socio-religious norms more persistent than those primarily born out of a need to address a collective action dilemma. As Douglass North (1990) notes, this is what makes informal institutions 'sticky'. Given their strong binding power, what then explains a change in socio-religious norms?

Norm change

The study of the mechanisms facilitating on-going reforms in Saudi Arabia toward liberal social norms highlights the significant role of a strategic planner. This is similar to the embedding of Wahhabi Salafi social norms in society. However, unlike that experience, the new social norms are not being formally enforced. Instead, individuals are free to choose whether or not they wish to exercise the newfound freedoms made available through the removal of former restrictions and the provision of infrastructure that enables new social and economic opportunities. As analysed in this volume, the current shift in social norms is driven by voluntary compliance and the active adoption of new norms by members of society. This is akin to how Bedouin-era social norms emerged as societal efforts to minimize collective action dilemmas. The on-going changes and shifts away from Wahhabi social norms are also a product of this process. They arise from society's efforts to minimize emerging collective action dilemmas, which are fuelled by the vastly different experiences and opportunities of the current generation compared to older generations. Both the state and older generations – parents and grandparents – recognize that the attitudes of the young have changed due to altered social contexts and opportunities resulting from economic development. This has led to an appreciation that, for social harmony, it's important to adapt the societal context to meet the expectations of the youth. Several factors have played a role in ensuring this smooth transition.

The first key factor in this transition has been the availability of infrastructure to support choices aligned with liberal social norms. The state's strong track record of providing security has been crucial in allowing women to enter the workforce and participate in the social sphere. Even conservative families are becoming more open to letting women seize these opportunities, reassured by the prevailing sense of safety that comes with following established rules and decorum. Concurrently, the rapid emergence of opportunities for entertainment and tourism has invigorated social spaces and encouraged widespread public participation. Without the swift development of this supporting infrastructure, the Crown Prince's policy announcements favouring social liberalism would have had limited real-world impact. Adding to this momentum is the high quality of the programmes being developed and the efficiency with which they are managed. Reliable, quick reimbursements in cases of non-delivery make a significant difference, encouraging society to engage swiftly with new opportunities. This has minimized personal risks associated with exploring newfound social and economic freedoms. Fathers, brothers and husbands don't have to feel pressured about ensuring the safety of women in public spaces, thanks to this strong sense of state-guaranteed security. The issue now boils down to the women's internal conviction to adhere to accepted behaviour.

The second critical factor has been that, although the new norms may appear to be in stark contrast to the original norms, they are in fact building on local traditions and culture without violating the core religious principles. For example, mixed-gender settings are now acceptable for economic activities, but sexual liberty is not. As analysed in Chapter 5, the swift acceptance of these new norms is largely because they offer liberal interpretations of minor debates within Islam while leaving the core tenets untouched. What has changed is only a small part of the overall religious belief system. To outsiders unfamiliar with the complete framework of Islamic beliefs, these changes could be misinterpreted as the society or state abandoning its core principles. Such an interpretation could wrongly suggest that material incentives have overridden all other considerations. This perspective might also incorrectly indicate that the 'ulama' have always been pragmatists, devoid of any deeper religious commitments. What we have actually observed at each level – society, state, and 'ulama' – is a far more complex behaviour. All parties are concerned with maximizing both material and religious rewards. Calculations have been made on what can be traded within the overall belief system without compromising the core. This nuanced approach has been recognized and adopted by the state, ensuring that its programmes align with public sentiment while also allowing the 'ulama' to help preserve the core beliefs while relaxing their positions on secondary concerns. Simultaneously, programmes designed to promote entertainment and tourism build on Saudi cultural traditions and aesthetics, rather than replacing them with Western influences. There is a genuine effort to blend both elements, creating something original but with a strong local flavour. This gives people the sense of societal progression, rather than feeling that their old norms are being eroded by new ones.

The third key factor in the on-going changes in Saudi Arabia is the pivotal role played by media, the internet and social apps. This highlights the significance of introducing new technology in institutional change (North 1990), especially technology that facilitates bridging ties between individuals. Whether it's the introduction of the printing press, news cables, television or more recently, social media and internet technologies, the adoption of these platforms has historically facilitated the spread of new ideas and societal shifts by connecting people who are not part of one's immediate network. These technologies not only bridge gaps between individuals but also ensure that people can easily rely on bridging ties to meet individuals of different profiles as opposed to merely drawing on bonding ties.[1] In the case of Saudi Arabia, these platforms have done more than just connect the youth; they have also provided a space for content creators to express and share their evolving social expectations and alternative worldviews without fearing persecution from the state or religious authorities. Furthermore, the ability to gauge public interest, whether through likes, shares or views, has bolstered confidence among users that their views are supported within society.

Measuring support for a new idea is significantly easier now than it was with traditional media. For example, the number of hits is displayed directly below a YouTube video, making it easier to ascertain its reach compared to the circulation of a magazine or the viewership of a TV show.

The fact that many social media posts analysed in Chapter 4 received millions of hits provided both the youth and the Crown Prince with an indication of changing tastes and attitudes. This data made it clear to state observers that societal attitudes to observance of strict norms are changing. However, the degree of this change and the number of people it affects remained unclear. This uncertainty underscores the importance of constant monitoring of social media reactions by the state agencies from the moment these changes were announced. It also highlights the state's on-going willingness to reverse course or make adjustments if society starts to impose sanctions against those adopting liberal norms.

Fourth, the concept of a 'tipping point' has also proven to be relevant (Gladwell 2002). While changes from the 1960s to the 1990s laid the groundwork for current shifts, the more dramatic alterations in social norms can be directly attributed to developments over the last ten to fifteen years. These developments include an emphasis on higher education and increased foreign exposure for both Saudi men and women due to ease of travel, as well as widespread access to social media and internet connectivity. Therefore, what may appear as a sudden institutional change is often the culmination of incremental shifts that have occurred over time. However, at a certain point, momentum accelerates because the groundwork has been laid for the shift to occur. Recognizing what can speed up society's move toward this tipping point is essential for predicting the pace of institutional change.

Also, another reason the pace of change seems so fast is that state enforcement of Wahhabi Salafi norms artificially delayed the shift by at least a decade. Around 2010, early videos expressing ideas in favour of more liberal norms began circulating on social media. The state's enforcement of Wahhabi religious norms contributed to a phenomenon referred to in literature as 'pluralistic ignorance': a process whereby 'individuals may believe others endorse a certain action while no one personally does' (Görges and Nosenzo 2020: 288). The rapid change in social norms in Saudi Arabia is also partly a product of this phenomenon. Pluralistic ignorance regarding others' changing attitudes was only overcome when increased connectivity among the youth through social media established a growing consensus for more liberal spaces. While the majority of the public, as is now evident in their participation in the social sphere, were open to the idea of increased women's participation in the workforce or participating in mixed-gender settings, they assumed that the majority of others still adhered to conservative norms. This perception was also evident in the caution demonstrated by the state when announcing the initial reforms.

The frequency as well as the extent of reforms gained speed once there was evidence that the initial reforms were well-received. A recent study measuring social norms surrounding female labour force participation in Saudi Arabia conducted a norm-elicitation experiment with young Saudi husbands. The study aimed to assess their attitudes towards female participation in the workforce (Bursztyn et al. 2020). The authors found that 90 per cent of men in the sample said it was appropriate for women to work outside the home. However, the same men assumed that support for female labour force participation among other Saudi men was very low. This finding supported the thesis of pluralistic ignorance, whereby the men were willing to let the women in their family work outside the home but chose otherwise due to the assumption that the majority of society does not support it. The authors also showed that once husbands were informed of higher approval rates among Saudi men in general regarding women working outside the home, their willingness to support their wives in securing jobs increased.

As noted in Chapter 3, my own interviews with young women in universities revealed a similar pattern: while recognizing that the society is conservative, they consistently reported that the men in their own families were very supportive of their economic and social preferences. Under normal conditions, the increased opportunities that have been becoming available would have led to automatic adjustments, as those who could access them would have gradually shifted toward liberal norms. However, because the state was endorsing conservative norms, people were reluctant to publicly express or exercise liberal choices, as the dominant position appeared to favour conservative norms. Without state endorsement of religious norms, these conservative norms would have begun to change earlier and more gradually, as has happened in many Muslim countries (Klugman et al. 2014). The fact that the norms were officially supported made it difficult for those desiring liberties to gauge how many people were actually ready for change.

Finally, in line with debates in the literature, we have seen that the role of a reformer is also crucial in discussions about institutional change (Liebowitz and Margolis 1995). To what extent can an individual lead to major societal shifts, and to what extent is change a product of evolutionary forces is an often-repeated question. As is often noted, both explanations are important. We thus see that the role of the Crown Prince as a strategic planner, who recognized the growing dissonance in society and initiated reforms, has also been critical to the current social opening. The efficient provision of infrastructure to facilitate the adoption of new norms could not have occurred without his active leadership. The state is also using its power to reform curricula, this time in favour of liberal norms, while purging texts of the Wahhabi excesses (Gold and al-Lawati 2023).

However, all these efforts would have remained at the policy level and not resulted in a normative shift, unless society was ready for these changes. The fact that society was prepared is a result of evolutionary changes, as people responded to opportunities that became available through modernization. Initial reforms – such as those by King Faisal, who pushed for girls' education in the early 1960s against the will of the Wahhabi establishment, or parents who sent their daughters to school at that time – could not have predicted where these actions would collectively lead society by 2016. It's unclear whether the early reformers would have endorsed all the liberties that are now available,[2] such as desert raves. Yet, these incremental changes, the result of people maximizing their interests in light of new opportunities, were key to laying the groundwork for major change.

Thus, what we see is that while religiously informed social norms, which can be referred to as ideational social norms, required strategic action for embedding, their decline is less a result of strategic design. We have observed that liberal social norms are not being imposed or enforced by the state, as was the case with Wahhabi norms. Instead, the state is simply guiding the social change that has been evolving due to evolutionary forces. The state plays a significant role in both strategic intervention and evolutionary design, but the mechanisms through which it shapes change differ in these two contexts. The first follows the course of the invention of tradition, while the latter is aligned with the economic and social modernization of society. The House of Saud has thus, over time, led change in opposing directions: first embedding social conservatism and then reversing it.

The discussion above offers practical insights into how policies aimed at social norms can be effective. To be successful, several factors must be in place: the necessary infrastructure must be provided, the ideology must be homegrown rather than imported or aimed at eroding the core ideology, the reformer must be committed and efficient, and the timing must be right, meaning that the groundwork leading up to it should have been laid. Additionally, there must be strong, legitimate mobilizers within society. These mobilizers should use the local language, respect traditions and have access to widely shared media platforms that can both disseminate and monitor support for new ideas. In the final section of this chapter, we will explore how the neglect of these factors frequently leads to the failure of development programmes, especially those aimed at changing social attitudes in Muslim societies. Meanwhile, the shift from conservative to liberal norms in Saudi Arabia not only informs our theoretical understanding of social norms, institutional persistence, and change but also raises another important question: What is it about the processes of modernization that leads to a decline in religious or conservative social norms? Specifically, why do conservative social norms, which allow more societal checks on individual behaviour, dominate in cases where state and market institutions are weak? Conversely, why does the development of state and market institutions result in the emergence of more liberal social norms, even in societies where religion remains a dominant force? In such contexts, more liberal interpretations of religious texts come to replace literalist readings. It is to this question that we now turn.

8.2. From conservative to liberal norms

Why economic development and modernization leading to secularization has been a central concern in the field of sociology. The literature on the subject is extensive, but there is a general consensus that economic modernization tends to result in secularization – a phenomenon often referred to as the 'secularization thesis'. Data and analysis from the World Values Survey (WVS) are particularly illuminating in this regard. Initiated in the 1970s, the WVS periodically measures values across societies and categorizes them on a continuum ranging from conservative to liberal values, which are also referred to as traditional or pro-family values and secular-rational values, respectively. The former set of values emphasizes religiosity, national pride, respect for authority, obedience and marriage – precisely the kind of values that characterized the Saudi social sphere until the recent reforms. The latter set of values opposes traditional values and prioritizes individual freedom of choice.

Ronald Inglehart, one of the primary academic leads for the WVS, has analysed global trends in these shifts across regions in his recent book, which explores the decline in global religiosity (Inglehart 2021). It is useful to examine his reasoning on this subject both to understand how the Saudi case fits within this broader framework and to address the concept of Muslim exceptionalism. While he notes a persistent trend toward reduced religiosity in the West, including the United States (which was long considered an exception to the secularization thesis), he also engages with the question of why Muslim societies might be different. Let us first consider his explanation for the factors driving this shift.

Inglehart's argument posits that the decline in religiosity as societies economically develop is attributable not just to material security but also to the emotional security that comes from being part of a stable society. Drawing on data, he demonstrates that societies tend to shift from traditional to secular-rational values as their sense of existential security increases. This security encompasses not only economic development but also law and order and societal stability. In traditional societies, religion becomes a powerful force because it nurtures values essential for survival in conditions marked by economic scarcity and an absence of state-enforced law and order. As was argued in the case of the emergence of Bedouin-era social norms, Inglehart (2021) contends that religious values in traditional societies tend to emphasize generosity, marriage, family and honour. These norms are necessary for survival within that traditional context. For example, norms of sharing become vital in a setting where there is no social security system or unemployment benefits. Similarly, the family assumes heightened importance, serving as a network of support in the absence of a robust state welfare system. Inglehart (2021) argues that as material and related psycho-emotional security increasingly become provided by the state, there is a corresponding decline in religiosity.

Furthermore, where his arguments become particularly interesting and relevant to the Saudi context is in his focus on the regulation of marriage and sexual freedom in traditional societies. According to him, the emphasis on these norms aimed to ensure that sexuality was used solely for reproduction and within the confines of a family. This gave mothers an incentive to invest in childcare and family well-being. His contention is that economic modernization and state-provided security lessen the dependence on family members for survival, thereby eliminating the incentives for limiting sexual liberty. In this new context, sex takes on a role beyond mere reproduction, serving as a means for personal gratification. What was once curtailed for survival reasons can now be indulged in, as survival is no longer dependent on its restriction.

He observes that throughout history, religion primarily shaped social norms, enforcing strong taboos against sexual behaviour not linked to reproduction and often confining women to reproductive roles. However, this dynamic has reversed in the Western world. He notes that the decline in pro-fertility norms, which had remained strong in most societies for a long time, is contributing to the on-going decline in religious observance. The argument posits that all major world faiths vigorously emphasize pro-fertility norms, presenting them as divine edicts the violation of which will result in eternal damnation. These sanctions need to be robust because pro-fertility norms require individuals to suppress strong natural urges. Commandments like 'Thou shalt not commit adultery' conflict with deep-rooted desires. However, since these norms are so central, they are among the last to be abandoned. And when society does finally let go of them, the decline in religiosity becomes quite permanent.

He thus explains the shift as a logical process. Although he doesn't use the same terminology, his analysis supports the idea that social norms, and even religious values, emerge to solve collective action dilemmas. These dilemmas are more frequent in the absence of a strong central state capable of providing law and order as well as economic security. Economic modernization allows for enhanced state security, and stronger state and market institutions reduce the nature and frequency of collective action dilemmas. With fewer needs for coordination, people find it less costly to exercise free choice, even if it disregards the wishes of others, starting with immediate family members. This explains the heavy reliance on family unity in developing countries and the emphasis on individualism in the West.

The Saudi case largely aligns with this analysis. However, his argument that these innate desires for sexual freedom are so strong that they override pro-fertility norms when economic security is attained doesn't entirely hold true when applied to Muslim societies. As we saw in the Saudi case, while it's consistent with his argument that pro-fertility norms are central to religious traditions and often carry strict sanctions (which is also true in Islam), there remains a clear reservation to embracing sexual freedom. This is largely because the prohibition on it is considered core to Islamic teachings. One could argue that the on-going social opening in Saudi Arabia will eventually lead to greater sexual liberty. Yet, we repeatedly encounter the same dilemma: in Muslim societies, unlike in Western ones, economic development and even social liberalization do not necessarily lead to a shift in social norms toward accepting sexual freedom or its related aspects, such as sex outside of marriage, single motherhood, or LGBT behaviour (Bano 2017; WVS 2023).

Simultaneously, it's noteworthy that the level of religiosity in Muslim societies remains exceptionally high, both in absolute and comparative terms (Inglehart

2021; WVS 2023). This trend stands in contrast to the West. In his analysis, Inglehart (2021) highlights a pronounced cultural zone pattern, showing that within Islamic societies in the Middle East, the emphasis on traditional values is especially strong. Time-series data from ten Muslim-majority countries, spanning an average of nearly sixteen years, reveals the highest levels of religiosity among any major cultural group. Moreover, the age-based differences in religiosity that exist in high-income countries are minimal in Muslim-majority nations. To illustrate the divergent worldviews across different cultural zones, examples of two survey questions aimed at measuring the emphasis a society's places on traditional versus secular-rational values are useful. When asked, 'How important is God in your life?', responses varied dramatically: while only 8 per cent considered God important in Confucian-influenced societies, the figure jumps to 99 per cent in Muslim-majority societies. When asked how important religion is in their lives, 79 per cent of respondents in Muslim-majority countries said it's 'very important', compared to 21 per cent in Catholic Europe and just 11 per cent in Protestant Europe. The question of whether the refusal to abandon pro-fertility norms is due to their centrality in Islam or whether adherence to Islam itself leads to the preservation of these norms is somewhat circular. What is clear, however, is that Islam exhibits a particular resilience in preserving pro-fertility norms and limiting sexual freedom at the societal level, as well as in sustaining its own relevancy and influence.

Inglehart (2021) attributes this persistence of Islamic prohibitions in Muslim societies partly to a lack of modernization and economic development. He contends that economic growth fosters pro-liberal norms only when it arises from education and employment, arguing that the oil wealth of Gulf states like Saudi Arabia distorts this process. However, as we have discussed in this volume, the current shift in social norms in Saudi Arabia is very much a product of the same factors he identifies as being important for the shift from conservative to liberal norms: education, employment, a strong sense of security and global connectivity. While he could dismiss these factors when writing the book in 2022, as noted throughout this volume, similar processes have played a role in triggering on-going changes in Saudi Arabia.

We thus need to review whether the social opening in Saudi Arabia is an exception to the normative assumptions about economic modernization leading to socially liberal norms. Specifically, what is it about Islam that makes it particularly resilient in restricting sexual liberty and preserving its own identity, even in the face of economic modernization? Although any answer can only be hypothetical, this volume concludes by offering some insights. These insights are garnered not only from rigorous observations of Muslim religiosity in the spiritual centres of Mecca and Medina, but also from interviews with numerous believers conducted across the various studies I have led over the past two decades across Muslim societies (Bano 2012, 2017, 2018c, 2018e, 2020). Understanding what allows Islam to maintain its hold also indirectly helps us address an often-asked question: why has Islam not undergone a reformation similar to that of Christianity?

8.3. Engineering social norms in Muslim societies

The question of why Islam has not undergone a reformation, unlike Western Christianity, has elicited two dominant responses. First, specialists in the Reformation in the West note that it was the product of complex socio-political and economic factors, unique to the time (Mastracci 2016; Fukuyama 2017a, 2017b, 2017c). Second, those answering from within the Islamic tradition argue that there has been a constant effort at internal reform within Islam (Hasan 2015; Akyol 2017; Zubaida 2016) – the emergence of the Wahhabi movement being one such effort. Both of these arguments have merit. At the same time, many would argue that the question is not worthy of attention, as it is Eurocentric and has a simplistic understanding of the factors that led to the decline of religion in the European public sphere and the rise of the modern nation-state, as well as its complex outcomes. I agree with this critique. However, since the question continues to provoke on-going debate, it is worth exploring if the analysis of the continued importance of religion in shaping public perception of the appropriate extent of reforms in Saudi Arabia, as recorded in the previous chapters, despite the declining authority of religious elites, provides insights into the resilience of the appeal of classical Islamic teachings.

In this section, I briefly outline what I have found compelling about Islam to believers during my fieldwork in Saudi Arabia, as well as my two decades of fieldwork with Muslim communities in multiple Muslim-majority sites and among Muslims in the diaspora. In *The Rational Believer: Choices and Decisions in the Madrasas of Pakistan* (Bano 2012), I examine in detail the appeal of madrasa education to parents and students in Pakistan. In *Female Islamic Education Movements: The Re-democratisation of Islamic Knowledge* (Bano 2017), I explore why Islam is particularly resilient in preserving itself in the face of modernization, demonstrated through the lens of believing women, with prolonged fieldwork with women mosque networks across Pakistan, northern Nigeria and Syria. This study particularly addresses the centrality of restraint on sexual transgressions as key to how these women differentiate the liberties they enjoy compared to what is deemed essential by modern Western feminism. In *The Revival of Islamic Rationalism: Logic, Metaphysics and Mysticism in Modern Muslim Societies* (2020), I examine the appeal of Islam to modern, educated young Muslims in the West who join Islamic networks promoting a more logic-based and mystical approach to Islam.

There are several dimensions of the appeal of Islam that have repeatedly emerged across these studies as well as in my discussions with local Saudis and pilgrims of different backgrounds in Mecca and Medina. The crux of it, in my experience, consistently goes back to the power of Islam's ʿaqidah and its emphasis on a direct relationship with God. This emphasis on establishing a direct connection with God proves very powerful, especially when it becomes a central part of the Islamic teachings received. This aspect has also often been cited as a reason for conversions from Christianity to Islam: notable converts to Islam, like Muhammad Asad,

Hamza Yusuf and Tim Winter, have highlighted this as a significant factor in their conversions (Asad 1982; Bano 2020). This focus also helps explain the potency of Wahhabi Salafi core teachings, which emphasize ʿaqidah, and their success in winning followers. However, across the populations covered in my studies, it is clear that different individuals find different ways to build their conviction in God. For some, the core Islamic rituals, including the daily five prayers and fasting, as well as other rituals such as the pilgrimage to Mecca, become the primary means to cultivate their faith, as I found with most of my respondents in madrasas in Pakistan (Bano 2012). For others, the mystical dimension of Islam, especially when linked with deeper philosophical questions, is the primary way to reach God, as was often the case for the young Muslims I studied in the West (Bano 2020) and the more modern, educated women in Muslim-majority countries, who were also pursuing higher-level Islamic education in private study circles (Bano 2017).

Sufi mystics like Ibn Arabi have delved deeply into single verses, such as 'Everywhere you turn there is the face of God' (2:115), producing complex works of mysticism (Chittick 1989). Meanwhile, the extensive body of studies in Islamic fiqh caters to those with a legalistic mindset. Although Wahhabi Salafi tradition is known for emphasizing direct engagement with the Quran and Sunnah, the appeal of rich fiqh literature (Hallaq 2009) remains strong among believing Muslims. This comprehensive body of Islamic legal scholarship clearly outlines rules and methods for categorizing major and minor sins and understanding proportionality. In my studies that I have quoted above, I have found that when adhering to specific rulings, people often justify them within the broader ethical framework of their cultural or religious context. Each belief is not an isolated idea; it makes sense within the larger moral framework provided by the religion, complete with specific dictates and levels of punishment. The highly developed tradition of fiqh allows for reasoned debate and argumentation, which, across my studies, appears to be important for my respondents in building conviction that Islam is a logical religion. Many of my respondents have repeatedly explained their conviction in Islam in terms of it being a logical religion (Bano 2012, 2017, 2020). Thus, the possibility of cultivating a direct connection with God, whether through a ritualistic or shariʿah-oriented approach or a more mystical route – which in a simplistic sense has historically shaped the ʿulama' and Sufi divide – has actually been quite effective in retaining individuals of different propensities within the Islamic fold.

The belief in the untampered nature of the Quran is also a key factor, in my observation, in explaining Islam's resilience. As I have found across my studies, believers consider everything mentioned in the Quran to be the untouched word of God, leaving no room for doubt. This has influenced how both the legal scholars, but also the public, have, over time, identified core versus secondary legal provisions. For example, public acceptance of sexual liberty struggles to gain traction in Muslim societies and communities, even as they modernize economically or live in the diaspora (Bano 2017, 2020), as also documented in the case of on-going social change in Saudi Arabia. The complete prohibition of sex outside marriage for both genders is firmly stated in the Quran, even though sexual pleasure within marriage is encouraged (Ali 2016). The importance given to what is explicitly stated in the Quran as core guidelines also explains why hadith and sunnah acquire such paramount importance in shaping Muslim actions, given that the instruction to follow the Prophet is repeatedly emphasized in the Quran (Verses 3:132; 4:79; 8:20; 24:54; 59:7).

The centrality of the belief in the Quran as the ultimate word of God, combined with the Quran's emphasis on following Muhammad's example, thus makes the Salafi method of reasoning, with its focus on direct engagement with the Quran and hadith, particularly compelling. Whether or not they belonged to the Salafi tradition, for my respondents across these studies, including the pilgrims and locals interviewed in Saudi Arabia, following the Prophet's example as understood through hadith and Sunnah is critical to their faith. In Medina, at the Prophet's Mosque, this reverence is constantly on display. How does one relate to the reverence the Prophet has for many Muslim believers, such as a woman who walks barefoot around the streets of Masjid-i-Nabawi because it is the city of the Prophet, and she might touch the same ground where the Prophet had stepped – as did one of my respondents from southern Punjab, Pakistan, whom I met at the door of Masjid-i-Nabawi? Similarly, a male respondent from India, acting as a tour guide during one of the activities I joined in Riyadh, criticized some of the entertainment projects, such as mixed raves, saying, 'but not here; it is the birthplace of my Nabi (a term of deep endearment for Prophet Muhammad).' The strong emotive dimension of the relation many Muslims feel with the Prophet, as also visible in the reactions to Prophet Muhammad cartoons, is quite a unique religious phenomenon in my assessment.

Finally, in my research, I've observed an important comparative institutional dimension. The West's advanced stage of development has provided other societies, including Muslim ones, with the opportunity to observe both the benefits and drawbacks of secularism (Bano 2017). I have documented this in detail, highlighting how educated Muslim women argue against the ideals of Western feminism (Bano 2017) and how the critique of excessive commercialism and materialism associated with Western-style modernity is central to the appeal of classical Islamic scholarly networks among educated young Muslims in the West (Bano 2020). This is especially evident at both the personal level, in terms of faith, and the societal level, concerning family life. One widely recognized drawback of modernization and individualism is the feeling of loneliness it can engender (Taylor 2007). The gradual encroachment of liberal cultural values is beginning to challenge strict, literalist interpretations of Islamic teachings, particularly among young Muslims educated in modern Western institutions. However, this shift cannot be interpreted as a decline in faith. On the contrary, exposure to Western lifestyles is also making many Muslims acutely aware of the limitations of materialism and the emotional void that can accompany a complete loss of faith (Bano 2017, 2020). This sense of inner emptiness, which Charles Taylor (2007) argues is driving many young people in the West back towards some form of spirituality, is also prompting more educated, modern Muslims to recognize the importance of preserving their faith.

There is thus little value in debates that expect the Muslim world to undergo a transformation akin to the Reformation in Christianity for a modern liberal sphere to emerge. Instead, we need to appreciate how Muslim societies are constantly evolving according to their social and material conditions, often leading to 'alternative modernities', as a steadily growing body of scholarship on women's Islamic piety movements is showing (Mahmood 2005; Abu-Lughod 2013; Bano and Kalmbach 2011). This is important, first and foremost, as a right of each society to develop its own moral debates, which, as we have seen in this volume, do evolve with socio-economic development. Evidence from Saudi Arabia, along with a growing number of empirical studies, shows how socially conservative gender interpretations of Islam relax when economic opportunities become available for women in Muslim societies to engage more broadly in society and economy (Hanmer et al. 2014). Moreover, understanding these dynamics is crucial for designing more effective development programmes for Muslim societies.

Against this backdrop, international development programmes often falter in Muslim societies because they adhere too rigidly to Western logic, reasoning, or moral frameworks (Nussbaum 2001; Wallace and Porter 2014). This is evident in standard gender empowerment initiatives (Nussbaum 2001; Hanmer et al. 2014) and the failure of Western NGOs to gain widespread support due to their Western-centric language and approaches (Wallace and Porter 2014). Moreover, reformers lack the necessary accountability as donor organizations don't take local value systems seriously (Nussbaum 2001; Wallace and Porter 2014). To craft more effective and realistic interventions, it's crucial to distinguish between what is considered a minor issue and what is deemed a major issue within a religious tradition. For instance, advocating for women's sexual liberty, as international development organizations do through funding NGOs to promote these demands in Muslim countries, is fundamentally different from promoting mixed-gender work settings. While both will prove controversial in a conservative Muslim setting, the latter is much more negotiable than the former, as seen in the case of on-going social change in Saudi Arabia and across the Muslim world. Female employment rates have climbed in recent decades with increased access to education, but social norms around sexuality, especially concerning sex outside marriage and same-sex relationships, remain largely unchanged. Understanding these nuances is vital not only for the on-going debate in international development between universal and local cultural preferences (Sen 1995; Nussbaum 2001) but also for gauging the likely level of societal and religious resistance to various reforms. This ability to differentiate between core and secondary principles is especially important for effective policymaking by governments wanting to make progressive changes while operating within an Islamic framework, such as the government's attempt to introduce the New Family Law in Morocco (Chaara 2011; Aldashev et al. 2012).

To craft effective interventions in Muslim societies, we must first gauge their current stage of societal development. As we have seen, factors like economic growth, educational opportunities and employment prospects, rather than religious ideology alone, often determine a society's readiness for certain social freedoms (Platteau 2000). A conservative Muslim community may be open to primary and secondary education for girls but resistant to coeducation, or it may accept women in the workforce but only in gender-segregated settings (Hanmer et al. 2014). Focusing on immediately attainable goals does not mean abandoning long-term objectives; rather, it acknowledges that social norms will only evolve if aligned with existing institutional frameworks.

Next, it's essential to identify credible reformers within the religious sphere. While a fully liberal reformer might advocate for sweeping changes, such efforts often fail to take root, as has historically been the case in multiple Muslim countries, including Turkey (Spannaus 2018b). Reformers who operate within the existing religious tradition and meet established criteria for legitimacy are generally more successful in enacting meaningful change (Aldashev et al. 2012; Hanmer et al. 2014). The reasons on-going reforms in Saudi Arabia have had a high degree of acceptance are that the state has not tried to force people to engage with spaces, which for many are contentious, such as dance raves, even though it is providing opportunities for them, thereby avoiding the imposition of an aggressive liberal agenda from the top. Furthermore, the importance of utilizing local traditions, vocabulary and symbols cannot be overstated. Doing so makes new ideas more relatable and more likely to be accepted by the community (Wallace and Porter 2014). The on-going social changes in Saudi Arabia illustrate this point well. By noting that, while much is changing, the importance of Islam for most of the public remains unchanged, the volume thus also helps shed light on why Muslim communities are likely to continue challenging the secularization thesis, as noted by World Values Survey results (Inglehart 2021), even as they undergo economic modernization.

GLOSSARY

'abayah 'cloak'; refers to a robe-like dress worn by Muslim women
adab Islamic norms of behaviour and comportment
adhan call to prayer
'alim (pl. 'ulama') Islamic scholar
amanat (Urdu) item left for safekeeping
'amir honorific title for a commander, prince or general
'ashrah literally 'ten'; in reference to the last ten days of Ramadan
'asr obligatory one of the five obligatory prayers, performed after the sun is half way between noon and sunset
al-asma' al-husna the divine names
al-sahwah al-Islamiyyah 'the Islamic awakening'; a movement by conservative 'ulama' asking for sociopolitical reform in Saudi Arabia (1960s–80s)
al-salaf al-salih the first three generations of righteous Muslims
al-wala' wa-l-bara' loyalty and disavowal
'aqidah Islamic creed, the Islamic science of theology
aqalliyyat minorities
'ayah a verse of the Quran, literally 'a sign'
bedouin Arab nomads
bid'ah religious innovation
da'i someone who proselytizes, preaches Islam
da'wah proselytizing, preaching of Islam
dhikr remembrance of Allah; repeated recitation of specific Quranic verses, names of God or certain prayers
dirah pasture land
du'a' supplication or invocation, seeking assistance from God
fajr dawn prayer
faqih (pl. *fuqaha'*) Islamic jurist
fatwa religious decrees; a formal but generally non-binding statement on an issue or question pertaining to Islamic law, issued by a *mufti* (from *ifta'*, 'to advise')
fiqh Islamic jurisprudence
fitna temptation, disorder, civil strife
fus-haa classical Arabic
hadar sedentary population; term used to refer to the Arabian tribes that developed small settlements around oases in the Arabian desert, as compared with the nomadic nature of Bedouin life
hadith reports describing the words, actions or habits of Prophet Muhammad
hafiz one who has memorized the entire Quran
hifz the act of memorization of the Quran
hajj the annual Muslim pilgrimage to Mecca

hakim ruler
halal legitimate; approved in Islamic law
halaqah teaching circle
Hanbali a legal school of Islamic law (*madhhab*) whose origins are attributed to Ahmad ibn Hanbal (d. 855/214)
Hanafi a legal school of Islamic law (*madhhab*) whose origins are attributed to Abu Hanifah (d. 767/150)
haram illegitimate; forbidden in Islamic law
haramayn 'the two sanctuaries'; Mecca and Medina
hay'ah Islamic religious police; also referred to as morality police
hijab head covering for women
hudud mandated divine punishments in Islamic law, including corporeal punishments and the death penalty
'ibadah ritual practices such as prayer, fasting
iftar evening meal marking the opening of the fast
ijtihad the process of legal reasoning in which the jurist applies maximum effort in order to derive a ruling, extrapolation of rulings from scriptural sources
Ikhwan 'brothers'; a term used to refer to Bedouin soldiers mobilized by the House of Saud, drawing on Wahhabi da'wah in the early twentieth century
imam prayer leader
iman faith
'isha' obligatory night prayer
ishraq optional prayer to be performed just after sunrise
jahiliyyah the age of ignorance; often used to describe the 'ignorant' way of life of Arabs before Islam
jihad to strive, to exert, to fight
Jum'ah Friday congregational prayer, where the imam gives the weekly sermon
Ka'bah a cube-shaped building located in Masjid-i-Haram (the Sacred Mosque in Mecca)
kafir unbeliever
kalam Islamic theology
khanqah a Sufi lodge; generally used for Sufi teachings and performance of rituals
khawarij 'seceders'; an early sectarian group that revolted against the Caliph Ali ibn Abu Talib (d. 661/ 40)
khutbah sermon given during the Friday midday service
kufr unbelief; in reference to the act of disbelief in God, the prophets and other pillars of faith in Islam
la ilaha illa Allah there is no god but Allah
laylat al-qadar 'night of power or decree'; the night when the Quran was revealed to Muhammad
madhhab 'way'; an Islamic legal school of thought
madrasah 'place of study'; an Islamic educational institution, a higher Islamic school
mahram unmarriageable kin, such that sexual intercourse would be considered incestuous
majlis gathering; formal or informal councils
makruh an act deemed unfavourable in Islamic law
Maliki a legal school of Islamic law (*madhhab*) whose origins are attributed to Malik ibn Anas (d. 795/179)

mataf the area immediately around the *Ka'bah* where *tawaf* takes place
mubtadi' innovator
mufti a learned scholar in Islamic law, qualified to give *fatwa*
mutawwi' 'volunteer'; the Saudi religious police
nafl a type of optional prayer, which is not obligatory but promises reward
niqab face veil
niyyah intention
qadi an Islamic judge
qadr predestination; the belief that God knows everything and has already decreed everything that will happen
qalb heart
qiyam al-layl praying during the night, ideally standing in prayer and reciting an extended portion from the Quran
Quran the Islamic sacred book
Quranic relating to the Quran
rak'ah a 'unit' of ritual prayer in Islam, consisting of a combination of certain prayers and actions. A full prayer (*salah*) is composed of multiple *rak'ah*s
rawdah same as *Riyad al-Jannah* (see below)
Riyad al-Jannah the area between the *minbar* (pulpit) and the chamber of Prophet Muhammad in the Masjid al-Nabawi, which is next to his grave. It is also referred to as the rawdah and is believed to be a part of heaven.
sahabah Prophet Muhammad's companions
salah ritual prayer; the five daily obligatory prayers in Islam
sahih authentic
salaf pious forbears, referring to the first three generations of Muslims (an abridgement of *al-salaf al-salih*, see above)
salawat to pray for divine blessing on Prophet Muhammad
sirah biography of the Prophet Muhammad
Shafi'i a legal school of Islamic law (*madhhab*) whose origins are attributed to Muhammad ibn Idris al-Shafi'i (d. 820/204)
shahadah the declaration of faith in monotheism and Muhammad's prophecy required to become Muslim
shari'ah God's eternal will for humanity that is considered binding, the ideal of Islamic law
sharif a descendant or relative of the Prophet
shirk 'association'; to associate partners to God in divinity or any one of the divine attributes, the gravest sin in Islam
suhur pre-dawn meal consumed at the start of the Muslim fast
sujud bowing down in worship; to prostrate
souq bazaar; market
sunnah practice of the Prophet Muhammad
tafsir 'clarification'; Quranic commentary and interpretation
tahajjud optional prayer offered during the night, ideally in the last third of the night
takfir excommunication; declaring someone non-Muslim
takfiri often in reference to one who excommunicates other Muslims in an excessive manner

tarawih special prayers said after *'isha'* prayer during Ramadan, often involving reading long portions of the Quran over the performance of many *rak'ah*s
tariqah 'way'; a Sufi order
tasawwuf Sufism, Islamic mysticism
tasbih rosary
tawaf one of the principal rites of the *'umrah* and *hajj*; refers to circumambulating or walking in circles around the Ka'bah in an anti-clockwise motion
tawhid divine unity and singularity; the oneness of God
tekke (Turkish) an Ottoman Sufi lodge
'ulama' Islamic scholars or clergy
ummah global Muslim community
'umrah optional Muslim pilgrimage to Mecca that can be performed any time during the year; often referred to as lesser hajj
'urf 'custom'; a theoretical consideration in legal interpretation based on social customs and realities
Vilayat-i-Faqih 'Guardianship of the Islamic jurist'; a religiopolitical doctrine adopted in the Islamic Republic of Iran, characterized by the exercise of political authority by religious clerics
wahdat al-wujud the 'unity of being'; the metaphysical view that there is a single existence coming from God that is shared by all creation, associated most prominently with Ibn 'Arabi
wajd state of religious ecstacy
wajib obligatory
wali guardian
waliyah male guardianship
waqf religious endowment
waqi' reality of the time
wasatiyyah a contemporary approach to Islamic jurisprudence that claims to tread a fine line between extreme conservatism (e.g. often attributed to Salafis) and reformism grounded in excessive reinterpretation of scripture to fit liberal values.
wudu' ablution
zakah obligatory giving; one of the five pillars of Islam
zuhr obligatory noon prayer

NOTES

Chapter 1

1 In this volume, the terms 'Wahhabism' and 'Saudi Salafism' are used interchangeably. For an understanding of how followers of Muhammad Ibn Abd al-Wahhab came to adopt the label of 'Salafi', see section 3.1 in Chapter 3; also see Commin (2015).

2 These media outlets, most noticeably, include CNN, *The Economist* and *The New York Times*. During 2023, these and other outlets have carried frequent articles on developments within Saudi Arabia, including offering cover page stories, see Slobodian (2023) and The Economist (2023c). This coverage is largely around social and economic change (Economist 2023c), the dynamism of the Saudi Sovereign Fund and the investments being made under it (Slobodian 2023), especially in the sports area (Blinder 2023; Woodyatt et al. 2023), and the appeal of its tourism projects (CNN Travel 2023).

3 Saudi Arabia has faced resistance from various Islamic groups over the decades. The most violent incident occurred in 1979 when a radical Islamic group took control of the Ka'bah (al-Sarhan 2015). For resistance posed by al-Qaida, see al-Saud (2021). For resistance by scholars advocating for greater political liberties within an Islamic framework, see Lacroix (2011) and al-Rasheed (2006, 2015).

4 Refer to Mouline (2014) for a comprehensive analysis of the constitution and functioning of the religious hierarchy in Saudi Arabia.

5 This religiopolitical doctrine adopted in the Islamic Republic of Iran is characterized by the control of political authority by religious clerics. Ayatollah Ruhollah Khomeini, who led the popular movement that toppled the government of the Shah of Iran (Muhammad Reza Pahlavi, 1941–1979), leading to the establishment of the clerical role, presented the main thinking behind it.

6 He is recorded to have fathered forty-five sons, of which thirty-six are estimated to have reached adulthood and established their own families. After the death of King Abdulaziz in 1953, the kingship passed to his sons in the following order: King Saud (1953–1964), King Faisal (1964–1975), King Khalid (1975–1982), King Fahd (1982–2005), King Abdullah (2005–2015), and King Salman (2015–). Crown Prince Muhammad bin Salman al-Saud is thus the first grandson primed to be the future King.

7 Some prominent members of the royal family, such as Prince Alwaleed bin Talal and ex-ministers, were placed under arrest at the Ritz-Carlton Hotel in Riyadh in November 2017 (BBC 2017b). While highlighting the divisions within the royal family and the high-stakes game played by the Crown Prince to consolidate his political power, which continued in subsequent periods (BBC 2020), the move did enhance the credibility of the Crown Prince among some youths. They believed his argument that this was a high-level effort to purge the system of corruption: Thompson (2019) notes that in the focus group discussions he held with young male Saudis across the country, some respondents were of the view that since

the Crown Prince has had a free hand to curtail corruption, there should now be no reason for failure to deliver on the goals promised under Vision 2030.

8 For a critique of the tendency among these authors to equate the observation of religious practices in Muslim societies with conservative Islam and excessive piety, see the 'Introduction' in Bano (2018a).

9 The Qatari approach to enforcing Wahhabi teachings has, however, been different, due in part to not having a powerful official Wahhabi establishment, unlike Saudi Arabia (Dorsey 2017).

10 The Ottoman Empire, for instance, historically relied on *Qanun* (rule), which tabulated administrative regulations that supplemented the Shari'ah and the discretionary authority of the sultan. When faced with increasing pressure from the rising military and scientific prowess of neighbouring European powers, it also introduced a system of legal reforms known as the Tanzimat reforms (1839–1876) (Britannica 2023b).

11 The driver I engaged in Dammam, originally from Indian Kashmir, was highly critical of the Crown Prince's neglect of the concerns of Indian Muslims, given his extensive efforts to foster economic ties with India. He expressed similar concerns about the Saudi royal family's, and other Gulf royal families', failure to use their economic influence to defend Muslims facing state persecution, including Muslims in China or the struggles of ordinary Palestinians at the hands of the Israeli state. Such views among Muslims about the wasted potential of the Gulf monarchies, including Saudi Arabia, are, in my experience, not an exception but the norm.

12 Rubin (2017) references the following verse (4:59) from the Quran to argue that the Islamic emphasis on obeying the ruler is particularly binding: 'O you who have believed, obey Allah and obey the Messenger and those in authority among you . . .' (Rubin 2017: 51). See the full discussion on pages 49–54, under the heading 'The Doctrine of Religious Legitimization in Islam and Christianity' in Chapter 3 (Rubin 2017).

13 President Obama was received at the airport by the governor of Riyadh, Prince Faisal bin Bandar al Saud, instead of the king. Unlike normal practice, the event was not broadcast live on Saudi TV. Commentaries within the Saudi media, as well as the international media, focused on how the two sides are forced to stay in an 'unhappy marriage' as outright 'divorce' will (for both) be too costly (Black 2016).

14 Based on an online survey with Saudi male youth, Thompson (2019: 170), who complemented this survey by holding focus group discussions with male Saudi youth, notes that 67 per cent were positive about the reforms and the future of the country. While many of them understand the risks and challenges that could hinder the realization of the promised reforms (see Thompson 2019: 170–2), it does underscore their positive attitude towards the Crown Prince's efforts to shift the Saudi state away from oil dependency and diversify the economy to ensure long-term economic stability.

15 Prominent female Muslim scholars, who have critiqued many gender-based restrictions as being a product of male clerical authority and have attempted to reinterpret the text to allow more agency to women; however, unlike Mernissi, they actively resist the label of Islamic feminist as they see the title feminist to be too tied to Western framing, for discussion on this see Bano (2017).

16 Najd refers to the central Arabian land, which is the home base of the Saudi royal family; this is juxtaposed against Hejaz (Yamani 2009), the land on the western border of the Arabian Peninsula comprising the holy land of Mecca and Medina.

Chapter 2

1 It opened on 21 November 2022 and was reportedly built in just eighty-two days (Time Out 2023).
2 For a more detailed explanation of these concepts, see Chapter 3. Also, see Maher (2016) for a detailed discussion of these concepts and how they are also specifically invoked by Salafi jihadi groups.
3 Verse 24:31: 'And say to the believing women that they should lower their gaze and guard their modesty; that they should not display their beauty and ornaments except what (must ordinarily) appear thereof; that they should draw their veils over their bosoms and not display their beauty except to their husbands, their fathers, their husbands' fathers, their sons, their husbands' sons, their brothers or their brothers' sons, or their sisters' sons, or their women, or the slaves whom their right hands possess, or male servants free of physical needs, or small children who have no sense of the shame of sex; and that they should not strike their feet in order to draw attention to their hidden ornaments. And O ye Believers! Turn ye all together towards Allah, that ye may attain Bliss.' For a detailed discussion on the importance of this verse and how classical jurists have justified the covering of hair and modest dressing for women as an obligatory part of Islamic dictates, see Alkiek (2023).
4 Javed Ahmad Ghamidi, a prominent reformist Islamic scholar from Pakistan who advocates this position and is also listed by Jahangir (2017) as one of the few scholars to do so, argues that Islamic dictates only require women to lower their gaze, wear modest clothing, cover their bosom with a piece of cloth and not display ornamental embellishments before unrelated men.
5 In my own fieldwork with madrasahs belonging to all five madrasah boards in Pakistan that were state-recognized in 2008, including those affiliated with the Shia board, there was a shared emphasis on the need for women to cover their head and body (Bano 2012). Despite clear differences on many issues of Islamic jurisprudence and Islamic history, and the notably high emphasis placed among Shia madrasahs on the use of *aql* (intellect) versus *naql* (copy) in teaching methodology, the emphasis on female covering in practice – as visible in female madrasahs in the dress of students and teachers and in their teachings – was the same (Bano 2012).
6 There have been reports of harassment of women participating in mixed-gender desert raves held on the outskirts of Riyadh (Usher 2021). However, as we will discuss later in this volume, this is an example of an extreme event from the perspective of Saudi society, even among those who appreciate the basic social liberalization agenda.
7 In justifying the social reforms, the Crown Prince has attributed the social conservatism marking the Saudi society pre-2017 reforms to measures the royal family had to put in place post the 'Mecca revolt' in order to counter the appeal of religious extremists. See al-Rasheed (2021) for a critique of this narrative being promoted by the Crown Prince.
8 The design of the concert hall, which is entirely made of glass, has won much acclaim.
9 This annual festival is being organized by a Saudi entertainment company, MDLBeast, which presents itself as the region's leading music promotion company (MDLBeast 2023).
10 These young female Saudi DJs are actively profiled in Saudi newspapers and presented as examples of hidden talent among Saudi women that needs to be nurtured. For the great opportunities these women see for themselves in current investments being

made by the state and private industry in promoting entertainment options, see al-Hamawi (2021); for profiles of some of these female DJs, see al-Hamawi (2021) and McIntrye (2021).

11 The reported turnout at the successive sandstorm festivals has been between 600,000 and 700,000 people (Bullen 2022; McIntyre 2021), but this also included visitors from the other Gulf states. In interviews, the festival was repeatedly referenced as an example of things going too far. However, it was also emphasized that the large turnout should not be interpreted as acceptance of this culture among the Saudi youth who attend. As one respondent noted, 'people go because they want to try it once, not because they endorse this culture'.

12 It is among the world's largest sovereign wealth funds with estimated assets of US$776 billion (£538 billion). For an analysis of the dynamism currently marking this fund, see The Economist (2023b), and Slobodian (2023).

13 Named 'Mukaab', which means 'cube', the project has proven controversial (Uddin 2023). For coverage of negative comments shared by Muslims from many countries on social media, see Fatima (2023).

14 For details on the historical importance of Old Jeddah as promoted by the Saudi government today, see Visit Saudi (2023b).

15 Edge of the World is the name of the 1,131 m high cliff that lies approximately 100 km from Riyadh, part of the Tuwaik Mountain range.

Chapter 3

1 For a first-hand account of how the Sharif family eventually led to the decline of Ottoman rule in the Arabian Peninsula, see Lawrence (2015).

2 Its law enforcers are also commonly referred to as mutawwiʿ. Established in 1940, the body exercised much authority, especially from the 1980s onwards, until King Salman curbed its powers in 2016 through the issuance of a royal decree.

3 For a demonstration of this in the case of al-Azhar University in Egypt, see Zeghal (2007), for example.

4 The ongoing textbook reforms are, according to a report produced by an independent Israel and UK-based institute, *Monitoring Peace and Cultural Tolerance in School Education (IMPACT-se)*, further purging books of any extremist ideas and promoting the acceptance of more tolerant values, including the normalization of relationships with Israel. For a summary of the report's findings, see Gold and al-Lawati (2023).

5 Salman al-Awda, for instance, was reported as having 14.6 million followers on his Twitter (now X) account in 2018 (Bruton 2018).

6 There have been public critiques made by some Saudi scholars who have gone into exile, and whose family members have reportedly been targeted by the state (Alam 2023; Akkad 2023), but none belong to the senior Wahhabi establishment.

Chapter 4

1 Thompson (2019: 115–16) provides details of how social media usage accelerated in Saudi Arabia in the past decade. By 2018, he notes, the number of internet users in Saudi Arabia had reached thirty million, which means that over 91 per

cent of the Saudi population has access to it. Drawing on local sources, he records that by 2014, there was already high usage of social media apps among the Saudi population: Facebook (80 per cent); Twitter (53 per cent); Instagram (43 per cent); YouTube (40 per cent). During 2017–2018, the following three were the most popular chat apps among users: WhatsApp (24.27 million); Facebook's Messenger (13.30 million); Snapchat (12.97 million).

Chapter 5

1 My respondent in al-Ula, for instance, was trying to convey that the ideal time to visit is late autumn but was mentioning the names of summer months according to the Gregorian calendar. He admitted that he cannot easily recall the correct names of months in the Gregorian calendar, as he organizes his life according to the Hijri calendar.
2 The United Arab Emirates (UAE), with 9 million people, of whom only 1.15 million are UAE citizens, has the second-largest population in the GCC countries after Saudi Arabia. The remaining countries, including Qatar, have populations of less than 4 million.

Chapter 6

1 The educational background of the lead imam of Masjid-i-Haram in 2022, Sheikh Yasir ad Dawsary, for example, is in line with that of members of the Wahhabi establishment (ITH 2019).
2 For an alternative interpretation of Ibn ʿAbd al-Wahhab's core teachings and intellectual legacy, see Wahhabi Islam (DeLong-Bas 2004). DeLong-Bas offers a revisionist reading that questions post-9/11 portrayals of Wahhabism as inherently militant, emphasizing themes of reform, moral renewal, and a restricted conception of jihad in Ibn ʿAbd al-Wahhab's writings instead. She further argues that key features associated with contemporary extremist movements—such as global jihad, martyrdom and the targeting of civilians—are not present in his work.
3 For insight into how many Salafi Wahhabi preachers still defend the original daʿwah of Abdul al-Wahhab, critiqued by Qadhi, including justifying the Ottomans as kafir, listen to the multi-episode commentary by the famous British Salafi preacher, Abu Khadeejah Abdul Wahid (Abdul Wahid 2023).

Chapter 7

1 King Saud, who reigned between 1953 and 1964, was arguably an exception. However, as discussed in the subsequent section, his tenure was consequently cut short.
2 Examples include the Justice and Development Party (AK Party) in Turkey, the Justice and Development Party (PJD) in Morocco, and the Pakistan *Tehreek-i-Insaf* (Movement for Justice) in Pakistan.

3 He maintains that popular legitimacy is best measured as the capacity of the system to cultivate and maintain the belief that the existing political institutions are the most appropriate ones for society.

Chapter 8

1 Bonding social networks bring 'together people who are like one another in important respects (ethnicity, age, gender, social class, and so on)' while bridging ties 'bring together people who are unlike one another' (Putnam and Goss 2002: 11).
2 It is well documented that early feminists in Europe actively resisted certain demands, including calls for sexual freedom, which became core to feminist struggle in the late twentieth century (Rendall 1985; Bano 2017).

BIBLIOGRAPHY

Abdelaal, M. 2015. ‘Leadership Accountability in Islam: Islamic Standards for Holding the Executive Accountable for Official Misconduct.’ *4 Global Journal of Comparative Law*. (11 May 2015). [Available Online: https://ssrn.com/abstract=2605103; Accessed 1 October 2023].

Abdo, G. 2017. *The New Sectarianism: The Arab Uprisings and the Rebirth of the Shia-Sunni Divide*. Oxford: Oxford University Press.

Abdul Wahid, A.K. 2023. ‘Kitab At-Tfawhid Explained by Shaykh Ahmad An-Najmi, Part 1.’ *Salafi Sounds*. Lecture Series by Abu Khadeejah Abdul Wahid. [Available Online: https://www.salafisounds.com/kitab-at-tawhid-explained-by-al-allamah-ahmad-an-najmi-complete-playlist-lecture-series-by-abu-khadee jah-abdul-wahid/; Accessed 20 September 2023].

Abueish, T. 2023. ‘Vision 2030, GASTAT: 63 Percent of Saudis Under the Age of 30.’ *Al-Arabiya News*. 31 May 2023. [Available Online: https://english.alarabiya.net/News/saudi-arabia/2023/05/31/GASTAT-63-percent-of-Saudis-under-the-age-of-30; Accessed 21 September 2023].

Abulof, U. 2017. ‘“Can’t Buy Me Legitimacy”: The Elusive Stability of Mideast Rentier Regimes.’ *Journal of International Relations and Development* 20: 55–79.

Abu-Lughod, L. 2013. *Do Muslim Women Need Saving?* Cambridge, MA: Harvard University Press.

Acemoglu, D., and Robinson, J.A. 2006. ‘Economic Backwardness in Political Perspective.’ *American Political Science Review* 100(1): 115–31.

Agrama, H.A. 2012. *Questioning Secularism: Islam, Sovereignty, and the Rule Of Law in Modern Egypt*. Chicago, IL: University of Chicago Press.

Akeel, M. 2004. ‘Khadija Center Helping Businesswomen.’ *Arab News*. 6 September 2004. [Available Online: https://www.arabnews.com/node/256202; Accessed 20 September 2023].

Akeel, M. 2017. ‘The Case for Gender Equality in the Muslim World.’ *al-Jazeera*. 26 April 2017. [Available Online: https://www.aljazeera.com/opinions/2017/4/26/the-case-for-gender-equality-in-the-muslim-world; Accessed 1 October 2023].

Akeel, M. 2021. ‘Saudi Women on the Rise but Gender Gap Remains 2021.’ *Arab News*. 18 August 2021. [Available Online: https://arab.news/2entb; Accessed 20 September 2023].

Akkad, D. 2023. ‘Saudi Arabia: Brother of Prominent Scholar Sentenced to Death Over Tweets.’ *Middle East Eye*. 25 August 2023. [Available Online: https://www.middleeast eye.net/news/saudi-arabia-saeed-ghamdi-brother-scholar-sentenced-death-tweets; Accessed 20 September 2023].

Akyol, M. 2017. ‘The Islamic World Doesn’t Need a Reformation.’ *The Atlantic*. 31 October 2017. [Available Online: https://www.theatlantic.com/international/archive/2017/10/muslim-reformation/544343/; Accessed 20 September 2023].

Alam, H.A. 2023. ‘Retired Teacher Sentenced to Death in Saudi Arabia after Tweeting Criticism.’ *CNN*. 1 September 2023. [Available Online: https://edition.cnn.

com/2023/08/31/middleeast/saudi-arabia-retired-teacher-death-sentence-intl/index.html; Accessed 20 September 2023].

Alamer, S. 2022. *The Saudi 'Founding Day' and the Death of Wahhabism. The Arab Gulf States Institute in Washington.* [Available Online: https://agsiw.org/the-saudi-founding-day-and-the-death-of-wahhabism; Accessed 18 July 2024].

al-Arabiya. 2020. 'This is How Cinemas in Saudi Arabia Looked 40 Years Ago.' *Al-Arabiya.* 20 May 2020. [Available Online: https://english.alarabiya.net/variety/2017/12/11/Pictures-Cinemas-in-Saudi-Arabia-40-years-ago; Accessed 27 September 2023].

al-Atrush, S. 2022. 'Saudi Crown Prince Mohammed bin Salman Appointed Prime Minister.' *The Financial Times.* 27 September 2022. [Available Online: https://www.ft.com/content/saudi-crown-prince-mohammed-bin-salman-appointed-prime-minister; Accessed 18 July 2024].

al-Azami, U. 2021. 'Legitimising Political Dissent: Islamist Salafi Discourses on Obedience and Rebellion after the Arab Revolutions.' In M. Bano (ed.) *Salafi Social and Political Movements: National and Transnational Contexts*, 61–86. Edinburgh: Edinburgh University Press.

al-Droubi, M. 2020. '"Overwhelming Support" for Saudi Arabia's Reforms.' *The National.* 4 January 2020. [Available Online: https://www.thenationalnews.com/world/gcc/overwhelming-support-for-saudi-arabia-s-reforms-1.959661; Accessed 20 September 2023].

al-Fahad, A.H. 2004. 'From Exclusivism to Accommodation: Doctrinal and Legal Evolution of Wahhabism.' *New York University Law Review* 79(2): 485–519.

al-Fahad, A.H. 2015. 'Raiders and Traders: A Poet's Lament on the End of the Bedouin Heroic Age.' In B. Haykel, T. Hegghammer and S. Lacroix (eds) *Saudi Arabia in Transition: Insights on Social, Political, Economic and Religious Change*, 231–62. Cambridge: Cambridge University Press.

al-Faisal, T. 2016. 'Mr Obama, We Are Not "Free Riders".' *Arab News.* 14 March 2016. [Available Online: http://www.arabnews.com/columns/news/894826; Accessed 20 September 2023].

al-Ghalayini, B.M.K. 2023. 'Saudi Arabis is Blessed with an Aspiring, Youthful Population.' *Arab News.* 4 June 2023. [Available Online: https://www.arabnews.com/node/2315821/saudi-arabia-blessed-aspiring-youthful-population; Accessed 21 September 2023].

al-Ghazali, A.H.M. 2009. *The Secrets of Pilgrimage: Kitab Asrar al-Hajj*. Kuala Lumpur: Ibrahim Books.

al-Hamawi, L. 2021. '"Music Connects Us All" Says SOUNDSTORM DJ.' *Arab News.* 19 December 2021. [Available Online: https://www.arabnews.com/node/1989641/lifestyle; Accessed 27 September 2023].

al-Hussein, E. 2019. 'Saudi Changes to Guardianship System Ease Restrictions on Women.' Arab Gulf States Institute in Washington. 7 August 2019. The Arab Gulf States Institute in Washington. [Available Online: https://agsiw.org/saudi-changes-to-guardianship-system-ease-restrictions-on-women/; Accessed 20 September 2023].

al-Jaser, M. 2023. '(@meshalaljaser): Instagram Photos and Videos.' [Available Online: https://www.instagram.com/meshalaljaser/; accessed 20 September 2023].

al-Jazeera. 2017. 'Saudia Arabia to Allow Women to Drive.' *al-Jazeera.* 27 September 2017. [Available Online: https://www.aljazeera.com/news/2017/9/27/saudi-arabia-to-allow-women-to-drive; Accessed 1 October 2023].

al-Jazeera. 2019. 'Who are the Key Sahwa Figures Saudi Arabia is Cracking Down On?' *al-Jazeera.* 5 June 2019. [Available Online: Who are the key Sahwa figures Saudi Arabia is cracking down on? | Religion | Al Jazeera; Accessed 18 July 2024].

al-Jazeera. 2020. 'Mohammed bin Salman: The Dark Side of Saudi Arabia's Crown Prince.' *al-Jazeera*. 9 March 2020. Available Online: https://www.aljazeera.com/news/2020/3/9/mohammed-bin-salman-the-dark-side-of-saudi-arabias-crown-prince.

al-Jazeera. 2021a. 'Saudi Minister Defends Volume Limit on Mosque Loudspeakers.' *al-Jazeera*. 1 June 2021. [Available Online: https://www.aljazeera.com/news/2021/6/1/saudi-minister-defends-volume-limit-on-mosque-loudspeakers; Accessed 1 October 2023].

al-Jazeera. 2021b. 'The Saudi Women's Rights Activists Who Remain Behind Bars.' 11 February 2021. [Available Online: https://www.aljazeera.com/news/2021/2/11/saudi-arabia-women-rights-activists-that-are-still-in-jail; Accessed 18 July 2024].

al-Kinani, M. 2020. 'The History of Makkah Grand Mosque's Expansion.' *Arab News*. 29 July 2020. [Available Online: https://www.arabnews.com/node/1711561/saudi-arabia; Accessed 20 September 2023].

al-Kinani, M. 2021. 'Saudi Business to Remain Open During Prayer Time.' *Arab News*. 16 July 2021. [Available Online: https://www.arabnews.com/node/1895481/saudi-arabia; Accessed 1 October 2023].

al-Mayman, H. 2021. 'First Saudi Woman to Participate in International Beauty Pageant: 'Believe in God, In Yourself, Set a Goal, and Everything Will come to You.' *Arab News*. 7 September 2021. [Available Online: https://www.arabnews.com/node/2369006/saudi-arabia; Accessed 28 July 2024].

al-Otaibi, N. 2020. 'Vision 2030: Religious Education Reform in the Kingdom of Saudi Arabia Special Report.' Riyadh: King Faisal Centre for Research and Islamic Studies (KFCRIS). [Available Online: https://kfcris.com/pdf/cc53a3201f65554c400886325b5f715e5f577d35934f7.pdf; Accessed 20 September 23].

al Qassemi, S. 2012. 'Tribalism in the Arabian Peninsula: It Is a Family Affair.' *Jadaliyya*. 1 February 2012. [Available Online: www.jadaliyya.com/Details/25199/Tribalism-in-the-Arabian-Peninsula-It-Is-a-Family-Affair; Accessed 18 July 2024].

al-Rasheed, M. 1996. 'The Politics of Encapsulation: Saudi Policy towards Tribal and Religious Opposition.' *Middle Eastern Studies* 32(1): 96–119.

al-Rasheed, M. 2002. *A History of Saudi Arabia*. Cambridge: Cambridge University Press.

al-Rasheed, M. 2006. *Contesting the Saudi State: Islamic Voices from a New Generation*. Cambridge: Cambridge University Press.

al-Rasheed, M. 2013. 'Saudi Arabia: Local and Regional Challenges.' *Contemporary Arab Affairs* 6(1): 28–40.

al-Rasheed, M. 2015. *Muted Modernists: The Struggle Over Divine Politics in Saudi Arabia*. London: Hurst & Company.

al-Rasheed, M. 2020. 'The New Populist Nationalism in Saudi Arabia: Imagined Utopia by Royal Decree.' *Middle East Centre*. [Available Online: https://www.lse.ac.uk/middle-east-centre/the-new-populist-nationalism-in-saudi-arabia-imagined-utopia-by-royal-decree; Accessed 18 July 2024].

al-Rasheed, M. 2021. *The Son King: Reform and Repression in Saudi Arabia*. Oxford: Oxford University Press.

al-Rasheed, M. 2024. 'Saudi Arabia: Who Will Mohammed bin Salman Appoint as Crown Prince?' *Middle East Eye*. 29 May 2024. [Available Online: https://www.middleeasteye.net/news/saudi-arabia-who-will-mohammed-bin-salman-appoint-crown-prince; Accessed 18 July 2024].

al-Saadi, S. 2008. 'Women Driving is Not in Conflict with Religion: Scholars.' *Arab News*. 21 February 2009. [Available Online: https://www.arabnews.com/node/309049; Accessed 20 September 2023].

al-Saggaf, Y. 2004. 'The Effect of Online Community on Offline Community in Saudi Arabia.' *Electronic Journal on Information Systems in Developing Countries* 16: 1–16.

al-Sarhan, S. 2015. 'The Struggle for Authority: The Shaykhs of Jihadi-Salafism in Saudi Arabia, 1997–2003.' In B. Haykel, T. Hegghammer and S. Lacroix (eds) *Saudi Arabia in Transition: Insights on Social, Political, Economic and Religious Change*, 215–41. Cambridge: Cambridge University Press.

al-Sarhan, S. 2016. 'The Saudis as Managers of the Hajj.' In E. Tagliacozzo and S.M. Toorawa (eds) *The Hajj: Pilgrimage in Islam*, 196–212. Cambridge: Cambridge University Press.

al-Saud, A.K. 2021. 'Wahhabi Salafism versus Islamic State: Age-old Traditions Appropriated by Modern-Day Terrorists.' In M. Bano (ed.) *Salafi Social and Political Movements: National and Transnational Contexts*, 171–87. Edinburgh: Edinburgh University Press.

al-Shahrani, H.A. 2016. 'A Brief History of the Internet in Saudi Arabia.' *TechTrends* 60: 19–20.

al-Shihabi, A. 2016. *The Saudi Kingdom: Between the Jihadi Hammer and the Iranian Anvil*. Princeton, NJ: Marcus Wiener Publishers.

al-Turki, N. 2022. 'Saudi Comedy "Sattar" Hits the Funny Bone at Premier.' *Arab News*. 28 December 2022. [Available Online: https://www.arabnews.com/node/2223506/saudi-arabia; Accessed 20 September 2023].

al-Ula Moments. 2023. 'Experience AlUla.' [Available Online: https://www.experiencealula.com/en/alula-moments; Accessed 20 September 2023].

Aldashev, G., Chaara, I., Platteau, J.-P., and Wahhaj, Z. 2012. 'Formal Law as a Magnet to Reform the Custom.' *Economic Development and Cultural Change* 60(4): 795–828.

Aldosary, A. S. Nahiduzzaman, K.M. and Rahman, M.T. 2021. 'Financing the Welfare State System in Saudi Arabia.' In C. Aspalter (ed.) *Financing Welfare State Systems in Asia*, 153–71. London: Routledge.

Alesa, M. 2015. '*Barbs*.' [Available Online: https://www.youtube.com/watch?v=soMOZdR5Z8g; Accessed 20 September 2023].

Alesa, M. 2016. '*Hawages* (Concerns).' [Available Online: https://www.youtube.com/watch?v=1rUn2j1hLOo; Accessed 20 September 2023].

Ali, K. 2016. *Sexual Ethics and Islam: Feminist Reflections on Qur'an, Hadith, and Jurisprudence*. London: Oneworld.

Alkiek, T. 2023. 'Is Hijab Religious our Cultural? How Islamic Rulings Are Formed.' Yaqeen Institute. 20 September 2023. [Available Online: https://yaqeeninstitute.org/read/paper/is-hijab-religious-or-cultural-how-islamic-rulings-are-formed; Accessed 27 September 2023].

Alotaibi, L. 2022. 'From Quantity to Quality: Restructuring Saudi Arabia's Scholarship Program.' The Arab Gulf State Institute in Washington. 2 June 2022. [Available Online: https://agsiw.org/from-quantity-to-quality-restructuring-saudi-arabias-scholarship-program/; Accessed 20 September 2023].

Alshamsi, M.J. 2011. *Islam and Political Reform in Saudi Arabia: The Quest for Political Change and Reform*. Abingdon: Routledge.

Amnesty International. 2022. 'Saudi Arabia Codifies Male Guardianship and Gender Discrimination.' *Amnesty International*. 9 December 2022. [Available Online: https://www.amnesty.org/en/latest/research/2022/12/saudi-arabia-codifies-male-guardianship-and-gender-discrimination/#:~:text=Musawah%2C%20a%20global%20movement%20for,(female%20or%20male); Accessed 20 September 2023].

Amnesty International. 2023a. 'End the Horror in Syria's Torture Prisons.' Amnesty International. [Available Online: https://www.amnesty.org/en/latest/campaigns/2016/08/syria-torture-prisons/; Accessed 1 October 2023].

Amnesty International. 2023b. 'Saudi Arabia: Alarming Crackdown on Online Expression.' Amnesty International. 14 February 2023. [Available Online: https://www.amnesty.org/en/latest/news/2023/02/saudi-arabia-alarming-crackdown-on-online-expression; Accessed 18 July 2024].

Amnesty International. 2024a. 'Defying Saudi Arabia's Kingdom of Repression.' *Amnesty International.* Available Online: https://www.amnesty.org/en/projects/saudi-arabia-kingdom-of-repression; Accessed 18 July 2024].

Amnesty International. 2024b. 'Saudi Arabia: Woman Jailed for 11 Years for Online Expression Supporting Women's Rights.' *Amnesty International.* 30 April 2024. [Available Online: https://www.amnesty.org/en/latest/news/2024/04/saudi-arabia-woman-jailed-for-11-years-for-online-expression-supporting-womens-rights/#:~:text=In%20the%20past%20two%20years,%2DQahtani%20(45%20years); Accessed 18 July 2024].

Amnesty International. 2024c. 'Ten Ways that Saudi Arabia Violates Human Rights.' *Amnesty International.* 5 March 2024. [Available Online: https://www.amnesty.org.uk/saudi-arabia-human-rights-raif-badawi-king-salman; Accessed 18 July 2024].

Arab News. 2016. 'Deputy Crown Prince Backs Women Driving.' *Arab News.* 23 April 2016. [Available Online: http://www.arabnews.com/featured/news/914356; Accessed 20 September 2023].

Arab News. 2020. 'The History of Makkah Grand Mosque's Expansion.' *Arab News.* 29 July 2020. [Available Online: https://arab.news/nv3pa; Accessed 20 September 2023].

Arab News. 2022a. 'Saudi Digital ID Holders can Travel within GCC After Obtaining Required Travel Documents.' *Arab News.* 18 December 2022. [Available Online: https://www.arabnews.com/node/2218101/business-economy; Accessed 20 September 2023].

Arab News. 2022b. 'Third Expansion of Makkah Grand Mosque Receives 19 million Worshippers.' *Arab News.* 1 May 2022. [Available Online: https://arab.news/8rwpk; Accessed 20 September 2023].

Arab News. 2023. 'Saudi Comedy "Sattar" to get UK Premier in London this Week.' *Arab News.* 8 February 2023. [Available Online: https://www.arabnews.com/node/2247216/lifestyle; Accessed 20 September 2023].

Arnosti, N., and Liu, A. 2018. 'Why Rural America Needs Cities.' Brookings. 30 November 2018. [Available Online: https://www.brookings.edu/articles/why-rural-america-needs-cities/; Accessed 24 July 2024].

Arts, W.A., and Gelissen, J. 2010. 'Models of the Welfare State.' In F.G. Castles (ed.) *The Oxford Handbook of the Welfare State*, 569–83. Oxford: Oxford University Press.

Asad, M. 1954. *The Road to Mecca.* New York: Simon and Schuster Inc.

Asad, M. 1982. *Islam at the Crossroads.* Gibraltar: Dar Al-Andalus.

Atassi, B. 2017. 'Saudi Music Video on Women's Rights Goes Viral.' *CNN.* 4 January 2017. [Available Online: https://www.cnn.com/2017/01/04/middleeast/saudi-song-women/index.html; Accessed 20 September 2023].

Bano, M. 2012. *The Rational Believer: Choices and Decisions in the Madrasas of Pakistan.* Ithaca, NY: Cornell University Press.

Bano, M. 2017. *Female Islamic Education Movements: the Re-democratisation of Islamic Knowledge.* Cambridge: Cambridge University Press.

Bano, M. 2018a. 'At the Tipping Point? Al-Azhar's Growing Crisis of Moral Authority.' *International Journal of Middle East Studies* 50(4): 715–34.

Bano, M. 2018b. 'Diyanet: Taking Center Stage.' In M. Bano (ed.) *Modern Islamic Authority and Social Change. Volume 1, Evolving Debates in Muslim-Majority Countries*, 271–92. Edinburgh: Edinburgh University Press.

Bano, M. 2018c. 'Introduction.' In M. Bano (ed.) *Modern Islamic Authority and Social Change. Volume 1, Evolving Debates in Muslim-Majority Countries*, 1–52. Edinburgh: Edinburgh University Press.

Bano, M. (ed.). 2018d. *Modern Islamic Authority and Social Change. Volume 1, Evolving Debates in Muslim-Majority Countries*. Edinburgh: Edinburgh University Press.

Bano, M. 2018e. 'Saudi Salafism Amid Rapid Social Change.' In M. Bano (ed.) *Modern Islamic Authority and Social Change, Volume 1, Evolving Debates in Muslim-Majority Countries*, 127–49. Edinburgh: Edinburgh University Press.

Bano, M. (ed.). 2018f. *Modern Islamic Authority and Social Change. Volume 2, Evolving Debates in the West*. Edinburgh: Edinburgh University Press.

Bano, M. 2020. *The Revival of Islamic Rationalism: Logic, Metaphysics and Mysticism in Modern Muslim Societies*. Cambridge: Cambridge University Press.

Bano, M. (ed.). 2021. *Salafi Social and Political Movements: National and Transnational Contexts*. Edinburgh: Edinburgh University Press.

Bano, M., and Benadi, H. 2017. 'Regulating Religious Authority for Political Gains: al-Sisi's Manipulation of al-Azhar in Egypt.' *Third World Quarterly* 39(8): 1604–21.

Bano, M., and Kalmbach, H.E. (eds) 2011. *Women, Leadership, and Mosques: Changes in Contemporary Islamic Authority*. Leiden: Brill.

Bano, M., and Sakurai, K. (eds). 2015. *Shaping of Global Islamic Discourses: Role of al-Azhar, al-Medina, and al-Mustafa*. Edinburgh: Edinburgh University Press.

Baldwin, K. 2016. *The Paradox of Traditional Chiefs in Democratic Africa*. New York: Cambridge University Press.

Bari, A. 2023. 'The First-Ever Islamic Arts Biennale is Starting Soon: The Milestone Event will be Hosted in Jeddah.' 22 January 2023. [Available Online: https://www.timeoutriyadh.com/art/first-islamic-arts-biennale-jeddah; Accessed 20 September 2023].

Barlas, A. 2019. *Believing Women in Islam: Unreading Patriarchal Interpretation of the Qur'an*. Austin: University of Texas Press.

BBC. 2017a. 'Crown Prince Says Saudis Want Return to Moderate Islam.' *BBC*. 25 October 2017. [Available Online: https://www.bbc.com/news/world-middle-east-41747476; Accessed 1 October 2023].

BBC. 2017b. 'Saudi Arabia Arrests: Anti-Corruption Drive "Just the Start".' *BBC*. 7 November 2017. [Available Online: https://www.bbc.com/news/world-middle-east-41894175; Accessed 1 October 2023].

BBC. 2020. 'Saudi Arabia Detains Three Senior Members of Royal Family.' *BBC*. 7 March 2020. [Available Online: https://www.bbc.com/news/world-middle-east-51778781; Accessed 1 October 2023].

BBC. 2021. 'Jamal Khashoggi: All You Need to Know about Saudi Journalist's Death.' *BBC*. 24 February 2021. [Available Online: https://www.bbc.co.uk/news/world-europe-45812399; Accessed 20 September 2023].

BBC. 2023. 'Mohammed bin Salman: "I Don't Care" About "Sports Sashing" Accusations.' *BBC*. 21 September 2023. [Available Online: https://www.bbc.co.uk/sport/66874723; Accessed 20 September 2023].

BBC. 2024. 'Manahel al-Otaibi: Saudi Women's Rights Activist Jailed for 11 Years.' *BBC*. [Available Online: https://www.bbc.co.uk/news/world-middle-east-68934913; Accessed 18 July 2024].

Beblawi, H. 1987. 'The Rentier State in the Arab World.' *Arab Studies Quarterly* 9: 383–98.

Beblawi, H., and Luciani, G. 1987. *The Rentier State*. London: Croom Helm.

Beckerle, K. 2016. 'Boxed In: Women and Saudi Arabia's Male Guardianship System.' *Human Rights Watch*. 16 July 2016. [Available Online: https://www.hrw.org/report/2016/07/17/boxed/women-and-saudi-arabias-male-guardianship-system; Accessed 20 September 2023].

Bell, C. 2015. 'What we Talk About When we Talk about Political Settlements. Towards Inclusive and Open Political Settlements in an Era of Disillusionment.' Political Settlement Research Programme [Available Online: https://psrpdev.law.ed.ac.uk/psrpx/wp-content/uploads/2017/09/201509_WP_1_Bell_What-We-Talk-About.pdf; Accessed 20 September 2023].

Bellin, E. 2004. 'The Robustness of Authoritarianism in the Middle East: Exceptionalism in Comparative Perspective.' *Comparative Politics* 36(2): 139–57.

Bicchieri, C. 2006. *The Grammar of Society: The Nature and Dynamics of Social Norms*. New York: Cambridge University Press.

Bicchieri, C. 2017. *Norms in the Wild: How to Diagnose, Measure, and Change Social Norms*. New York: Oxford University Press.

Bicchieri, C., and Xiao, E. 2009. 'Do the Right Things but Only if Others Do So.' *Journal of Behavioural Decision Making* 22: 191–208.

Bing Videos. 2024. "National Anthem of Saudi Arabia | An-Nasid Al-Wataniy As-Su Udi | Kingdom of Saudi Arabia." *Bing Videos*. Available Online: https://www.bing.com/videos/search?q=National+Anthem+of+Saudi+Arabia; Accessed 18 July 204].

Black, I. 2016. 'Obama's Chilly Reception in Saudi Arabia Hints at Mutual Distrust.' *The Guardian*. 20 April 2016 [Available Online: https://www.theguardian.com/world/2016/apr/20/barack-obama-saudi-arabia-visit-king-salman-relationship; Accessed 20 September 2023].

Blinder, A. 2023. 'How Saudi Arabia Took on Pro-Golf and Won.' *The New York Times*. 15 June 2023. [Available Online: https://www.nytimes.com/2023/06/15/podcasts/the-daily/saudi-liv-golf-pga.html; Accessed 20 September 2023].

Bloomberg. 2019. 'So How Far-Reaching are Social Reforms in Saudi Arabia?' *Arabian Business*. 6 August 2019. [Available Online: https://www.arabianbusiness.com/industries/travel-hospitality/425387-even-saudi-arabias-most-conservative-heartland-is-starting-to-sing; Accessed 20 September 2023].

Boghani, P. 2019. 'The Paradox of Saudi Arabia's Social Reforms.' *Frontline*. 1 October 2019. [Available Online: https://www.pbs.org/wgbh/frontline/article/the-paradox-of-saudi-arabias-social-reforms/; Accessed 20 September 2023].

Boiler, S. 2018. 'Young Saudi Pin Their Hope on Crown Prince.' *DW*. 3 May 2018. [Available Online: https://learngerman.dw.com/en/saudi-arabia-the-crown-prince-and-the-generation-gap/a-42795556; Accessed 20 September 2023].

Bourguignon, F., and Verdier, T. 2000. 'Oligarchy, Democracy, Inequality and Growth.' *Journal of Development Economics* 62(2): 285–313.

Brancati, D. 2014. 'Democratic Authoritarianism: Origins and Effects.' *Annual Review of Political Science* 17: 313–26.

Brett, R. 2024. 'Doing Short-Term Ethnography.' In D. Oswald and L. olde Scholtenhuis (eds). *Embracing Ethnography: Doing Contextualised Construction Research*, 173–86. London: Routledge.

Briggs, A. 1961. 'On the Welfare State: An Historical Perspective.' *European Journal of Sociology* 2(2): 221–58.

Britannica. 2023a. 'How Many Countries are There in the World?' *Britannica*. [Available Online: https://www.britannica.com/story/how-many-countries-are-there-in-the-world; Accessed 20 September 2023].

Britannica. 2023b. 'The Tanzimat Reforms (1839–76).' *Britannica*. [Available Online: https://www.britannica.com/place/Ottoman-Empire/The-Tanzimat-reforms-1839-76; Accessed 1 October 2023].

Brockopp, J.E. 2020. *Muhammad's Heirs: The Rise of Muslim Scholarly Communities, 622–950*. Cambridge: Cambridge University Press.

Brown, N.J. 2012. 'Why Won't Saudi Arabia Write Down Its Laws?' *Foreign Policy*. 23 July 2023. [Available Online: https://foreignpolicy.com/2012/01/23/why-wont-saudi-arabia-write-down-its-laws/; Accessed 20 September 2023].

Bruton, F.B. 2017. 'Tinder, Dating and Sex in Saudi Arabia – Where Love Is a "Sin".' *NBC News*. 22 December 2017. [Available Online: www.nbcnews.com/news/world/tinder-dating-sex-saudi-arabia-where-love-sin-n824101; Accessed 18 July 2024].

Bruton, F.B. 2018. 'Saudi Cleric Salman al-Awda Called for Reform. Now He's in Solitary Confinement.' *NBC News*. 27 January 2018. [Available Online: https://www.nbcnews.com/news/mideast/saudi-cleric-salman-al-awda-called-reform-now-he-s-n840916; Accessed 1 October 2023].

Bsheer, R. 2018. 'A Counter-Revolutionary State: Popular Movements and the Making of Saudi Arabia.' *Past & Present* 238(1): 233–77.

Bsheer, R. 2020. *Archives Wars: The Politics of History in Saudi Arabia*. Redwood City: Stanford University Press.

Buckley, J. 2019. 'Saudi Arabia Allows Unmarried Couples to Share Hotel Rooms.' *CNN*. 7 October 2019. [Available Online: https://edition.cnn.com/travel/article/saudi-arabia-unmarried-couples-female-travelers/index.html; Accessed 20 September 2023].

Bullen, C. 2022. 'More than 600,000 People attend Star-Studded Festival in Saudi Arabia.' *Mail Online*. 14 December 2022. [Available Online: https://www.dailymail.co.uk/tvshowbiz/article-11516017/More-600-000-people-attend-star-studded-MDLBEAST-Soundstorm-festival-Saudi-Arabia.html; Accessed 20 September 2023].

Bunzel, C.M. 2023. *Wahhābism: The History of a Militant Islamic Movement*. Princeton, NJ: Princeton University Press.

Bursztyn, L., González, A.L., and Yanagizawa-Drott, D. 2020. 'Misperceived Social Norms: Women Working Outside the Home in Saudi Arabia.' *American Economic Review* 110(10): 2997–3029.

Business and Human Rights Resource Centre (BHRSC). 2023. Saudi Activist's Killing Exposes Local Tensions over Neom Construction. [Available Online: https://www.business-humanrights.org/en/latest-news/saudi-activists-killing-exposes-local-tensions-over-neom-construction/; Accessed 20 September 2023].

Butt, G. 2017. 'Mohammed bin Salman's Rise Marks Climax of Leadership Revolution.' *BBC*. 21 June 2024. [Available Online: https://www.bbc.com/news/mohammed-bin-salmans-rise-marks-climax-of-leadership-revolution; Accessed 18 July 2024].

CBS News. 2023. 'Saudi Arabia Invests in Sports as it Tries to Reshape its World Image.' *CBS News*. 25 June 2023. [Available Online: https://www.cbsnews.com/news/saudi-arabia-invests-in-sports-as-it-tries-to-reshape-its-world-image-60-minutes-2023-06-25/; Accessed 20 September 2023].

Chaara, I. 2011. 'Pro-Women Legal Reform in Morocco: Is Religion an Obstacle?' Proceedings of the German Development Economics Conference, Berlin 2011, No. 17, ZBW. [Available Online: https://www.econstor.eu/bitstream/10419/48301/1/17_chaara.pdf; Accessed 16 July 2024].

Champion, D. 2003. *The Paradoxical Kingdom: Saudi Arabia and the Momentum for Reform*. New York: Columbia University Press.

Charles, S. 2023. 'Saudi Arabia is Throwing Everything it Can at the Coffee Industry.' *Coffee Intelligence*. 8 November 2023. [Available Online: https://intelligence.coffee/2023/11/saudi-arabia-coffee/; Accessed 17 July 2024].

Chaudhary, S. 2016. The Role of Social Media as a Decisive Actor in Saudi Arabia. In B. Gunter, M. Elareshi and K. al-Jaber (eds) *Social Media in the Arab World: Communication and Public Opinion in the Gulf States*, 25–44. London: I.B. Tauris.

Chaudhry, K.A. 1997. *The Price of Wealth: Economies and Institutions in the Middle East*. Ithaca, NY: Cornell University Press.

Chilton, N. 2023. 'Diriyah: The Latest "Giga Project" Aiming to Transform Saudi Arabia.' *CNN*. 22 February 2023. [Available Online: https://www.cnn.com/travel/article/saudi-arabia-diriyah/index.html; Accessed 20 September 2023].

Chittick, W.C. 1989. *The Sufi Path of Knowledge: Ibn Al-'Arabi's Metaphysics of Imagination*. Albany: State University of New York Press.

Chulov, M. 2017. 'I Will Return Saudi Arabia to Moderate Islam, Says Crown Prince.' *The Guardian*. 24 October 2017. [Available Online: https://www.theguardian.com/world/2017/oct/24/i-will-return-saudi-arabia-moderate-islam-crown-prince; Accessed 20 September 2023].

CNN Travel. 2023. 'Journey to the "Edge of the World".' [Available Online: https://www.cnn.com/videos/travel/2023/05/10/saudi-arabia-edge-of-world-spc-intl.cnn; Accessed 27 September 2023].

Coleman, J.S. 1990. *Foundations of Social Theory*. Cambridge, MA: Harvard University Press.

Commins, D. 2009. *The Wahhabi Mission and Saudi Arabia*. London: I. B. Tauris.

Commins, D. 2015. 'From Wahhabi to Salafi.' In B. Haykel, T. Hegghammer and S. Lacroix (eds) *Saudi Arabia in Transition: Insights on Social, Political, Economic and Religious Change*, 151–66. Cambridge: Cambridge University Press.

Coogle, A. 2018. 'Saudi Arabia's "Reforms" Don't Include Tolerance of Shia Community.' *Human Rights Watch Dispatches*. 21 September 2018. [Available Online: https://www.hrw.org/news/2018/09/21/saudi-arabias-reforms-dont-include-tolerance-shia-community; Accessed 18 July 2024].

Cook, S. A. 2023. 'Saudi Arabia Is Mysteriously Absent in the Israel-Hamas War. Foreign Policy.' [Available Online: https://foreignpolicy.com/2023/10/26/saudi-arabia-mbs-israel-hamas-war-strategy-policy-diplomacy/; Accessed 24 July 2024].

Crawford, M. 2014. *Ibn 'Abd al-Wahhab*. London: Oneworld Publications.

Crystal, J. 1995. *Oil and Politics in the Gulf: Rulers and Merchants in Kuwait and Qatar*. Cambridge: Cambridge University Press.

Dagher. S, 2024. 'Saudi Arabia Steps Up Gaza-Related Arrests as Israel Ties Edge Closer.' *The Japan Times*. [Available Online: https://www.japantimes.co.jp/news/2024/05/02/world/politics/saudi-arabia-gaza-arrests-israel-ties/; Accessed 24 July 2025].

Dale, S.F. 2010. *The Muslim Empires of the Ottomans, Safavids, and Mughals, New Approaches to Asian History*. Cambridge: Cambridge University Press.

D'arcy, D. 2016. '"Barakah Meets Barakah": Berlin Review.' *ScreenDaily*. 18 February 2016. [Available Online: https://www.screendaily.com/reviews/barakah-meets-barakah-berlin-review/5100622.article; Accessed 1 October 2023].

Davin, C. 2019. 'Resources for Measuring Social Norms: A Practical Guide for Programme Implementers.' *Align Platform*. [Available Online: https://www.alignplatform.org/resources/resources-measuring-social-norms-practical-guide-programme-implementers; Accessed 20 September 2023].

Dawn. 2009. 'Criticism of Co-education: Saudi Scholar Sacked.' DAWN. 6 October 2009. [Available Online: http://beta.dawn.com/news/855298/criticism-of-co-education-saudi-scholar-sacked; Accessed 20 September 2023].

DeLong-Bas, N.J. 2004. *Wahhabi Islam: From Revival and Reform to Global Jihad*. Oxford: Oxford University Press.

Destination KSA. 2023. 'AlUla Reveals the 2023 Calendar of Events.' [Available Online: https://destinationksa.com/alula-reveals-the-2023-calendar-of-events/; Accessed 20 September 2023].

de Wit, J.R., and Lisciandra, C. 2021. 'Measuring Norms Using Social Survey Data.' *Economics and Philosophy* 37: 188–221.

Dickinson, E. 2017. 'Can Saudi Arabia's Young Prince Wean the Welfare State?' *Foreign Policy*. 5 June 2017. [Available Online: https://foreignpolicy.com/2017/06/05/is-saudi-arabias-massive-economy-reform-coming-off-the-rails-mohammed-bin-salman/; Accessed 20 September 2023].

Diriyah Biennale Foundation (DBF). 2023. 'Diriyah Biennale Foundation.' [Available Online: https://biennale.org.sa/; Accessed 20 September 2023].

Diriyah Gate Project (DGP). 2023. 'Diriyah.' [Available Online: https://www.vision2030.gov.sa/v2030/v2030-projects/diriyah-gate/; Accessed 20 September 2023].

Diwan, I. 2019. 'A Landing Strategy for Saudi Arabia.' Project on Middle East Political Science (POMEPS) Studies 33: *The Politics of Rentier Sates in the Gulf*. [Available Online: https://pomeps.org/a-landing-strategy-for-saudi-arabia; Accessed 1 October 2023].

Diwan, K. 2021. 'Salafi Leadership Outside Saudi Arabia: Hakim al-Mutairi and the Umma Party of Kuwait.' In M. Bano (ed.) *Salafi Social and Political Movements: National and Transnational Contexts*. Edinburgh: Edinburgh University Press.

Diwan, K.S. 2016. *Youth Appeal of Saudi Vision 2030*. The Arab Gulf States Institute in Washington. 6 May 2016. [Available Online: www.agsiw.org/youth-appeal-of-saudi-vision-2030; Accessed 18 July 2024].

Diwan, K.S. 2018. *Mohammed bin Salman's Media Obsession – and What It Means for Dissent*. The Arab Gulf States Institute in Washington. 30 October 2018. [Available Online: https://agsiw.org/mohammed-bin-salmans-media-obsession-and-what-it-means-for-dissent; Accessed 18 July 2024].

Dorsey, J.M. 2017. 'Qatari Wahhabism vs. Saudi Wahhabism And the Perils of Top-Down Change.' *HuffPost*. 4 December 2017. [Available Online: https://www.huffpost.com/entry/qatari-wahhabism-vs-saudi-wahhabism-and-the-perils_b_5a257240e4b05072e8b56b29; Accessed 27 September 2023].

Dresch, P., and Piscatori, J. 2013. *Monarchies and Nations: Globalisation and Identity in the Arab States of the Gulf*. London: I. B. Tauris.

Dunning, T. 2008. *Crude Democracy: Natural Resource Wealth and Political Regimes*. Cambridge: Cambridge University Press.

DW. 2018. 'Young Saudis Pin Their Hopes on Crown Prince.' *DW*. 3 March 2018. [Available Online: https://learngerman.dw.com/en/saudi-arabia-the-crown-prince-and-the-generation-gap/a-42795556; Accessed 20 September 2023].

Ebrahim, N. 2022. 'Why the Birthplace of Islam is Hosting One of the World's Biggest Raves.' *CNN*. 30 November 2022. [Available Online: https://edition.cnn.com/2022/11/30/middleeast/saudi-arabia-biggest-rave-mime-intl/index.html; Accessed 20 September 2023].

Ebrahim, N., and al-Masri, D. 2023. 'Space Pods and Flying Dragons: How Saudi Arabia Wants to Transform its Capital.' *CNN*. 21 February 2023. [Available Online: https://edition.cnn.com/2023/02/20/middleeast/saudi-arabia-mukaab-mime-intl/index.html; Accessed 20 September 2023].

Economist. 2018. 'Shias are Doing Better in Saudi Arabia.' *The Economist*. 30 August 2018. [Available Online: https://www.economist.com/middle-east-and-africa/2018/08/30/shias-are-doing-better-in-saudi-arabia; Accessed 18 July 2018].

Economist. 2019. 'The Unlikely Rise of Book Fairs in the Gulf.' *The Economist*. 6 July 2019. [Available Online: https://www.economist.com/books-and-arts/2019/07/06/the-unlikely-rise-of-book-fairs-in-the-gulf#; Accessed 2 October 2023]

Economist. 2023a. 'Arab Petrostates Must Prepare Their Citizens for a Post-Oil Future.' *The Economist*. 9 February 2023. [Available Online: https://www.economist.com/leaders/2023/02/09/arab-petrostates-must-prepare-their-citizens-for-a-post-oil-future; Accessed 2 October 2023].

Economist. 2023b. 'Meet the World's Most Flirtatious Sovereign-Wealth Fund.' *The Economist*. 29 June 2023. [Available Online: https://www.economist.com/business/2023/06/29/meet-the-worlds-most-flirtatious-sovereign-wealth-fund#; Accessed 2 October 2023].

Economist. 2023c. 'The New Middle East: More Money and Less Mayhem, For Now.' *The Economist*. 18 September 2023. [Available Online: https://www.businessreview.global/latest/6503e8f3c6208476286e5aa6; Accessed 2 October 2023].

Eibl, F., and Hertog, S. 2023. 'From Rents to Welfare: Why Are Some Oil-Rich States Generous to Their People?' *American Political Science Review*. 1–20.

England, A., and A. al-Omran. 2019. 'Nationalism on the Rise as Saudi Arabia Seeks Sense of Identity.' *The Financial Times*. 7 May 2019. Available Online: https://www.ft.com/content/5d6f372e-7013-11e9-bf5c-6eeb837566c5; Accessed 18 July 2024].

Esanov, A., Raiser, M., and Buiter, W. 2004. 'Nature's Blessing or Nature's Curse: The Political Economy of Transition in Resource-Based Economies.' ZEF Discussion Papers on Development Policy, No. 81. [Available Online: https://www.econstor.eu/bitstream/10419/84743/1/zef_dp81.pdf; Accessed 20 September 2023].

Esposito, J.L., and Voll, J. O. 1996. *Islam and Democracy*. New York: Oxford University Press.

Experience al-Ula. 2023. Five Senses Sanctuary. [Available Online: https://www.experiencealula.com/en/alula-moments/alula-wellness-festival/five-senses-sanctuary; Accesses 27 September 2023].

Eyre, G. 2021. 'Scholastic Salafism in Morocco Since the Arab Spring.' In M. Bano (ed.) *Salafi Social and Political Movements: National and Transnational Contexts*, 113–34. Edinburgh: Edinburgh University Press.

Fahmy, D. 2018. 5 Facts About Religion in Saudi Arabia. Pew Research Center. [Available Online: https://www.pewresearch.org/short-reads/2018/04/12/5-facts-about-religion-in-saudi-arabia/; Accessed 20 September 2023].

Fareed, A. 2019. 'First Saudi Opera House to Open in Jeddah.' 23 February 2019. [Available Online: https://www.arabnews.jp/en/saudi-arabia/article_1104/; Accessed 20 September 2023].

Farhat, B. 2024. 'Saudi Arabia to Make Debut at Miss Universe Pageant.' *Al-Monitor*. 27 March 2024. [Available Online: https://www.al-monitor.com/originals/2024/03/saudi-arabia-make-debut-miss-universe-pageant; Accessed 28 July 2024].

Farouk, Y.. and Brown, N. J. 2021. 'Saudi Arabia's Religious Reforms Are Touching Nothing but Changing Everything.' In F. Wehrey (ed.) *Islamic Institutions in Arab States: Mapping the Dynamics of Control, Co-option, and Contention*. Carnegie Endowment for International Peace. [Available Online: https://carnegieendowment.org/2021/06/07/saudi-arabia-s-religious-reforms-are-touching-nothing-but-changing-everything-pub-84650; Accessed 20 September 2023].

Farquhar, M. 2017. *Circuits of Faith: Migration, Education, and the Wahhabi Mission*. Stanford, CA: Stanford University Press.

Fatima, S. 2022. 'Saudi Arabia Reports Divorce Cases Every 10 Minutes in 2022.' *The Siasat Daily*. 29 October 2022. Available Online: https://www.siasat.com/saudi-arabia-reports-divorce-cases-every-10-minutes-in-2022-2444503/#; Accessed 20 September 2023].

Fatima, S. 2023. 'Saudi's Cube-Shaped Project Lands in Controversy Over "Replicating Kaaba".' *The Siasat Daily*. 24 February 2023. [Available Online: https://www.siasat.com/saudis-cube-shaped-project-lands-in-controversy-over-replicating-kaaba-2534191/; Accessed 27 September 2023].

FII. 2024. FII 8th Edition 2024. 'Infinite Horizons: Investing Today, Shaping Tomorrow.' [Available Online: https://fii-institute.org/conference/fii8; Accessed 25 November 2024].

Foley, S. 2019. *Changing Saudi Arabia: Art, Culture and Society in the Kingdom*. Boulder, CO: Lynne Rienner Publishers Inc.

Fortes, M., and Evans-Pritchard, E. 2015. 'Introduction.' In M. Fortes and E. Evans-Pritchard (eds) *African Political Systems*, 1–23. Routledge Revivals. New York: Routledge.

Fouad, H. 2021. 'Salafism: The Core Critiques.' In M. Bano (ed.) *Salafi Social and Political Movements: National and Transnational Contexts*, 33–51. Edinburgh: Edinburgh University Press.

French, N. 2023. 'Saudi Reforms Are Softening Islam's Role, but Critics Warn the Kingdom Will Still Take a Hard Line Against Dissent.' *The Conversation*. 5 September 2024. [Available Online: https://www.theconversation.com/saudi-reforms-are-softening-islams-role-but-critics-warn-the-kingdom-will-still-take-a-hard-line-against-dissent; Accessed 18 July 2024].

Frey, B.S., and Oberholzer-Gee, E. 1997. 'The Cost of Price Incentives: An Empirical Analysis of Motivation Crowding Out.' *American Economic Review* 87(4): 746–55.

Friedman, T.L. 2015. 'Iran and the Obama Doctrine.' *The New York Times*. 5 August 2015. [Available Online: http://www.nytimes.com/2015/04/06/opinion/thomas-friedman-the-obama-doctrine-and-iran-interview.html?_r=1; Accessed 20 September 2023].

Fukuyama, F. 2017a. 'Political Consequences of the Protestant Reformation, Part I.' *The American Interest*. [Available Online: https://www.the-american-interest.com/2017/10/31/political-consequences-protestant-reformation-part/; Accessed 20 September 2023].

Fukuyama, F. 2017b. 'Political Consequences of the Protestant Reformation, Part II.' *The American Interest*. [Available Online: https://www.the-american-interest.

com/2017/11/02/political-consequences-protestant-reformation-part-ii/; Accessed 20 September 2023].

Fukuyama, F. 2017c. 'Political Consequences of the Protestant Reformation, Part III.' *The American Interest*. [Available Online: https://www.the-american-interest.com/2017/11/06/political-consequences-protestant-reformation-part-iii/; Accessed 20 September 2023].

Fuller, G.E., and Francke, R.R. 2000. *The Arab Shi'a: The Forgotten Muslims*. Basingstoke: Macmillan.

Gambetta, D., and Hertog, S. 2018. *Engineers of Jihad: The Curious Connection between Violent Extremism and Education*. Princeton, NJ: Princeton University Press.

Gary, J. 2023. 'Saudi Arabia's Crown Prince Understands the Modern World. His Western Suitors Do Not.' The New Statesman. [Available Online: https://www.newstatesman.com/comment/2023/09/saudi-arabia-crown-prince-modern-world; Accessed 1 October 2023].

Gerring, J., Wig, T., Veenendaal, W., Weitzel, D., Teorell, J., and Kikuta, K. 2021. 'Why Monarchy? The Rise and Demise of a Regime Type.' *Comparative Political Studies* 54: 585–622.

Gerschewski, J. 2013. 'Three Pillars of Authoritarian Regime Durability.' *Democratization* 20(1): 13–38.

Gharem, A. 2023. 'Ajlan Gharem.' Personal website. [Available Online: http://www.ajlangharem.com; Accessed 1 October 2023].

Gharem Studio. 2023a. '(@gharemstudio): Instagram Photos and Videos.' Available Online: https://www.instagram.com/gharemstudio/; Accessed 20 September 2023].

Gharem Studio. 2023b. 'Gharem Studio Website.' [Available Online: http://www.gharemstudio.com; Accessed 20 September 2023].

GIWPS and PRIO. 2017. *Women Peace and Security Index 2017/2018: Tracking Sustainable Peace through Inclusion, Justice, and Security for Women*. Washington, DC: Georgetown Institute for Women, Peace and Security and Peace Research Institute Oslo.

Gladwell, M. 2002. *The Tipping Point: How Little Things Can Make a Big Difference*. Boston, MA: Black Bay Books.

Goffman, E. 1966. *Behavior in Public Places: Notes on the Social Organization of Gatherings*. New York: Free Press.

Goffman, E. 1971. *Relations in Public: Microstudies of the Public Order*. New York: Basic Books.

Gold, H., and al-Lawati, A. 2023. 'Saudi Arabia Is Quietly Changing Its Textbooks. Could that lead to Acceptance of Israel?' *CNN*. 19 June 2023. [Available Online: https://edition.cnn.com/2023/06/19/middleeast/saudi-textbooks-israel-mime-intl/index.html; Accessed 20 September 2023].

Görges, L., and Nosenzo, D. 2020. 'Measuring Social Norms in Economics: Why It Is Important and How It Is Done.' *Analyse & Kritik* 42: 285–312.

Gould, E.R. 2006. *Money Talks: The International Monetary Fund, Conditionality and Supplementary Financiers*. Stanford, CA: Stanford University Press.

Government of Saudi Arabia (GoSA). 1992. 'King Fahd's Speech on the Issuance of the Basic Law of Governance.' [Available Online: https://www.saudiembassy.net/king-fahds-speech-issuance-basic-law-governance; Accessed 1 October 2023].

Government of Saudi Arabia (GoSA). 2016. 'Vision 2030: Kingdom of Saudi Arabia.' 25 April 2016. [Available Online: https://www.vision2030.gov.sa/media/rc0b5oy1/saudi_vision203.pdf; Accessed 1 October 2023].

Government of Saudi Arabia (GoSA). 2023a. 'Basic Law of Governance. The Embassy of the Kingdom of Saudia Arabia.' [Available Online: https://www.saudiembassy.net/basic-law-governance; Accessed 1 October 2023].
Government of Saudi Arabia (GoSA). 2023b. 'General Entertainment Authority.' [Available Online: https://www.gea.gov.sa/en/; Accessed 20 September 2023].
Government of Saudi Arabia (GoSA). 2023c. 'Human Rights Commission.' [Available Online: https://www.my.gov.sa/wps/portal/snp/agencies/agencyDetails/AC156/!ut/p/z0/04_Sj9CPykssy0xPLMnMz0vMAfIjo8zivQIsTAwdDQz9LQwNzQwCnS0tXPwMvYwNDAz0g1Pz9L30o_ArAppiVOTr7JuuH1WQWJKhm5mXlq8f4ehsaGqmX5DtHg4A6D1KYw!!/; Accessed 20 September 2023].
Graham-Harrison, E. 2019. 'Saudi Arabia Allows Women to Travel Without Male Guardian's Approval.' *The Guardian*. 2 August 2019. [Available Online: https://www.theguardian.com/world/2019/aug/01/saudi-women-can-now-travel-without-a-male-guardian-reports-say.; Accessed 20 September 2023].
Gray, M. 2011. 'A Theory of "Late Rentierism" in the Arab States of the Gulf.' *CIRS Occasional Papers*. Available Online: https://ssrn.com/abstract=2825905; Accessed 18 July 2024].
Greif, A. 2006. *Institutions and the Path to the Modern Economy: Lessons from Medieval Trade*. New York: Cambridge University Press.
Gritten, D. 2022. 'Saudi Crown Prince Mohammed bin Salman Named Prime Minister.' *BBC*. 28 September 2022. [Available Online: https://www.bbc.com/news/saudi-crown-prince-mohammed-bin-salman-named-prime-minister; Accessed 18 July 2024].
Guardian. 2023. 'UN Rights Experts Denounce Planned Saudi Executions of Megacity Opponents.' *The Guardian*. 3 May 2023. [Available Online: https://www.theguardian.com/world/2023/may/03/un-rights-experts-denounce-planned-saudi-executions; Accessed 20 September 2023].
Guardian Culture. 2016. 'Saudi Arabian Artists Confront Islamophobia on US Road Trip: Crossing the Line.' YouTube Video. [Available Online: https://www.youtube.com/watch?v=67OwgwynClo; Accessed 20 September 2023].
Guardian Glass. 2023. 'No, It's Not a Mirage. It's the Maraya Concert Hall.' [Available Online: https://www.guardianglass.com/me/en/insights/maraya-concert-hall-the-worlds-largest-mirrored-building; Accessed 1 October 2023].
Guase III, F.G. 2015. 'Oil and Political Mobilization: Technopolitics and Power.' In B. Haykel, T. Hegghammer and S. Lacroix (eds) *Saudi Arabia in Transition: Insights on Social, Political, Economic and Religious Change*, 117–32. Cambridge: Cambridge University Press.
Gunter, B., Elareshi, M., and al-Jaber, K. (eds). 2016. *Social Media in the Arab World: Communication and Public Opinion in the Gulf States*. London: I.B. Tauris.
Haber, S., and Menaldo, V. 2011. 'Do Natural Resources Fuel Authoritarianism? A Reappraisal of the Resource Curse.' *American Political Science Review* 105(1): 1–26.
Habermas, J. 1989 (1962). *The Structural Transformation of the Public Sphere: An Inquiry into a Category of Bourgeois Society*. Cambridge, MA: MIT Press.
Hagmann, J. 2022. 'Saudi Arabia's Urban Development: The Crown Prince's Bulldozers.' *Qantara.de*. 16 February 2023. [Available Online: https://en.qantara.de/content/saudi-arabias-urban-development-the-crown-princes-bulldozers; Accessed 20 September 2023].
Hallaq, W. 2009. *Sharia: Theory, Practice, Transformations*. New York: Cambridge University Press.

Half Million (1/2 Million). 2023. 'Know Our Story: Half Million.' [Available Online: https://halfm.sa/about/; Accessed 20 September 2023].

Hammond, A. 2021. 'Reordering Saudi Religion: MBS is Defanging Wahhabism, not Dethroning it.' *Maydan*. 20 September 2021. [Available Online: https://themaydan.com/2021/09/reordering-saudi-religion-mbs-is-defanging-wahhabism-not-dethroning-it/; Accessed 20 September 2023].

Hanmer, L.C., Hasan, T., Klugman, J. McCleary-Sills, J., Santamaria, J., and Twigg, S. 2014. *Voice and Agency: Empowering Women and Girls for Shared Prosperity*. Washington, DC: World Bank Group.

Hasan, M. 2015. 'Why Islam Doesn't Need a Reformation.' *The Guardian*. 17 May 2015. [Available Online: https://www.theguardian.com/commentisfree/2015/may/17/islam-reformation-extremism-muslim-martin-luther-europe; Accessed 20 September 2023].

Hassan, H. 2022. 'The "Conscious Uncoupling" of Wahhabism and Saudi Arabia.' *New Lines Magazine*. 22 February 2023. [Available Online: https://newlinesmag.com/argument/the-conscious-uncoupling-of-wahhabism-and-saudi-arabia/; Accessed 20 September 2023].

Haykel, B. 2015. 'Oil is Saudi Arabian Culture and Politics: From Tribal Poets to Al-Qaeda's Ideologues.' In B. Haykel, T. Hegghammer and S. Lacroix (eds) *Saudi Arabia in Transition: Insights on Social, Political, Economic and Religious Change*, 53–71. Cambridge: Cambridge University Press.

Haykel, B., Hegghammer, T., and Lacroix, S. 2015a. 'Introduction.' In B. Haykel, T. Hegghammer and S. Lacroix (eds) *Saudi Arabia in Transition: Insights on Social, Political, Economic and Religious Change*. Cambridge: Cambridge University Press.

Haykel, B., Hegghammer, T., and Lacroix, S. (eds) 2015b. *Saudi Arabia in Transition: Insights on Social, Political, Economic and Religious Change*. Cambridge: Cambridge University Press.

Hegghamer, T. 2015. '"Classical" and "Global" Jihadism in Saudi Arabia.' In B. Haykel, T. Hegghammer and S. Lacroix (eds) *Saudi Arabia in Transition: Insights on Social, Political, Economic and Religious Change*, 133–50. Cambridge: Cambridge University Press.

Herb, M. 2009. 'A Nation of Bureaucrats: Political Participation and Economic Diversification in Kuwait and the United Arab Emirates.' *International Journal of Middle East Studies* 41(3): 375–95.

Hertog, S. 2010. *Princes, Brokers, and Bureaucrats: Oil and the State in Saudi Arabia*. Ithaca, NY: Cornell University Press.

Hertog, S. 2015. 'National Cohesion and the Political Economy of Regions in Post-World War II Saudi Arabia.' In B. Haykel, T. Hegghammer and S. Lacroix (eds) *Saudi Arabia in Transition: Insights on Social, Political, Economic and Religious Change*, 72–95. Cambridge: Cambridge University Press.

Hertog, S. 2019. 'What Would the Saudi Economy have to Look Like to be "Post-Rentier"?' Project on Middle East Political Science (POMEPS) Studies 33: *The Politics of Rentier Sates in the Gulf*. [Available Online: https://pomeps.org/what-would-the-saudi-economy-have-to-look-like-to-be-post-rentier; Accessed 20 September 2023].

Hickey, S., and Hossain, N. 2019. 'The Problem of Education Quality in Developing Countries.' In S. Hiskey and N. Hossain (eds) *The Politics of Education in Developing Countries: From Schooling to Learning*, 1–31. Oxford: Oxford University Press.

Hirschkind, C. 2009. *The Ethical Soundspace: Cassette Sermons and Islamic Counterrepublics*. New York: Columbia University Press.

Hirwani, P. 2019. 'Everything You Need to Know About Saudi Arabia's Winter at Tantora Festival.' *Vogue*. 8 December 2019. [Available Online: https://en.vogue.me/culture/winter-at-tantora-festival/; Accessed 27 September 2023].

Hobsbawm, E. 2012. 'Introduction: Inventing Traditions.' In. E. Hobsbawm and T. Ranger (eds) *The Invention of Tradition*, 1–14. New York: Cambridge University Press.

Hodgetts, R. 2024. 'Why Saudi Arabia's Red Sea coast could be the next big luxury tourism destination.' *CNN*. 3 January 2024. [Available Online: Why Saudi Arabia's Red Sea Coast Could be the Next Big Luxury Tourism Destination | CNN; Accessed 18 July 2024].

Hodgson, M.G.S. 1977. *The Venture of Islam: Conscience and History in a World Civilization*. Chicago, IL: University of Chicago Press.

Hoteit, L., and Radsch, C.C. 2009. 'Saudi Cleric Sacked Over Co-Ed University Spat.' *Al Arabiya News*. 4 October 2009. [Available Online: https://www.alarabiya.net/articles/2009%2F10%2F04%2F86923.html; Accessed 20 September 2023].

Hubbard, B. 2017. Saudi Arabia Agrees to Let Women Drive. *The New York Times*. 25 September 2017. [Available Online: https://www.nytimes.com/2017/09/26/world/middleeast/saudi-arabia-women-drive.html; Accessed 1 October 2023].

Hubbard, B., and Kirkpatrick, D.D. 2018. 'Behind Prince Mohammed bin Salman's Rise, Two Loyal Enforcers.' *The New York Times*.14 November 2018. Available Online: https://www.nytimes.com/2018/11/14/world/middleeast/saudi-mbs-enforcers.html; Accessed 18 July 2024].

Human Development Report (HDR). 2019. 'Inequalities in Human Development in the 21st Century: Saudi Arabia.' United Nations Development Programme (UNDP). [Available Online: https://www.undp.org/sites/g/files/zskgke326/files/migration/sa/ab6b0bf382777ea4a354b67591f04dab61d20dd61da6f256828bdb07440dc982.pdf; Accessed 1 October 2023].

Human Rights Careers (HRC). 2023. '20 Organizations Fighting Female Genital Mutilation.' [Available Online: https://www.humanrightscareers.com/issues/organizations-fighting-female-genital-mutilation/; Accessed 20 September 2023].

Human Rights Watch (HRW). 2014. 'All According to Plan: The Rab'a Massacre and Mass Killings of Protesters in Egypt.' *HRW*. August 2014. [Available Online: https://www.hrw.org/sites/default/files/reports/egypt0814web_0.pdf; Accessed 20 September 2023].

Human Rights Watch (HRW). 2019. 'The High Cost of Change: Repression Under Saudi Crown Prince Tarnishes Reforms.' *HRW*. 4 November 2019. Available Online: https://www.hrw.org/report/2019/11/04/high-cost-change/repression-under-saudi-crown-prince-tarnishes-reforms; Accessed 1 October 2023].

Human Rights Watch (HRW). 2022. 'Saudi Arabia: Events of 2022.' Available Online: https://www.hrw.org/world-report/2023/country-chapters/saudi-arabia; Accessed on 18 July 2024].

Human Rights Watch (HRW). 2023. 'Saudi Arabia: Law Enshrines Male Guardianship.' *HRW*. 8 March 2023. [Available Online: https://www.hrw.org/news/2023/03/08/saudi-arabia-law-enshrines-male-guardianship; Accessed 20 September 2023].

Hussain, L. and Smith, S. 2017. 'Saudi Arabia Hosts First Concert by Female Performer in Country's History.' *NBC News*. 7 December 2017. [Available Online: https://www.nbcnews.com/news/world/saudi-arabia-hosts-first-concert-female-performer-country-s-history-n827306; Accessed 20 September 2023].

Hunt, K. 2017. 'Work, Not Sex? The Real Reason Chinese Women Bound Their Feet.' *CNN*. 21 May 2017. [Available Online: https://edition.cnn.com/2017/05/21/health/china-foot-binding-new-theory/index.html; Accessed 20 September 2023].

Ibn Abdul al-Wahhab, M. 1996. *Kitab at-Tawhid*. Riyadh: Dar us Salam Publications. [Available Online: https://www.kalamullah.com/Books/Kitab-At-Tauhid-The-Book-of-Monotheism-Sh.-Muhammad-bin-Abdul-Wahhab.pdf; Accessed 20 September 2023].

IMDb. 2016. 'Wasati.' [Available Online: https://www.imdb.com/title/tt6620846/; Accessed 20 September 2023].

IMDb. 2023. 'Masameer County.' [Available Online: https://www.imdb.com/title/tt14936146/; Accessed 20 September 2023].

Inge, A. 2017. *The Making of a Salafi Muslim Woman: Paths to Conversion*. New York: Oxford University Press.

Inglehart, R.F. 2021. *Religion's Sudden Decline. What's Causing it, and What Comes Next?* New York: Oxford University Press.

Inside the Haramain (ITH). 2019. 'Sheikh Yasir Ad Dawsary.' Facebook.com. [Available Online https://www.facebook.com/insharifain/; Accessed 20 September 2023].

International Crisis Group (ICG). 2005. *The Shiite Question in Saudi Arabia*. Middle East Report 45.

ISHR (International Service for Human Rights). 2024. 'Civil Society Reiterates Their Call on Saudi Authorities to Release Jailed Women's Rights Activists.' *International Service for Human Rights*. 8 March 2024. [Available Online: https://ishr.ch/latest-updates/civil-society-reiterates-their-call-on-saudi-authorities-to-release-jailed-womens-rights-activists; Accessed 18 July 2024].

Ismail, R. 2016. *Saudi Clerics and Shī'a Islam*. New York: Oxford University Press.

Ismail, R. 2021. *Rethinking Salafism: The Transnational Networks of Salafi 'Ulama in Egypt, Kuwait and Saudi Arabia*. New York: Oxford University Press.

Jahangir, J. 2017. '5 Muslim Scholars on The Permissibility of Not Wearing The Headscarf.' *HuffPost*. 10 January 2017. [Available Online: https://www.huffpost.com/entry/5-muslim-scholars-on-the-permissibility-of-not-wearing-the-heads_b_610874fde4b0497e67026d7c; Accessed 27 September 2023].

Jankowicz, M. 2023. 'Saudi Arabia Is Planning to Execute Three Local Tribe Members Who Opposed its Futuristic Neom-Megacity Project, UN Experts Warn.' 4 May 2023. [Available Online: https://www.businessinsider.com/saudi-tribe-members-death-sentence-opposing-neom-megacity-un-2023-5?r=US&IR=T; Accessed 20 September 2023].

Jeffrey, B. and Troman, G. 2004. 'Time for Ethnography.' *British Educational Research Journal* 30: 535–48.

Jezebel. 2017. 'Saudi Women Mock Trump, Beg God to "Rid Us of Men" in Gorgeous Viral Music Video.' *Jezebel*. 6 January 2017. [Available Online: https://jezebel.com/saudi-women-mock-trump-beg-god-to-rid-us-of-men-in-gor-1790844649; Accessed 20 September 2023].

Jiffry, F. 2013. '"Saudi Schools Lack Quality Science and Math Teaching".' *Arab News*. 19 July 2013. Available Online: https://www.arabnews.com/news/458491; Accessed 20 September 2023].

Johnson, C. 1999. 'The Developmental State: Odyssey of a Concept.' In M. Woo-Cumings (ed.) *The Developmental State*, 32–60. Ithaca, NY: Cornell University Press.

Jones, C.W. 2017. *Bedouins into Bourgeois: Remaking Citizens for Globalization*. Cambridge: Cambridge University Press.

Jones, C.W. 2019. 'Social Engineering in Rentier States.' Project on Middle East Political Science (POMEPS) Studies 33: *The Politics of Rentier Sates in the Gulf*. [Available Online: https://pomeps.org/social-engineering-in-rentier-states; Accessed 20 September 2023].

Jones, K. 2018. 'Ahmed Mater: The Edge Becomes the Center.' *Art Asia Pacific*. Available Online: https://www.ahmedmater.com/press/the-edge-becomes-the-center; Accessed 20 September 2023].

Jones, T.C. 2015. 'The Dogma of Development: Technopolitics and Power in Saudi Arabia.' In B. Haykel, T. Hegghammer and S. Lacroix (eds) *Saudi Arabia in Transition: Insights on Social, Political, Economic and Religious Change*, 96–116. Cambridge: Cambridge University Press.

Jütting, J.P., Morrisson, C., Dayton-Johnson, J., and Drechsler, D. 2008. 'Measuring Gender (In)Equality: The OECD Gender, Institutions and Development Data Base.' *Journal of Human Development* 9(1): 65–86.

Karolak, M. 2016. 'Identity and Culture in the 21st Century Gulf: Overview.' *Gulf Affairs. Identity and Culture in the 21st Century Gulf.*

Kattan, F. 2017. 'A Review and Critique of the Saudisation Metanarrative: Bringing "the Citizen" into Focus.' In M.C. Thompson and N. Quilliam (eds) *Policy Making in the GCC: State, Citizens and Institutions*, 89–106. London: I.B. Tauris.

Kerwin, C.M., and Furlong, S.R. 2018. *Rulemaking: How Government Agencies Write Law and Make Policy*. London: Sage Publications Ltd.

Khambalah 2015. 'Filter of a Nation.' YouTube.com. [Available Online: https://www.youtube.com/watch?v=iGr4DGxfcJM; Accessed 20 September 2023].

Khambalah. 2023. 'Khambalah YouTube Channel.' YouTube.com. [Available Online: https://www.youtube.com/user/khambalah; Accessed 20 September 2023].

Kinninmont, J. 2017. 'Vision 2030 and Saudi Arabia's Social Contract: Austerity and Transformation.' London: Chatham House. [Available Online: https://www.chathamhouse.org/sites/default/files/publications/research/2017-07-20-vision-2030-saudi-kinninmont.pdf; Accessed 20 September 2023].

Kirchgaessner, S. 2021. 'US Finds Saudi Crown Prince Approved Khashoggi Murder but does not Sanction Him.' *The Guardian*. 26 February 2021. [Available Online: https://www.theguardian.com/world/2021/feb/26/jamal-khashoggi-mohammed-bin-salman-us-report; Accessed 20 September 2023].

Klugman, J., Hanmer, L., Twigg, S., Hasan, T., McCleary-Sills, J., and Santamaria, J. 2014. *Voice and Agency: Empowering Women and Girls for Shared Prosperity*. Washington, DC: World Bank.

Knutsen, C.H., and Rasmussen, M. 2018. 'The Autocratic Welfare State: Old-Age Pensions, Credible Commitments, and Regime Survival.' *Comparative Political Studies* 51(5): 659–95.

Kostiner, J. 1993. *The Making of Saudi Arabia, 1916–1936: From Chieftaincy to Monarchical State*. New York: Oxford University Press.

Krämer, G., and Schmidtke, S. (eds). 2006. *Speaking for Islam: Religious Authorities in Muslim Societies*. Leiden: Brill.

Krane, J. 2019. 'Subsidy Reform and Tax Increases in the Rentier Middle East.' Project on Middle East Political Science (POMEPS) Studies 33: *The Politics of Rentier Sates in the Gulf.* [Available Online: https://pomeps.org/subsidy-reform-and-tax-increases-in-the-rentier-middle-east; Accessed 20 September 2023].

Krell, D. 2025. *Islamic Law in Saudi Arabia*. Boston, MA: BRILL.

Künkler, M., and Stewart, D.J. (eds). 2018. *Female Religious Authority in Shi'i Islam*. Edinburgh: Edinburgh University Press.

Kuran, T. 2010. *The Long Divergence: How Islamic Law Held Back the Middle East*. Princeton, NJ: Princeton University Press.

Kuru, A.T. 2019. *Islam, Authoritarianism, and Underdevelopment: A Global and Historical Comparison*. Cambridge: Cambridge University Press.

Lacroix, S. 2004. 'Between Islamists and Liberals: Saudi Arabia's New "Islamo-Liberal" Reformists.' *Middle East Journal* 58: 345–65.

Lacroix, S. 2011. *Awakening Islam: The Politics of Religious Dissent in Contemporary Saudi Arabia*. Cambridge, MA: Harvard University Press.

Landau, J.M. 1971. *The Hejaz Railway and the Muslim Pilgrimage: A Case of Ottoman Political Propaganda*. London: Routledge.

Lashitew, A.A., and Werker, E. 2020. 'Do Natural Resources Help or Hinder Development? Resource Abundance, Dependence, and the Role of Institutions.' *Resource and Energy Economics* 61: 101183.

Lawrence, T.E. 2015. *Seven Pillars of Wisdom*. London: Penguin.

Le Renard, A. 2014. *A Society of Young Women: Opportunities of Place, Power, and Reform in Saudi Arabia*. Stanford, CA: Stanford University Press.

Le Renard, A. 2015. 'Engendering Consumerism in the Saudi Capital: A Study of Young Women's Practices in Shopping Malls.' In B. Haykel, T. Hegghammer and S. Lacroix (eds) *Saudi Arabia in Transition: Insights on Social, Political, Economic and Religious Change*, 214–33. Cambridge: Cambridge University Press.

Liakos, C., Popalzai, E., Akbarzai, S., Tawfeeq, M., and Kottasová, I. 2022. 'Major Foreign Aid Groups Suspend Work in Afghanistan After Taliban Bars Female Employees.' *CNN*. 26 December 2022. [Available Online: https://edition.cnn.com/2022/12/25/asia/afghanistan-ngos-suspend-programs-taliban-work-ban-intl/index.html; Accessed 1 October 2023].

Liebowitz, S.J., and Margolis, S.E. 1995. 'Path-Dependence, Lock-In, and History.' *Journal of Law, Economics, and Organization* 1: 205–26.

Lippman, T.W. 2012. *Saudi Arabia on the Edge: The Uncertain Future of an American Ally*. Council of Foreign Relations Book. Washington, DC: Potomac Books, Inc.

Lippman, T.W. 2013. 'Support for el-Sisi: What's in it for al-Saud?' Middle East Institute. 3 September 2012. [Availble Online: https://www.mei.edu/publications/support-el-sisi-whats-it-al-saud; Accessed 20 September 2023].

Louër, L. 2021. 'Social Citizenship in the Gulf Monarchies: Beyond the Rentier State Paradigm.' SciencesPo Center for International Studies. December 2021. [Available Online: https://www.sciencespo.fr/ceri/en/content/dossiersduceri/social-citizenship-gulf-monarchies-beyond-rentier-state-paradigm; Accessed 20 September 2023].

Luca, D., Terrero-Davila, J., Stein, J., and Lee, N. (2023). 'Progressive Cities: Urban–Rural Polarisation of Social Values and Economic Development Around the World.' *Urban Studies*, *60*(12), 2329–50.

Macaulay, E. 2015. 'The Kaaba.' Smarthistory: The Center for Public Art History. [Available Online: https://smarthistory.org/the-kaaba/; Accessed 1 October 2023].

Macdonald, H., Baker, N., Muller, G., and Lopresti, L. 2023. 'How Saudi Arabia's Crown Prince Mohammed bin Salman Rose to Power – and Why It Matters.' *ABC News*. 8 February 2023. [Available Online: https://www.abc.net.au/news/how-saudi-arabias-crown-prince-mohammed-bin-salman-rose-to-power; Accessed 18 July 2024].

Madain Project. 2023. 'Expansion Chronology of Masjid-i-Nabawi.' [Available Online: https://madainproject.com/expansion_chronology_of_masjid_al_nabawi#:~:text=(7%20Hj.)-,629%20CE%3A%20Expansion%20by%20Prophet%20Muhammad,construction%20ends%20in%20this%20direction; Accessed 20 September 2023].

Mahdavy, H. 1970. 'The Patterns and Problems of Economic Development in a Rentier State: The Case of Iran.' In M.A. Cook (ed.) *Studies in Economic History of the Middle East*, 428–67. London: Oxford University Press.

Maher, S. 2016. *Salafi-Jihadism: The History of an Idea*. London: Penguin Random House UK.

Mahmood, S. 2005. *Politics of Piety: The Islamic Revival and the Feminist Subject*. Princeton, NJ: Princeton University Press.

MAI. 2023. 'Misk Art Institute (MAI).' [Available Online: https://miskartinstitute.org/; Accessed 20 September 2023].

Malik, A. 2017. 'Rethinking the Rentier Curse.' In G. Luciani (ed.) *Combining Economic and Political Development: The Experience of MENA*, 49–69. Leiden: Brill.

Malkiel, N.W. 2018. *"Keep the Damned Women Out": The Struggle for Coeducation*. Princeton, NJ: Princeton University Press.

Mandaville, P.G. (ed.). 2022. *Wahhabism and the World: Understanding Saudi Arabia's Global Influence on Islam*. New York: Oxford University Press.

Manning, J.P. 1998. *Threats to the Saudi Arabian Monarchy*. Carlisle, PA: US Army War College.

Marca Monitor. 2021. 'Saudi Arabia Dress Code for Visit of FI Sparks Hugh Controversy.' Marca. 18 October 2021. [Available Online: https://www.marca.com/en/f1/2021/10/18/616dba0122601dfc398b45d5.html#; Accessed 1 October 2023].

Mastracci, D. 2016. 'Islam Doesn't Need the Reformation Western Pundits are Demanding.' *The Islamic Monthly*. [Available Online: https://www.theislamicmonthly.com/islam-doesnt-need-the-reformation-western-pundits-are-demanding/; Accessed 20 September 2023].

Matthiesen, T. 2009. 'Diwaniyyas, Intellectual Salons, and the Limits of Civil Society.' *Middle East Institute*. [Available Online: https://www.mei.edu/publications/diwaniyyas-intellectual-salons-and-limits-civil-society; Accessed 20 September 2023].

Matthiesen, T. 2015. *The Other Saudis: Shiism, Dissent and Sectarianism*. New York: Cambridge University Press.

Maududi, S. A. 2000. 'The Political Theory of Islam.' In M. Moaddel and K. Talattof (eds) *Contemporary Debates in Islam*, 209–21. New York: St. Martin's.

McIntrye, C. 2021. '"We're a Part of Change" Saudi Festival Attended By 732,000 Praised By "Proud" Female DJs.' *Express*. 22 December 2021. [Available Online: https://www.express.co.uk/entertainment/music/1539616/saudi-arabia-mdlbeast-soundstorm-732000-change-david-guetta-female-dj-eli-and-fur; Accessed 27 September 2023].

MDLBeast. 2023. 'The Region's Leading Music Platform' [Available Online: https://mdlbeast.com; Accessed 1 October 2023].

Meijer, R. (ed.). 2009. *Global Salafism: Islam's New Religious Movement*. New York: Columbia University Press.

Ménoret, P. 2014. *Joyriding in Riyadh: Oil, Urbanism, and Road Revolt*. Cambridge: Cambridge University Press.

Ménoret, P. 2020. *Graveyard of Clerics: Everyday Activism in Saudi Arabia*. Stanford, CA: Stanford University Press.

Mernissi, F. 1991. *Women and Islam: An Historical and Theological Enquiry*. London: Blackwell.

Mernissi, F. 1995. *Fear of the Imam. Islam and Democracy: Fear of the Modern World*. New York: Addison-Wesley.

Metcalf, B.D. 1982. *Islamic Revival in British India: Deoband, 1860–1900*. Princeton, NJ. Princeton University Press.

Middle East Monitor (MEM). 2019. 'Amnesty: Saudi Cleric Ouda Faces Possible Death Penalty for Peaceful Activism.' *Middle East Monitor*. 27 July 2019. [Available Online: https://www.middleeastmonitor.com/20190727-amnesty-saudi-cleric-ouda-faces-possible-death-penalty-for-peaceful-activism/; Accessed 20 September 2023].

Middle East Monitor (MEM). 2023. 'Saudi Arabia Imposes Restrictions on Ramadan Practices, Limiting Loudspeakers and Surveiling Worshippers.' *Middle East Monitor*. 8 March 2023. [Available Online: https://www.middleeastmonitor.com/20230308-saudi-arabia-imposes-restrictions-on-ramadan-practices-limiting-loudspeakers-and-surveiling-worshippers/; Accessed 1 October 2023].

Miller, C. 2005. 'Saudi Arabia: In al-Qaida's Sights.' *Council on Foreign Relations*. 7 February 2005. [Available Online: https://www.cfr.org/backgrounder/saudi-arabia-al-qaedas-sights; Accessed on 1 October 2023].

Mirza, M. 2018. '9 of the Most Popular Saudi Sheikhs on Twitter.' *Lovin Saudi*. 11 August 2018. [Available Online: https://lovinsaudi.com/lifestyle/technology/9-of-the-most-popular-saudi-sheikhs-on-twitter; Accessed 18 July 2024].

Moore, M. 2004. 'Revenues, State Formation, and the Quality of Governance in Developing Countries.' *International Political Science Review* 25: 297–319.

Moran, M., Rein, M., and Goodin, R.E. (eds) 2006. *The Oxford Handbook of Public Policy*. Oxford: Oxford University Press.

Mortiz, J. 2019. 'Oil and Social Quiescence: Rethinking Casual Mechanisms in Rentier State Theory.' Project on Middle East Political Science (POMEPS) Studies 33: *The Politics of Rentier Sates in the Gulf*. [Available Online: https://pomeps.org/oil-and-societal-quiescence-rethinking-causal-mechanisms-in-rentier-state-theory; Accessed 20 September 2023].

Mouline, N. 2014. *The Clerics of Islam: Religious Authority and Political Power in Saudi Arabia*. New Haven, CT: Yale University Press.

Mouline, N. 2015. 'Enforcing and Reinforcing the State's Islam: The Functioning of the Committee of Senior Scholars.' In B. Haykel, T. Hegghammer and S. Lacroix (eds) *Saudi Arabia in Transition: Insights on Social, Political, Economic and Religious Change*, 166–84. Cambridge: Cambridge University Press.

Munt, H. 2014. *The Holy City of Medina: Sacred Space in Early Islamic Arabia*. Cambridge: Cambridge University Press.

Murphy, C. 2013. 'Young Saudis and the Kingdom's Political Future.' Wilson Center. February 2013. [Available Online: https://www.wilsoncenter.org/publication/young-saudis-and-the-kingdoms-political-future; Accessed 20 September 2023].

Nakash, Y. 2006. *The Shi'a in the Modern Arab World: Reaching for Power*. Princeton, NJ: Princeton University Press.

Nasrallah, T. 2021. 'Businesses in Saudi Arabia May No Longer Need to Close During Prayer Time.' *Gulf News*. 20 June 2021. [Available Online: https://gulfnews.com/world/gulf/saudi/businesses-in-saudi-arabia-may-no-longer-need-to-close-during-prayer-time-1.80065767; Accessed 1 October 2023].

Nasrallah, T. 2022. 'Saudi Arabia Reports Alarming Increase in Divorce Rates: 7 Cases Every Hour.' *Gulf News*. 27 October 2023. [Available Online: https://gulfnews.com/world/gulf/saudi/saudi-arabia-reports-alarming-increase-in-divorce-rates-7-cases-every-hour-1.91541159; Accessed 20 September 2023].

Netflix. 2020. 'Netflix Draws Curtain on "Six Windows in the Desert."' *Netflix*. 12 February 2020. [Available Online: https://about.netflix.com/en/news/netflix-draws-curtains-on-six-windows-in-the-desert; Accessed 20 September 2023].

Niblock, T. 2006. *Saudi Arabia: Power, Legitimacy and Survival, Contemporary Middle East*. London: Routledge.

Niskanen Center. 2019. 'Explaining the Urban-Rural Political Divide.' [Available Online: https://www.niskanencenter.org/explaining-the-urban-rural-political-divide/; Accessed 24 July 2024].

Nizami, A. F. 1983. 'A. Madrasahs, Scholars and Saints: Muslim Response to the British Presence in Delhi and the Upper Doab 1803–1857.' DPhil thesis. University of Oxford.

North, D.C. 1990. *Institutions, Institutional Change and Economic Performance*. New York: Cambridge University Press.

North, D.C., Wallis, J.J., and Weingast, B.R. 2009. *Violence and Social Orders: A Conceptual Framework for Interpreting Recorded Human History*. New York: Cambridge University Press.

Norton Rose Fulbright (NRF). 2021. 'Saudi Arabia Implements Wide Ranging Legislative and Judicial Reforms.' [Available Online: https://www.nortonrosefulbright.com/en/knowledge/publications/8b9a1182/saudi-arabia-implements-wide-ranging-legislative-and-judicial-reforms; Accessed 20 September 2023].

Nussbaum, M.C. 2001. 'Symposium on Amartya Sen's Philosophy: 5 Adaptive Preferences and Women's Options.' *Economics and Philosophy* 17: 67–88.

Nusuk. 2023a. 'Madinah.' [Available Online: https://www.nusuk.sa/destination/madina?gclid=CjwKCAjwp6CkBhB_EiwAlQVyxZTTi7z1enel2deXEDuAmigq9LsSWZCmAaHnXXfOXGx-dddbnOqwUxoCnIAQAvD_BwE&gclsrc=aw.ds; Accessed 20 September 2023].

Nusuk. 2023b. 'Makkah.' [Available Online: https://www.nusuk.sa/destination/makkah?gclid=CjwKCAjwp6CkBhB_EiwAlQVyxetLvlMBvk-09TxsFKY7na-XAJe5op_Ed16QI4Pgmn2w32JBVbL1CRoCMEgQAvD_BwE&gclsrc=aw.ds; Accessed 8 February 2023); Accessed 20 September 2023].

Obeid, G. 2022. 'Saudi's Misk Forum Highlights Need to Narrow Generation Gap to Transform Societies.' *Al-Arabiya News*. 9 November 2022. [Available Online: https://english.alarabiya.net/News/saudi-arabia/2022/11/09/The-Misk-Global-Forum-kicks-off-in-Saudi-Arabia-s-Riyadh; Accessed 20 September 2023].

Ober, J. 2008. *Democracy and Knowledge: Innovation and Learning in Classical Athens*. Princeton, NJ: Princeton University Press.

OECD. 2023. 'Education in Saudi Arabia.' [Available Online: https://www.oecd-ilibrary.org/sites/76df15a2-en/1/3/1/index.html?itemId=/content/publication/76df15a2-en&_csp_=52c9984cac4fdeba56b32f54ff82555e&itemIGO=oecd&itemContentType=book; Accessed 20 September 2023].

Olson, M. 1993. 'Dictatorship, Democracy, and Development.' *American Political Science Review* 87: 567–76.

Olson, M. 2000. *Power and Prosperity: Outgrowing Communist and Capitalist Dictatorships*. New York: Basic Books.

O'Malley, 2017. 'Saudi Arabia Finally Hosts Its First-Ever Concert by a Female Performer.' *Elle*. 8 December 2017. [Available Online: https://www.elle.com/uk/life-and-culture/culture/news/a40411/saudi-arabia-first-ever-concert-female-performer/; Accessed 20 September 2023].

Opp, K.-D. 2018. 'Externalities, Social Networks, and the Emergence of Norms: A Critical Analysis and Extension of James Coleman's Theory.' *Social Research* 85: 167–96.

O'Reilly, K. 2012. 'Ethnographic Returning, Qualitative Longitudinal Research and the Reflexive Analysis of Social Practice.' *Sociological Review* 60(3): 518–36.

Ottaway, D.B. 2018. 'Will Saudi Arabia's Social Revolution Provoke a Wahhabi Backlash?' Wilson Center. May 2018. [Available Online: https://www.wilsoncenter.org/publication/will-saudi-arabias-social-revolution-provoke-wahhabi-backlash; Accessed 20 September 2023].

Ottaway, D.B. 2021a. 'Saudi Crown Prince Lambasts His Kingdom's Wahhabi Establishment' Wilson Center. 6 May 2021. [Available Online: https://www.wilsoncenter.org/article/saudi-crown-prince-lambasts-his-kingdoms-wahhabi-establishment; Accessed 20 September 2023].

Ottaway, M. 2021b. 'The Conundrum of Political Parties in the Gulf Countries: Unwanted but Inevitable.' Wilson Center. 25 June 2021. [Available Online: https://www.wilsoncenter.org/article/conundrum-political-parties-gulf-countries-unwanted-inevitable; Accessed 20 September 2023].

Oxford Business Group (OBG). 2022. 'How Saudi Arabia is Reforming Education through Technological Investment.' [Available Online: https://oxfordbusinessgroup.com/reports/saudi-arabia/2022-report/education-training/bright-future-a-raft-of-reforms-and-restructuring-of-the-education-system-boosts-technological-proficiency-and-equips-students-to-thrive/; Accessed 20 September 2023].

Paglayan, A.S. 2021. 'The Non-Democratic Roots of Mass Education: Evidence from 200 Years.' *American Political Science Review* 115(1): 179–98.

Peterson, J.E. 2018. *Saudi Arabia under Ibn Saud: Economic and Financial Foundations of the State*. London: I.B. Tauris & Co. Ltd.

Pew Research Centre (PRC). 2023. 'Muslim-Majority Countries.' [Available Online: https://www.pewresearch.org/religion/2011/01/27/future-of-the-global-muslim-population-muslim-majority/; Accessed 20 September 2023].

Pierret, T. 2013. *Religion and State in Syria. The Sunni Ulama from Coup to Revolution*. Cambridge: Cambridge University Press.

Platteau, J.-P. 2000. *Institutions, Social Norms and Economic Development*. London: Routledge.

POMEPS. 2019. *Project on Middle East Political Science (POMEPS)*. Studies 33: *The Politics of Rentier Sates in the Gulf*. [Available Online: https://pomeps.org/pomeps-studies-33-the-politics-of-rentier-states-in-the-gulf;Accessed 20 September 2023].

Public Statement. 2023. 'Navigating Differences: Clarifying Sexual and Gender Ethics in Islam.' [Available Online: https://navigatingdifferences.com/clarifying-sexual-and-gender-ethics-in-islam/; Accessed 20 September 2023].

Putnam, R., and Goss, K.A. 2002. 'Introduction.' In R. Putnam (ed.) *Democracies in Flux. The Evolution of Social Capital in Contemporary Society*, 3–19. Oxford: Oxford University Press.

Qadhi, Y. 2013. 'Reconciling Reason and Revelation in the Writings of Ibn Taymiyya (d. 728/1328): An Analytical Study of Ibn Taymiyya's 'Dar' Al-Ta'arud." PhD dissertation. New Haven, CT: Yale University.

Qadhi, Y. 2018. 'Reformation or Reconstruction: Dr Hatem al-Awni's Critiques of Wahhabism.' Paper presented at The Future of Salafism conference, 5–7 December 2018. Oxford: University of Oxford.

Qadhi, Y. 2019. 'Dr. Yasir Qadhi on Why He left Salafi or Wahabi Movement of Muhammad Ibn Abd al-Wahab.' [Available Online: https://www.youtube.com/watch?v=Xo8ykbyYIgI; Accessed 20 September 2023].

Qiblawi, T. 2019. 'MBS Once Sought Advice from this Cleric. Now Saudi Prosecutors Want him Executed.' *CNN*. 25 July 2019 [Available Online: https://edition.cnn.com/2019/07/25/middleeast/saudi-cleric-sheikh-salman-al-awda-intl/index.html; Accessed 20 September 2023].

Quadango, J. 1987. 'Theories of the Welfare State.' *Annual Review of Sociology* 13: 109–28.
Ramirez, F.O. and Boli, J. 1987. 'The Political Construction of Mass Schooling: European Origins and Worldwide Institutionalization.' *Sociology of Education* 60(1): 2–17.
Rappeport, A. 2019. 'Saudi Arabia Embraces Western Sports to Rehabilitate Global Image.' *The New York Times*. 2 December 2019. Available Online: https://www.nytimes.com/2019/12/02/business/economy/saudi-arabia-image-sports.html; Accessed 20 September 2023].
Razavian, C.P. 2018a. 'Post-Salafism: Salman al-Ouda and Hatim al-Awni.' In M. Bano (ed.) *Modern Islamic Authority and Social Change, Volume 1. Evolving Debates in Muslim-Majority Countries*, 150–70. Edinburgh: Edinburgh University Press.
Razavian, C.P. 2018b. 'Yasir Qadhi and the Development of Reasonable Salafism.' In M. Bano (ed.) *Modern Islamic Authority and Social Change, Volume 2. Evolving Debates in the West*, 173–92. Edinburgh: Edinburgh University Press.
Rendall. J. 1985. *The Origins of Modern Feminism. Women in Britain, France, and the United States, 1780–1860*. Basingstoke: Macmillan.
Reuters. 2019. 'FACTBOX-Saudi Arabia's Key Economic and Social Reforms.' [Available Online: https://www.reuters.com/article/saudi-investment-reforms-idUKL5N2763K6; Accessed 20 September 2023].
Reuters. 2021a. 'Saudi Crown Prince Says He Will Further Centralise Policy-Making.' *Reuters*. 28 April 2021. [Available Online: https://www.reuters.com/article/saudi-crown-prince-centralises-policy-making; Accessed 18 July 2024].
Reuters. 2021b. 'Saudi Minister Defends Order to Turn Down the Volume on Mosques.' *Reuters*. 31 May 2021. Available Online: https://www.reuters.com/world/middle-east/saudi-minister-defends-order-turn-down-volume-mosques-2021-05-31/; Accessed 1 October 2023].
Riedel, B. 2013. 'Saudi Arabia Cheers the Coup in Egypt.' Brookings. 7 July 2013. [Available Online: https://www.brookings.edu/articles/saudi-arabia-cheers-the-coup-in-egypt/; Accessed 20 September 2023].
Riyadh Season. 2021. 'All You Need to Know About Riyadh Season Activities.' [Available Online: https://saudivisitors.com/en/riyadh-season-2022/; Accessed 20 September 2023].
Riyadh Tours 2023. 'A Moderate without Moderation (Arabic: Wasati Bila Wasatiah).' Available Online: https://www.facebook.com/Experbia/videos/a-moderate-without-moderation-arabic-wasati-bila-wasatiah-is-a-saudi-theatrical-/714957305905148/; Accessed 20 September 2023].
Robbins, M. 2015. 'After the Arab Spring: People Still Want Democracy.' *Journal of Democracy* 26(4): 80–9.
Roberts, D.B. 2014. 'Qatar, the Ikhwan, and Transnational Relations in the Gulf.' Paper Presented at Visions of Gulf Security Workshop, 9 March 2014. *POMEPS*. [Available Online: https://pomeps.org/qatar-the-ikhwan-and-transnational-relations-in-the-gulf; Accessed 27 September 2023].
Robinson, F. 2001. *The 'Ulama of Farangi Mahall and Islamic Culture in South Asia*. London: Hurst.
Rock-Singer, A. 2022. *In the Shade of the Sunna: Salafi Piety in the Twentieth-Century Middle East*. Oakland: University of California Press.
Rosenberg, G. 2008. *The Hollow Hope: Can Courts Bring About Social Change?* Chicago, IL: University of Chicago Press.
Ross, M. 2001. 'Does Oil Hinder Democracy?' *World Politics* 53(3): 325–61.

Ross, M.L. 2004. Does Taxation Lead to Representation? *British Journal of Political Science* 34: 229–49.
Rubin. J.T. 2017. *Rulers, Religion, and Riches: Why the West Got Rich and the Middle East Did Not*. New York: Cambridge University Press.
Russell, N. 2021. 'Between Da'wa and Politics: The Changing Dynamics of Egypt's Ansar al-Sunna, 2011–2013.' In M. Bano (ed.) *Salafi Social and Political Movements: National and Transnational Contexts*, 189–210. Edinburgh: Edinburgh University Press.
Said-Moorhouse, L. 2016. 'Saudi Arabia Strips Religious Police of Arrest Powers.' *CNN*. 14 April 2016. [Available Online: https://www.cnn.com/2016/04/14/middleeast/saudi-arabia-religious-police-powers/index.html; Accessed 20 September 2023].
Samin, N. 2015. *Of Sand and Soil: Genealogy and Tribal Belonging in Saudi Arabia*. Princeton, NJ: Princeton University Press.
Samson, M., van Katwyk, S., Fröling, M., and Ndoro, R., 2015. 'Methods of Measuring the Impacts of Social Policy in Political, Economic and Social Dimensions.' UNRISD Working Paper 2015–4. Available Online: https://www.econstor.eu/bitstream/10419/148748/1/861283775.pdf; Accessed 20 September 2023.
Sanchez, R. 2018. 'Saudi Women Do Not Need to Wear Black Abayas, Mohammed bin Salman Says Ahead of Trip to US.' *The Telegraph*. 19 March 2018. Available Online: https://www.telegraph.co.uk/news/2018/03/19/saudi-women-do-not-need-wear-black-abayas-mohammed-bin-salman/; Accessed 20 September 2023].
Saudi Scoop. 2023. 'Discover the Magic of Boulevard World: Riyadh Season 2023.' Available Online: https://saudiscoop.com/lifestyle/discover-boulevard-world-riyadh/; Accessed 21 September 2023].
Savat, S. 2020. 'The Divide Between US: Urban-Rural Political Differences Rooted in Geography.' *The Source*. Washington University in St. Louis: Newsroom. [Available Online: https://source.washu.edu/2020/02/the-divide-between-us-urban-rural-political-differences-rooted-in-geography/; Accessed 24 July 2023].
Schaer, C. 2021. 'Saudi Arabia Reforms: Royal Power Play or Meaningful Change?' *DW*. 27 June 2021. Available Online: https://www.dw.com/en/saudi-arabia-reform-royal-family/a-58017860; Accessed 20 September 2023].
Schmidt-Feuerheerd, B. 2023. ' "The Pandemic Was a Global Exam, and Our Country Came in First": Autocratic Performance Legitimacy in Saudi Arabia.' *Perspectives on Politics*.
Sedgwick, M.J.R. 1997. 'Saudi Sufis: Compromise in the Hijaz, 1925–40.' *Die Welt Des Islams* 37(3): 349–68.
Sen, A. 1995. 'Gender Inequality and Theories of Justice.' In M. Nussbaum and J. Glover (eds) *Women, Culture and Development*, 259–73. Oxford: Clarendon Press.
Sewell, W.H. 1996. 'Three Temporalities: Towards and Eventful Sociology.' In T.J. McDonald (ed.) *The Historic Turn in the Human Sciences*. Ann Arbor: University of Michigan Press.
Sinn, H.W. 1994. *A Theory of the Welfare State*. National Bureau of Economic Research (NBER) Working Paper Series. Working Paper No. 4856. Cambridge, MA: NBER.
Slobodian, Q. 2023. How Saudi Arabia is buying the World. *The New Statesman*. 19 July 2023. [Available Online: https://www.newstatesman.com/long-reads/2023/07/saudi-arabia-capitalsim-buying-world; Accessed 20 September 2023].
Spannaus, N. 2018a. 'Evolution of Saudi Salafism.' In M. Bano (ed.) *Modern Islamic Authority and Social Change. Volume 1, Evolving Debates in Muslim-Majority Countries*, 102–26. Edinburgh: Edinburgh University Press.

Spannaus, N. 2018b. 'Religion in the Service of the State: Diyanet and Republican Turkey.' In M. Bano (ed.) *Modern Islamic Authority and Social Change. Volume 1, Evolving Debates in Muslim-Majority Countries*, 247–70. Edinburgh: Edinburgh University Press.

Stenslie, S. 2012. *Regime Stability in Saudi Arabia: The Challenge of Succession*. Abingdon: Routledge.

Sunier, T. 2024. *Making Islam Work: Islamic Authority Among Muslims in Western Europe*. Leiden: Brill.

Swedberg, R. 1990. *Economics and Sociology: Redefining Their Boundaries: Conversations with Economists and Sociologists*. Princeton, NJ: Princeton University Press.

Tashkandi, H. 2019. 'Top Egypt Musician Sees Bright Future for a Saudi National Orchestra.' *Arab News. Arab News*. 3 March 2019. [Available Online: https://www.arabnews.com/node/1460811/saudi-arabia; Accessed 20 September 2023].

Taylor. C. 2007. *A Secular Age*. Cambridge, MA: Harvard University Press.

Telfaz11. 2023a. 'A Creative Media Studio.' [Available Online: https://telfaz11.com/; Accessed 20 September 2023].

Telfaz11. 2023b. 'Traditional Music Videos.' [Available Online https://www.youtube.com/watch?v=p0Gw-smKqhc; Accessed 20 September 2023].

TGM Research. 2021. 'Saudi Arabia's Statistics Through a Magnifying Glass.' [Available Online: https://tgmresearch.com/ksa-population-population-of-saudi-arabia-gdp-and-saudis-people.html; Accessed 20 September 2023].

The New Arab. 2018. 'Coverings for Women "Not Mandatory", Says Saudi Crown Prince Ahead of US Charm Offensive.' *The New Arab*. 20 March 2018. [Available Online: https://www.newarab.com/news/abayas-not-mandatory-women-says-saudi-crown-prince; Accessed 20 September 2023].

The New Arab. 2021. Saudi Arabia Backtracks on Strict Dress Code at Jeddah F1 Grand Prix. *The New Arab*. 30 October 2021. [Available Online: https://www.newarab.com/news/saudi-arabia-backtracks-strict-dress-code-grand-prix; Accessed 1 October 2023].

TheWanderingQuinn. 2020. '16 BEST Things to do in Riyadh as a Tourist and Like a Local in 2023.' *The Wandering Quinn Travel Blog*. [Available Online: https://thewanderingquinn.com/things-to-do-in-riyadh/; Accessed 20 September 2023].

TIFF Trailers. 2015. 'Barakah Meets Barakah.' [Available Online: https://www.youtube.com/watch?v=vK9V_n4i_CY; Accessed 20 September 2023].

Time Out. 2023. 'Boulevard World is Back at Riyadh Season 2023.' *Time Out*. 17 September 2023. [Available Online: https://www.timeoutriyadh.com/attractions/boulevard-world-riyadh-season; Accessed 21 September 2023].

Thesiger, W. 2007. *Arabian Sands*. With an introduction by Rory Stewart. Penguin Classics. London: Penguin.

Thompson, M.C. 2014. *Saudi Arabia and the Path to Political Change: National Dialogue and Civil Society*. London: Bloomsbury Publishing.

Thompson, M.C. 2019. *Being Young, Male and Saudi: Identity and Politics in a Globalized Kingdom*. Cambridge: Cambridge University Press.

Thurston, A. 2016. *Salafism in Nigeria: Islam, Preaching, and Politics*. Cambridge: Cambridge University Press.

Uddin, R. 2023. '"New Kaaba": Saudi Arabia Plans To Build Giant Cube Building in Riyadh.' *Middle East Eye*. 17 February 2023. [Available Online: https://www.middleeasteye.net/news/saudi-arabia-mukaab-giant-cube-riyadh-new-kaaba; Accessed 27 September 2023].

UNESCO. 2023. 'Al-Ahsa Oasis, an Evolving Cultural Landscape.' UNESCO World Heritage Centre. [Available Online: https://whc.unesco.org/en/list/1563/; Accessed 20 September 2023].
UNICEF. 2020. 'Participatory Research Toolkit for Social Norms Measurement.' [Available Online: https://www.unicef.org/documents/participatory-research-toolkit-social-norms-measurement; Accessed 20 September 2023].
UNICEF. 2023. 'UNFPA-UNICEF Joint Programme on the Elimination of Female Genital Mutilation.' Available Online: https://www.unicef.org/protection/unfpa-unicef-joint-programme-eliminating-fgm; Accessed 20 September 2023].
Valeri, M. 2009. *Oman: Politics and Society in the Qaboos State*. London: Hurst Publishers.
van der Ploeg, F. 2011. 'Natural Resources: Curse or Blessing?' *Journal of Economic Literature* 49: 366–420.
Vasil'ev, A. 2000. *The History of Saudi Arabia*. London: Saqi.
Viator. 2023. '"Walk in Moses" Footsteps – Tour between Tabuk and The Red Sea.' [Available Online: https://www.viator.com/tours/Tabouk/Walk-in-Moses-Footsteps-in-Bedouin-Style/d51790-322037P1; Accessed 20 September 2023]
Visit Saudi. 2023a. 'Al-Ahsa, 2023.' [Available Online: https://www.visitsaudi.com/en/see-do/destinations/al-ahsa; Accessed 20 September 2023].
Visit Saudi. 2023b. 'Celebrating Ramadan in Jeddah.' [Available Online: https://www.visitsaudi.com/en/do/culture/ramadan-in-jeddah; Accessed 20 September 2023].
Visit Saudi. 2023c. 'Events All Around Saudi: Calendar.' [Available Online: https://calendar.visitsaudi.com/en?gclid=Cj0KCQiA14WdBhD8ARIsANao07i16b9hXKvSwghDhi2OoVsJSmv-jBhIRQdpFVfUI4JE87I55_Eyy00aAvPMEALw_wcB&gclsrc=aw.ds; Accessed 20 September 2023].
Visit Saudi. 2023d. 'Historic Jeddah.' [Available Online: https://www.visitsaudi.com/en/see-do/destinations/jeddah/summer-night-adventures-in-al-balad; Accessed 1 October 2023].
Visit Saudi. 2023e. 'The History of Saudi's Trade Routes.' [https://www.visitsaudi.com/en/do/culture/the-history-of-saudi-s-trade-routes; Accessed 20 September 2023].
Vitalis, R. 2009. *America's Kingdom: Mythmaking on the Saudi Oil Frontier*. London: Verso.
Vivarelli, N. 2023. 'Saudi Wrestling Comedy "Sattar" Breaks Home Box Office Record for Local Titles.' *Variety*. [Available Online: https://variety.com/2023/film/global/saudi-wrestling-comedy-sattar-breaks-box-office-record-1235482080/; Accessed 20 September 2023].
Vogel. F.E. 2000. *Islamic Law and Legal System: Studies of Saudi Arabia*. Leiden: Brill.
Vogue Arabia. 2021. 'Everything to Know About Winter at Tantora Festival's Return to Al Ula.' *Vogue Arabia*. Available Online: https://en.vogue.me/culture/winter-at-tantora-festival-al-ula/; Accessed 20 September 2023].
Wade, R.H. 2018. 'The Developmental State: Dead or Alive?' *Development and Change* 49: 518–46.
Wadud, A. 2006. *Inside the Gender Jihad: Women's Reform in Islam*. Oxford: Oneworld.
Wagemakers, J. 2012. *A Quietist Jihadi: The Ideology and Influence of Abu Muhammad al-Maqdisi*. Cambridge: Cambridge University Press.
Walbridge, J. 2010. *God and Logic in Islam: The Caliphate of Reason*. Cambridge; Cambridge University Press.
Walker, P. 2016.'Saudi Prince Mohammed bin Salman "buys £452m yacht" but Slashes Public Spending.' *Independent*. 18 October 2016. [Available Online: https://www.inde

pendent.co.uk/news/world/middle-east/saudiprincemohammedbinsalmanyachtfrancenewyorktimes-a7365261.html#; Accessed 1 October 2023].

Wallace, T., and Porter, F. (eds). 2014. *Aid, NGOs, and the Realities of Women's Lives: A Perfect Storm*. London: Practical Action Publishing.

Wehrey, F. (ed.). 2021. Islamic Institutions in Arab States: Mapping the Dynamics of Control, Co-Option, and Contention. Carnegie Endowment for International Peace. [Available Online: https://carnegieendowment.org/2021/06/07/islamic-institutions-in-arab-states-mapping-dynamics-of-control-co-option-and-contention-pub-84647; Accessed 20 September 2023].

Western University. 2023. 'Saudi Arabia King Abdullah Scholarship Program.' [Available Online: https://grad.uwo.ca/finances/saudi_bureau.html#:~:text=King%20Abdullah%20Scholarships%20provide%20financial,directly%20to%20the%20educational%20institution; Accessed 20 September 2023].

Witherspoon, J. 2023. 'Diriyah: Inside the €57 Billion "Giga-Project" Set to Transform the Birthplace of Saudi Arabia.' *Euronews*. 6 May 2023. [Available Online: https://www.euronews.com/travel/2023/05/06/diriyah-inside-the-57-billion-giga-project-set-to-transform-the-birthplace-of-saudi-arabia; Accessed 20 September 2023].

Whitaker, B. 2015. 'Saudi Arabia is Worried – And Not Just About its King.' *The Guardian*. 29 September 2015. [Available Online: https://www.theguardian.com/commentisfree/2015/sep/29/saudi-arabia-king-salman-spending-gulf; Accessed 20 September 2023].

Woodyatt, A., Shveda, K., and Cubero, A.J. 2023. 'Saudi Arabia is Trying to Disrupt Soccer's World Order. The Reasons Why Might Surprise You.' *CNN*. [Available Online: https://edition.cnn.com/2023/09/20/sport/saudi-arabia-soccer-spl-bin-salman-intl-spt-cmd-dg/index.html; Accessed 20 September 2023].

World Values Survey (WVS). 2023. 'World Values Survey Site.' [Available Online: https://www.worldvaluessurvey.org/wvs.jsp; Accessed 20 September 2023].

Worth, R.F. 2009. 'For Saudi Liberals, a Ripple of Hope in a Sea of Tradition.' *The New York Times*. 3 March 2009. [Available Online: https://www.nytimes.com/2009/03/03/world/middleeast/03saudi.html; Accessed 20 September 2023].

Wright J., and Escriba-Folch, A. 2012. 'Authoritarian Institutions and Regime Survival: Transitions to Democracy and Subsequent Authoritarian Regimes.' *British Journal of Political Science* 42(2): 283–309.

Yamani, M. 1997. *To Be a Saudi*. London: Janus Publishing Company.

Yamani, M. 2000. *Changed Identities: The Challenge of the New Generation in Saudi Arabia*. London: Royal Institute of International Affairs.

Yamani, M. 2009. Cradle of Islam: *The Hijaz and a Quest for Identity in Saudi Arabia*. London: I.B. Tauris.

Yee, V. 2020. 'Art Rises in the Saudi Desert, Shadowed by Politics.' *The New York Times*. 11 February 2020. [Available Online: https://www.nytimes.com/2020/02/11/arts/design/Desert-X-AlUla-saudi-arabia.html; Accessed 20 September 2023].

Yizraeli, S. 2016. 'Al Saud: An Ambivalent Approach to Tribalism.' In U. Rabi (ed.). *Tribes and States in a Changing Middle East*, 111–28. London: C. Hurst & Co.

Young, E. 2013. 'Intelligence Testing: Accurate or Extremely Biased.' *The Euroethics Blog*. Emory Center for Ethics. 24 September 2013. [Available Online: http://www.theneuroethicsblog.com/2013/09/intelligence-testing-accurate-or.html; Accessed 20 September 2023].

Young, H.P. 2007. 'Social Norms and Public Policy.' Brookings. [Available Online: https://www.brookings.edu/articles/social-norms-and-public-policy/; Accessed 20 September 2023].

Zand, R. 2018. 'MiSK Art Institute: A Symbol of Saudi Arabia's Grassroots Art Scene.' *Sothebys*. 29 May 2018. [Available Online: https://www.sothebys.com/en/articles/misk-art-institute-a-symbol-of-saudi-arabias-grassroots-art-scene; Accessed 20 September 2023].

Zeghal, M. 2007. 'The "Recentering" of Religious Knowledge and Discourse: The Case of al-Azhar in Twentieth Century Egypt.' In R.W. Hefner and M.Q. Zaman (eds) *Schooling Islam: The Culture and Politics of Modern Muslim Education*, 107–34. Princeton, NJ: Princeton University Press.

Zubaida, S. 2016. 'Islamic Reformation?' *openDemocracy*. 5 January 2016. [Available Online: https://www.opendemocracy.net/en/author/sami-zubaida/; Accessed 20 September 2023].

INDEX